Gender, Religion, & Family Law

BRANDEIS SERIES ON GENDER, CULTURE, RELIGION, AND LAW

Series editors: Lisa Fishbayn Joffe and Sylvia Neil

This series focuses on the conflict between women's claims to gender equality and legal norms justified in terms of religious and cultural traditions. It seeks work that develops new theoretical tools for conceptualizing feminist projects for transforming the interpretation and justification of religious law, examines the interaction or application of civil law or remedies to gender issues in a religious context, and engages in analysis of conflicts over gender and culture/religion in a particular religious legal tradition, cultural community, or nation. Created under the auspices of the Hadassah-Brandeis Institute in conjunction with its Project on Gender, Culture, Religion, and the Law, this series emphasizes cross-cultural and interdisciplinary scholarship concerning a range of religious traditions.

For a complete list of books that are available in the series, visit www.upne.com

Lisa Fishbayn Joffe and Sylvia Neil, editors, *Gender, Religion, and Family Law: Theorizing Conflicts between Women's Rights and Cultural Traditions*

Chitra Raghavan and James P. Levine, editors, *Self-Determination and Women's Rights in Muslim Societies*

Janet Bennion, *Polygamy in Primetime: Media, Gender, and Politics in Mormon Fundamentalism*

Ronit Irshai, *Fertility and Halakhah: A Gender Analysis*

Jan Feldman, *Citizenship, Faith, and Feminism: Jewish and Muslim Women Reclaim Their Rights*

EDITED BY LISA FISHBAYN JOFFE AND SYLVIA NEIL

Gender, Religion, & Family Law

Theorizing Conflicts between Women's Rights and Cultural Traditions

BRANDEIS UNIVERSITY PRESS WALTHAM, MASSACHUSETTS

Brandeis University Press
An imprint of University Press of New England
www.upne.com

Manufactured in the United States of America
Designed by Mindy Basinger Hill

Typeset in 11/14 Garamond Premier Pro by Walton Harris
University Press of New England is a member of the Green Press Initiative. The paper used in this book meets their minimum requirement for recycled paper.

Library of Congress Cataloging-in-Publication Data

Gender, religion, and family law : theorizing conflicts between women's rights and cultural traditions / edited by Lisa Fishbayn Joffe and Sylvia Neil.
p. cm. — (Brandeis series on gender, culture, religion, and law)
Includes bibliographical references and index.
ISBN 978-1-61168-325-7 (cloth : alk. paper) — ISBN 978-1-61168-326-4 (pbk. : alk. paper) — ISBN 978-1-61168-327-1 (ebook)
1. Domestic relations. 2. Legal polycentricity. 3. Jews—Legal status, laws, etc. 4. Muslims—Legal status, laws, etc. 5. Customary law. 6. Domestic relations—South Africa. I. Joffe, Lisa Fishbayn. II. Neil, Sylvia.

K670. G435 2012
346.01'5—dc23
2012011027

5 4 3 2 1

CONTENTS

PART THREE Narratives of Innovative Law Reform

PREFACE

This anthology, based on the initial conference of a new academic project I founded and chair at Brandeis University called the Project on Gender, Culture, Religion, and the Law, is part of a new book series that I co-edit with Lisa Fishbayn Joffe, the project director.

My reason for founding the Project on Gender, Culture, Religion, and the Law can be simply put: the status of women is the cause of our time. The mission of the project is more complicated—we seek to identify ways to work through what can seem like the unbridgeable abyss between women's rights, religious law, and cultural norms in order to alleviate and hopefully one day eliminate the negative effects of religion and custom on the status of women.

Controversies about the status of women arise in all societies. The manifestations of these conflicts occur when religious and cultural practices that are debilitating to women intersect with public or civic life; when religious or customary norms are enforced or accommodated through the application of civil law; when religions play a mediating role in the distribution of services; and when civil laws protecting women are not enforced due to prevailing customary and religious views. The result is that virtually every aspect of women's lives is influenced, and in some societies controlled, by religious and customary proscriptions.

Nonetheless, an essential assumption of the Project on Gender, Culture, Religion, and the Law is that religion and culture are positive values in society. We recognize and embrace that religion and tradition have been important forces in women's lives, and that religion can be a vehicle for social justice, activism, and change. Therefore it should be no surprise that many women choose to remain within the paradigm of their cultural and religious norms, and no surprise that we would look to religion for some answers. As Dr. Fishbayn Joffe describes, the goal is to "engage cultural communities in the processes of reevaluating their discriminatory practices and identifying egalitarian solutions that will be both legitimate and enforceable."

To this end we have adopted the model of transformative dialogue promoted by a number of theorists of gender and multiculturalism where political agreement and progress is reached through a process that appeals to values internal to one's own comprehensive doctrines—in addition to analyzing external values as applied to guaranteeing basic justice and equality for women. To this end we aggressively foster intercultural and intracultural dialogue to uncover best practices, bringing together academics and activists, taking academic theories into the real world, and, vice-versa, bringing facts on the ground to theory. Our initial conference, Untying the Knots, the starting place of this anthology, was an opportunity to debate the project's founding principles and relate real life examples and theoretical analyses in various contexts. The Brandeis Series on Gender, Culture, Religion, and Law, which this anthology is part of, builds on this interactive dialogue model, attracting a diverse array of activists and scholars from various countries and cultures, who are engaged in vibrant debate and cross-seeding of ideas.

The reason I sought to place the Project on Gender, Culture, Religion, and the Law at Brandeis University, particularly at the Hadassah-Brandeis Institute rather than a law school or human rights institute, is that Brandeis is a university self-consciously based on Jewish values where the status of Jewish women within religion and culture is being aggressively addressed first hand. Therefore it is here that a transformative dialogue with others can take place in an atmosphere of shared experiences and within a paradigm of parity. Careful honing has resulted in a broad diversity of faces and voices from academia, religions, and social justice organizations around the world involved in every aspect of our work, freely discussing difficult personal and cultural issues, sometimes passionately disagreeing in approach, but open-mindedly grappling with untying the knots of female realities in an atmosphere of safety and acceptance.

On a personal note, one of the project's programs is the Diane (Dina) Markowicz Memorial Lecture named after my sister who died while she was a student at Brandeis. She was an exceptional teenager who inspired people of all ages to pursue social justice. The inaugural Markowicz Lecture was held on the first evening of the Untying the Knots conference, which featured Nobel Peace Prize laureates Shirin Ebadi and Jody Williams, who both exemplify the unprecedented impact that can result from advocacy and activism for change in human rights and women's rights. The evening was an apt introduction to the thoughtful and cutting-edge ideas presented by scholars and activists from around the world the next day at the conference. Their work comprises the core of this volume, with an overview by Dr. Fishbayn Joffe.

The idea for the Project on Gender, Culture, Religion, and the Law flowered in discussions with friends and family to whom I owe many thanks, particularly my husband, Dan Fischel. I am very grateful to Jehuda Reinharz, the former president of Brandeis University, for his personal encouragement and support, and to Shula Reinharz, the Jacob Potofsky Professor of Sociology and co-director of the HBI, who embraced the idea with enthusiasm and energy. I would also like to thank the board and staff of HBI; its co-director Professor Sylvia Barack Fishman; Phyllis Deutsch, editor in chief of UPNE; and Brandeis University Press for their unfaltering commitment to the project and book series. Finally, the success of the project is due to the extraordinary Lisa Fishbayn Joffe, whose leadership and scholarship is actualizing our vision.

Sylvia Neil

LISA FISHBAYN JOFFE

Introduction Theorizing Conflicts between Women's Rights and Religious Laws

Why Are Women's Equality Claims So Often at the Heart of Multicultural Conflicts?

Open the newspaper or surf the net any day and you will find a range of stories, both domestic and international, involving conflicts between women's rights and religious or cultural traditions. Many of these raise challenging questions about the scope of freedom of religion and the role of the state in balancing the rights of individuals, religious authorities, and the broader community. A representative sample might include stories like these:

- Women who ride the B110 bus from Williamsburg to Borough Park in Brooklyn are made to sit in a women's section at the back of the bus to prevent immodest mixing with men.[1] The bus operates with a license from the state of New York. Does this policy violate the rights to equality of women who ride the bus? Would putting a stop to it deny the freedom of religion of those who support separate seating? Does allowing this practice to go on mean that the state is supporting the establishment of religion?
- The Iranian women's soccer team is banned from competing in Olympic trials because team members wear headscarves in violation of the sport's uniform rules.[2] Should an exemption be made when participants believe the rule is in conflict with their religious obligations? Should the rule be rethought, with a more diverse group of participants in mind?
- An immigrant couple now living in the United States is divorcing. They were married in Pakistan, and the husband has divorced the wife there under Islamic laws that provide her with no right to alimony. The wife sues in a Maryland court for the maintenance and property she would be entitled to under state law. Can the state courts help her or does respect for

the integrity of other states or of other religions mean they must honor the terms of the Islamic marriage contract?[3]

- A suburban family in Utah that practices polygamy agrees to be part of a reality show about their lives, in part to show how ordinary they are. Prosecutors in Utah begin an investigation into whether the husband is violating state laws against bigamy.[4] The family flees the state but later sues, arguing that the law is being used to persecute polygamists unfairly. Does polygamy harm women by allowing them to be treated as unequals? Does a ban on polygamy violate the freedom of religion of those who freely choose to practice it?
- The leader of a fundamentalist Mormon sect is given a life sentence for the statutory rape of young girls he took as his "spiritual brides." Should polygamous marriages be viewed differently when they involve underage girls in a closed fundamentalist community? Can these girls be said to freely choose polygamy if they are given limited education and are groomed to marry men chosen for them by the "prophet"?[5] Should respect for religious difference excuse practices that would otherwise be characterized as heinous crimes?

The challenge of accommodating religious and cultural difference pervades many areas of our shared public life. An awareness of the central role that our religious faith and cultural ties play in the formation of personal identity and the pursuit of a satisfying life has prompted a broad range of legal and policy reforms and a continuing stream of new controversies. Our religious identity affects what we wear, how we educate our children, how we marry and divorce, and how we engage with or avoid the world around us. Whether accommodation takes the form of public financial support for faith-based institutions, affirmation of the right to wear religiously required attire in public spaces, or the integration of religious norms into aspects of state law, the impact of these strategies on the rights and roles of women is frequently at issue.

Asserting control over family law and the lives of women that are so intimately regulated by it is a frequent feature of demands for religious toleration. Whether by discouraging community members from using civil courts, demanding recognition of religious courts or contracts in liberal states, or seeking to replace secular law with religious law, how we regulate relationships in marriage and family says a lot about who we understand ourselves to be. Shifts in the way we regulate the family send a clear message to ourselves and others about this changed identity. Two recent examples demonstrate how this ideological shorthand has been used. In post-apartheid South Africa, recognizing African customary marriages and Muslim marriages that had been treated as legally invalid during the apartheid era was an important symbol of what it meant to be a new, nonracial, South Africa.[6] In the period after the Arab Spring of 2011, reasserting the primacy of Sharia law was also an important sign that power had shifted to the people. For example, one of the first acts of the transitional government in Libya after the overthrow of the Qaddafi regime was to announce that laws prohibiting polygamy had been abolished in order to restore Sharia as the basic source of the nation's laws.[7] While this act and similar alterations of religious law made clear that a new regime was in power, Muslim feminists warn that it will be women who pay a disproportionate price for these changes.[8]

Concern over the impact that policies for accommodating religious difference might have on women is expressed both by cultural insiders and by external observers. In the eyes of members of a religious or cultural group, women's rights often appear at the heart of conflicts between tradition and equality because women bear a disproportionate share of the burden of representing a community's collective identity to itself.[9] Anthropologist Anne McClintock has described this as a gendered distribution of symbolic labor, which solves the riddle of how a group can exist, simultaneously, as the natural embodiment of age-old traditions and as a self-conscious, modern community seeking worldly political power. The community may see men as representing growth and responsiveness to changing contemporary circumstances, while women are characterized as expressing the natural, authentic, and essential nature of a community and its traditions.[10] This association of women with a communal essence can have negative consequences for women. It may be overtly expressed in doctrines that deem women the repository of family or communal honor, which requires that women's behavior be carefully monitored and controlled.[11] It may also justify the exclusion of women from participation in the culture's rituals of public worship or structures of public power, on the theory that women do not need the experience of being shaped by these cultural institutions because they naturally manifest the virtues such practices are meant to inculcate.[12]

Leaving the symbolic realm and returning to the practical world, women may actually follow a more traditional lifestyle than men in their communities precisely because they have been excluded from the public sphere of work and politics and from exposure to alternative ways of being. Women's symbolic association with the notion of tradition may be enhanced because women play an important role in creating cultural continuity through their role as mothers who reproduce and educate a new generation.[13] Given these deep and pervasive associations, initiatives to change women's status under religious or customary law may be perceived as threats not only to entrenched power relations within the group, but also to the very possibility of perpetuating a shared set of social practices and the shared narrative of identity that justifies it.

For outsiders to the religious or cultural group, concern over the place of women in minority cultures can provide an apparently legitimate avenue for the expression of ambivalence, if not outright hostility, toward the distinctive practices and worldviews of these groups.[14] Such ambivalence may be expressed in popular media, academic discourse, or official state policy regarding the social and political integration of minorities. The content of a recent Canadian citizenship guide for prospective immigrants is instructive in this regard. In Canada, it explains, "men and women are equal under the law. Canada's openness and generosity do not extend to barbaric cultural practices that tolerate spousal abuse, 'honour killings,' female genital mutilation, or other gender-based violence. Those guilty of these crimes are severely punished under Canada's criminal laws."[15] While a laudable (if perhaps somewhat aspirational) statement of contemporary civic values, this account says as much about the suspicions of the fearsome practices of incoming minorities as it does about the values of the receiving country. Similar guides, reflecting similar anxieties, have been published in recent years in other Western countries.[16]

Outright expressions of contempt for religious and racial minorities, allegedly justified in part by the poor treatment they accord to women, is often now part of racist "White nationalist" discourse in Europe and North America. A controversial "Code of Conduct" passed by the rural town of Herouxville, Québec in 2007 instructed immigrants to adapt to the local culture and abandon their "barbaric cultural practices" that victimize women.[17] English racists calling themselves the English Defence League have defended race rioting against Muslims in the town of Luton by citing their suspicions that Muslims beat their wives and want to impose Sharia law.[18] Similar concerns may lie behind proposals to pass legislation barring the application of Sharia law in Canada[19] and in a dozen jurisdictions in the United States.[20]

For scholars of political and legal theory, women's rights are often at the heart of multicultural toleration debates because they are key issues in legal disputes involving regulation of the family. For members of the cultural majority and religious minorities, the family is an important nexus between private practices and public values. The resolution of family law disputes often involves reconciling competing desires for individual flourishing and familial and communal solidarity. Arguments over the rights of women to exert power over property and children in the family, to set the terms for their entry into marriage, and to seek to exit from marriage, often bring competing worldviews about the role of women into sharp relief.

These disputes are sometimes characterized as involving irreconcilable clashes of cultural visions, but lawyers, judges, policymakers, religious leaders, and the individuals involved can and do find ways of working through these conflicts, often in creative and innovative ways. The work collected in this anthology reflects this commitment to find effective solutions to these intractable problems. The authors move beyond polemics to seek concrete strategies to integrate the dual commitments to women's rights to gender equality and multicultural toleration. The anthology brings together the work of an international and interdisciplinary group of scholars grappling with knotty questions at the intersection of civil rights and religious law. Should religious law be an entirely private matter, or should it be recognized by the state? If the state chooses to recognize religious family laws, should these be interpreted and applied by the state's own courts or by religious courts staffed by clergy? Regardless of whether the courts are secular or religious in nature, should they also be required to comply with the rights contained in the Constitution? If the religious laws conflict with constitutional norms, which should take precedence? When commitment to equality demands changes to religious norms, how can these be implemented in ways that community members will find legitimate?

The contributions to this volume go beyond theory to explore in concrete terms how conflicts between women's rights and religious law are being addressed in a range of nations around the world. While demonstrating a sophisticated grasp of developments in legal and political theory, these authors also bring to bear their expertise as lawyers, activists, and religious authorities to provide fresh insight into how these theories translate into real change on the ground. While much past work in this field has pointed to case studies to illustrate the ways in which women can be disadvantaged by religious and cultural norms, the pieces in this anthology explore what happens when proposals for multicultural toleration and initiatives to improve women's rights are actually applied in states around the world. In their chapters, leading theorists Martha Minow and Ayelet Shachar address the challenge of finding the right balance between commitment to the principles of equality between men and women and equality between religious groups by exploring how these competing concerns are reflected in a number of recent public controversies. The conflicts discussed in these chapters and those that follow emerge from several different religious traditions. Susan Weiss, Michal Roness, and Irit Koren discuss Jewish law in Israel. Rashida Manjoo and Pascale Fournier explore how Muslim law is applied in the secular states of South Africa, the United States, and Canada, while Fatou Kiné Camara looks at strategies for changing women's status in Senegal, where Islamic law is the law of the land. Likhapha Mbatha and I consider the case of African Customary Law, the traditional, tribally based quasi-religious, quasi-political rules used to govern the family relationships of Black Africans in South Africa. Linda C. McClain provides a comparative evaluation of how American courts deal with disputes emerging from a range of traditions, including cases involving conservative interpretations of Christian marriage doctrine that are no longer embodied in American law.

The case studies also deal with a variety of ways of configuring the relationship between religious law and state law. In Israel and Senegal, religious norms are enforced by the state as part of a regime of personal law. In the United States and Canada, religious norms are, at least formally, relegated to the private sphere but can be brought into the legal realm through the private acts of the spouses if they decide to make and rely on a religious marriage contract or refer their family law dispute to a religious tribunal for arbitration. Several authors make the point that enhanced recognition of religious tribunals or religious doctrines by civil courts would create a new hybrid of these two models. These case studies provide an occasion to interrogate the utility of recent theoretical models for engaging with gender and multicultural conflicts, to explore contextual differences, and to analyze and celebrate stories of successful initiatives that have transformed legal and cultural norms.

The Place of Gender in Multicultural Theory

While the challenge of negotiating the place of gender in religious and multicultural conflicts is now widely recognized by theorists in law and political theory,[21] this has not always been the case. A brief account of this history will set the stage for the exploration of conflicts over gender and religious accommodation that is the focus of this book. There have been three moments in the development of the political theory of multiculturalism that have culminated in a focus on questions of gender. The first stage saw the emergence of a communitarian critique of the notion of cultural identity in liberal political theory. In the second stage, theorists responded to the communitarian challenge by elaborating a distinctly liberal justification for multicultural toleration. A third phase has been marked by attempts to identify the lacunae in this liberal conception with regard to the rights of minorities within minorities and has resulted in an approach that seeks to grapple with the concerns of women.[22]

The communitarian critique developed as a corrective to what its proponents took to be an overemphasis on the role of the autonomous individual in liberal theory. Communitarians object both to a liberal ethics that prioritizes respect for rights over the pursuit of the good and the phenomenology of consciousness upon which these ethics are based. Liberalism relies upon a conception of the person as one whose capacity for reasoned autonomy preexists any determinate objectives she might have. If one accepts this model, communitarians argue, a vision of the good life, whether drawn from secular reason or religious revelation, cannot be constitutive of an individual's identity in any deep way. All commitments are seen as being deliberately adopted at some discrete point in time by an individual whose primary identity is merely that of a choosing consciousness.

Communitarians argue that our actual experience of consciousness is quite different, in that it includes a sense of being encumbered by the values, connections, and points of view in which we are embedded as members of familial, religious, cultural, and political communities. Moreover, the exercise of autonomy relies on our already having these commitments in order to be able to engage in the process of evaluation and action through which a liberal self is constructed. While one may define oneself in opposition to one's social context, one cannot do so independent of any context. One cannot in fact exercise the power of choice without some preexisting evaluations and preferences that one aims to satisfy and develop in so choosing.[23]

If their critique stopped there, few liberals would object to this corrective account. However, communitarians go on to argue that the state ought to be structured to protect these cultural conceptions from outside influence and from destructive internal critique and revision. Rather than encouraging people to exercise autonomy in the quest for some illusory critical distance upon their values, political life should create conditions under which individuals can gain a deeper and more complex understanding of these constitutive attachments. Thoroughgoing rejection of one's cultural values is undesirable, as it would see individuals render themselves rudderless in a moral universe to no great advantage.[24] In this second moment in the development of multicultural theory, liberal multiculturalists accept the need of each individual for a cultural context but argue that if culture is important because it is instrumental to autonomy, culture's claims will pale when cultural practices themselves place unreasonable limits on autonomy.

Liberal multiculturalists do not characterize the duty to respect and accommodate cultural difference as a counterpoint to liberalism but as derivative of the central liberal commitment to autonomy. They argue that this commitment is both the source of the duty to respect cultural difference and the limit upon the extent of the duty to do so. The liberal political vision is organized around creating the conditions under which individuals can exercise their capacity to develop and revise conceptions of the good life. One of these conditions is the opportunity to be involved in a cultural community.

In developing a conception of the good, we do not create conceptions out of whole cloth, but contemplate and critique the values, roles, and institutions revealed to us by our socialization into our cultural community.[25] A complex awareness of the traditions of our community is thus a precondition for making intelligent choices about how to live our lives.[26]

A commitment to autonomy is supplemented by a commitment to secure benefits such as autonomy to all on an equal basis. Liberals are thus obliged to equalize the capacities of individuals who are disadvantaged through no fault of their own. The fact that most modern nations are culturally plural, containing a range of religious, ethnic, and cultural groups, means that there is often inequality in access to culture understood as a resource in this way. While members of the dominant cultural group can meet their need for a cultural structure with little effort because it is woven into the fabric of public life, members of minority cultural groups must expend financial, political, and emotional resources to create a sphere in which they can participate in their own culture. The values of the dominant cultural group are reflected in everything from the rhythm of the workweek, to the content of school curricula and the obligations of the laws of marriage. While it might be difficult, in practical terms, to avoid conferring such benefits on the majority group, it is appropriate to offer exemptions from general rules or additional assistance to members of minorities who are disenfranchised by these rules.

On this model, a group might be entitled to seek assistance from the state in resisting apparently neutral state policies that have the effect of disabling the capacity of minorities to participate in their own cultural structures. This might mean that the state should change what was intended to be a neutral rule barring wearing scarves while playing in a soccer match because it prevents observant Muslim women from participating. The rule might be an attempt to achieve an unobjectionable goal but has an unfair impact on members of some religious groups. If the same objective can be achieved through a less restrictive rule, the law should be changed to accommodate this difference.

Conversely, a group cannot claim to be entitled to seek assistance or immunity from the law in order to prevent individual dissentient members from seeking to change the character of the community by revising or rejecting its traditional values.[27] The young girls coerced into "spiritual marriage" by Warren Jeffs in accordance with his sect's interpretation of Mormon doctrine are entitled to characterize this treatment as rape and to have the state prosecute it as such, without deference to the sensibilities of Jeffs or his adherents. A liberal state may thus be obligated to cushion the impact of policies set outside the community but not to take positions that thwart processes of internal change within the community or deny the rights of community members. In practice, it has often proved difficult to map this distinction. Is the regulation of family life under religious regimes of marital law a central cultural practice that should be protected from the impact of inconsistent national family and human rights legislation, or should the gender differentiated rights under such regimes be seen a prime example of internal restrictions that the state is justified in redressing?[28]

The third moment in the development of multicultural theory is the emergence of this feminist critique regarding the rights of minorities within minorities. If the duty to tolerate and accommodate religious and cultural difference is predicated on the important roles these institutions play in fostering personal autonomy, then customs and traditions that obstruct the development or exercise of this capacity for some members of the community based on their sex cannot be justified.

The Place of Individual Agency in Debates over Gender, Law, and Multiculturalism

Some of the questions that emerge in translating a commitment to women's rights into the transformation of impugned aspects of religious law are highly theoretical: How can philosophical conceptions of a good life that are predicated on enabling individual autonomy be reconciled with religious or cultural conceptions that are organized around pursuing virtue, often by complying with highly gendered normative codes? In the context of a multicultural society, how should a concern for equality between religious and cultural groups be balanced against claims for equality among men and women within a particular group? How should courts understand the nature of women's interests when women themselves hold a diverse range of views on the merits of such practices?

Some of the questions that arise are more tactical in nature: How should courts and commentators respond to the fact that some women and men may choose to exercise their personal autonomy to comply with religious rules that others might finding limiting and even demeaning? How can advocates for legal change devise strategies to ameliorate women's disadvantage that will be both subtle enough to take account of the role that cultural and religious practices play in people's lives and effective enough to make a real difference?

In the opening chapter of this collection, Martha Minow elegantly frames the challenge to reconcile the tactical and theoretical questions that run through the book as the "paradox of liberalism." The accommodation of religious groups may sometimes be read as a compromise of principle; in others, it may be the expression of a principled embrace of the ideal of the coexistence of multiple normative traditions. Minow argues that approaching these conflicts in a spirit of humility, flexibility, and cooperation can lead to outcomes that are both more satisfying and more effective. This supple approach to identifying and developing opportunities for change informs the narratives of diverse legal regimes' responses to cultural difference that follow.

While there may be general agreement that just laws and social policies should demonstrate respect for women's individual autonomy, in practice there is often ambivalence about how such respect should be manifested. Regardless of gender, the actual choices we make may not reflect our deepest preferences, for a range of reasons. Everyone's choices are constrained by their circumstances, their entitlements, and their conflicting obligations. However, women's choices may be constrained in ways that are distinctly unfair. They may be educated to believe that few preferences they might hold are legitimate and that few choices are open to them. They may also be prevented by illegitimate coercion from pursuing some preferences that they do genuinely hold. In situations where women appear to make choices that reflect a diminished sense of possibility for their lives or an acquiescence to coercion, those committed to respecting women's capacity to make their own lives must consider whether this is best achieved through accepting women's actual choices without comment or by also trying to identify and change the background circumstances that condition these unappealing choices.[29]

This ambivalence is expressed very clearly in the persistent debates about the acceptability of wearing Islamic veils in public spaces. Nations with very different attitudes toward the toleration of cultural and religious difference seem to agree that this mode of attire is a problem that needs to regulated. In nations committed to state neutrality toward all religious practices, the wearing of veils is seen as a symbol of cultural difference that impedes commitment to shared civic values. In nations committed to policies of multicultural accommodation, some more restrictive forms of veiling, like the niqab, which covers the face, are prohibited where they are found to impede job performance or impair legitimate government interests in identifying individuals at the voting booth or airport check-in line.

Feminist commentators differ on their evaluations of whether such policies enhance or impair the autonomy of women. Some Islamic feminists praise such bans, like those on headscarves in Turkey and face veils in France, because it empowers women who are inclined to resist community pressure to adopt a practice they do not believe in. However, others argue that such bans prevent them from manifesting their genuine belief that veiling is a binding religious obligation. Indeed, they suggest that such bans harm the prospects for altering objectionable elements of Islamic practice because it may force powerful, educated women who could provide leadership in negotiating the tension between traditional norms and women's educational, professional, and political aspirations out of the public sphere.

Something that may go unremarked in these debates is the way in which such bans valorize the treatment of women's bodies and women's attire as potent cultural symbols rather than as expressions of the intentions and aspirations of the individuals who wear them. The women who may themselves accept or reject the veil for complex reasons can disappear from these debates as anything other than mute pawns carrying the banner for one or another ideological viewpoint. Their actions may have multiple and contradictory meanings, perhaps as affirmations of tradition, rejection of what they perceive to be the racism or sexism of the dominant culture, or a personal bid to occupy space as a powerful political actor on the public stage.[30] Observing this practice may also allow them to be taken more seriously by those in authority as they try to transform discriminatory practices in their community.[31]

Recognizing women's agency thus entails recognizing the ways in which women may deploy tradition strategically. Religious and cultural norms may be invoked, subverted, or transformed as community members seek to achieve their personal and collective objectives. In the context of her analysis in this collection of the way doctrines from foreign religious law regimes are enforced in American courts, Linda McClain points out not only how the distribution of power between religious bodies and civil courts can serve to disadvantage women by empowering male elites, but also how women can and do use the interplay between regimes strategically to secure their best advantage. Attempts to shop among available forums in order to seek one's advantage are a constant factor in such plural family law regimes. Any changes made to distribution of powers over family law jurisdiction between these regimes will not end competition and conflict between plural regimes, but will channel it in a different fashion that may have different impacts on different stakeholders.

Like McClain, Pascale Fournier's chapter analyzes the ways in which American and Canadian courts deal with doctrines drawn from religious family law. She parses the range of doctrinal approaches developed toward Islamic *mahr* contracts, which provide for financial gifts from husband to wife upon marriage, in conflicts of laws jurisprudence. Fournier focuses on the ways these doctrines enable or hamper the agency of the parties. While courts may treat these complex issues as ones requiring the careful reconciliation of legal and moral principle, the parties themselves are generally acting strategically to maximize their personal material benefit. Fournier asks us to consider these cases from the perspective of the "bad man" or "bad woman" who seeks to maximize his or her economic advantages at the expense of coherence between the moral and legal principles invoked. Viewed from the perspective of those who care "only about what the law might *do* to him, not what it *is* abstractly for him," she urges us to consider the distributive impacts of legal decisions as of equal importance to their ideological significance.

It is possible, however, to push this interest in identifying the capacity for agency of individuals in even the most constrained circumstances too far. In her chapter in this anthology, Ayelet Shachar cautions that many of the features that make negotiating disputes with the help of lawyers or mediators rather than taking a case before a judge a desirable option in the context of civil family law may not be present in religious courts. Women may lack an effective voice, effective representation, or access to legal language in which to frame their claims in proceedings before religious tribunals. The law applied may be substantively unfair, however able the woman is in presenting her case. Even the possibility of review by a civil court judge of suspect decisions by religious bodies may fail to adequately compensate for the disadvantage women may experience before religious courts. Shachar argues for what she has called "transformative accommodation" of these religious tribunals, such that recognition of their decisions as binding law is made contingent upon their applying state-sanctioned human rights norms to their own actions and doctrines.

The parties may not be the only ones seeking their best advantage when decisions are being made about whether to resolve family law disputes with the help of religious authorities or through the civil courts. Religious law authorities also have a stake in the resolution of these conflicts. Patriarchal elites are motivated to defend both their institutional power and the substantive discriminatory doctrines that secure that power. From her perspective as a "cause lawyer" litigating to develop a feminist divorce jurisprudence in Israel, Susan Weiss provides an intriguing example of how women can get caught up in the struggle over jurisdiction between secular and religious courts in plural law regimes. While the modern state of Israel initially granted exclusive jurisdiction over family law matters to religious courts, this power has been gradually whittled down, as civil courts have been granted concurrent jurisdiction over most matters, with the exception of the dissolution of marriage. Many couples engage in a race to the courthouse[32] where women seek to bring their cases under the more egalitarian civil law, while men seek their best advantage by bringing their actions in rabbinical courts. Weiss describes how rabbinical courts react to the erosion of their sphere of influence through developing ever more draconian devices for asserting their authority. Through a series of civil suits in tort for damages for failure to grant a religious divorce, Weiss explains how her Center for Women's Justice is enabling women to use secular law as a platform to comment upon and redress their mistreatment under religious law.

Resolving Conflicts between Multicultural Toleration and Women's Rights

Feminist critics of multiculturalism agree that in cases of conflict, guarantees of gender equality must take precedence over claims rooted in culture and religion. While it has sometimes been argued that it might be best if cultures wedded to the patriarchal oppression of women within their midst were to become extinct, most theorists argue that the primacy of equality should be established by encouraging communities to identify ways in which their discriminatory practices can be integrated with gender equality norms.[33] Several chapters in this book consider the attempt to develop institutional forms that will ensure the priority of gender equality and make such reflection possible. The opportunity for judicial review of the actions of religious courts by civil tribunals can both alleviate disadvantage at the hands of religious law courts and encourage dialogue between legal regimes and within law-following communities about the possibilities for law reform.

A key theme that runs through the book is a consideration of the role structural devices for dividing jurisdiction can play in alleviating conflicts between public equality and private religious or cultural norms.[34] Religious law may operate in at least three ways. It may be the basis for general family law throughout the nation, as it was in eighteenth-century England[35] and as it is now in many Muslim majority states.[36] In a second model, multiple regimes of religious family law may be permitted to operate side by side within an otherwise secular state, exercising jurisdiction over members of those religious communities, as in contemporary Israel, India, and Kenya. In modern versions of these plural law regimes, some elements of family law, like the distribution of property or custody of children, may also be covered by civil laws, giving rise to the possibility of the sort of race to the courthouse described by Weiss. In a third approach, principles of religious family law may be incorporated into an otherwise secular regime by the private acts of individuals, who may choose to contract marriages solemnized under religious law and to take family law or other disputes to religious tribunals. Shachar has pointed out how rules for resolving conflicts between jurisdictions can be used to create or alleviate pressure on religious law bodies to change their norms or risk losing recognition for their authority and the allegiance of their followers.[37] In her chapter for this volume, Minow suggests that the creative and critical deployment of traditional governance devices for the management of plural nations may serve to contain or defer conflicts that cannot or need not be resolved through state coercion or state deference. McClain cautions, however, that enhanced recognition of religious law may throw the fragile balance struck by American courts between civil rights and religious norms out of balance in ways that will disadvantage women.

To illustrate the risks involved in delegating power over family law to religious authorities in the name of accommodating religious or cultural difference, chapters by Rashida Manjoo and by Likhapha Mbatha and myself consider recent efforts to address women's inequality while reforming the plural family law regime in South Africa. Until the demise of apartheid, South Africa divided jurisdiction over family law between the state and tribal authorities but provided only partial recognition to a stunted conception of African tribal family law and refused all recognition to marriages contracted under Islamic law. Both chapters address the tension between seeking to affirm equality between previously disenfranchised Black and Muslim communities and the privileged White minority in the face of a history of grievous disenfranchisement and the need to turn a critical eye on the internal practices of both the African and Muslim legal regimes. The fact that neither regime was recognized under apartheid has had the perverse effect of making it more difficult to change the official accounts of patriarchal legal doctrine, as no formal mechanisms have existed for doing so. In this difficult context, Mbatha and I examine the decision of post-apartheid South Africa to grant recognition to the institution of polygamous marriage. We explore the reasons that a newly democratic South Africa chose to recognize this practice in the face of clear evidence of its pernicious effects on African women. We also consider how such recognition has, nevertheless, formed the basis for incremental reforms to the institution of polygamy.

Manjoo, a former member of the South African Gender Commission and now UN Special Rapporteur on Violence against Women, describes another legislative proposal in the new South Africa, which would redress the refusal to recognize Islamic law by codifying the principles of Muslim Sharia family law and the role of Islamic tribunals in resolving family disputes. She argues that equality between religious traditions can be achieved through affirming the legitimacy of Islamic law institutions without entrenching the more extreme patriarchal norms that have been promulgated by legally unrecognized Sharia courts. She urges the adoption of mechanisms that will ensure that a recognized South African conception of Sharia can be reshaped in the light of the equality guarantees in the new Constitution and South Africa's commitments under international human rights laws.

Contesting the Notion of "Culture" in Multiculturalism

It is sometimes argued that eradicating practices that deny women power over key aspects of their lives is fundamentally inconsistent with essential elements of some cultural traditions. Changing these practices may thus put at risk the possibilities of perpetuating important forms of life in which they are enmeshed. However, this notion elides the ways in which religious and cultural traditions constantly undergo a process of interpretation, selection, and refinement. While certain elements may be conceived of as essential to a cultural worldview at a given point in time, the nature of the practice, its meaning, and its role have often changed over time. The tradition may also have been variously shaped by the practices of the broader communities in which minorities live. Even within the official discourse of a religion, there are often recognized countertendencies, alternative interpretations, and insurgent schools of thought competing for dominance.[38]

Arguments that multicultural toleration requires the uncritical preservation of authentic, traditional practices thus rely on an anthropologically naïve conception of how cultural identities are formed and maintained.[39] This naïve conception characterizes culture as the way of life of a discrete people whose essence is expressed through a coherently interlinked set of ideas and practices. Individuals are slotted into defined roles within the community and express what agency they have in elaborating the performance and meaning of these roles and the rules that undergird them. On this model, culture is a fragile organic structure that flourishes if left alone, but can be destroyed through even small changes.[40]

A model of culture that captures the genuine dynamism of cultural practice and cultural identity through time looks rather different. A culture is not an organic whole but a shifting set of religious and cultural texts, symbols, and practices that has no central core features. The link between these materials and a particular people is wrought by history rather than logical or biological necessity. A cultural group maintains this sense of identity through collaborative elaboration of a narrative that pulls these materials together in a coherent way. The group identity is constituted by this collaborative activity, but it is predicated on the shared effort to find meaning together, not on a shared consensus of what these materials meant in the past or what their implications are for the future. Legal and policy interventions by outside authorities may change the terms of this struggle over meaning in the community, empowering some and disadvantaging others who previously enjoyed more privileged positions, but this does not render the culture thereby produced necessarily less authentic in an anthropological sense.

It may, however, be substantially less legitimate in the eyes of key stakeholders in the community because it has been produced outside the accepted mechanisms for normative change within the community and does not appear to cohere with its stated values.[41] A key strategy for working through conflicts between women's rights to equality and the preservation of religious and cultural structures is, therefore, to explore the dissonant voices within the tradition in order to uncover ways in which human rights values might be seen as consistent with internal cultural values.[42] Even where such analysis reveals that there is no indigenous norm that parallels important human rights norms, this process of collaborative deliberation may reduce the scope of the apparent inconsistency. This dialogue may be initiated through public policy discussions, through internal educational campaigns, or through women's increased involvement in areas of ritual or legal life. It may also come about through the law reform process itself. Litigation or legislative reform aimed at bringing religious and cultural practices in line with human rights norms may provide the impetus for working through conflicts that might otherwise remain inchoate and therefore apparently intractable.

While we all need cultural materials to do the work of identity formation and normative deliberation, these materials do not need to come from a single integrated normative vision and rarely do so.[43] Many women experience their normative lives as constituted by the interweaving of obligations from multiple sources. As Minow notes, a legal approach that seeks to work through this complexity rather than slide over it may be more effective in resolving both women's real-life conflicts and conflicts of principle.

How do women seek to change the practices of their culture from within? The chapters by Koren, Roness, and Camara take a deeper look into the experience of religiously observant women who seek to transform the religious law that governs them. The authors describe both the ways in which women involved in initiating legal change understand their practices and how they endeavor to justify them to other stakeholders in their religious and cultural communities. These pieces discuss women defining new roles as participants in key religious rituals, in developing the credentials to be recognized interpreters of religious doctrine, and as designers of new institutions to articulate egalitarian cultural narratives. As Irit Koren describes it, these are women who may have the option to exit their religious community to join the secular world but who make a conscious decision to seek change from within. Koren's work explores women's attempt to transform the Jewish marriage ritual, particularly the symbolic motifs that reflect the notion that the husband is acquiring rights of ownership and dominion over the wife. Just as Minow urges legal theorists to live with the tension between affirming equality and accommodating difference, Koren argues that these transgressive brides are distinguished by their ability to contain the dissonance in their own identities between their religious and feminist selves.

From her unique perspective as a member of one of the first cohorts of trained *yoatzot halakhah*, or female Jewish law advisors, Michal Roness describes the emerging recognition of women as authorities on the application of Jewish laws relating to menstruation and marital intimacy. She considers how proponents of this novel legal role for women were able to successfully negotiate the shoals of expanding women's authority as guides to the application of religious law and securing acceptance by the community and rabbinate in the Modern Orthodox world. Roness demonstrates how social change initiated by religious women with detailed knowledge of the community, high status among existing leadership, and commitment to its values can be successful. She suggests that attempts to fraction legal transformation agendas into incremental steps may thereby reduce the potential for conflict that may accompany it.

In the final chapter in this section, Fatou Kiné Camara writes about an innovative program to undermine resistance to feminist reform of Muslim family law in Senegal. Camara demonstrates how notions of an indigenous matriarchal and egalitarian tradition are disseminated as a corrective to invocations of Islamic heritage. Like Mbatha and Fishbayn Joffe, she argues that the legacy of colonialism for African family law can only be eroded through careful attention to the role the commingled values of indigenous custom and formal law play in the regulation of African family life.

This anthology aims both to capture a sense of the diversity of forms that conflicts between gender equality and practices justified in terms of cultural and religious norms might take and to offer a sense of the creative and innovative theoretical models and practical strategies that are being deployed to understand and deal with these conflicts. The contributors demonstrate a complex grasp of the challenges posed by having multiple religious and civil normative systems operating within one society. They reflect with sophistication upon the interplay between individual agency and the structures that distribute power to religious groups or centralize power in a secular state. They consider the legacy that relations of colonial domination, racial hierarchy, and gender inequality have on the possibilities for effective transformation of laws that disadvantage women. Finally, they provide examples of the ways in which women within communities that retain discriminatory patriarchal norms are working from the inside to integrate their personal commitments to both gender equality and religious law. The role of law may not always be to resolve the tensions between women's rights and religious law, but it can shift the terms of the debate in ways that put greater power into the hands of the female leaders, plaintiffs, and advocates who seek to implement these changes.

Acknowledgments

The idea for this collection grew out of the inaugural conference of the Project on Gender, Culture, Religion and the Law of the Hadassah-Brandeis Institute, held at Brandeis University in 2008. The Project on Gender, Culture, Religion and the Law is funded by a grant from the Dan Fischel and Sylvia Neil Philanthropic Fund. I am grateful to the project founder, Sylvia Neil, for her vision, confidence, and friendship. We are grateful to the HBI directors, Shulamit Reinharz and Sylvia Barack Fishman, for their support and encouragement. Lenore Weitzman was an enthusiastic advisor. Sarah Twichell, HBI coordinator, was enormously helpful in running the conference and pulling together the final contributions to the book. Phyllis Deutsch was an engaged and wise editor. Thanks also to our collaborators on the conference: Elisheva Baumgarten of the Fanya Gottesfeld Heller Center for the Study of Women in Judaism at Bar Ilan University; Leigh Swigart at the International Center for Ethics, Justice and Public Life at Brandeis University; Kelly Ready and the Gender Working Group at the Heller School for Social Policy at Brandeis; the Schusterman Center for Israel Studies at Brandeis University; and the Office of the President of Brandeis University. Excellent research assistance for the conference and this anthology was provided by Shayna Weiss, Katherine Romanow, and Marley Weiner through the HBI Lily Safra Internship Program; by Becca Wasser and Navah Rosenbaum through the Brandeis Women's Studies Research Center Student-Scholar Partnership; and by Rasha Azoni through the Project on Gender, Culture, Religion and the Law. The conference was supported by major gifts from the Neil-Fischel Philanthropic Fund and the Weinberg Fund.

Notes

1. Christine Haughney, "At Front of Brooklyn Bus, a Clash of Religious and Women's Rights," *New York Times*, October 19, 2011. Women on the #56 bus in Jerusalem are subject to the same coercion, even though the Supreme Court of Israel has declared the practice illegal. Maayan Lubell, "Women Fight 'Back of the Bus' Battle in Jerusalem: Segregation of Sexes Has Been Spreading in Ultra-Orthodox Jewish Areas," MSNBC.com, November 14, 2011.

2. Thomas Erdbrink, "Olympics 2012: FIFA Bans Headscarves for Iranian Women's Soccer Team," *Washington Post*, June 6, 2011.

3. See discussion of the *Aleem* case in Linda C. McClain's chapter in this volume.

4. "'Sister Wives' Family: Bigamy Law Hurting, Not Helping," Associated

Press, October 18, 2011. For an extended discussion, see Janet Bennion, *Polygamy in Primetime: Media, Gender and Politics in Mormon Fundamentalism* (Waltham, MA: Brandeis University Press, 2012).

5. *Texas: Polygamist Leader Gets Life Sentence*, Associated Press, August 9, 2011.

6. See chapters in this volume by Rashida Manjoo and by Likhapha Mbatha and Lisa Fishbayn Joffe.

7. Richard Spencer, "Libya's Liberation: Interim Ruler Unveils More Radical than Expected Plans for Islamic Law," *Telegraph*, October 23, 2011. http://www.telegraph.co.uk/news/worldnews/africaandindianocean/libya/8844819/Libyas-liberation-interim-ruler-unveils-more-radical-than-expected-plans-for-Islamic-law.html

8. *Women Living under Muslim Laws Statement on Libya*, October 25, 2011, http://www.wluml.org/action/women-living-under-muslim-laws-statement-libya.

9. Ayelet Schachar, "Group Identity and Women's Rights in Family Law: The Perils of Multicultural Accommodation," *Journal of Political Philosophy* 6 (1998): 285, 293.

10. Anne McLintock, *Imperial Leather: Race, Gender and Sexuality in the Colonial Context* (New York: Routledge 1995), 359.

11. L. Abu-Odeh, "Comparatively Speaking: The 'Honor' of the 'East' and the 'Passion' of the 'West,'" *Utah Law Review*, 1997, 287–307.

12. Judith Hauptman, *Rereading the Rabbis: A Woman's Voice* (Boulder, CO: Westview Press, 1998), 225.

13. Ayelet Shachar, *Multicultural Jurisdictions: Cultural Differences and Women's Rights* (Cambridge: Cambridge University Press, 2001), 50.

14. Sherene Razack, *Casting Out: The Eviction of Muslims from Western Law and Politics* (Toronto: University of Toronto Press, 2008), 146.

15. *Discover Canada* (Citizenship and Immigration Canada). http://www.cic.gc.ca/english/resources/publications/discover/section-04.asp.

16. See, for example, *Life in the United Kingdom: A Journey to Citizenship*, 2nd ed. (United Kingdom Stationery Office, 2009).

17. See 2007 Herouxville Town Charter. A slightly amended version is at http://herouxville-quebec.blogspot.com/2007/03/about-beautiful-herouxville-quebec.html.

18. Lauren Collins, "England, Their England," *New Yorker*, July 4, 2011, 30. Interestingly, a Muslim leader rejects the notion of assimilation on much the same basis, saying, "We're not required to look like you, be like you—especially when we look at the state of you. You get drunk, you beat up your wives, you sell drugs" (ibid., 32).

19. See discussion of debates over faith-based arbitration in family law in Ontario in the chapters by Minow, Shachar, and McClain in this volume.

20. Michel Martin, "States Move to Ban Islamic Sharia Law," NPR, March 11, 2011, http://www.npr.org/2011/03/11/134458058/States-Move-To-Ban-Islamic-Sharia-Law.

21. See, for example, Shachar, *Multicultural Jurisdiction*; Monique Deveaux, *Gender and Justice in Multicultural Liberal States* (Oxford: Oxford University Press, 2006); Sarah Song, *Justice, Gender and the Politics of Multiculturalism* (Cambridge: Cambridge University, 2007); Anne Phillips, *Gender and Culture* (Cambridge: Polity Press, 2010).

22. Susan Moller Okin, "Is Multiculturalism Bad for Women?" in *Is Multiculturalism Bad for Women?* ed. Joshua Cohen et al. (Princeton: Princeton University Press, 1999); Avigail Eisenberg and Jeff Spinner-Halev, eds., *Minorities within Minorities: Equality, Rights and Diversity* (Cambridge: Cambridge University Press 2005).

23. Michael Sandel, *Liberalism and the Limits of Justice* (Cambridge: Cambridge University Press, 1998), 161–65.

24. Ibid., 214.

25. Will Kymlicka, *Liberalism Community and Culture* (Oxford: Oxford University Press, 1989), 164–65.

26. Ibid.

27. Ibid., 198.

28. Okin, *Is Multiculturalism Bad for Women?*, 13.

29. "In order to account for women's consciousness . . . feminism must grasp that male power produces the world before it distorts it. Women's acceptance of their condition does not contradict its fundamental unacceptability if women have little choice but to become persons who freely choose women's roles." Catharine A. MacKinnon, "Feminism, Marxism, Method and the State," *Signs: Journal of Women in Culture and Society* 7 (1983): 515–42.

30. Seyla Benhabib, *Another Cosmopolitanism* (Oxford: Oxford University Press, 2006), 53. Wearing the veil may be a strategic choice that allows women to be taken seriously while advocating for reform of religious norms. Asifa Quirashi, "Western Advocacy for Muslim Women: It's Not Just the Thought That Counts," paper presented at *Working from the World Up: Equality's Future,* University of Wisconsin Law School, Madison, WI, March 14–15, 2008.

31. This ambivalence about women's capacity for autonomous decision making is not limited to the sphere of religious law disputes. See, for example, recent moves by American courts to protect women from the possibility of making abortion

decisions about which they may someday feel remorse or regret; Jeannie Suk, "The Trajectory of Trauma: Bodies and Minds of Abortion Discourse," *Columbia Law Review* 110 (2010): 1193.

32. Susan Weiss and Netty Gross, *Israel's Civil War: Jewish Marriage and Divorce* (Brandeis University Press, forthcoming 2012).

33. Joseph Raz, *The Morality of Freedom* (Oxford: Oxford University Press, 1986), 408; Okin, *Is Multiculturalism Bad for Women?*, 7. Okin emphasized her preference for using human rights law as a guidepost for internal reform of discriminatory practices in her later work. See Susan Okin, "Multiculturalism and Feminism: No Simple Questions, No Simple Answers," in *Minorities within Minorities*, 67–89 at 72–75. See also Martha Nussbaum, "A Plea for Difficulty," in *Is Multiculturalism Bad for Women?*

34. A role elegantly highlighted by Shachar, *Multicultural Jurisdictions*.

35. Between the passage of *Lord Hardwicke's Marriage Act* of 1753 and the *Marriage Act* of 1836, valid marriages could only be solemnized under the auspices of the Church of England, with special dispensations made for Jews and Quakers; Carolyn Hamilton, *Family, Law and Religion* (London: Sweet and Maxwell, 1995), 43.

36. It is not a coincidence that this model persists in these former English colonies once subject to indirect rule. See Lisa Fishbayn, "Litigating the Right to Culture: Family Law in the New South Africa," *International Journal of Law, Policy and the Family* 13, no. 2 (1999): 147. Nations throughout the Arab world, for example, developed family law codes based on Sharia law throughout the last century, beginning with the Ottoman Empire in 1917 and continuing, most recently, with Qatar in 2006; Lynn Welchman, *Women and Muslim Family Laws in Arab States* (Amsterdam: Amsterdam University Press, 2007), 12–13.

37. Shachar, *Multicultural Jurisdictions*.

38. See, for example, Jan Feldman's discussion of the assumption in Jewish law that conflicting opinions about interpretation are inevitable and potentially simultaneously correct; Jan Feldman, *Citizenship, Faith and Feminism: Jewish and Muslim Women Reclaim Their Rights* (Waltham, MA: Brandeis University Press, 2011), 57–58.

39. Will Kymlicka, *Multicultural Odysseys* (Oxford: Oxford University Press, 2007), 101.

40. See Lisa Fishbayn, "Culture, Gender and the Law: Recent Thinking and Practical Strategies," in *Gender and Human Rights in the Commonwealth* (London: Commonwealth Secretariat, 2004), 36–37.

41. Commenting on the recent judgment of the Supreme Court of the

United Kingdom in *R (E) v Governing Body of JFS* [2010] 2 AC 728, [2010] 2 WLR 153, that a school admissions policy based on the doctrines of Jewish law was discriminatory based on race, Simon Hochhauser, president of the United Synagogue for Orthodox Judaism, commented, "Essentially, we must now apply a non-Jewish definition of who is Jewish." Jewish School Loses Appeal," Guardian Online December 16, 2009.

42. James Tully, *Constitutionalism in the Age of Diversity* (Cambridge: Cambridge University Press, 1995); Thandabantu Nhlapo, "African Family Law under an Undecided Constitution: The Challenge of Law Reform in South Africa," in *The Changing Family: Family Forms and Family Law*, ed. John Eekelaar and Thandabantu Nhlapo (Oxford: Hart Publishing, 1998), 625; Abdullahi An-Naim, *Islam and the Secular State* (Cambridge: Harvard University Press, 2008).

43. Jeremy Waldron, "Minority Cultures and the Cosmopolitan Alternative," in *The Rights of Minority Cultures*, ed. Will Kymlicka (Oxford: Oxford University Press, 1995), 93, 99–101.

Part One

The Ethics of Recognizing Religious Family Law in Secular Societies

MARTHA MINOW

Chapter One Principles or Compromises Accommodating Gender Equality and Religious Freedom in Multicultural Societies

Introduction

The "paradox of liberalism," often phrased as the problem of how to "tolerate the intolerant,"[1] is not only a problem of theorists but a practical problem for those who are committed both to gender equality and to religious freedom. To pursue gender equality is to encounter the frequent objections that challenged practices rest on religious grounds; to defend religious freedom is to confront objections that a religious school's decision to fire a pregnant teacher or religious practices such as covering a woman's hair, or face, or entire body discriminate or degrade individuals on the basis of gender.[2] Middle-ground solutions — like exempting private religious schools but not public schools from gender discrimination norms and permitting women to cover their hair but not their faces — may offer practical working solutions but not a strong rationale. Is there a principled way to resolve apparent conflicts between gender equality and religious freedom — and if not, can compromises be justified?

A prime context for this question arises with conflicts between women's equality advanced by national constitutions and international human rights, on the one hand, and state deference to traditional cultural and religious norms, on the other. These conflicts lie just beneath the surface of recent high-profile debates in Great Britain and Canada. Calls for the resignation of the Dr. Rowan Williams from the post of Archbishop of Canterbury erupted after he suggested that Great Britain consider including some parts of Sharia

(Islamic religious law) under a jurisdiction parallel to secular law in order to acknowledge religious differences and also aid social cohesion.[3] A firestorm of protest terminated a proposal to permit use of Islamic law in arbitration and mediation of family disputes in Ontario, Canada.[4]

The treatment of women is a central concern here; social and legal regulation of what women wear or do not wear, for example, has become the subject of national and international political and legal debates. Largely secular democracies in particular are struggling to maintain gender equality while respecting religious freedom, as recent immigrants to European and North American communities bring religious traditions that differ from the ones dominant in their host countries — and the encounter with the host country leads some of the immigrants' children to seek more religious orthodoxy and some to seek less.

Some of the tensions arise within religious communities over degrees of overt religious observance and as advocates on various sides use the arenas of public policy as well as community and peer pressure. Hence, a growing majority seeks greater room for religious expression in public life in Turkey and threatens to dismantle the constitutionally mandated secularism in that country. A ban on religious head coverings in the public university has given rise to action by Turkey's highest court and by the European Court of Justice, with reactions by the Turkish parliament and then more reaction by the nation's supreme court — and then due to political support, universities in Turkey now informally permit women to wear headscarves.

The United States Supreme Court's recent reinterpretations of the Establishment Clause also allow more religion in public life[5] and more public aid to religion,[6] but the courts and hence public officials continue to debate the precise line to draw between religious accommodation and guarding against governmental establishment of religion.[7] Israel is experiencing intense debate over that country's assignment of exclusively religious control over family law, including women's status in that context.[8] Meanwhile, feminists' struggles for gender equality in South Africa, Ethopia, and Central Asia garner some success using domestic constitutions and international human rights. But those very victories set a collision course with legal and human rights recognizing cultural and religious freedom.

Québec launched a province-wide exploration of cultural accommodation in 2007 and identified sharp public controversies over whether human rights call for the provision of prayer rooms in state-supported schools, whether there should be an exemption from the no-weapons rule for a student who wants to carry a Kirpan (ceremonial knife used by Sikhs) to school, and whether Muslim voters wearing the niqab or burka should be allowed to vote without showing their faces as identification.[9] Incidents in Québec, Istanbul, Paris, and London raise the question whether accommodating the veiling of a Muslim woman respects her human rights and personal liberty or subjects her to internal group hierarchy and confinement. How much room should a secular democracy ensure for religious and ethnic subgroups, and should it do this as a matter of normative principle or instead as a compromise of principles? Does focusing on individual choice express the ultimate regard for another, socialization pressures, the neglect of the significance of group identity and tradition, or the imposition of Western imperialism? Is the "self" in any particular instance free to be self-determining?

These problems emerge because of growing encounters between people who identify with different religious or ethnic traditions — and also between people within the same tradition who develop contrasting views about how to navigate local and cosmopolitan worlds. Potentially tense encounters due to these kinds of diversity increasingly arise, given immigration patterns to North America and Europe; increasing religious diversity within local communities produces clashes between new groups and dominant rules while also offering options — and potential conflict — within religious communities.[10] In this period of massive migration and what some provocatively call a "clash of civilizations,"[11] we need to ask how much room a secular democracy should ensure for religious and ethnic subgroups. Given enough room to be exempt from otherwise emerging norms against gender discrimination, religious groups could claim protection under principles of religious freedom, personal autonomy, or freedom of association, but from the perspective of gender equality concerns, such exemption could be understood as a compromise of principles, however explained. When do accommodations of religious groups represent compromise of principle,[12] and when instead do they represent a further principle of pluralism, affirmatively embracing as a positive good the coexistence of multiple normative traditions?

These are old as well as new questions. Many countries, including the United States, embraced pluralism — a commitment to respecting multiple religious and secular traditions — long ago in allowing religious figures to officiate at marriages that have a civil effect and in permitting parents to select religious schools to satisfy their children's compulsory schooling requirement. Nonetheless, prior and contemporary waves of migration generated heated contests over the scope of pluralism and the requisites of unity in this country and elsewhere.[13] These contests, past and present, raise issues about coordination and conflict between secular and religious legal arrangements.

Do accommodations of cultural or religious subgroups, such as Ontario's now-defunct proposal to permit arbitrations of family disputes to follow Islamic law, fall short of defensible principle in pursuing a form of coexistence and recognition for different religious groups within a country committed to preventing gender discrimination? When do accommodations for minority groups represent a compromise of principles of a constitutional democracy, and when do they fulfill those principles, which include both gender equality and religious freedom? And do structural commitments to preserving pluralism involve merely practical concerns or instead normative ideals?[14] What is possible when societies encounter tensions between cultural pluralism and gender equality?[15] Should we want compromise, steadfast ideals, or something else?

Buried within these questions are five linked but still distinct issues that I pursue in this chapter: (1) when should state accommodations of cultural and religious difference be viewed as a compromise; (2) what is so bad about compromises: when are they not wrong and when even admirable; (3) if compromise is suboptimal, when might convergence be possible in the form of solutions that both attend to gender equality and accord respect for customary practices, rather compromise of one or the other; (4) when are differences too profound to find points of convergence; and (5) in the absence of convergence and due to concerns about compromised principles, what alternatives can be devised to manage or avoid collisions over pluralism and guarantees of individual equality?

Comparing Two Treatments of Religious Difference

At the urging of reformers concerned with the treatment of women, the state of New York modified its own divorce law to withhold secular divorce if there is an impediment to a religious divorce pursued by the same party. The New

York law was designed to prevent husbands from securing a secular divorce while withholding a document required by Jewish law for a religious divorce; it is written broadly enough to apply in comparable situations involving other religions.[16] One commentator observed, "Despite the controversial nature of the New York Get Law, it serves as an apt illustration of a compromise between competing religious and civil interests. The law recognizes the indispensability of religious law for some persons while preserving the state's interest in marriage and the ability of adults to marry freely."[17]

Hence, some people view New York's law as a compromise, although it might better be described as an effort to align secular and religious laws. The New York divorce law is a concession to religious law, in the sense that it acknowledges and makes room for religious legal systems rather than treating only the law of New York and the United States as the exclusive source of norms. Such acknowledgment of other normative systems could seem threatening to a government that seeks to be the exclusive source of binding norms for the people in its realm. Professor Robert Cover suggested that the modern state may be especially jealous of rival normative regimes.[18] For the jealous state, even recognizing and accepting the parallel operation of religious law would seem a compromise. The New York law could seem a compromise in a different sense to those who want to keep the government far away from particular religious practices to ensure there is no hint of government endorsement of that religion or religion in general, given the constitutional ban on government establishment of religion.[19] Due to this concern about staying far from religious matters, courts have foreclosed questions raised by divorcing parties that appear to cross the line into religious issues.[20]

In this example, the state law acknowledges the existence of another legal system. It ensures that the state's divorce process will not be used in conjunction with religious practices to undermine the gender equality otherwise ensured in secular law. Under traditional Jewish law, a marriage is a contract, and the only way a married couple could divorce would be if the husband of his own free will gives the wife a legal document dissolving the marriage — and without such a document, the marriage continues, even if the couple is granted a civic divorce. The New York law prevents secular divorce until the parties have eliminated any impediment to a religious divorce, and in so doing the state sharply reduces the risks that observant Jewish women will be cast into the difficult status of an abandoned but not divorced woman or forced to bargain away property entitlements in exchange for avoiding that status.[21] The state thereby ensures that its gender equality norm will not be undone by the religious divorce process — and in so doing, extends some protection for women into the religious community. New York takes a religious community's laws and practices into account and aligns the options available within the religious and secular settings.

If this is a compromise, the sole "concession" from the secular side is to acknowledge the existence of the religious world; the secular law trumps any contrary religious practice (much to the satisfaction of many religious individuals who lobbied for the change). There is no compromise of or departure from a requirement of otherwise existing New York law. No secular substantive norm relevant to the availability or terms of divorce is altered by the New York law; it simply alters the prospects for a woman who otherwise would risk real problems without a religious divorce.[22] The state provides the overarching umbrella within which religious freedom is protected, but so are secular values of gender equality and fairness.

The Canadian Supreme Court offered a similar analysis in deciding to enforce a privately negotiated "consent to corollary relief," in which a Jewish husband agreed to attend a rabbinical court to obtain a *get*.[23] His failure to comply for fifteen years gave rise to a damage suit by his ex-wife, and the Canadian Supreme Court reversed an appellate decision that the obligation at issue could not be enforced by the courts because it was religious in nature.[24] The judgment delivered by Justice Abella reasoned that a voluntary agreement meant to have legal consequences by two consenting adults is appropriate for judicial consideration; the agreement itself is valid under Québec law because individuals can transform a moral obligation into a legally valid and binding one; and the agreement itself is not contrary to public order.[25] Indeed, the agreement "harmonizes with Canada's approach to religious freedom, to equality rights, to divorce and remarriage generally," preventing impairment of the wife's freedom of religion and ability to remarry and have children according to her religious beliefs.[26]

A contrasting proposal to permit use of Islamic law in arbitration and mediation of family disputes in Ontario, Canada, erupted in a firestorm of protest.[27] The former attorney general of the province developed the proposal after the Islamic Institute of Civil Justice requested religiously based arbitrations similar to those used by Jews and Catholics under a 1991 law permitting voluntary arbitrations, subject to court ratification.[28] Attracting international attention, the proposal produced heated debate and protests.[29] Not only was it defeated; the controversy prompted the Ontario legislature to revoke authority for the use of any religious law in arbitrations and to require Canadian law instead.[30]

In one sense, the Ontario proposal presented no more compromise of the public law than did New York's divorce law or Canada's enforcement of a private agreement. The Ontario proposal took account of a religious world by proposing to allow lawyers, retired judges, and religious scholars to serve as arbitrators in the alternative dispute process already established by law while requiring that the process and result of any such process be consistent with Canadian law.

Yet, a compromise of secular values would in fact emerge if the norms used to resolve the family disputes depart from the laws of Ontario or the Canadian Charter of Rights and Freedoms and if the arbitration plan foreclosed access to a Canadian-government decision maker to ensure compliance with Canadian law. The proposal called for reference to Sharia (Islamic law), which itself is subject to multiple interpretations and conclusions. Some of those interpretations could well depart from Canadian law, notably with regard to women's status and rights. The arbitration plan, organized to authorize private control over the selection of dispute resolution, would have permitted foreseeable departures from secular guarantees. Although resort to arbitration formally would be voluntary, the proposal lacked any provision for government monitoring to ensure truly voluntary election of religious arbitration. The absence of government oversight would be especially a concern with regard to parties lacking independent economic resources or social connections outside the Islamic subcommunity, and many women within immigrant communities would fit that description. One critic declared that use of Islamic family law arbitration would create "an under-class of underprivileged people who can go into their ghettos and deal with issues and not bother them."[31] Even if intended as an accommodation for minority groups, privatizing dispute resolution could permit systematic subordination of some individuals within the group, effectively undermining their individual rights.[32]

Opposition to the proposal, however, raised concerns about anti-Islamic attitudes because the arbitration option had already been used by members of other religious groups. The proposal to permit Islamic arbitration emerged as an amendment of the already existing law, and despite that law's origin in commercial matters, it had been used for family matters by Jewish and Catholic groups.[33] The argument for equal treatment for Islamic groups ultimately was persuasive, but given the new concerns raised about how the Islamic arbitration could depart from Canadian norms, the government decided to treat the religious subcommunities equally by eliminating altogether the option of any religiously based arbitration for any group.

This series of events signaled suspicion by the dominant community toward Muslims. Concerns that Islamic norms depart from Canadian ones raised questions about alien norms in a way that Jewish and Christian arbitration had not. Lack of familiarity with Islam on the part of many in the community combined with the larger global setting. Domestic fears of rising forms of Islamic fundamentalism and terrorist activities associated with some Islamic groups affected local Canadian politics. Yet it is also possible that as compared with the Jewish and Catholic groups, the Muslim advocates of religious arbitration may have provided less overt assurance that they would abide by Canadian law.[34]

This episode at the same time reveals the limitations of government law in a society with vibrant religious subgroups. When Ontario ended statutory authorization for religious arbitration, it did not prohibit and did not halt the use of even more informal private religious resolution of family disputes, including mediation by religious figures or others guided by religious principles.[35] If anything, foreclosing public recognition of private family arbitration in effect pushes the use of informal mediation, remote from secular legal guarantees, further from oversight of government authorities or public knowledge than the arbitration option would have produced. Advocates of the pluralist arbitration process — and advocates of women's equality — thus might well have been wiser to press for meaningful judicial review of arbitrated family disputes to make the option of religious arbitration viable and consonant with the secular commitments of the constitutional democracy.[36]

Central to this story is the fear that women's rights would be compromised by enforcement of Islamic rather than Canadian principles. Feminists often treat as a compromise any coordination of religious and secular norms around family and gender issues and imagine that either the state's norms supplant religious ones or the religious ones supplant state norms.[37] Although the Ontario Arbitration proposal expressed the secular values of private dispute resolution, religious freedom, and multicultural accommodation, it seemed to open an avenue for religious norms supplanting state ones. A state ban on a religious practice, such as polygamy, would be the reverse, supplanting of a religious norm by a secular one. Either way, a norm is surrendered, compromised, unfulfilled. The negative meanings of compromise deserve attention here; do they invariably accompany efforts to make room for religious and cultural groups within a constitutional democracy? When is it possible to make room for religious or cultural practices without sacrificing secular values — and vice versa?

Yet sometimes, rather than compromise, convergence between competing norms is possible.[38] The New York and Canadian treatments of religious impediments to secular divorce exemplify convergence, not the state supplanting religious norms or religious norms supplanting state rules. In these examples, the women involved were able to remain as active members in their own minority communities while also retaining access to rights guaranteed by the government.[39] This contrasts with other settings where women face the choice between remaining within a religious community or else asserting their rights guaranteed by the state at the cost of remaining within the religious community. For many religious communities would view the judicial exercise of individual rights, guaranteed by the state, as a decision to exit the religious community and reject religious law and religious institutions.

Some might object that even the New York statute and Canadian decision involved compromises of religious norms. The men in New York and the husband in the Canadian case lost the prerogative to withhold the religious divorce. That prerogative was permitted — but not required — under religious law. Leave it to theological debates within the Jewish tradition to explore when it is just or fair to withhold the *get* and when it is instead an act of unfairness or abuse. From the vantage point of New York or Canadian law, no burden on religious belief or practice is required to eliminate an option (withholding the *get*) in order to ensure equal access to the divorce for religious as well as nonreligious members of the community. Members of the religious community may view forgoing an option in order to comply with secular law as a compromise, and some secularists may see compromise in the effort to frame state law with cognizance of religious norms. If these minimal forms of accommodation are compromise, what is troubling about compromise itself? The very assumption that compromise involves second-best or worse deserves scrutiny.

What's Wrong with Compromise?

If "compromise" means departure from principle, by definition, it produces a shortfall; measured by principle, compromise is definitionally inadequate or even corrupt. Compromise in this sense means unprincipled; uncompromising means principled. Compromise and accommodation imply abandonment of principles, rights, and commitments.[40] Widespread discomfort with compromise may explain the American reliance on institutions, such as the jury, that do the compromising behind closed doors.

Yet "uncompromising" can also mean "unyielding" in the less positive sense of intransigent or rigid. With this meaning, its opposite does not look so bad. Compromises should not always be castigated when they signal the flexibility that is often a virtue and a concomitant of good results. Flexibility involves creativity, willingness to change, or dexterity in achieving accommodations between prior commitments and justifiable impediments. Practically speaking, accommodation is indispensable for stability and mutual learning in a diverse polity and for peace between diverse nations.

The practical need for accommodation may only suggest that compromise is inevitable, not that it is desirable. The important question is when compromise or accommodation should be resisted and when instead it should be advanced. Compromise can seem messy, unguided, emotional, or political; it can seem to abandon what the very notion of "rights" would command. More precisely, compromise can seem undesirable for three reasons: (1) it can seem to sacrifice important ideals for the sake of avoiding conflict; (2) it can seem to involve middle positions that are more incoherent or less defensible than the rejected alternatives; or (3) it can require "dealing with the devil" who uses illicit tactics that should not be rewarded. Let us take each problem in turn.

Sacrificing important ideas to avoid conflict? Simply avoiding conflict is not a sufficient rationale for sacrificing important principles, especially in the context of constitutional and human rights. The very aspiration of rights is to alter how people might be otherwise inclined to treat one another. Constitutional or human rights fail at the starting gate if they collapse in the face of the conflicts they foreseeably provoke. Yet the conflict that rises to the level of violent instability itself can jeopardize the realization of any rights. Peace and social stability are potentially the predicates and the outcome of a functioning constitutional society. Desire to reduce or eliminate conflict cannot silence calls for human rights, but nor is cessation of conflict irrelevant to the realizing of human rights.

Women's equality requires struggle in societies that have not guaranteed it (that is, most societies), yet women themselves often care deeply about maintaining relationships and involvement in religious and ethnic communities where gender equality has not prevailed. Struggles that destroy those ties are counterproductive both for those women and for the society as a whole. Struggles for women's equality that force women to disrupt or depart their own communities violate women's dignity, choice, and meaning, as well as alienate the intended beneficiaries. Processes of accommodation and balancing are indispensable given the multiple values of importance in people's lives. Accommodation and balancing are techniques that help individuals navigate multiple commitments.

Accommodation of competing principles similarly is often the predicate of peace and social stability necessary for realizing all ideals and norms for a society as whole. Compromise does not become acceptable simply if it avoids conflict, but pursuit of peaceful relationships can be a reason to work for a compromise that is otherwise justifiable and acceptable.

Middle positions: In a perhaps apocryphal case, a judge heard a plaintiff and defendant argue over which one rightfully owned a herd of cattle; unable to decide in the face of two plausible claims, the judge ordered the herd divided between the two parties — only to be reversed by the appellate court for failing to do the job of judging. It is a faulty view of judging, though, that imagines only all-or-nothing conclusions. In a sophisticated view of judging, the decision need not always result in an all-or-nothing result but instead can apportion ownership, or blame, or liability across multiple parties.[41]

Granted, at times a middle position can be simply worse than either alternative. Just as painting a room half one color and half the other may be worse aesthetically than picking one of the colors, allowing officials discretion about what private expression to permit in a public space (on a bus or on a plaza) can be worse than permitting or restricting all speech in that space. But these examples do not prove that the middle ground is invariably worse. In fact, some middle positions are defensible and embody their own principles, for example: abortion should be legal but rare; race-conscious governmental categories can be justifiable but only when narrowly tailored to serve a compelling public interest.[42] The fact that these examples reflect commitments to multiple values does not make them unprincipled; instead, a principled position can embody considered apportionment of commitments to multiple and at times competing values.

Dealing with the devil: A different objection to compromise attaches when it arises in the face of violence or other illegitimate threats. Negotiating with kidnappers or terrorists compromises principled opposition to their behavior even though it may be necessary to save lives or produce peace. Peace and life are values just as much as the principles condemning kidnapping and terrorism. But recognizing peace and life as legitimate goals does not alter the danger that negotiating solutions with kidnappers and terrorists creates incentives rather than deterrents for future kidnapping and terrorism. Hence, even when such negotiations are sought and heralded, they are tainted by charges of "dealing with the devil" and warnings of failure to hold firm against tactics that should not be rewarded.[43] The problem is, however, morally complicated. Refusing to negotiate can produce immediate and potentially severe effects. Hence, it may be an understandable and even justifiable compromise to negotiate with kidnappers or terrorists in order to save lives. It is a compromise in the sense of forgoing steadfast adherence to the principle that condemns the tactics pressuring for such negotiation even as it may be a victory for the protection of human life.[44]

So what may initially seem to be an abandonment of principle may instead be an acknowledgment of and tribute to multiple values, yet what may seem an acknowledgment of multiple values may instead be capitulation to illicit pressures. Compromising in response to a threat can be defended given limited available options, but this kind of compromise is not likely to comport with the ideals of constitutional and human rights. But then the negative connotations properly apply to the poverty of the options more than to the selection of one. In contrast, if accommodating multiple principles is in fact a compromise, it can be defensible precisely because comparably valuable principles compete; the effort to balance competing principles itself should not be viewed as a departure from principle itself.[45] In the context of international conflict, giving up on rights claims in order to avoid conflict does not help realize rights, but working out accords that secure peace can in fact be crucial to making human rights possible.[46] Compromise and accommodation should not be viewed as inevitably unprincipled or undesirable in general, and in the context of human rights, these are important elements of an ongoing process for elaborating, debating, and accommodating differences.

Similarly, in a domestic context, where conflicts between a group and the nation are intense, processes of accommodation produce the stability that can hold the nation together.[47] Who speaks for the group in such accommodations is a fair question, to which I will need to return. But it is worth pushing for something better than compromise, when possible, and that lies in the possibility of convergence.

The Possibility of Convergence

Of course, better than compromise would be solutions where no one on competing sides has to give in because each finds common ground without sacrificing principles. That is convergence. Rather than trimming on principle, find a point of connection. Convergence of principles may seem elusive in conflicts over cultural accommodations, but religious and secular leaders found convergence despite a conflict over San Francisco's policy mandating that its contracting partners provide domestic partner benefits equal to those that they offer spouses.[48] Among the organizations affected, the Salvation Army did not have a direct problem with the policy because it provided no benefits, but the Roman Catholic Archdiocese immediately registered opposition and sought an exemption. As Archbishop William Levada later explained:

> I pointed out that the ordinance as written created a problem of conscience for agencies of the Catholic Church (and perhaps others), because it required that we change our Church's internal benefits policies to recognize domestic partnership as equivalent to marriage.
>
> This requirement, I argued, amounted to government coercion of a church to compromise its own beliefs about the sacredness of marriage, and seemed to violate the First Amendment protection guaranteed to religion by our Constitution.[49]

The archbishop made it clear he would sue on free exercise grounds if the policy were enforced against church agencies.[50] But he also went further and drew on church teachings to criticize the city's policy as inadequate in policy terms:

> I am in favor of increasing benefits, especially health coverage, for anyone. As the Catholic bishops of the U.S. stated in 1993, "Every person has a right to adequate health care." I would welcome the opportunity to work with city officials to find ways to overcome what I believe is a national shame, the fact that so many Americans have no health coverage at all. I can be counted on to raise my voice in support of universal health coverage nationally and locally. I feel sure I could make common cause with city officials in working toward this truly urgent need.[51]

In response to Archbishop Levada's comments, Mayor Willie Brown and four members of the San Francisco Board of Supervisors asked to meet with the archbishop to see if they could reach "a mutually acceptable solution to the problem."[52] They met, they talked, and they negotiated a solution that addressed the concerns of both sides.[53] As a result, the city now deems a contracting party to be in compliance if it "allows each employee to designate a legally domiciled member of the employee's household as being eligible for spousal equivalent benefits."[54] As the city currently explains in its overview of the ordinance, contracting parties can achieve compliance in different ways:

> Some contractors comply with the requirements of the Ordinance by offering benefits to spouses, domestic partners and other individuals. One company, for example, has created a policy that extends some benefits to "other individuals if the relationship with [the employee] is especially close and it would be normal for them to turn to [the employee] for care and assistance." Other contractors comply by allowing each employee to extend benefits to one adult living in their household. Compliance also is possible where the benefits offered do not extend to spouses or domestic partners, or where no employee benefits are offered.[55]

The archbishop acknowledged criticism of the solution, but he defended it. Hence, he explained:

> [T]o those like my local Catholic critic who say that we implicitly give recognition to domestic partnerships by not excluding them from benefits, I must demur. Under our plan, an employee may indeed elect to designate another member of the household to receive benefits. We would know no more or no less about the employee's relationship with that person than we typically

> know about a designated life insurance beneficiary. What we have done is to prohibit local government from forcing our Catholic agencies to create internal policies that recognize domestic partnerships as a category equivalent to marriage.[56]

The solution avoided costly and potentially bitter litigation between the city and the church, and the two parties worked together, as the archbishop said, to "help address many pressing social needs."[57] San Francisco's health benefit resolution kept the Catholic providers in contractual relations with the city.[58] Both the religious and governmental leaders in San Francisco proceeded with a willingness to find common ground and a stance of collaborative problem solving — without ceding principle.[59] Crucial to the outcome, the opposing sides treated one another with the virtues of respect, flexibility, and humility, even when the stakes seemed high and the cause just.[60] Accommodating someone's religious practices through an exception to a general rule is not a compromise but an acknowledgment of higher commitments. Yet, it is not always easy to distinguish compromise from convergence. Ironically, perhaps the announcement of higher principles can get in the way. Sometimes there are also real and profound differences in beliefs, commitments, and worldviews that make multicultural accommodations difficult, impossible, or paradoxical, as I explore next.

What Disagreements Undermine Both Convergence and Compromise?

Some clashes between gender equality and religious accommodation defy compromise as well as elude convergence. Consider the dilemmas posed by the case of Leyla Sahin. She enrolled at the medical school at Istanbul University before the university issued an order excluding students if they wore clothes "symobli[zing] any religion, faith, race or political or ideological persuasion."[61] Denied the ability to pursue her studies, Sahin filed a challenge to the university's order, pursued court action in Turkey without success, and then pressed for consideration in the European Court of Human Rights. There, the government of Turkey and the university recounted the historical background that included the effort by Turkey, alone with Senegal among all other Islamic nations, to elevate secularism as part of its constitution.[62] But because 99 percent of Turkey's population is Muslim, religious tension often takes the form of conflicts over degrees of religious observance. A woman who goes uncovered is at risk of derision or worse by fellow citizens who are more orthodox, unless the government creates a space where she is not allowed to cover her hair. The state is deeply engaged in the project of secularism, but this does not mean that it separates itself from religion; indeed, the Turkish government pays the salaries of sixty thousand imams and dictates the contents of their sermons.[63] After a military coup in 1980, the political party regained democratic control in 1983 and relaxed restrictions on religious expression.[64] Subsequent leaders have pressed for greater room for religious expression while trying to contain religious fundamentalism.[65]

In 2005, the European Court of Human Rights agreed that the ban interfered with Sahin's right to manifest her religion, but the court nonetheless affirmed the ban — in the name of pluralism, broad-mindedness, and tolerance. The European Court reasoned that to advance those values, the government of Turkey needed to act as an impartial arbiter protecting democracy, and in that role, it could adopt the ban as a proportional means to advance such legitimate aims.[66] British, German, French, and Dutch universities would not adopt such a ban and would instead construe pluralism, broad-mindedness, and tolerance to require accommodating the religious dress of its students, observed the European Court of Human Rights.[67] Nonetheless, the court reasoned that the Turkish government would know better how to advance these goals in its national context.[68]

This result and the struggle leading up to it could be viewed as a classic example of cultural relativism at work: a specific group claims and gets exemption from otherwise prevailing norms because of its history and commitments. Yet, it could instead be understood as an exemplar of the process of mediation and cross-cultural dialogue through which human rights — and the freedom and respect they are meant to effectuate — depend upon context. Turkey's rule clearly restricted religious freedom for those women who wanted to wear a head covering but also enlarged freedom for those who did not want to do so; the rule also restricted the autonomy of some individual women while enhancing the autonomy for others. Centrally, the rule created a secular space, removed from religious pressures one way or the other. The very ambiguity in interpreting this example could be frustrating; the paradoxes are obvious. But the shift in attention to the process of mediation and cross-cultural dialogue underscore that even with possibilities for compromise and convergence, real clashes will persist, with no answers satisfactory to all.

The struggle within Turkey continues. The Parliament in February 2008 approved a potential constitutional amendment removing the ban on Islamic headscarves in universities, but then in June 2008, the Constitutional Court rejected the Parliament's proposed amendment and ruled that removing the ban would run counter to official secularism — even though the court historically only assessed proposed amendments in terms of procedural correctness.[69] The government — reflecting electoral pressure — asserted support for students wearing headscarves on university campuses, and informally, universities in Turkey by 2011 permitted women to wear headscarves.[70]

This issue in Turkey reflects growing conflict between an earlier generation's vision of secularism and emerging power of overtly religious practices in the lives of voters even as it also implicates a struggle over what kind of Turkey would Europeans welcome into the European Union. Disputes over the relationship between state and religion and between gender equality and religion thus can implicate relationships among coreligionists in one country, relationships between different countries that have majority populations of different religions and background, and relationships within societies confronting new kinds and degrees of population diversity.

The relationship between the individual and overlapping groups is unavoidably altered by the approach taken by a nation to the issues of gender equality and religious freedom. Once again, Turkey provides a vivid example as it struggles to find a path between Islamic fundamentalism and secular fundamentalism.[71] Recep Tayyip Erdoğan, Turkey's prime minister at the time of the Sahin decision, sent his two daughters to attend school in the United States in order to avoid the headscarf restrictions in Turkish universities.[72] This bit of irony exposes and emphasizes how exit and migration possibilities alter what may have once seemed simply domestic issues. Those options reflect the effects of global communications and transportation and collapse the differences in struggles over human rights within a nation and across the world. Erdoğan, still prime minister in 2008, pushed for a revision of the country's constitution to ensure that women could cover in the universities and triggered both public protests and rejection of the amendment by critical reactions by the courts and the military;[73] the constitutional amendment itself must be approved by the Turkish court.[74] When an electoral response ushered in an administrative solution, permitting headscarves on campus, the issue of majority versus minority views resurfaced. What should be the proper focus for analysis: individuals or groups, and rights or duties? Theorists may imagine ways to meld individuals and groups as well as rights and duties, but theoretical solutions do not overcome the perception of real differences along just these lines, differences that track commitments animating debates over cultural accommodation.

INDIVIDUALS OR GROUPS?

One of the touchiest points of contention involves whether individuals or groups are the primary unit of analysis and protection for human rights. This is the moment to return to questions about who speaks for the group, as well as to surface issues of genuine consent and voluntariness for individuals within the group when there are real risks of harm. Using "harm" as the undeniable touchstone obscures the question of harm to whom: the group or the individual? The difficulty is that for many individuals, the strength of the group matters enormously. It is, therefore, of concern to both individuals and groups whether and when harm to a group defined by religion, ethnicity, or family should rise to the level of harm deserving protection.[75] Even for those who view the individual as sacrosanct, the most vexing problems pertain to the group affiliations of those individuals. Professor An-Na'im has asked, if advocates "encourage young women to repudiate the integrity and cohesion of their own minority culture, how can the theorists then help to sustain the identity and human dignity of these women?"[76] Given the choice, some women may choose to exit their groups, but many will not. Martha Nussbaum offers a particularly deft embrace of individual rights embedded in social life by framing universal human rights as a way to afford women solidarity and affiliation, often with other women.[77] Threading the group dimension through the individual rights-holder is the solution in the work of Will Kymlicka and Michael Walzer; this approach largely makes the choice between individual or group recede in questions of accommodation.[78]

There is a paradox that makes this solution more than sleight of hand: we all share our isolation. Gary Larson, the cartoonist, has a popular image of a room full of identical penguins; one in the back has a song bubble shouting,

"I gotta be me." Asked to print it up as a poster, a printer was confused and colored the singing penguin yellow; he missed the entire point of the universality of the individual experience.[79]

But even with clever connections between individuals and groups, there remain knotty issues about the governance of self-identified groups within a liberal state. Many of the most debated issues focus on women's lives and choices, although those involving children are even more difficult. For example, should every child face a requirement to attend schooling devised by the state, or instead can parents or community leaders frame an education suited to a subcommunity's way of life?[80] Should a religious tribunal supervise divorce and child custody determinations, with results to be accorded state recognition? Should such a tribunal be allowed to perform such a role only if its norms match those of the larger state? And when if ever can the vitality or survival of the group serve as a justification for reducing or denying protection for an individual — for example, when membership in an Indian tribe passes through the father's line, can the self-preservation and self-governance of the group justify denying access to a federal court for a sex discrimination claim?[81] The Supreme Court of the United States, in an opinion written by Justice Thurgood Marshall, answered yes, relying on a reading of congressional action.[82] The court relied on statutory interpretation in denying Mrs. Martinez access to the federal courts, but the court also pointed to the crucial role of the tribe itself in determining who could be its members. This self-determination is both definitional and also especially important for a group struggling with legacies of subordination and conquest.[83]

Despite the possible overlap between individual rights and group rights, there remain areas that diverge; the different starting points could prove obstacles to negotiation, mediation, or other efforts to bypass clashes around the meaning and shape of human rights. Many people may think that respecting the individual is the irreducible touchstone and also the significance of group membership. Yet, the resources and coordination needed to sustain groups at times may call for acknowledging and supporting groups apart from their affiliation through individuals. If I need to pray with nine others, my individual right is not enough if I am not allowed to join with others. Even to exercise my right to marry, I need another. And the structures of secularism and rights themselves require collective effort in order to enable individuals to exercise their rights.

RIGHTS, DUTIES, OR COMPASSION IN THE RECOGNITION OF HUMAN DIGNITY?

The focus on individuals recurs in concerns about "rights" rather than "duties" or "compassion." "Rights" connote and may even entail the Western liberal tradition, associated with John Locke and others, that life, liberty from arbitrary rule, and property are inherent entitlements that people surrender to the state in order to form a social contract to protect precisely these interests. To many, this is a problematic conception if it means:

- Ignoring or suppressing people's intimate and social relationships
- Entrenching preexisting distributions and practices
- Neglecting conflicts among rights, such as the right to protection against discrimination on the basis of gender versus the right to free exercise of religion; or the right of free speech versus the right to not be a target of degradation
- Missing a focus on responsibilities and compassion, whether viewed as the necessary reciprocal to fulfill rights or the richer resource for protecting and enhancing human dignity

These goals may seem consonant with "rights." Yet some people find the very notion of "rights" neglects and may even suppress the sense of duty, or community membership, or care and compassion that is or should be the wellspring of respect for others. A step toward reconciling these different views can come by locating rights as part of a pattern of social relationships that in turn involve duties toward and care of others.[84] Yet the conception of the individual at the core of a right diverges from the conception of relationships of care and duty. Different dreams and fears as well as different grounds for compromise and intransigence emerge when relationships rather than individuals are the focus.

Perhaps an overlapping consensus can emerge about how to respect human dignity, whatever the wellspring or motive.[85] Such solutions in real life require processes of negotiation, assessment, debate, and judgment to overcome conflicting views about what a woman should wear in public, whether an employer should be allowed to hire children, or whether officials engaged in humanitarian military interventions should be seen as culpable of crimes against humanity for "collateral damage" (otherwise known as killing people).

The stakes when cultural and religious worldviews diverge can indeed include death, meaning, and fundamental beliefs. What, then, can be done when differences elude a search for points of agreement?

When Neither Convergence Nor Compromise Is Possible: Governance Devices for Pluralism

When neither convergence nor compromise seems possible, legal frameworks and lawyers can be helpful. It is not because lawyers are smarter than other people; it is just that lawyers have developed methods for managing interminable disputes and deep conflicts through devices like burden of proof and through institutions like the jury. Legal and political devices of governance can enable coexistence among diverging ways of life while preserving avenues for limiting that divergence. These devices include federalism, with decentralized authorities empowered to make parallel and conflicting decisions, and privatization, according power to private actors to arrange their own affairs away from public view and differently than a public process would do. Both implicitly reflect the adage: in the face of conflicting values, shift the decision maker. Federalism and privatization offer a way through highly charged conflicts over what constitute fundamental rights. Each permits alternatives to all-or-nothing solutions to moral and legal conflicts; each structures avenues for coexistence of diverging groups while retaining processes for collective restrictions of extreme practices. Each allows multiple answers to coexist.

Decentralization in the form of federalism is a common solution in the United States. In the United States, federal courts have permitted states to adopt certain restrictions on abortion rights and vouchers authorizing public funding for religious schools, but they do not require either; instead the choice is left with state governments, with the result that diverging practices emerge in different states.[86] Even without leaving decisions to the states, the national government can use decentralization to defuse a dispute over values. For example, the federal courts have incorporated reference to local community standards to resolve disputes over free speech challenges to restrictions on obscenity rather than pick one standard for the whole nation.[87] Decentralization permits multiple answers to a contested question. This device is troubling to those who insist there is only one acceptable answer. However, it is an attractive solution for minority groups unable to win across the whole country, but with sufficient concentration to influence the local practice.

The distinction between public and private realms affords another a technique for permitting and managing coexistence of diverging cultural and religious groups, even though the very notion of a "private realm" is more compatible with some worldviews and religions than others. Many of the current conflicts over Islamic practices in Europe reveal the particularly Christian form of the public-private distinction that has emerged in Europe.[88] Nonetheless, some imagined distinction can separate the shared spaces where people with different cultures, traditions, and languages coexist and cooperate from private spaces where people can organize their time and practices according to their own embraced culture and tradition.[89] Even if this implies a distinction between public and private that not all religious groups or nations use, it also offers a strategy for coexistence in which groups can flourish. There is a difference between the religious group's effort to use the state to impose its rules on everyone and its effort to find space to practice its rules apart from the rest of the society.[90]

In this respect, law governing private ordering can construct and enhance pluralism. Law professor Carol Weisbrod has shown how utopian communities in nineteenth-century America used contract and property laws to construct spaces for their own practices.[91] Legal structures permitting the organization of corporations, fraternal groups, and families similarly enable pluralism.[92] The legal structures create spaces where the diversity and pluralism within a religious group can itself flourish rather than be suppressed in a struggle against the state or other groups. A more complex set of possibilities emerges than simply one division between the public and private realm. Instead of a single public/private divide, the line between "public" and "private" is not natural but instead a resource for law, politics, and advocacy. The public resource of law can be an instrument of multiple efforts by groups of people to preserve and invent distinctive ways of life. The line between workplace and home has warranted regulation of the workplace that would not proceed in the family, even though both are "private" in relation to government itself. Yet over time, feminists successfully moved violence in the home from the private to the public side.[93] Public laws governing tort and crime now apply in the United

States to conflicts within families. Government enforcement of private arrangements through contract and property tools allows groups to arrange their use of resources; laws permitting private schools and private dispute resolution can enable religious and cultural groups to manage their own social reproduction and conflict management. In a sense, the government's law in all these ways can provide an umbrella under which individuals and groups can organize for their own purposes.

Yet the image of the state as umbrella is too static to capture the dynamism permitted by negotiation over public and private spaces; it also implies wrongly that the harsh elements come only from outside the state rather than acknowledging that the state itself can be a threat to those it claims to protect. More apt, perhaps, than an umbrella is the image of a computer operating system that serves as a resource to users and programs, controlling and allocating memory for use, facilitating networking and management of information, and permitting other programs and devices to send inputs and outputs. The operating system is hardly neutral. For operating systems set parameters, enabling some kind of activities and curbing others. Then users can deploy the operating system for their own purposes, even to alter the operating system, although like a constitution, an operating system can have a protected mode, limiting the content and procedures for changes to itself. By analogy, varying degrees of governmental oversight can be produced to adjust the state's power to veto or influence the private communities; private communities in turn can work through public processes to influence the public norms used to supervise their conduct as well as norms applicable to everyone. The potential rivalries between such groups and the organized state will not go away.[94]

An answer given by the U.S. Supreme Court is not the final answer for a religious group that looks elsewhere for final authority. Conflicts over values and communal practices will arise and often remain insoluble, even with governance devices that permit pluralism. But the public governance devices help to channel and shape those conflicts. The field of law makes central the processes of accommodating and supervising cultural pluralism. Law itself is inevitably distorted if the only focus is on the state law and sources, and unnecessarily limited if only public norms, rather than private law or customs, are addressed. The formal law of a nation-state or the convention of international law can enable, manage, and at times restrict pluralism, while the formal law can also countenance, foster, or reject compromises along the way.

From the vantage point of a nation-state, the use of governance devices like federalism and the public-private distinction ensures final control by the nation-state; but from the vantage point of plural groups, enabled by and taking advantage of these legal structures, the nation-state's answers are not the final ones. The group may resort to civil disobedience, conflict, or exit when they lose a battle in the courts, agencies, or legislatures. This lack of a single hierarchy of authority thus exists within nation-states. The lack of a single hierarchy of authority is even more obviously present in the international context, where conflicts between nations at best give rise to multilateral accords, depending on the consent of the separate nations. Negotiating is the inevitable tool to avoid or resolve such conflicts. The possibility of convergence deserves special attention. So does the potential use of compromise as a human rights strategy sometimes borne of necessity and sometimes nourishing individual freedom and meaning in human lives. The very meanings and shapes of individual identity can shift over time, as can the contours and commitments of groups and nations.

Now, is all of this just a modus vivendi, a pattern of necessity, or instead a path to a pluralism that enriches human experience? To begin to answer so big a question, I turn to the wisdom of that great philosopher and comedian Lily Tomlin, who said, "It's my belief we developed language because of our deep inner need to complain."[95] What we can't change, we complain about, and when we complain, we also shift our own stances toward the difficulty. Human beings may be creatures especially adept at complaining about what we cannot change, but we are also gifted in celebrating features of our lives whether or not we can change them. When it comes to the pluralism exhibited by contrasting cultural and religious groups, the fact of diversity cannot be changed, but our stance toward it can, with palpable consequences for the scale and valence of conflicts, the prospects for peaceful coexistence, and the opportunities for enriching encounters. Adlai Stevenson, a failed candidate for U.S. president, but a witty and perceptive thinker, said that he believed "that if we really want human brotherhood to spread and increase until it makes life safe and sane, we must also be certain that there is no one true faith or path by which it may spread."[96] Paradoxically, to find our shared brotherhood and sisterhood, we will have to pursue more than one path.

Notes

1. See, e.g., Thomas Nagel, "Moral Conflict and Political Legitimacy," *Philosophy and Public Affairs* 16 (1987): 215–401; Jeremy Waldron, "The Theoretical Foundations of Liberalism," *Philosophical Quarterly* 37 (April 1987): 147.

2. For discussion of the tension and spirited argument about the right response, see the essays collected in Susan Moller Okin et al., *Is Multiculturalism Bad for Women?* (Princeton, NJ: Princeton University Press, 1999). See also Gila Stopler, "A Rank Usurpation of Power: The Role of Patriarchal Religion and Culture in the Subordination of Women," *Duke Journal of Gender Law & Policy* 15 (2008); Gila Stopler, "Countenancing the Oppression of Women: How Liberals Tolerate Religious and Cultural Practices That Discriminate against Women," *Columbia Journal of Gender and Law* 12 (2003): 154. For an argument that dominant institutions have accentuated gender hierarchies within minority communities, see Sarah Song, *Justice, Gender, and the Politics of Multiculturalism* (Cambridge: Cambridge University Press, 2007).

3. Ruth Gledhill and Joanna Sugden, "Archbishop of Canterbury 'Should Resign' Over Sharia Row," *The Times,* February 8, 2008, accessed June 27, 2011, http://www.timesonline.co.uk/tol/news/uk/article3335026.ece?token=null&offset=0.

4. CBC News, "Global Groups Unite against Islamic Arbitration in Ontario," *CBC News*, September 4, 2005, accessed June 27, 2011, http://www.cbc.ca/canada/story/2005/09/04/islamic_arbitration20050904.html.

5. See Van Orden v. Perry, 545 U.S. 677 (2005).

6. Zelman v. Simmons-Harris, 536 U.S. 639 (2002).

7. Current disputes include whether public officials can approve a Ten Commandments monument while disapproving a proposed monument with seven aphorisms from the religious group (see Pleasant Grove City v. Summum, No. 07–665); whether religious groups should be exempt from employment discrimination laws when the groups receive public funding (see Martha Minow, "Should Religious Groups be Exempt from Civil Rights Laws?" *Boston College Law Review* 48 [2007]:781); whether a public school's refusal to recognize a proposed Bible study club requiring members to sign a statement of faith violates students' free exercise of religion — or whether the contrary decision would violate the Establishment Clause (see Truth v. Kent School District, No. 04–35786, available online at http://www.ninthcircuitopinions.com/2008/04/25/truth-v-kent-school-district/).

8. See other chapters in this volume. See also Ayelet Shachar and Ran Hirschl,

"Constitutional Transformation, Gender Equality, and Religious/National Conflict in Israel: Tentative Progress through the Obstacle Course," in *The Gender of Constitutional Jurisprudence*, ed. Beverly Baines and Ruth Rubio-Marin (Cambridge: Cambridge University Press, 2005): 205–29.

9. "Seeking Common Ground: Quebecers Speak Out: Consultation Document," Commission de Consultation sur les Practiques D'Accommodement Reliées Aux Differences Culturelles, accessed June 27, 2011, http://www.accommodements.qc.ca/documentation/document-consultation-en.pdf.

10. For information on developments in the United States, see "Resources by Tradition," The Pluralism Project at Harvard University, accessed June 27, 2011, http://www.pluralism.org/resources/tradition/index.php.

11. Samuel P. Huntington, "The Clash of Civilizations?" *Foreign Affairs* 72 (1993): 22–49. For critiques, see generally Paul Berman, *Terror and Liberalism* (New York: W.W. Norton & Co., 2003), and Amartya Sen, *Identity and Violence: The Illusion of Destiny* (New York: W.W. Norton & Co., 2006).

12. "Compromise" carries these two basic definitions: "settlement of differences reached by arbitration or by consent reached by mutual concessions" and "a concession to something derogatory or prejudicial." *Merriam-Webster's Collegiate Dictionary*, 11th ed. (Springfield, MA: Merriam-Webster, Inc., 2008): 256.

13. See Milton Ridvas Konvitz, *The Legacy of Horace M. Kallen* (Madison, NJ: Fairleigh Dickinson University Press, 1987), discussing debates in the United States in the early twentieth century; Dalia Tsuk Mitchell, *Architect of Justice: Felix S. Cohen and the Founding of American Legal Pluralism* (Ithaca, NY: Cornell University Press, 2007), on the same; and Maria Rosa Menocal, *The Ornament of the World: How Muslims, Jews, and Christians Created a Culture of Tolerance in Medieval Spain* (Boston: Little, Brown, and Company, 2002), exploring a moderate form of pluralist tolerance in intergroup relations in fourteenth-century Spain.

14. Pluralism here means "a conviction that various religious, ethnic, racial, and political groups should be allowed to thrive in a single society." *American Heritage New Dictionary of Cultural Literacy*, 3rd ed. (Boston: Houghton Mifflin, 2005), http://dictionary.reference.com/browse/pluralism. A system arranging a hierarchy, subordinating one group to another in terms of freedoms, status, and resources, is not pluralist.

15. I follow in the path set by others, notably, Carol Weisbrod (*Emblems of Pluralism: Cultural Differences and the State* [Princeton, NJ: Princeton University Press, 2002]: 7, 29, 49), offering an account of the relations between individuals, groups, and the state, with emphasis on the cultural resonances of those relationships, and comparing a state-centered hierarchical model, illustrated by

American legal treatment of Mormon and a horizontal state-subgroup model, in which groups are accorded more recognition and autonomy.

16. See N.Y. Dom. Rel. Law § 253 (McKinney 1999) (requiring a party married by clergy seeking a divorce to verify that no barriers to remarriage exist by the time the final court judgment is entered); N.Y. Dom. Rel. Law § 236b (McKinney 1999) (directing divorce courts to consider actions by one spouse created a barrier to remarriage by the other spouse when setting spousal maintenance [alimony] and property division maintenance ["equitable distribution"]). The legislature also gives divorce courts discretion to consider the effect of a barrier to remarriage in making equitable distribution of property. Idem § 253.

17. Laureve Blackstone, "Note: Courting Islam: Practical Alternatives to a Muslim Family Court in Ontario," *Brooklyn Journal of International Law* 31 (2005): 207, 228.

18. Robert M. Cover, "The Supreme Court, 1982 Term — Forward: *Nomos* and Narrative," *Harvard Law Review* 97 (1983): 4, 11.

19. Tanina Rostain, "Permissible Accommodations of Religion: Reconsidering the New York Get Statute," *Yale Law Journal* 96 (1987): 1147, 1149. Yet, even in the absence of a statute like New York's, a New Jersey court approved a judicial directive telling a husband to deliver a *get* in order to permit completion of the secular divorce process. *Minkin v. Minkin*, 434 A.2d 665, 668 (N.J. Super Ct. Ch. 1981). A similar judicial approach recently emerged in Canada.

20. *Sieger v. Sieger*, No. 6975/98, 2005 N.Y. Misc. LEXIS 1808, at *61 (N.Y. Sup. Ct. June 29, 2005) (concluding that the Establishment Clause precluded the Court from inquiring into the propriety of the husband's pursuit of a ruling from a religious court regarding the wife's refusal to accept the husband's notice of divorce).

21. See idem at 1166–67 (noting that "[c]ivil divorce impeded some women's ability to marry within Judaism").

22. T. Rostain, "Permissible Accommodations of Religion," 1166–68.

23. Marcovitz v. Bruker, 2007 SCC 54.

24. Idem, 33, 36 (noting that the obligation was unenforceable because it was religious in nature).

25. Idem, 47, 51, 60–63.

26. Idem, 63. The court also cited analogous protections for Jewish women from husbands who refuse to provide a religious divorce in the European Commission of Human Rights, France, the United Kingdom, Australia, Israel, and New York. Idem, 73, 83–89.

27. CBC News, "Global Groups Unite."

28. See Asia Pacific News Service, "Canada to Allow Islamic Courts," *Asian Pacific Post,* May 19, 2004, http://www.asianpacificpost.com/portal2/40288191 0674ebab010674f4c17b13b3.do.htm; Mona Eltahawy, "Ontario Must Say 'No' to Islamic Law," *Christian Science Monitor*, February 2, 2005, http://www.csmonitor.com/2005/0202/p09s01-coop.html; Faisal Kutty, "In Praise of Marion Boyd's Report: Ontario Report Affirms Right to Use Islamic Principles in Arbitration," *Catholic New Times,* January 30, 2005, accessed June 27, 2011, http://goliath.ecnext.com/coms2/gi_0199-3694320/In-praise-of-Marian-Boyd.html#abstract.

29. Lee Carter, "Protests over Canada Sharia Move," *BBC News*, September 8, 2005, accessed June 27, 2011, http://news.bbc.co.uk/2/hi/americas/4215182.stm.

30. Jehan Aslam, "Judicial Oversight of Islamic Family Law Arbitration in Ontario: Ensuring Meaningful Consent and Promoting Multicultural Citizenship," *NYU Journal of International Law and Politics* 38 (2006): 841, 842–43.

31. See CBC News, "Global Groups Unite" (quoting Tarek Fatah of the Canadian Muslim Congress); see also Shauna Van Praagh, "Bringing the Charter Home," *McGill Law Journal* 38 (1993): 233 (reviewing John Tibor Syrtash, *Religion and Culture in Canadian Family Law* [Toronto: Butterworth-Heinemann, 1992]).

32. See Ayelet Shachar, *Multicultural Jurisdictions: Cultural Differences and Women's Rights* (Cambridge: Cambridge University Press, 2001) (noting that multicultural accommodation can in some cases nullify an individual's citizenship rights); Judith Resnik, "Dependent Sovereigns: Indian Tribes, States, and the Federal Courts," *University of Chicago Law Review* 56 (1989): 671 (examining the differences in sovereignty between states and Indian tribes and their relationship to the federal courts); Martha Minow, "About Women, About Culture: About Them, About Us," *Daedalus* 129 (2000): 125 (reflecting on why women's issues predominantly arise as clashes of cultural conflict).

33. Arbitration Act, 1991 S.O., ch. 17 (Can.), available at http://www.canlii.org/on/laws/sta/1991c.17/20080215/whole.html.

34. Hence, the Ontario Bet Din, which managed Jewish arbitrations, explicitly adopted a rule to abide by Canadian law in case of a conflict with Jewish law, while at least some of the advocates of Islamic arbitration called for shielding the arbitrated disputes from Canadian law. Conversation with Professor Ayelet Shachar (Dec. 20, 2007); see also Ayelet Shachar, "Entangled: State, Religion, and the Family" (unpublished article, on file with *Connecticut Law Review*).

35. Note this comment on a blog by Saffiyah:

> What will this mean for Canadian Muslims? Very little. It would have been complicated to try and develop these religious tribunals for Muslims in Ontario,

> precisely because the supporting structures are underdeveloped and our imams do not have adequate training to be able to carry out their duties in a manner that stands up to public scrutiny. But mediation will continue despite the legal prohibition on religious tribunals. So if a couple wants to resolve a conflict and chooses to go to their imam to do so? They can go right ahead. The process will be unsupervised and informal, and one wonders whether this will not set the stage for greater rights violations than might be suffered within the context of the religious tribunal itself.

Posting of Thoughts, Rants and Passions of a Young Muslim Woman Seeking Soulful Enlightenment in Cyberspace to "Law Prohibits Religious Arbitration in Ontario," http://www.safiyyah.ca/wordpress/?cat=20 (Feb. 17, 2006, 4:41 EST). In mediation, the parties design their own agreement with the help of a neutral third-party; in arbitration, the third party resolves the dispute between the couple, but only within the range of options that the parties could elect themselves; hence, neither criminal sanctions nor a divorce can be issued by arbitration. Natasha Bakht, "Arbitration, Religion and Family Law: Private Justice on the Backs of Women," *National Association of Women and the Law Working and Research Papers* (March 2005): 7–8, http://www.nawl.ca/ns/en/documents/Pub_ReligArb05_en.rtf. Nothing by law would prevent arbitration of disputes over child support, custody, access to children, and religious education of children (Ibid. 11)

36. This would have required more explicit authorization for judicial review of arbitrated agreements; absent agreement by the parties to provide for judicial review, the Arbitration Act had limited bases for juridical review. Arbitration Act, 1991 S.O., ch. 17 (Can.), § 45(1), § 46(1).

37. See, for example, Susan M. Okin, "Is Multiculturalism Bad for Women?" in *Is Multiculturalism Bad for Women?* ed. Susan Moller Okin et al. (Princeton, NJ: Princeton University Press, 1999): 9–24.

38. Convergence is "the process of coming together or the state of having come together toward a common point." See *The American Heritage Medical Dictionary* (Boston: Houghton Mifflin, 2007), accessed June 27, 2011, http://medical-dictionary.thefreedictionary.com/convergence.

39. Compare with Ayelet Shachar, "The Puzzle of Interlocking Power Hierarchies: Sharing the Pieces of Jurisdictional Authority," *Harvard Civil Rights–Civil Liberties Law Review* 35 (2000): 385, 399–400, 405–6 (explaining that women should not have to choose between their rights as citizens and their group identities, and offering jurisdiction as the key to achieving both of these goals).

40. See Theodore M. Benditt, "Compromising Interests and Principles," in

Compromise in Ethics, Law, and Politics, ed. J. Roland Pennock and John William Chapman (New York: New York University Press, 1979): 26, 31–36.

41. See Summers v. Tice, 199 P.2d 1, 2–3, 5 (1948) (finding defendants to be jointly liable); Page Keeton, "Products Liability — Some Observations About Allocation of Risks," *Michigan Law Review* 64 (1966): 1329, 1330–31, 1334, 1339 (examining the shifting and allocation of losses in products liability cases); David L. Sunding and David Zilberman, "Allocating Product Liability in a Multimarket Setting," *International Review of Law and Economics* 18 (1998): 1–3 (considering the efficiency of various liability rules); see also David M. Dudzinski, "Tobacco Litigation: Statistics Permitted for Proof of Causation and Damages in Class Action," *Journal of Law, Medicine & Ethics* 31 (2003): 161–63 (allowing statistical proof and extrapolation to find proof of causation).

42. President Bill Clinton and others in the 1990s advanced the position that abortion should be "legal, safe, and rare." The Lancet, "Making Abortion Safe, Legal, and Rare," *Lancet* 370 (2003): 291. For the view that governments can use racial categories but only if narrowly tailored to serve a compelling governmental interest, see Parents Involved in Community Schools v. Seattle School District No. 1., 127 S. Ct. 2738, 2789, 2797 (2007) (J. Kennedy, concurring in part and concurring in the judgment). Thanks to Adrian Vermeuele for this point.

43. Robert Mnookin, "Dealing with the Devil" (presentation at a Harvard Law School Faculty Workshop, July 2007).

44. Similar issues arise for the prosecutor of international courts who may be invited to negotiate with human rights abusers who offer to halt their abuse in exchange for delaying or avoiding prosecution, though here protection of the roles of the court and prosecutor may add to the reasons not to negotiate.

45. Working out a way to acknowledge and respect two principles is itself not a compromise unless refusal to accommodate rises to the level of a principle that itself should not be sacrificed. Sadly, such refusals often seem the price of not only adhering to principle, but being seen to do so. Even being seen talking with an opponent in some quarters can be viewed as a compromise either because withholding the approval implied by the conversation is part of expected condemnation or because the conversation may make compromise too tempting. Candidates for national political office, thus, argue over whether meeting with dictators or heads of rogue states would be too compromising — either because the sheer act of meeting grants too much approval or due to fear that a substantive compromise of principle could be the only outcome of such a meeting.

46. Cf. Gabriella Blum, *Islands of Agreement: Managing Enduring Armed Rivalries* (Cambridge, MA: Harvard University Press, 2007) (identifying and

forging agreements on narrow issues can provide a predicate for stability even if the larger conflict is not resolved).

47. See Rhonda Parkinson, "The Meech Lake Accord," November 2006, accessed June 27, 2011, http://www.rhondaparkinson.com/meech-lake-accord.htm (describing failed constitutional amendments to address relationship between Québec and rest of Canada).

48. See Nondiscrimination in City Contracts Chapters 12B and 12C of the San Francisco Administrative Code, http://www.sfgov.org/site/sfhumanrights_index.asp?id=4584 (last visited Mar. 31, 2008) ("The Human Rights Commission enforces San Francisco's Nondiscrimination in Contracts Laws. These laws include provisions prohibiting discrimination in employee benefits and public accommodations based on marital and domestic partner status and in most cases require that City contractors provide domestic partner benefits equal to those offered to spouses of their employees."). See Minow, "Should Religious Groups Ever Be Exempt from Civil Rights Laws?"

49. William J. Levada, "The San Francisco Solution," *First Things: The Journal of Religion, Culture, and Public Life* (1997): 17–19, accessed June 27, 2011, http://www.firstthings.com/article.php3?id_article=3724.

50. Ibid.

51. Ibid. That statement continued:

> But I reject the notion that it discriminates against homosexual, or unmarried heterosexual, domestic partners if they do not receive the same benefits society has provided to married employees to help maintain their families. If it is a question of benefits, why should not blood relatives, or an elderly person or a child who lives in the same household, enjoy these same benefits? Under the city's new ordinance, however, blood relatives are excluded from the benefits that the city's new ordinance extends to domestic partners.
>
> Historically social legislation providing spousal benefits for married persons has recognized the role that women traditionally exercised as wives and mothers, and the important function they contribute to the future of society by their unpaid work in the home raising their families. Even with today's changes in the workplace, to seek to equate domestic partnership with the institution of marriage and family runs contrary to Catholic teaching, indeed to the beliefs of most religious and cultural traditions, and as recent polls have shown, to the basic convictions of the great majority of Americans.

52. Ibid.

53. See ibid. (discussing the city's regulations).

54. Ibid.

55. "Overview," San Francisco Human Rights Commission, accessed March 31, 2008, http://www.sfgov.org/site/sfhumanrights_page.asp?id=5921 (describing the Equal Benefits Ordinance, also known as the City's Nondiscrimination in Contracts Ordinances [Chapters 12B and 12C of the San Francisco Administrative Code]).

56. Levada, "The San Francisco Solution."

57. Ibid.

58. See ibid. (discussing the agreement reached with San Francisco to allow the archdiocese to comply with the new ordinance).

59. See ibid. (examining the "mutually acceptable solution" reached by the city and the archdiocese).

60. Let us distinguish those who seek space for private freedom and those who seek to impose their own views on everyone else. A free society should offer not untrammeled but more latitude of the first kind than the second. See Carol Weisbrod, "Family, Church and State: An Essay on Constitutionalism and Religious Authority," *Journal of Family Law* 26 (1988): 741, reprinted in *Kindred Matters*, ed. D. Meyers et al. (Ithaca, NY: Cornell University Press, 1993.

61. See Christopher D. Belelieu, "Note: The Headscarf as a Symbolic Enemy of the European Court of Human Rights' Democratic Jurisprudence: Viewing Islam through a European Legal Prism in Light of the *Sahin* Judgment," *Columbia Journal of European Law* 12 (2006): 573, 606 (citing Sahin v. Turkey, 44 Eur. Ct. H.R. 5, ¶ 47 [2005]).

62. Ibid., 577.

63. Ibid., 581 (quoting Nicole Pope and Hugh Pope, *Turkey Unveiled: A History of Modern Turkey* [Woodstock, NY: Overlook Press, 2004]: 317).

64. Ibid.

65. See ibid., 582 (describing Prime Minister Erdogan's efforts to maintain a secular-religious balance).

66. Ibid., 607–8 (citing Sahin v. Turkey, No. 44774/98, ¶¶ 78, 98–99, 108, 113–114, 117–21 (Eur. Ct. H.R. Nov. 10, 2005).

67. *Sahin*, App. No. 44774/98, ¶¶ 55–59, 61.

68. Belelieu, "The Headscarf as the Symbolic Enemy," 589–92, 607–10 (citing *Sahin*, App. No. 44774/98, ¶¶ 78, 98–99, 108, 113–14, 117–22, discussing the court's reliance on Turkey's case law, and noting the concept of "the margin of appreciation" used by the court to allow latitude for member states in their decision making and adherence to the Convention on Human Rights).

69. Pierre Atlas, "Secularism vs Democracy in Turkey," *RealClear Politics*, June

15, 2008, accessed June 27, 2011, http://www.realclearpolitics.com/articles/2008/06/secularism_vs_democracy_in_tur.html.

70. Jonathan Head, "Quiet End to Turkey's College Headscarf Ban," *BBC News*, Dec. 31, 2010, http://www.bbc.co.uk/news/world-europe-11880622.

71. Marvine Howe, *Turkey Today: A Nation Divided over Islam's Revival* (Boulder, CO: Westview Press, 2000): 248.

72. Belelieu, "The Headscarf as the Symbolic Enemy," 583.

73. Grenville Byford, "Fighting the Veil: Turkey Is Bitterly Divided over Government Efforts to Ease Its Headscarf Ban. What Will the Courts Do Now?" *Newsweek*, February 4, 2008, accessed June 27, 2011, http://www.newsweek.com/id/107941; Noah Feldman, "Veiled Democracy?" *New York Times*, February 8, 2008, accessed June 27, 2011, www.nytimes.com/2008/02/08/opinion/08feldman.html; Gareth Jenkins, "Turkey's Constitutional Changes: Much Ado about Nothing?" *Eurasia Daily Monitor* 5 (February 11, 2008), accessed June 27, 2011, http://www.jamestown.org/single/?no_cache=1&tx_ttnews%5Btt_news%5D=33371.

74. Pierre Tristan, "Leila Sahin and Turkey's Battle over the Islamic Head Scarf: How Political Islam Is Challenging the World's Most Secular Muslim Democracy," About.com: Middle East Issues, accessed April 26, 2008, http://middleeast.about.com/od/turkey/a/me080210.htm.

75. See Carolyn Fluehr-Lobban, "Cultural Relativism and Universal Human Rights," *Anthro Notes* 20 (1998), accessed June 27, 2011, http://anthropology.si.edu/outreach/anthnote/Winter98/anthnote.html (explaining the use of the harm principle in making a distinction between universal human rights and cultural relativism).

76. Abdullahi An-Na'im, "Promises We Should All Keep in Common Cause," in *Is Multiculturalism Bad for Women?* ed. Susan Moller Okin et al., (Princeton, NJ: Princeton University Press, 1999): 59.

77. Martha C. Nussbaum, *Sex and Social Justice* (New York: Oxford University Press, 1999): 49.

78. Will Kymlicka, *Multicultural Citizenship: A Liberal Theory of Minority Rights* (Oxford: Clarendon Press, 1995); Michael Walzer, "The Communitarian Critique of Liberalism," in *New Communitarian Thinking: Persons, Virtues, Institutions, and Communities*, ed. Amitai Etzioni (Charlottesville: University Press of Virginia, 1995): 52.

79. "Our Name," Colorful Penguin, accessed May 12, 2008, http://www.colorfulpenguin.com/our_name.html (discussing Gary Larson and penguin drawing); "Movie Review: Happy Feet," NY Movie Reviews, accessed May 12,

2008, http://nymoviereviews.com/?page_id=116 (discussing Gary Larson and penguin drawing).

80. See generally Wisconsin v. Yoder, 406 U.S. 205 (1972).

81. Santa Clara Pueblo v. Martinez, 436 U.S. 49 (1978); see Resnik, "Dependent Sovereigns," 672–75 ("[A]ccording to the Court, if federal courts were to imply power to 'intervene' in tribal decisions, the courts would undermine the authority of a group whose powers have already been limited"); see also Martha Minow, "About Women, About Culture: About Them, About Us," in *Engaging Cultural Differences: The Multicultural Challenge in Liberal Democracies*, ed. Richard Shweder et al. (New York: Russell Sage Foundation, 2002): 252–67.

82. Santa Clara Pueblo v. Martinez, 436 U.S. 49, 51–52, 72 (1978).

83. Idem.

84. See Martha Minow, *Making All the Difference: Inclusion, Exclusion, and American Law* (Ithaca, NY: Cornell University Press,1990): 110–12 ("[T]he social-relations approach assumes that there is a basic connectedness between people, instead of assuming that autonomy is the prior and essential dimension of personhood"); Martha Minow and Mary Lyndon Shanley, "Relational Rights and Responsibilities: Revisioning the Family in Liberal Political Theory and Law," *Hypatia* 11 (1996): 4–6 suggesting a view of family law that takes into account the deeply involved relationships of interdependency and mutual responsibility in families); Jennifer Nedelsky, "Reconceiving Rights as Relationships," *Review of Constitutional Studies* 1 (1993): 1–19 (arguing for an understanding of rights as relationships).

85. See John Rawls, *Political Liberalism* (New York: Columbia University Press, 1993): 134 (describing political liberalism as an overlapping consensus of reasonable comprehensive doctrines wherein the reasonable doctrine endorses a single political conception, but each from its own point of view); see also Cass R. Sunstein, "Commentary: Incompletely Theorized Agreements," *Harvard Law Review* 108 (1995): 1733 (identifying possibilities for convergence on specific resolutions of certain problems even in the absence of greater theoretical disagreement).

86. See Zelman v. Simmons-Harris, 536 U.S. 639 (2002) (finding an Ohio Pilot Project Scholarship Program that provided tuition aid allowing low-income students to elect private religious schools did not violate the Establishment Clause); Planned Parenthood v. Casey, 505 U.S. 833 (1992) (affirming the central holding of *Roe v. Wade* but permitting states to require written informed consent from the woman twenty-four hours before the abortion); see generally Martha Minow, "The Government Can't, May, or Must Fund Religious Schools: Three

Riddles of Constitutional Change for Laurence Tribe," *Tulsa Law Review* 42 (2008): 101–27.

87. Miller v. California, 413 U.S. 15 (1973).

88. See generally Olivier Roy, *Secularism Confronts Islam*, trans. George Holoch (New York: Columbia University Press, 2007) (discussing the tensions between secularism and private religious beliefs).

89. See generally Shachar, *Multicultural Jurisdictions*.

90. See generally Weisbrod, "Family, Church, and State"; Weisbrod, *Emblems of Pluralism* (particularly the chapter "Practical Polyphony"). There is still a further alternative of private space for separate practices that is nonetheless still conditioned upon compliance with fundamental protections that the secular state or human rights norms establish for everyone.

91. Weisbrod, *Emblems of Pluralism*, 61–63, 68.

92. Ibid., 166, 175–77.

93. See generally Elizabeth Schneider, *Battered Women and Feminist Lawmaking* (New Haven: Yale University Press, 2000).

94. Robert Cover argued that the nation-state will periodically seek to destroy normative subcommunities from jealousy or desire for overall control, even while acknowledging that the subcommunities may at times take steps that should — from an outside perspective — be stopped. Cover, "The Supreme Court, 1982 Term," 6–11, 68.

95. "The Search for Signs of Intelligent Life in the Universe," directed by John Bailey (1991, Los Angeles, CA, Orion Classics) (performed by Tomlin and written by Jane Wagner).

96. See Richard Henry, "Adlai Stevenson," accessed March 31, 2008, http://www.uua.org/uuhs/duub/articles/adlaistevenson.html.

AYELET SHACHAR

Chapter Two Privatizing Diversity A Cautionary Tale from Religious Arbitration in Family Law

Demands to accommodate religious diversity in the public sphere have recently intensified. The debates surrounding the Islamic headscarf (hijab) in Europe vividly illustrate this trend. We also find a new challenge on the horizon: namely, the request to "privatize diversity" through alternative dispute resolution processes that permit parties to move their disputes from public courthouses into the domain of religious or customary sources of law and authority. The recent controversies in Canada and England related to the so-called Sharia tribunals demonstrate the potential force of the storm to come. In this chapter, I offer an alternative to the presently popular vision of private diversity. This alternative is based on a deep commitment to women's identity and membership interests as well as their dignity and equality. Women's legal dilemmas often arise (at least in the family arena) from their allegiance to various overlapping systems of identification, authority, and belief — in this case, those arising from religious and secular law. I argue that only recognition of women's multiple affiliations, and the subtle interactions among them, can help resolve these dilemmas. The recognition of multiple legal affiliations does not sit well with the traditional view that a clear line can be drawn between public and private, official and unofficial, secular and religious, or positive law and traditional practice. Instead, to recognize multiple affiliations is to require greater access to and coordination among these once competing sources of law and identity. Once we conceive of citizenship more richly, it becomes apparent that individuals and families should not be forced to choose between the rights of citizenship and group membership; instead, they should be afforded the opportunity to express their commitment to both. I offer a vision of how such an alternative might be realized.

> The title of this series of lectures ["Civil and Religious Law in England"] signals the existence of what is very widely felt to be a growing challenge in our society — that is, the presence of communities which, while no less "law-abiding" than the rest of the population, relate to something other than the British legal system alone. — *The Archbishop of Canterbury (Feb. 7, 2008)*[1]

Introduction

In discussions about citizenship, we repeatedly come across the modernist schema of privatizing identities: we are expected to act as undifferentiated citizens in the public sphere but remain free to express our distinct cultural or religious identities in the private domain of family and communal life. Yet multiple tensions have exposed cracks in this privatizing identities formula; for instance, where precisely does the "private" end and the "public" begin?[2] What happens when cultural and religious customs extend beyond the home into the spaces of our shared citizenship, such as the school, the workplace, or the voting booth? The recent debates surrounding the hijab (the headscarf worn by some Muslim women), which have engulfed courts and legislatures from Germany to France to Turkey, vividly illustrate these tensions.[3]

We are also starting to see a new type of challenge on the horizon: namely, the request to "privatize diversity" through alternative dispute resolution processes that permit parties to move their disputes from public courthouses into the domain of religious or customary sources of law and authority. The recent controversies in Canada and England related to the so-called Sharia tribunals demonstrate the potential force of the storm to come. Acceptance of privatized diversity may indirectly make room for non-state norms to operate authoritatively within what are otherwise secular legal systems. It could also immunize such processes from the regulatory reach of statutory or constitutional norms of gender equality. These potentially far-reaching alterations to the legal system cannot be fully captured by the old and rigid vocabulary of "private" versus "public"; if anything, these changes challenge the very logic of this distinction. But what are the normative and prudential implications of this attempt to realign secular and religious law, public and private justice, citizenship and diversity? Who is likely to gain, and who may stand to lose from such changes? These are the questions that I will explore in the following pages.

In this chapter, I offer an alternative to the presently popular vision of "privatized diversity." Instead of resorting to a traditional public model, however, I explore the idea of permitting *regulated interaction* between religious and secular sources of law, so long as the baseline of citizenship-guaranteed rights remains firmly in place.[4] Unlike the strict separation model, which is willfully blind to the intersection of manifold affiliations in individuals' lives — to their state, religion, gender, and so on — I take this multiplicity as the point of departure for my analysis. These overlapping "belongings" offer religious women a significant source of meaning and value; at the same time, they may also make them vulnerable to a double or triple disadvantage, especially in a legal and governance system that categorically denies cooperation between their overlapping sources of obligation.

Although limiting intervention by the courts in cases where religious and civil worlds collide has had a long history, the urgency of my plea for rethinking this approach is informed by the contemporary revival of demands for privatized diversity in Canada, England, and elsewhere. The reincarnation of this debate raises a slew of important questions for our conception of citizenship in contemporary societies in the context of a wider trend toward the privatization of justice in family law. Consider the following examples: Should a court be permitted to enforce a civil divorce contract that also has a religious aspect — namely, a promise by a Jewish husband to remove all barriers to remarriage by granting his wife the religious *get* (Jewish divorce decree)? Is it legitimate to establish private religious tribunals — as alternative dispute resolution (ADR) forums — in which consenting adults arbitrate family law disputes according to the parties' religious personal laws in lieu of the state's secular family laws? And, is there room for considerations of culture, religion, national origin, or linguistic identity in determining a child's best interests in cases of custody, visitation, education, and so on? None of these examples are hypothetical. They represent real-life legal challenges raised in recent years by individuals and families who are seeking to redefine the place of culture and religion in their own private ordering and, indirectly, in the larger polity as well.[5]

Family law serves as a casebook illustration of these tensions. Take, for example, the situation of observant religious women who may wish — or feel bound — to follow the requirements of divorce according to their community of faith, in addition to the rules of the state, in order to remove barriers to remarriage. Without the removal of such barriers, women's ability to build new families, if not their very membership status (or that of their children), may be adversely affected. This is particularly true for Muslim and Jewish women living in secular societies who have entered into the marital relationship through a religious ceremony — as permitted by law in many jurisdictions. For them, a civil divorce is merely part of the story; it does not, and cannot, dissolve the religious aspect of the relationship. Failure to recognize their "split status" position — namely, that of being legally divorced according to state law, though still married according to their faith — may leave these women prey to abuse by recalcitrant husbands who are well aware of the adverse effect this situation has on their wives, as they fall between the cracks of the civil and religious jurisdictions.[6]

Ignoring this multiplicity of affiliations may be compatible with an abstract public/private divide, but it misses the mark for these embedded individuals. Even the bulk of theoretical literature on multiculturalism seems to lose sight of this type of concerns, engaging instead in intricate attempts to delineate the boundaries of *public, state-sponsored accommodation of diversity.*[7] As if the public accommodation dilemma did not present enough of a hurdle for policymakers seeking to build a pluralist society, pressing at the edges is another, less easily categorized challenge, which I will here refer to, for the sake of clarity and simplicity, as *privatized diversity.* The main claim raised by advocates of privatized diversity is that what respect for religious freedom or cultural integrity requires is not inclusion in the public sphere, but exclusion from it. This leads to a demand that the state adopt a hands-off, noninterventionist approach, placing civil and family disputes with a religious or cultural aspect fully *outside* the official realm of equal citizenship.

To illustrate this growing trend, I focus on an acrimonious debate that recently broke out in Canada following a community-based proposal to establish a "Private Islamic Court of Justice" (*darul-qada*) to resolve family law disputes among consenting adults according to Sharia principles. This proposal didn't come to the fore in the usual way, through democratic deliberation, constitutional amendment, or a standard law-reform process. Instead, a small and relatively conservative nongovernmental organization, named the Canadian Society of Muslims, declared in a series of press releases its intention to establish the said *darul-qada*, or Sharia tribunal, as this proposal came to be known in the ensuing debate.[8] In a nutshell, their idea was to rely upon a preexisting legal framework, the Arbitration Act, which (at the time) permitted a wide array of family-law disputes to be resolved under its extensively open-ended terms.[9] The envisioned tribunal would have permitted consenting parties not only to enter a less adversarial, out-of-court, dispute resolution process, but also to use the act's "choice of law" provisions to apply religious norms to resolve family disputes, according to the "laws (*fiqh*) of any [Islamic] school, e.g. Shiah or Sunni (Hanafi, Shafi'i, Hambali, or Maliki)."[10]

Instead of debating in the abstract whether to permit or prohibit the tribunal, I approach this privatized diversity challenge from a different angle. My point of departure is a grounded commitment toward respecting women's identity and membership interests as well as their dignity and equality.[11] I then ask what is owed to those women whose legal dilemmas (at least in the family arena) often arise from the fact that their lives are *already* affected by the interplay between overlapping systems of identification, authority, and belief. I suggest that only recognition of their multiple legal affiliations, and the subtle interactions among them, can help resolve these dilemmas. The idea of recognizing the multiplicity of individuals' legal affiliations does not sit well with the traditional view of hermetically separated spheres divided along the presumably clear-cut axes of public/private, official/unofficial, secular/religious, positive law / traditional practice. Instead, recognition calls for greater access to and coordination between these multiple sources of law and identity. In this richer conception of citizenship, individuals and families should be afforded greater options to express both their citizenship and group membership, rather than be forced to sacrifice one for the sake of the other.

The discussion proceeds in four parts. It opens with a typology of the "privatized diversity" family of claims, explaining why the Sharia tribunal's proposal represents a new phase in the debate about relations between secular and religious jurisdictions. This is precisely because of the tribunal's advocates' reliance on a positive law conception of "private ordering" through alternative dispute resolution (ADR). Identifying and assessing the implications of this "intermingling" of secular ADR mechanisms with religious privatized-diversity claims lies at the heart of my discussion. This fast-emerging set of challenges adds a whole new dimension to debates over multicultural or "differentiated" citizenship, placing them in the context of a broader trend that could see the ceding of state power in the sphere of marriage in favor of increased private ordering through contract and arbitration.

Turning to the Sharia tribunal example, in part 2 I use this particular narrative as a means to explore deeper concerns about the interrelationship between the privatization of justice, religious family law, and gender equality. I will elucidate three possible sources of feminist concerns that arise from the tribunal's proponents' espoused variant of privatized diversity: consent, inter- and intra-communal pressures, and the inadequacy of the exit option. I then explain how the Sharia tribunal debate revealed a slippage from a critique of privatization of justice per se (the legal framework allowing consenting parties to remove family disputes from the courts to ADR forums, or what I call "phase 1") to opposition to privatized diversity, which goes beyond phase 1 by calling for the introduction of customary or religious principles as relevant sources for family arbitration (phase 2). The convergence of these two strands of critique galvanized opposition to the tribunal, in the process concealing the validity of concerns expressed by religious women whose legal situation cuts across the idealized civil/religious divide.

In part 3 I argue that what is called for is a more context-sensitive analysis that sees women's freedom and equality as partly *promoted* (rather than inhibited) by recognition of their "communal" identity. Such a vision can help inform creative paths for cooperation that begin to match the actual complexity of lived experience in our diverse societies. I demonstrate the possibility of implementing such a vision by reference to a recent decision by the Supreme Court of Canada, *Bruker v. Marcovitz.* Finally, in revisiting the Sharia tribunal example in the last part of the chapter, I distinguish between ex ante and ex post regulatory oversight mechanisms, explaining why the former is preferable to the latter in the context of family arbitration. I close by reflecting on the government's chosen policy to *ban* any type of family arbitration by faith-based tribunals, thus reaffirming the classic public/private divide. While this decision is politically and symbolically astute, it does not necessarily provide protection for those individuals most vulnerable to their community's formal and informal pressures to turn to "unofficial" dispute-resolution forums in resolving marital issues. The decision may instead push these non-state tribunals underground where no state regulation, coordination, or legal recourse is made available to those who may need it most.

I. Privatized Diversity in Context

Here's a stark "privatized diversity" dilemma: how should a secular state respond to claims by members of religious minority groups seeking to establish private arbitration tribunals in which consenting members of the group will have their legal disputes resolved in a binding fashion — according to religious principles — under the procedural umbrella of ADR? To those seeking to establish a radically pluralistic legal system in which claims of culture or religion always trump other considerations or those endorsing a fully privatized regulation of our social interactions (permitting little if any room for government-created and government-enforced law), this strong vision of privatized diversity may appear quite attractive.[12] Yet for others who endorse a strict separationist approach, or "blindness" toward religious or cultural affiliation, the idea that we might find unregulated "religious islands of binding jurisdiction" mushrooming on the terrain of state law is seen as evidence of the dangers of accommodating diversity, potentially chipping away, however slightly, at the foundational, modernist citizenship formula of "one law for all."[13] Add to the mix two inflammatory components in today's political environment — religion and gender — and the stirrings of disagreement, likely followed by polarization, will soon be heard.[14]

This is what recently happened in Canada, with the debate over the so-called Sharia tribunal. This tale will serve as the basis for my analysis of the surprising lacuna that lies at the heart of multicultural theory: the manner in which we should deal with demands for respecting diversity, which are not raised as calls for fair and just *inclusion* in the public sphere — the latter vividly captured by Iris Young's image of a "heterogeneous public, in which persons stand forth with their differences acknowledged and respected."[15] Rather, what we are dealing with here is a different category of claims for *opting out of*, or seceding from, the effects of the polity's public laws and norms. Let us call the former pattern of multicultural inclusion *public accommodation*, and the latter, *privatized diversity*. My particular interest lies in exploring the scope and limits of privatized diversity, especially in those situations where claims for religious-based arbitration intersect and interact with concerns about power disparities between men and women in the resolution of family-law disputes.

A. FROM PUBLIC ACCOMMODATION TO PRIVATIZED DIVERSITY

To understand the significance of the privatized diversity claim, we must place it in a broader context. To begin with, as just mentioned, it is clearly distinguishable from the vision of public accommodation, which is "intended to help ethnic groups and religious minorities express their cultural particularity and pride without it hampering their success in the economic and political institutions of the dominant society."[16] Privatized diversity, by contrast, is not designed to ensure greater inclusion in the dominant society's institutions; instead, it offers an *alternative* to these institutions. This vision is also different from state-accommodationist legal structures that we find in countries like Israel, Kenya, or India, which publically and officially recognize and facilitate a degree of diversity in the regulation of the family.[17] In these countries the legislature vests recognized customary and religious communities with legal powers over certain matters of personal status; in the privatized diversity model, individuals *contract out* of the secular regime by turning to a private (i.e., non-state) dispute-resolution forum. Contrast this with the situation in Israel, for example, where judges sitting in Rabbinical or Sharia courts are appointed according to a state-defined selection process and are thus subject to closer scrutiny than any out-of-court third-party arbitrator chosen by the parties to resolve their legal disputes.[18] What is more, even in these more pluralistic family law regimes, the government does not leave the field of family regulation unchecked; it typically sets in motion a set of universally applied statutory limits (e.g., minimal age restrictions or equitable property-division presumptions) that apply across the board, effectively limiting the forms of marriage and divorce agreements that can be lawfully solemnized by representatives of the various identity communities.[19]

Neither is the privatized diversity model analogous to the situation found in many Arab and Muslim countries, where the Sharia informs *national* family-law legislation: this typically involves a process of codification of Islamic sources by a secular legislature in the post-independence period, which has in some places led to the adoption of more gender-equitable readings of the religious tradition, as manifested in the recent family-law reforms in Egypt and Morocco.[20] These liberalizing reforms have been advocated by a nontraditional alliance of feminist organizations, civil court functionaries, and moderate religious authorities.[21] This kind of coalition building on the ground has permitted the reshaping of a (state-codified) Islamic family-law framework from *within* the religious tradition as it interacts with national and transnational claims for justice and human dignity — in lieu of asserting a rigid opposition between Islamic texts and feminist demands for greater equality and fairness in the family.[22]

B. THE NEW TERRAIN: DIVERSITY AND THE PRIVATIZATION OF JUSTICE IN FAMILY LAW

One final distinction is appropriate as we identify the distinct features of the privatized diversity family of claims: standard notions of ADR, which often refer to business or commercial disputes, typically emphasize the values of autonomy, agency, and consent in selecting a non-adversarial forum. Some of these assumptions become increasingly tenuous when we shift our gaze to the family-law arena, with its specific baggage of charged gendered power relations. To this we must add, in the debate over the Sharia tribunal, the array of concerns associated with defining an alternative source of *substantive* law drawn from religious texts and their various schools of interpretation. Importantly, the turn to privatized diversity of this kind does not by itself provide a conclusive answer to determining how secular and religious norms should interact in governing the family; they may stand in tension with one another, point in different directions, or lead to broadly similar results.

But this sterile description conceals the actual political issue at hand: the Sharia tribunal proposal was seen as challenging the normative and juridical authority, not to mention legitimacy, of the secular state's asserted mandate to represent and regulate the interests and rights of *all* its citizens in their family-law affairs, irrespective of communal affiliation.[23] It was therefore seen by some as a foundational debate about some of the most basic questions concerning hierarchy and lexical order in the contexts of law and citizenship: which norms *should* prevail, and who, or what entity, ought to have the final word in resolving value conflicts between equality and diversity, if they arise. The vision of privatized diversity, in its full-fledged "unregulated islands of jurisdiction" variant, thus poses a challenge to the superiority of secular family law by its old adversary — religion.

Indeed, the prospect of tension, if not a direct clash, between religious and secular norms governing the family — and the fear that women's hard-won equal rights would be the main casualties of such a showdown — largely informed the opposition to the Sharia tribunal variant of privatized diversity. Add to that the charged political environment surrounding Muslim minorities in North America and Europe in the post-9/11 era, and we can easily understand why this tribunal initiative became a lightning rod for the much larger debate about what unites us as citizens and what may divide us. And were this not enough to create an explosive situation on its own, we must take account of the fact that once these charged gender and religious questions caught the attention of the mass media, they quickly fell prey to reified notions of the inherent contrast between (idealized) secular norms and (vilified) religious traditions. The recent storm in the United Kingdom that followed the "civil and religious law" speech by the archbishop of Canterbury (quoted at the beginning of this chapter) exhibits the same pattern at work.[24] In this war of images, secular family laws were automatically presented as unqualified protectors of equality as well as the deterrents to destitution or dependency (though they may leave women and children in a far poorer state than divorced husbands, for example); by contrast, religious principles were uncritically defined as inherently reinforcing inequality and as the source of disempowerment for women (although certain interpretations could lead to results that are equitable and respectful to the divorcing spouses).[25] Eventually, the Sharia tribunal came to represent a polarized oppositional dichotomy that allows *either* protecting women's rights *or* promoting religious extremism. Under these conditions, it is not surprising that the government chose the former over the latter. But were there other, less oppositional, alternatives that were missed in this politicized debate, alternatives that might better have responded to devout women's multiple affiliations and identities as group members and citizens of the larger polity? I return to this question in the final part of my discussion.

C. SETTING STRAIGHT MISGUIDED "EITHER/OR" CHOICES IN LAW AND IDENTITY

For the tribunal's principal advocates, the Canadian Society of Muslims, what seemed to matter most was not so much the theoretical ingenuity of privatized diversity's intermingling with the larger trend of "private justice" as it was the pragmatic bottom-line result that this permitted: in their words, it would allow Muslims living in a non-Muslim country to "live our faith to the best of our ability."[26] But the tribunal's advocates further argued (alarming many critics in the process) that once the possibility of turning to a Sharia tribunal becomes readily available, it *should* represent a clear choice for Muslim Canadians: "Do you want to govern yourself by the personal laws of your religion, or do you prefer governance by secular Canadian family law?"[27] It is here that the difficulty lies with the envisioned tribunal: it quickly came to represent an "either/or" choice for group members, dividing them between loyalty to the faith and governance by the state. This is an artificially constructed dichotomy, however, which in many ways replicates the logic of a rigid public/private divide. Let me provide two quick illustrations of the "cracks" in this "either/or" vision. For one, the advocates of the tribunal argued that any arbitral awards rendered by their proposed religious tribunal would be enforceable by the *secular* court system.[28] Though described as a selling point to its potential users,[29] this partial reliance on (or interaction with) the state and its legal system to enforce the tribunal's legal "product" created much public confusion on the ground. It also revealed the tribunal's selective, if not opportunistic, "disengagement" with state institutions. While they sought to escape the normative order of the state, the tribunal's advocates at the same time wanted to procedurally rely on Canada's (public) court system to enforce their "private" tribunal's awards. This is a shaky proposition: using state law inevitably brings with it certain public values of fairness and accountability; it is not an empty vessel to be used as dictated by convenience. Furthermore, the expectation that parties will turn to the private arbitration tribunal (in lieu of the state's public system) as an expression of *their* loyalty to the community, as implicitly and explicitly asserted by the tribunal's advocates, itself relies on an over-unified vision of the "Muslim community" in Canada. This community consists of members who hold different degrees of identification with religiosity, subscribe to a range of linguistic and cultural traditions, and originate from a wide variety of countries. Instead of recognizing multiplicity of affiliation, the tribunal's variant of privatized diversity, by posing a dichotomous choice — "Do you want to govern yourself by the personal laws of your religion, or do you prefer governance by the secular state's family laws?" — contributed to creating a presumably unbridgeable chasm between one's identity as citizen and as group member.

These issues become even more charged when the gendered dimension is added. The main concern here is that the push toward privatized diversity places disproportionate pressure on women to prioritize their communal loyalty over and above shared citizenship, given their often heightened responsibility as emblems of culture and "bearers" of tradition.[30] This last point is intensified by the fact that we are focusing on the family, a site that has become deeply intertwined with struggles over communal identity and expressions of "loyalty."[31] A central concern thus lies in the interplay between unequal power relations within the community and the tribunal's self-proclaimed mandate to represent the path that a "good Muslim" ought to choose.[32] It is here that the question of whether and how the state responds to such claims becomes crucial. The tribunal's opponents were rightly alarmed by the risk that once a privatized diversity route is recognized or permitted by the state, women who fail to agree to adjudicate family-law matters according to the norms of their own religious traditions (or those who reject the tribunal's authority to arbitrate their family disputes) may increasingly be portrayed by the more conservative elements in their communities as somehow lacking loyalty to their religious tradition or its localized manifestation.[33]

II. Women, ADR, and Privatized Diversity in the Family Arena

Concerns about pressure to enter into religious family arbitration processes are part of a larger story. As just mentioned, the most controversial claim raised by the tribunal's advocates was the suggestion that once Sharia family arbitration services become available, "any Muslims who continued to opt for civil law procedures should be regarded as failing in their religious duties [or communal obligations]."[34] The danger here is that arguments in favor of privatized diversity, especially when advanced by self-appointed "guardians of the faith," may all too quickly become intertwined with idealized images of gender and the family, as well as "loyalty" and "authenticity."[35] Under such conditions, feminist scholars and activists have ample reasons for concern. I wish to highlight here three of these major sources of concern: consent; inter- and intra-communal pressures (and their tendency to fossilize a living tradition under conditions of "reactive culturalism"); and the inappropriateness of the "exit" option as a magic-bullet answer. I do not claim that these are the sole pivotal issues that need to be taken into account; rather, they are used here as examples to illustrate the potential dangers associated with the privatized diversity route.

A. CONSENT

First, we must tackle the question of consent. It is well-known that the issue of consent — as expressed, for example, by signing an agreement to enter into an arbitration procedure — serves as the core legitimizing principle for contracts and other private justice mechanisms.[36]

The debate here turns on whether subjection to a religious arbitration forum can indeed be characterized as an act freely chosen or is an end result of complex and subtle social processes of coercion that eventually restrict the agent's free will — especially for those who are in more marginalized or subordinated positions within the group.[37] The problem of consent and coercion is one of the oldest on the books, though it is not unique to religious arbitration. However, religious arbitration involves both removing the case from the public courtroom and permitting choice-of-law provisions that introduce religious principles as the relevant authorities for resolving family-law disputes. Clearly, the concern about free choice can also arise simply when we shift from a public arena to an area of *private* dispute resolution.[38] This I will label "phase 1," which involves the choice of forum. But debates about free choice typically become more pronounced when we enter "phase 2," which involves the double layers of choice of forum *and* choice of law.

In the Canadian Sharia arbitration debate, these two choices were often challenged together by various women's advocacy groups, adding fuel to an already explosive controversy. Indeed, the tribunal's leading opponents argued against *any* type of privatization of justice in the family-law context. In this respect, a proposal raised by a minority community (or certain sectors thereof) as a way to address what they saw as the unmet demands of religious diversity (by utilizing phase 2) soon became a spur to resistance by those who saw *any* turn away from the courts (within the parameters of phase 1) as, by definition, eroding the very protections to which women should have access if they undergo a divorce proceeding. In other words, the tribunal debate served as an opportunity to reopen and invigorate opposition to phase 1 — allowing parties the freedom to turn to an out-of-court dispute-resolution mechanism, even if they still remain bound by the *secular* statutory regime governing family relations. Thus, even without adding religious or cultural factors to the mix, the very idea of "privatizing" dispute resolution in the family-law context raised the ire of the tribunal's opponents. They proposed an alternative model: to re-"universalize" the authority of the public courts as the only legitimate adjudicators of *any* family-law dispute. The inspiration for this particular demand, which we might call a return to "phase 0" — prohibiting *both* choice of forum and choice of law — came from Québec's Civil Code. Here, Article 2369 provides that "disputes over the status and capacity of persons, family law matters or other matters of public order may *not* be submitted to arbitration."[39]

The rationale for imposing this public-policy exception is a concern with power inequalities and information asymmetries in families, which, on this account, may become exacerbated in private dispute resolution that requires unequal parties to bargain. This approach stands in contrast to court-based proceedings where a sitting judge has the public authority to make final (and, ideally, fair and just) determinations in shaping the post-divorce rights and obligations of the parties. The counterresponse here, vigorously articulated by members of the family-law bar, is that channeling every family-law dispute through the courts (even where the parties have no difficulty reaching a balanced settlement) is both paternalistic and inefficient. It is estimated that the vast majority of divorce cases are resolved through *secular* ADR mechanisms that operate in the "shadow of the law."[40] At least in theory, this means that both parties bargain in the *same* shadow; they are equally informed by the state's defined legislative benchmarks, such as the commitment to equitable division, which then serves as the starting point that informs their respective "bargaining" positions and ultimate compromises, formalized in a separation agreement or arbitral awards.[41] This reality on the ground made the phase 0 option a moot response to the challenge posed by the proponents of the Sharia tribunal.

B. INTER- AND INTRA-COMMUNAL TENSIONS

This leads to a second set of concerns, which relate to the charged and often complex interactions between inter- and intra-communal pressures. Most relevant to our discussion is the recognition that a growing level of intercommunal tension and lack of mutual trust may contribute to renewed pressures on women in their intragroup relations, a phenomenon I have elsewhere called "reactive culturalism."[42] This may translate into a chorus of voices recommending the adoption of stricter and more rigid interpretations of shared religious norms and practices — a call that is justified internally in the name of upholding the autonomy and "authenticity" of the minority community vis-à-vis an externally hostile majority in situations of deep inter-communal tensions. In this scenario, immense pressure is likely to be imposed on women to turn to community-based tribunals, as a way of expressing their "loyalty" to the group. (This is yet another reason why reliance on the notion of nominal, free consent has become ever more contested by the critics of the tribunal.)

For a complex set of reasons, women and the family often serve a crucial symbolic role in constructing group solidarity vis-à-vis society at large.[43] Under such conditions, women's indispensable contribution in transmitting and manifesting a group's collective identity is coded as both an instrument and symbol of group integrity. As a result, idealized and gendered images of women as mothers, caregivers, educators, and moral guardians of the home come to represent the ultimate and inviolable repository of "authentic" group identity. These carefully crafted, gendered images of devout religiosity then become cultural markers that help erase internal diversity and disagreement, while at the same time allowing both minority and majority leaders to politicize selective and often invented boundaries between the "self" and the "other."[44]

Such hardening of the borders of inclusion and exclusion may unfortunately serve as a ready-made rationale for conservative group leaders to impose further restrictions on women; this may occur in the name of the collective effort to preserve the group's distinct identity in the face of (real or imagined) external threats. It may also motivate aggressive responses by the majority community, which may feel threatened by the resurgence and radicalization of religious minority-group identity. In this way, the conflation of increasingly "revivalist" claims of culture, involving gendered images of idealized womanhood, becomes a focal point for an unprecedented spate of state versus religion conflicts over foundational collective identity and basic citizenship questions.

C. THE INADEQUACY OF "EXIT"

The third area of potential trouble, which I will only flag here, is that the concerns surrounding the degree of freedom that individuals experience as a result of inter- and intra-communal tensions and power relations become more pronounced in the context of religious or other *nomoi* groups — precisely because the group member may *wish to remain within the group* (rather than utilizing the "exit" option favored by some).[45] Those with limited desire or ability to leave may feel that the spectrum of options that are realistically available to them is restricted not only by familiar factors such as economic or informational asymmetry (which inform those favoring phase 0 — namely, banning any forum of private dispute resolution in the family), but also by distinctive identity-based or communal pressures.

Therefore, even if arbitration in family-law disputes may be relevant and legitimate in the purely secular context where the pressures are more individualized (phase 1), the tripartite set of concerns that I have just presented — consent, inter- and intra-communal tensions, and the failure of the exit option — become even more pronounced in phase 2. This involves not only a move away from the public courts, but also a demand to enforce in the alternative forum an alternative body of law, which is itself derived from religious sources.

III. The (Lost) Non-dichotomous Route

With this background in mind, I now turn to consider whether the challenges presented by the Sharia tribunal proposal could have been resolved in ways that address these feminist concerns without necessarily leading to the conclusion — eventually adopted by the government — that the answer to such complex law and identity challenges lies in relegating these religious traditions to the margins, labeled as unofficial, exotic, or even dangerous (unrecognized) law. My objective in doing this is motivated by the desire to provide alternatives for devout women within religious communities who may find little solace in the "exit" option — women who are simultaneously culture-bearers *and* rights-bearers.[46] For them, the almost automatic rejection of the tribunal's proposal may respond to the protection-of-rights dimension of their lives but does little to address the cultural/religious affiliation issue. The latter may well be better addressed by a non-state tribunal. This is particularly true for observant women who have solemnized their marriage relationship according to the requirements of their religious tradition and who may now wish —

or feel bound — to receive the blessing of this tradition for the dissolution of that relationship. In the Canadian debate, this constituency also inserted a transnational element, suggesting that in families with roots in more than one country, a divorce agreement that complies with the demands of the faith (as a non-territorial identity community), in addition to those of the state of residence, is somehow more "transferable" across different Muslim jurisdictions.[47] In technical terms, this need not be the case — private international law norms are based on the laws of states, not of religions.[48] But what matters here is the perception that a faith-based tribunal may provide a valuable legal service to its potential clientele, a service that the secular state — by virtue of its formal divorce from religiosity — simply cannot provide.

The traditional legal approach is to turn a blind eye to these intersections, in line with the idealized public/private divide. Relegating family disputes with certain religious aspects beyond the reach of the secular courts need not, however, be the sole or even primary response to such dilemmas, especially when "non-intervention" effectively translates into immunizing wrongful behavior by more powerful parties. These parties may refuse to remove barriers to religious remarriage (as in the Jewish *get* situation, discussed below), to pronounce a *talaq* after the wife obtains a civil divorce, or fail to honor a commitment to pay a woman her *mahr*, thus impairing the woman's ability to build a new family or establish financial independence after divorce (which is the case in some Islamic matrimonial disputes and divorce proceedings).[49]

Instead of ignoring these gendered disadvantages, in *Bruker v. Marcovitz*, the Supreme Court of Canada has recently shown itself willing to break old habits.[50] The basic facts are as follows: a divorce proceeding between Stephanie Bruker and Jessel Marcovitz, a Jewish couple, was commenced by the wife before a civil court. A settlement agreement was negotiated and signed by the parties. It included various terms and trade-offs regarding custody, support payments, and so on. Most importantly for our discussion, this separation agreement also included a commitment by both parties to appear before a Jewish *beth din* (a three-member rabbinical panel) in order to obtain a religious divorce decree (the *get*). According to Canada's Divorce Act and Ontario's Family Law Act, the secular side of divorce can only be affirmed by the civil court, as the court did in this case, incorporating the terms of the settlement agreement between the parties into the final divorce decree. The obligation to turn to the rabbinical authorities thus became part of the terms that *enabled* the civil divorce by a public, state entity. Once the husband had the secular divorce decree in hand, however, he failed to honor the agreement he had signed to remove religious barriers to his wife's remarriage. For fifteen long years, Mr. Marcovitz *refused* to appear before the rabbinical authorities, leaving Ms. Bruker in the situation known as the *agunah*, or "chained wife." The consequences of this legal situation are severe. Despite being civilly divorced, the woman is unable to remarry or have children that are recognized as members of the faith.[51]

This was the sad situation in which Ms. Bruker found herself. For a decade and a half, the ex-husband refused to issue her the *get*, knowingly preventing her from availing herself of a crucial term of the agreement that had facilitated the issuance of the civil divorce decree in the first place. After nine years of waiting in vain, the wife decided to sue her husband. She turned to the court system in Québec, claiming damages in compensation for the husband's noncompliance (namely, the breach of contractual obligation to appear before the *beth din*). Whereas in New York the courts have recognized the *ketubah* (or prenuptial agreement) as requiring the husband to grant the wife a Jewish divorce in addition to a civil divorce and have intervened to grant specific performance of such agreements, in this case Ms. Bruker did not ask the secular court system to use its powers to compel the husband to appear before the *beth din*.[52] Her legal claim was more minimalist; it focused instead on a standard civil-damages claim for breach of contract.[53]

What is a court to do under such circumstances? The hands-off approach demands nonintervention, suggesting that the problem lies in the religious, not the secular sphere. The trial judge did not take this approach. After hearing the evidence, he ruled that the civil contract entered into by the parties was valid and binding, notwithstanding the fact that it had a religious aspect to it. As the trial judge succinctly put it, "The pith and essence of what is being asked for in this case is not religious."[54] This analysis permitted the wife to get her day in court, utilizing the "naming, claiming, blaming" mechanisms of civil litigation against the wrongful party (the husband). To reach this conclusion, the trial judge had to engage in the familiar tango of *delineating* the secular from the religious, a dance that had significant implications in favor of Ms. Bruker in this case. Recognizing the harm and suffering caused to her by the husband's refusal to fulfill his *civil* commitment to remove the religious barriers to remarriage, the trial judge ordered him to pay the sum of $47,500 in damages.

The husband appealed. He argued that *his* right to exercise his religious belief and freedom had been breached by the secular court's intervention in his allegedly private dispute with his wife over the religious divorce decree. He saw himself exonerated from liability for this reason. Mr. Marcovitz further argued that the promise he had made in the contract was merely moral, not legal, and therefore could not serve as the basis for a damages claim for breach of contract. The Court of Appeal accepted the husband's position. It held that "the substance of the . . . obligation is religious in nature, irrespective of the form in which the obligation is stated,"[55] consequently ruling that the contract was unenforceable. Judicial intervention under such circumstances, the Québec Court of Appeal continued, would be inconsistent with recognition of the husband's right to freely exercise his religious beliefs as he saw fit. Any harm suffered by the wife as a result of the husband's (in)action here was "private"; it was not a matter for public law to address.

The final twist in this saga occurred when Ms. Bruker turned to the Supreme Court of Canada. The substance of her argument was that nonintervention in the name of her ex-husband's freedom of religion under these circumstances amounted to a license to deny her, and similarly situated women, the right to *their* religious freedom (to comply with what they perceive as obligations of their faith) and to equality in family life. The husband's promise to remove the barriers to religious remarriage affected the trade-offs agreed to by the parties during the divorce negotiations. Immunizing the husband (the contract breacher) ex post from the legal consequences of his harmful act was tantamount to injustice, allowing him an unwarranted advantage to achieve concessions at the divorce (in exchange for the promise to remove barriers to religious remarriage) and then renege on his commitment while causing severe and gendered harms to his wife. The court, in a majority opinion, accepted these arguments. It held that the fact that a dispute had a religious aspect did not by itself make it nonjusticiable. Equally important for our discussion, the court rejected the simplistic "privatizing identities" formula. Instead, it ruled in favor of "[r]ecognizing the enforceability by civil courts of agreements to discourage religious barriers to remarriage, [addressing] the gender discrimination those barriers may represent and [alleviating] the effects they may have on extracting unfair concessions in a civil divorce."[56]

The significance of the *Marcovitz* decision for our discussion thus lies in its recognition that *both* the secular *and* the religious aspects of divorce matter greatly to observant women if they are to enjoy gender equality, articulate their religious identity, enter new families after divorce, or rely on contractual private ordering just like any other citizen.[57] This "intersectionist" or joint-governance framework offers us a vision in which the secular system may be called upon to provide remedies in order to protect religious women from husbands who might otherwise cherry-pick their religious and secular obligations as they see fit. This is a clear rejection of the simplistic either-your-culture-or-your-rights approach, offering instead a more nuanced and context-sensitive analysis that begins from the ground up. This requires identifying who is harmed, and why, and then proceeding to find a remedy that matches, as much as possible, the need to recognize the (indirect) intersection of law and religion that contributed in the first place to the creation of the harm for which legal recourse is now sought.

Achieving such a balance does not mean that the state must — or indeed may — rule on matters of religious doctrine or precept. In this example, the husband had freely agreed to turn to the rabbinical *beth din*. The Supreme Court was not in a position to order specific performance ("forcing" the husband to implement his promise); instead, it merely imposed monetary damages for the *breach* of the contractual promise in ways that harmed the wife personally and affected the public interest generally. What *Marcovitz* demonstrates is the possibility of employing a standard legal recourse (damages for breach of contract, in this example) in response to specifically gendered harms that arise out of the *intersection* between multiple sources of authority and identity in the actual lives of women who are members of religious minority communities and larger, secular states as well.

What conclusions can be drawn from the *Marcovitz* case, with its focus on a civil contract with a religious aspect, in relation to the Sharia tribunal debate? I shall briefly identify a few of the possible implications, referring to the distinctions between entry into a contractual agreement (with a religious aspect) as affirmed by a secular court and entry into a binding non-state arbitration forum; between ex post judicial review and ex ante regulatory oversight; and between self-restraint exercised by non-state religious tribunals and government-imposed statutory restrictions. Each of these distinctions has its own theoretical significance, though they may overlap and crosscut in practice. I discuss each in turn.

(i) Entry into a secular agreement (with a religious aspect) versus entry into a community-based, semi-private tribunal with binding authority over consenting members: Both of these situations involve the intersection of law and religion to some degree, but the former appears to offer more protections to women (or other potentially vulnerable parties) because of the publicity and legal advice that are part and parcel of the affirmation of the contract. This ensures more veto points as well as review options. Furthermore, unlike the religious tribunal arbitration award, the court-affirmed contract is negotiated in the shadow of the state's family laws.[58] At least in principle, the state's family laws are committed to equitable norms at divorce; in contrast, this is true for some (but not all) interpretations of religious personal law traditions. Cumulatively, then, the tribunal's privatized-diversity formula appears to offer fewer protections for women than entry into a civil contract with a religious aspect to it. The tribunal's provision of actual protections that respond to the concerns identified earlier relating to consent, intra- and inter-communal pressure, and the inadequacy of "exit" leave much to be desired.

(ii) Ex post judicial review versus ex ante regulatory control: The literature on institutional design distinguishes between different forms or techniques of oversight. In the context of congressional oversight of executive-agency activities, for example, Mathew McCubbins and Thomas Schwarz famously argued that we must distinguish between what they label *police patrol* oversight (involving centralized, active and direct oversight) and *fire alarm* oversight, which is less centralized and involves less active or direct oversight.[59] Instead of actively and directly monitoring administrative agencies (a costly and complex "police patrol" process), the fire-alarm oversight technique decentralizes regulation. It does so by enabling individual citizens and stakeholders, as well as organized interest groups, to examine administrative decisions, to charge executive agencies with violating stated goals, and to seek review or remedy (where relevant) by turning to the courts or the legislature.[60] In the context of our discussion, once the hands-off approach is rejected (as I think it should be), we can identify a related set of choices regarding regulatory oversight that need to be made.

The classic approach in arbitration is to allow *minimal* oversight; the idea is that the consenting parties intentionally removed their dispute from the public system, preferring instead an out-of-court process. In the case of severe breaches of procedural justice, however, most arbitration laws (including Ontario's Arbitration Act that was so central to the Sharia tribunal debate) permit the arbitrating parties to seek judicial review.[61] This represents a classic "fire alarm" procedure. Instead of having the courts or legislatures actively monitor the arbitration process, the burden of identifying alleged violations is passed on to those who are best informed about the process and who possess the strongest interest in identifying and reporting such breaches: the parties themselves. While the fire-alarm model, which in this context is better described as "ex post judicial review," might in theory fit the realm of commercial or civil arbitration with its strong emphasis on party autonomy, agency, and parity, it may fail miserably in the family arbitration context. Here, there is a serious concern about power and representation inequities, which disrupt the ex post judicial review model's basic assumption about both parties being equally positioned to "pull" the fire alarm and call attention to potential breaches in the arbitration process. (We earlier encountered similar concerns raised by those advocating the phase 0 response.) Given the gendered concerns identified in part 2 above, the idea of placing the burden of initiating the process of ex post review on the more vulnerable parties, which may have been semi-coerced in the first place into consenting to the tribunal's authority, is implausible. If anything, it provides an (unintended) guarantee that very few, if any, of the most serious violations will ever be reported. This result stands in direct contravention of the logic of active agency that lies at the basis of this oversight mechanism, making it a less attractive option to respond to the complex gendered and communal pressures at issue. Instead of merely relying on ex post judicial review, it appears that a complementary technique of regular oversight is required once we move to the realm of family arbitration.

This indeed was the conclusion reached by a major governmental review committee (the "Boyd Report"), which was set up to examine the interrelationships between private arbitration, religion, and protection of women's rights.[62] While the Boyd Report received criticism for a host of reasons, including its unhelpful "murkiness" in defining the appropriate conditions for intervention by secular courts in response to religious arbitral awards that appear to breach the reasonable margins of interpretation of family law statutory provisions (as would have been permitted in the secular system), it is important to note that this line of criticism *assumes* that oversight must reside primarily in the ex post judicial review model. A more charitable reading of the report's recommendations illuminates another pattern at work. Although the ex post model remains viable, the report initiates a conceptual shift toward the adoption of extensive ex ante oversight in family arbitration (responding to the phase 1 critique), thus moving to a more active and centralized "police patrol" regulatory model.[63]

Evidence for this shift is plentiful; indeed, it informed many of the procedural legislative amendments to the Arbitration Act (the government response to the tribunal debate), which were adopted in 2006, and was articulated through the Family Arbitration Regulation of 2007. Examples of the shift toward ex ante oversight include a mandatory training and licensing program for arbitrators; the requirements that any party entering a family arbitration process must receive counsel by an independent legal advisor before entering the arbitration; that files be kept by the arbitrator, containing both the evidence presented and notes taken during the hearings; and that separate screening of the parties to detect signs of domestic violence must take place, any such concerns categorically prohibiting the use of arbitration.[64]

These various reforms demonstrate an important organizing principle: instead of placing the burden of initiating the ex post judicial review on those who may be least able to challenge their family or community's norms or pressures (by turning to a secular court for judicial review), it is preferable under these circumstances of unequal power relations to adopt across-the-board, ex ante oversight techniques. While not without its shortcomings, I believe this is a wise move in this context. It places the burden on the arbitrators themselves to show that they have complied with the government's predefined standard rules and procedures, rather than placing the responsibility of taking action on a particular individual who may already be experiencing heightened vulnerability. Notably, this shift in regulatory emphasis does not require or entail total abandonment of the ex post review model. The two models can live happily side by side.

In Canada, the option of judicial review of arbitration remains open for those who wish — or feel sufficiently empowered — to utilize it. On this score, we can imagine additional reforms as well (assuming that family arbitration continues to exist — namely, rejecting the phase 0 option). For instance, instead of applying the hands-off approach typically adopted by the courts when asked to intervene in legal matters resolved through arbitration, we can envisage a relaxing of the standing requirement for such court review, allowing amicus or interveners to pursue the legal challenge in those instances where the affected party wants to challenge a religious arbitral award but fears that challenging the tribunal directly, in her own name, would expose her to intense pressure to withdraw the claim.

(iii) Voluntary agreement by faith-based tribunals to comply with statutory restrictions ("self-restraint") versus imposition by state fiat: The last set of issues that I wish to address here relates to the thorny challenge of tackling the potential for conflict between secular and religious norms governing family disputes. Recall that a significant part of the anxiety that surrounded the Sharia tribunal debate was the fact that its advocates never fully clarified what would happen if their interpretation of customary or religious personal laws provided women with less equitable divorce settlements than those that could have been obtained under the state's secular family laws. According to the tribunal's opponents, nothing less than an attempt to use a technique of "privatized diversity" to redefine the relationship between state and religion in regulating the family was under way. This is an "existential" threat that no secular state authority is likely to accept with indifference, not even in tolerant, multicultural Canada. And so, after much contemplation, the response chosen to the challenge presented by the proposed tribunal was to quash it with all the legal force the authorities could muster. This took the shape of an absolutist solution: prohibiting by decree the operation of *any* religious arbitration process in the family law arena. Such a response, which relies on imposition by state fiat, sends a strong symbolic message of unity, albeit a unity that is manufactured by ensuring compliance with a single monopolistic jurisdictional power holder.

A less heavy-handed approach might have required religious tribunals themselves to determine, through their actions and deeds, whether to enjoy the benefits of binding arbitration — including the boon of public enforcement of their awards — if they *voluntarily* agreed to comply with statutory thresholds and default rules defined in general family legislation. These safeguards typically establish a "floor" of protection, above which significant room for variation is permitted. These basic protections were designed in the first place to address concerns about power and gender inequities in family relations, concerns that are not typically absent from religious communities, either. If anything, they probably apply with equal force in the communal context as in the individualized, secular case. Under this "self-restraint" scenario — which offers an alternative to the top-down prohibition model that was eventually chosen by the government — if a resolution by a religious tribunal falls within the margin of discretion that any secular family-law judge or arbitrator would have been permitted to employ, there is no reason to discriminate against that tribunal solely for the reason that the decision maker used a different tradition to reach a permissible resolution. Put differently, the operative assumption here is that, in a diverse society, we can safely assume that at least some individuals might prefer to turn to their "communal" institutions, knowing that their basic state-backed rights are protected by these alternative forums. Add to this the guarantee that any solution reached through a dispute resolution process that was the result of duress, coercion, or violence will automatically be invalidated as a matter of law. Against this backdrop, permitting community members to turn to a faith-based tribunal may, perhaps paradoxically, provide the conditions for promoting a moderate interpretation of the tradition, as authorized by religious arbitrators themselves. The prospect for such "change from within" — or what I have elsewhere labeled *transformative accommodation*[65] — in this context may translate into a recognition by the tribunal's arbitrators themselves that if they wish to issue final and binding decisions (which permit parties to turn to the state for enforcement where needed), they cannot breach the basic protections to which each woman is entitled by virtue of her equal citizenship status. To ignore these entitlements is to lose the ability to provide relevant legal services to members of the community.[66] Counterintuitively, the qualified recognition of the religious tribunal by the secular state may ultimately offer an effective, noncoercive encouragement of egalitarian and reformist change from within the religious tradition itself. The state system, too, is transformed from strict separation to regulated interaction. In this way, the "multilayered" or intersectionist identity of the individuals involved may be fostered. This approach also discourages an underworld of unregulated religious tribunals and offers a path to transcend the "either/or" choice between culture and rights, family and state, citizenship and islands of privatized diversity.

A final observation is warranted before I conclude my discussion. In the midst of the explosive tribunal debate, it was repeatedly argued that if the Jewish *beth din* or the Catholic or Ismaili community can set up arbitration panels to regulate certain aspects of family affairs, then, mutatis mutandis, so should members of the Muslim community be permitted to set up the Sharia tribunal. This is a potent claim of formal equality among religions. What often gets lost in the discussion is the recognition that formal equality among religions is only part of the picture. It doesn't tell us how the potential value conflicts between these non-state actors and secular norms are to be resolved. It is, however, worth mentioning that the Orthodox Jewish Beis Din of Toronto, which had operated for a number of years in compliance with the Arbitration Act's requirements (before its amendment in 2006), voluntarily self-restricted its jurisdictional mandate by asking the parties that sought its advice in family matters to sign a binding agreement that held that any religious divorce (*get*) settlement or award by the tribunal must be made in accordance with the civil requirements of Canada's national and provincial family legislation.[67] This solution effectively means that beyond the removal of barriers to remarriage, which must comply with the parties' personal laws (assuming that a civil divorce has already been, or is about to be, obtained), general family law norms take priority over matters of property decisions and related material disputes. This self-restriction route permits the religious community to protect its most cherished *identity* (or demarcating) aspects of family law, while complying with state norms in divorce-related matters of distribution of assets, obligations, and responsibilities.[68] This approach is obviously less intrusive than a government-issued order that compels non-state tribunals to comply with secular family law provisions, or an all-out ban that prohibits their official operations altogether. In order to stand a fighting chance of success, this voluntary compliance model must espouse a considerable degree of trust and a desire to avoid dangerous clashes. Both of these conditions were in short supply in the highly politicized debate surrounding the Sharia tribunal proposal.

IV. Banning Privatized Diversity: Future Trajectories

The government ultimately decided to respond to the Sharia tribunal challenge by barring the operation of *any* faith-based family arbitration process. Such a universal ban ensures that Islam is not singled out as being more (or less) friendly to women's interests than any other religious or customary tradition. It further aims to realign the regulation of the family exclusively within the state, leaving no room (except for informal religious mediation, which has no legal effect in the eyes of civil courts or legislatures) for communities' own institutions and authorities to exercise any formal role in defining the parties' marriage and divorce status. In effect, this resolution reasserts a strict public/private divide, thus shutting down — rather than encouraging — coordination or dialogue between civil and religious jurisdictions. The government's legislative response thus stands in tension with the *Marcovitz* decision, which did not take the route of recommending that the wife's damages claim be dropped simply because the operation of the *beth din* (the only authority that can supervise the granting of a Jewish *get* decree) is not recognized in the eyes of state law.

In the Sharia-arbitration saga, the attempt to find creative, non-dichotomous solutions initially gained momentum. This became fruitless, however, once the public debate over the tribunal became highly politicized and polarized. Under these conditions, there was little room left for nuance or even open dialogue. It was at this moment that the government reinstated its sole authority to govern these disputes, to the exclusion of any potentially overlapping or competing (here, religious) sources of law.[69] The chosen alternative of legally *banning* the operation of religious tribunals by secular decree may turn out to be a wise political decision, but it is not an ideal normative and jurisprudential solution. Even though they are officially nonexistent, these faith-based institutions can unofficially operate as providers of mediated (rather than arbitrated) solutions, which may never be subject to regulation by state norms if they remain unchallenged by the parties. This may lead to an unintended consequence, leaving precisely those group members who may be most in need of the protections offered by joint-governance resolutions in an extremely vulnerable position — namely women, who for familial, cultural, religious, economic, political, or related reasons might feel obliged to have at least some aspects of their marriage and divorce regulated by religious principles and communal institutions.

A cynic might add that the government's decision to explicitly reassert the authority of the state over any potential competition can also be seen as a calculated attempt to inhibit diversity when it becomes too costly — not necessarily to women's rights, but to social peace. The government response can plausibly be explained along these lines: once the "difference" matter had been perceived (politically) as being too dangerous and disruptive to social peace and stability, the subsequent move was to reinstate the classic liberal divide between the *public* realm of citizenship and the *private* realm of group membership. This may look like a magic-bullet solution at first blush. It also sends a strong symbolic equality message: there is "one law for all" in the context of family disputes. Yet the problem is that this approach assumes that women are not bearers of culture or religion and that these identities are not worthy of public recognition. It also ignores the significant variation in actual agreements that is permitted and upheld under the growing trend of standard (i.e., secular) "private ordering" of the family.[70] This line of thinking leads to realignment of the "alternative" jurisdiction (here, religious-based arbitration) within the realm of an exotic non-law or unrecognized tradition. But this has not necessarily been the feminist inclination on these matters; many advocates share the concern that the most penetrating violations, if not outright abuses, of women's rights will occur precisely in artificially shielded "private" domains. A resolution of the tribunal debate that merely sweeps the problem of intersectional identities under the rug may satisfy some as a neat solution. But beneath the surface, for the most vulnerable group members, the re-crowning of the civil justice system as the sole regulator of family law — coupled with the relegation of group-based dispute-resolution processes to a no-man's land of shadowy, unofficial systems — may prove fatal. This "out of sight, out of mind" approach will probably not be of much assistance to vulnerable group members in blocking communal pressures to resolve family disputes by turning to "their" group's authorities, which, now legally unrecognized, remain free of any regulatory oversight, whether ex ante or ex post. The real concern here is that those most in need of the benefits of intercultural dialogues and pluralistic legal regimes — those whose lives genuinely manifest overlapping and potentially conflicting belongings — will become the "collateral" of a reasserted and rigid divide between (public) citizenship and (private) group membership.

Conclusion

Debates about the merits and pitfalls of what I have called "privatized diversity" may appear merely technical at first sight. However, they are anything but. Given the complex relationship between religion and state in almost every country around the globe, these dilemmas have become a flashpoint for exploring deeper questions about the relationship between gender and culture, rights and responsibilities, law and tradition in an increasingly complex social reality where the "ties that bind" citizens are themselves at issue. What makes the Sharia tribunal proposal particularly interesting is that it foregrounds these ancient questions, bringing them into the heart of those contemporary political communities that have committed themselves to secular statehood. It is no surprise that the process of addressing these complex dilemmas of privatizing diversity has revealed many unresolved tensions. The unexpected result of the Canadian debate has not been the re-relegation of religious sources into the realm of the unofficial. This pattern fits well with the traditional "public/private" divide in the realm of citizenship and identity. But what nobody foresaw was the renewed interest that this debate has generated in the larger question of whether *any* type of private or alternative dispute resolution ought to govern the inevitably sensitive and semi-public dilemmas that surround the state's involvement in governing and dissolving families in a fair and just way. Here, concern about the place of religion has in fact led to a significant revision of the *secular*: in 2006, the ex ante safeguards recommended by the Boyd Report were incorporated as legislative amendments to the Arbitration Act, and they now affect all family arbitration processes, which must be governed by the secular laws of recognized Canadian jurisdictions.[71] This solution means that no religious authority is permitted to set up family arbitration tribunals, nor can any foreign (national) source of personal law be incorporated into an arbitration process that occurs in Canada.

Despite the resounding verdict against the religious tribunal, the attention it gained has ultimately, and perhaps unexpectedly, led to a reclaiming of the *public* aspect of family law — even in mere phase 1–type dispute resolution. The legislative revisions that were engendered by this debate have further (and unambiguously) clarified that certain provisions protecting a more equitable conception of marriage are nonnegotiable. In this schema, religion is not singled out; *no one* is permitted to extend their margins of choice of law or contractual freedom in a manner that would override core statutory provisions that shape the post-divorce relations between the parties or their obligations toward the children they conceived together. What remains to be seen, however, is whether these new mechanisms will stick. While the adoption of ex ante oversight is an important and promising step that responds to potential inequalities in the process, the *tout court* relegation of religious divorce to the realm of the unregulated "private" sphere may prove problematic, rendering invisible precisely those power relations and informal legal agreements that occur under the shield of religious mediation. If comparative experience can teach us anything, it is that we may expect to see at least some devout women try to fulfill their obligations to both the secular and religious authorities, especially when creating (or dissolving) their families.[72] This effectively means that we might witness the operation of a dual-status system with no communication between the two branches. If this proves to be a correct assessment, then the debate over the Sharia tribunal is not truly over; we are merely witnessing a pause in an ongoing renegotiation.

Notes

This chapter is based on an article that was first published in *Theoretical Inquiries in Law* as "Privatized Diversity: A Cautionary Tale from Religious Arbitration in Family Law" and is reprinted here by permission of the publisher.

1. Rowan Williams, Archbishop of Canterbury, "Islam in English Law; Civil and Religious Law in England," February 2008, accessed August 23, 2011, http://news.bbc.co.uk/2/shared/bsp/hi/pdfs/07_02_08_islam.pdf.

2. This is one of the oldest questions on the books of contemporary feminism. See generally Frances E. Olsen, "The Family and the Market: A Study of Ideology and Legal Reform," *Harvard Law Review* 96 (1983): 1497.

3. For instance, the German Federal Constitutional Court addressed the hotly contested question of religious attire in public education in the *Ludin* case (2003). See BVerfG, I BvR 792/03, 30 July 2003. In the United Kingdom, the matter was addressed by the House of Lords in *Shabina Begum* (2006). See R. (Shabina Begum) v. Governors of Denbigh High School [2007] 1 A.C. 100 (H.L.). Even the European Court of Human Rights was reluctantly dragged into this matter in its *Leyla Sahin v. Turkey* decision (2006), in which it affirmed Turkey's ban on the wearing the hijab. See 19 BHRC 590 [2006] ELR 73 [European Court of Human Rights]). In France, the longstanding hijab drama culminated in 2004 with the introduction of a national law that banned the display of any "conspicuous religious symbols," including the Islamic headscarf, in public schools. See Law No. 2004–228 of Mar. 15, 2004, Journal Officiel de la République Française [J.O.] [Official

Gazette of France], Mar. 17, 2004, p. 5190. For an illuminating overview, see Dominic McGoldrick, *Human Rights and Religion: The Islamic Headscarf Debate in Europe* (Oxford: Hart Publishing, 2006).

4. "Citizenship rights" here apply to anyone who resides in the territory, irrespective of their formal membership status.

5. I discuss the latter set of challenges in Ayelet Shachar, "Is There Room for 'Culture' in the Courtroom?" in *Criminal Law and Cultural Diversity*, ed. Will Kymlicka and Claes Lernestedt (Oxford: Oxford University Press, forthcoming 2012).

6. This "split status" problem was explicitly addressed by Canada's Parliament prior to the introduction of amendments to the Divorce Act, 1985 R.S.C., ch. 3 (Supp. II), amendments that were based on consultations with the leaders of fifty religious groups in Canada. See House of Commons Debates, vol. 6, 34th Parl., 2d Sess., Feb. 15, 1990, at 8375–77. See also J. David Bleich, "Jewish Divorce: Judicial Misconceptions and Possible Means of Civil Enforcement," *Connecticut Law Review* 16 (1984): 201; David Pearl and Werner Menski, *Muslim Family Law* (London: Sweet & Maxwell, 1998): 78.

7. The major exception here is the work of feminist scholars engaged in the multiculturalism debate; for discussion of this fast-emerging body of scholarship, see Ayelet Shachar, "Feminism and Multiculturalism: Mapping the Terrain," in *Multiculturalism and Political Theory*, ed. Antony Simon Laden and David Owen (Cambridge, UK: Cambridge University Press, 2007): 115.

8. Syed Mumtaz Ali, "Establishing an Institute for Islamic Justice (*Darul Qada*)," Canadian Society of Muslims News Bulletin, Oct. 2002, accessed August 23, 2011 http://muslimcanada.org/news02.html.

9. Arbitration Act, 1991 S.O., ch. 17 (Ont.). The act "allows the parties to choose the law applicable to their disputes. . . . It does so by allowing the parties to vary or opt out of the applicability and choice of law sections." See John D. Gregory et al., "Faith-Based Arbitration" (paper presented at the Uniform Law Conference of Canada, Civil Section, August 21–25, 2005, St. John's, Newfoundland, Canada).

10. Ali, "Establishing an Institute for Islamic Justice."

11. For further elaboration, see Ayelet Shachar, *Multicultural Jurisdictions: Cultural Differences and Women's Rights* (Cambridge, UK: Cambridge University Press, 2001): 1–62 (2001); Shachar, *Feminism and Multiculturalism.*

12. This position is lucidly expressed by Talia Fisher, Bryan Caplan and Edward Stringham, and John Hasnas: Talia Fisher, "Nomos without Narrative," *Theoretical Inquiries in Law* 9 (2008): 473; Bryan Caplan and Edward Stringham, "Privatizing the Adjudication of Dispute," *Theoretical Inquiries in* Law 9(2008):

503; John Hasnas, "The Depoliticization of Law," *Theoretical Inquiries in Law* 9 (2008): 529.

13. Brian M. Barry, *Culture and Equality: An Egalitarian Critique of Multiculturalism* (Cambridge, MA: Harvard University Press, 2001); Jeremy Waldron, "One Law for All? The Logic of Cultural Accommodation," *Washington & Lee Law Review* 59 (2002): 3.

14. See Ayelet Shachar, "Religion, State, and the Problem of Gender: New Modes of Citizenship and Governance in Diverse Societies," *McGill Law Journal* 50 (2005): 49.

15. Iris Marion Young, *Justice and the Politics of Difference* (Princeton, NJ: Princeton University Press, 1990): 119. An exception to the emphasis on public accommodation is found in the careful analysis of the claims of "reclusive" groups offered by Jeff Spinner-Halev, *Surviving Diversity: Religion and Democratic Citizenship* (Baltimore: Johns Hopkins University Press, 2000). Another author who resists the notion of public accommodation is Chandran Kukathas, whose work challenges the legitimacy of the state's authority to grant group-differentiated rights in the first place. Instead, he envisions a libertarian-like "archipelago of different communities operating in a sea of mutual toleration." See Chandran Kukathas, *The Liberal Archipelago: A Theory of Diversity and Freedom* (Oxford: Oxford University Press, 2003): 8.

16. Will Kymlicka, *Multicultural Citizenship: A Liberal Theory of Minority Rights* (Oxford: Clarendon Press, 1995): 31 (emphasis added). Kymlicka here refers to the category of "ethnic groups" rather than "national minorities." The tribunal's advocates would fit under the former rather than the latter definition in Kymlicka's typology.

17. This pattern I elsewhere call the "religious particularist" model. See Shachar, *Multicultural Jurisdictions.*

18. Arbitration typically does not require that the written records of the process be maintained, nor does it define the specific skills/training that arbitrators should possess. A law degree, for example, is not a prerequisite.

19. Israeli legislation and case law in family law, addressing issues such as the regulation of minimal age or equitable distribution, illustrate this point. See Marriage Age Law, 5710–1950, 4 LSI 158 (1950); Spouses (Property Relations) Law, 5733–1973, 27 LSI 31 (1972–73); HCJ 1000/92 Bavli v. High Rabbinical Court [1994] IsrSC 48(2) 221; HCJ 2222/99 Gabai v. High Rabbinical Court [2000] IsrSC 54(5) 401. The debate in these jurisdictions typically turns on whether the government's legislation is too intrusive or too deferential to the religious communities involved, as manifested in the *Shah Bano* saga in India and its

aftermath (i.e., legislative overturn of the court's decision, and then *Latifi* and more recent case law restoring much of the protection offered to Muslim women before the legislative overturn of *Shah Bano*). See Mohd. Amhed Khan v. Shao Bano Begum, A.I.R. 1985 S.C. 945; Danial Latifi v. Union of India, A.I.R. 2001 S.C. 3958.

20. Egypt's family-law reform took place in 2000; Morocco's in 2004. For commentary, see Lama Abu-Odeh, "Modernizing Muslim Family Law: The Case of Egypt," *Vanderbildt Journal of Transnational Law* 37 (2004): 1043; Ran Hirschl, "Constitutional Courts vs. Religious Fundamentalism: Three Middle Eastern Tales," *Texas Law Review* 82 (2004): 1819; Leon Buskens, "Recent Debates on Family Law Reforms in Morocco: Islamic Law as Politics in an Emerging Public Sphere," Islamic Law and Society 10 (2003): 70; Laura A. Weingartner, "Family Law and Reform in Morocco — The Mudawana: Modernist Islam and Women's Rights in the Code of Personal Status," *University of Detroit Mercy Law Review* 82 (2004): 687. Obviously, not all countries follow this path of reform in family law. See, e.g., Saskia E. Wieringa, "Comparative Perspectives Symposium: Islamization," *Signs* 32 (2006): 1. Other countries have experienced, however, the opposite trend of restrictive interpretations of Sharia principles under national family-law legislation. The reasons for these different paths of modification versus radicalization lie beyond the scope of this chapter.

21. This coalition has been criticized by some as advancing women's rights in the family-law arena at the expensive "cost" of altogether weakening secularism. See, e.g., Lama Abu-Odeh, "Egyptian Feminism: Trapped in the Identity Debate," *Yale Law Journal* 16 (2004): 145.

22. See Ann Elizabeth Mayer, "The Islam and Human Rights Nexus: Shifting Dimensions," *Muslim World Journal of Human Rights* 4 (2007). Available online at http://www.bepress.com/mwjhr/vo14/iss1/art4 (accessed August 23, 2011).

23. This position was best expressed by the Canadian Council of Muslim Women (CCMW), which stated that "CCMW sees no compelling reason to live under any other form of law in Canada, as we want the same laws to apply to [Muslim women] as to other Canadian women." See "Position Statement on the Proposed Implementation of Sections of Muslim Law [Sharia] in Canada," Canadian Council of Muslim Women, revised May 25, 2004, accessed August 23, 2001, http://www.ccmw.com/activities/act_arb_muslimlaw_sharia.html. See also Lorraine E. Weinrib, "Ontario's Sharia Law Debate: Law and Politics under the Charter," in Richard Moon, ed., *Law and Religious Pluralism in Canada* (Vancouver: UBC Press, 2008).

24. Williams, "Islam in English Law."

25. These economic patterns of decline in the standard of living of women

and children after divorce in the United States, for example, and a correlated improvement in the standard of living for men are documented in many studies. See, e.g., Lenore J. Weitzman, *The Divorce Revolution: The Unexpected Social and Economic Consequences for Women and Children in America* (New York: Free Press, 1985); Richard P. Peterson, "A Re-evaluation of the Economic Consequences of Divorce," *American Sociological Review* 61 (1996): 528. Similar patterns were found in other jurisdictions as well. See John Eekelaar and Mavis Maclean, *Maintenance after Divorce* (New York: Oxford University Press, 1986).

26. "Interview: A Review of the Muslim Personal/Family Law Campaign," Canadian Society of Muslims, written August, 1995, accessed August 23, 2011, http://muslimcanada.org/pfl (interview with Syed Mumtaz Ali, President of the Canadian Society of Muslims); see also "*Darul-Qada*: Beginnings of Muslim Civil Justice System in Canada," Canadian Society of Muslims News Bulletin, written April 2003, accessed August 23, 2011, http://muslimcanada.org/news03.html; Judy Van Rhijn, "First Steps Taken for Islamic Arbitration Board," *Law Times,* Nov. 24, 2003, accessed August 23, 2011, http://www.freerepublic.com/focus/f-news/1028843/posts; Syed Mumtaz Ali and Rabia Mills, "*Darul Qada* (The Beginnings of a Muslim Civil Justice System in Canada)," Canadian Society of Muslims, accessed August 23, 2011 http://muslimcanada.org/DARLQADAform2andhalf.

27. "Interview: A Review of the Muslim Personal/Family Law Campaign."

28. Ali, "Establishing an Institute for Islamic Justice."

29. See Van Rhijn, "First Steps Taken for Islamic Arbitration Board."

30. See notes 42–44; I briefly discuss the reasons for these concerns in Shachar, "Religion, State, and the Problem of Gender," 73–77.

31. See Syed Mumtaz Ali, "The Reconstruction of the Canadian Constitution and the Case for Muslim Personal/Family Law: A Submission to the Ontario Civil Justice Review Task Force," Canadian Society of Muslims, 1994, accessed August 23, 2011, http://muslimcanada.org/submission.pdf.

32. "Ali's Interview with 'The Ambition,'" May 23, 2004, accessed August 23, 2011, http://muslimcanada.org/ambitioninterview.html (interview with Syed Mumtaz Ali by *The Ambition*, a Canadian young Muslims' Journal).

33. See Shahnaz Khan, "Canadian Muslim Women and Shari'a Law: A Feminist Response to 'Oh! Canada!'" *Canadian Journal of Women and the Law* 60 (1993): 6 ("[N]o doubt [Muslim women] would experience a certain amount of pressure to conform. . . . [S]hould they decline to be governed by Muslim Personal Status Laws . . . [they could] find themselves ostracized by their families and their community"; responding to an earlier attempt to introduce Sharia principles to govern Canada's

Muslim population). See Syed Mumtaz Ali and Anab Whitehouse, "Oh! Canada: Whose Land? Whose Dream? Sovereignty, Social Contracts, and Participatory Democracy: An Exploration into Constitutional Arrangements," Canadian Society of Muslims, 1991, accessed August 23, 2011, http://muslimcanada.org/ocanada.pdf.

34. See Anne Phillips, *Multiculturalism without Culture* (Princeton: Princeton University Press, 2007): 170 (citing Avigail Eisenberg, "Religious Arbitration and Multiculturalism: The Debate over Sharia Law in Canada," in *Sexual Justice/Cultural Justice: Critical Perspectives in Political Theory and Practice*, ed. Barbara Arneil, Avigail Eisenberg, Monique Deaveux, and Rita Dhamoon [New York: Routledge, 2007]).

35. See Shachar, "Religion, State, and the Problem of Gender."

36. In Canada, this view was most strongly manifested in the legal discourse by the Supreme Court's 2004 *Hartshorne* decision, which emphasized the legitimacy of using secular contractual mechanisms (known as "domestic contracts") that allow parties to stray away from statutory equitable default rules found in governing family-law statutes. What was categorized as an unfair agreement was later reinstated by the Supreme Court, in part through reliance on the logic of consent. As the country's top justices ruled: the "courts should be reluctant to second-guess the arrangement on which [private parties, here the husband and wife] reasonably expected to rely. Individuals may *choose* to structure their affairs in a number of ways, and it is their prerogative to do so." Hartshorne v. Hartshorne, [2004] 1 S.C.R. 550, para. 36 (emphasis added).

37. This objection was put forth powerfully by the Canadian Council of Muslim Women, a national nongovernmental organization, which stated in their objection to the Sharia tribunal that "the 'voluntary' nature of the woman's agreement may be colored by the coercion put upon her that she is being a 'good' Muslim by following some arbitrator's interpretation of Sharia/Muslim family law." See "Position Statement on the Implementation of Sections of Muslim Law in Canada."

38. In Canada, leading women's organizations, such as NAWL, expressed the concern that *any* type of private dispute resolution in the family-law arena may undermine women's bargaining position or equality protection, since there are "no public records detailing the nature of the dispute or the terms of the agreement," and that family mediation or arbitration is "removed from state regulation and public scrutiny." See generally Sandra A. Goundy, Yvonne Peters, and Rosalind Currie, *Family Mediation in Canada: Implications for Women in Canada* (Ottawa: The Status of Women Canada, 1998). Others may see this position as paternalistic and lacking in respect for women's agency and their ability to make informed choices for themselves. See generally Linda R. Singer, *Settling Disputes: Conflict*

Resolution in Business, Families, and the Legal System (Boulder, CO: Westview Press, 1994) (emphasizing the importance of parties' agency in different "private ordering" contexts — rather than their caricatured representation as eternal victims).

39. Québec Civil Code, S.Q., ch. 64, art. 2369 (1991).

40. In this particular debate, the governing provincial legislation casting the "shadow" under which the parties bargain is the Family Law Act, R.S.O., ch. F-3 (1990) (Ont.). See Marion Boyd, "Religiously-Based Alternate Dispute Resolution: A Challenge to Multiculturalism," *Canadian Diversity* 4 (2005): 71.

41. See the now-classic contribution by Robert H. Mnookin and Lewis Kornhauser, "Bargaining in the Shadow of the Law: The Case of Divorce," *Yale Law Journal* 88 (1979): 950.

42. On "reactive culturalism," see Shachar, *Multicultural Jurisdictions*, 35–37.

43. See, e.g., ibid., 45–62. My work is part of an emerging interdisciplinary body of literature now exploring the relationship between gender/sexuality and the construction of collective identity. See Nira Yuval-Davis, Floya Anthias, and Jo Campling, *Woman-Nation-State* (New York: St. Martin's Press, 1989); Hélie-Lucas, "The Preferential Symbol for Islamic Identity," in *Feminist Theory Reader: Local and Global Perspectives*, ed. Carole R. McCann and Seung-Kyung Kim (New York: Routledge Press, 2003); Deniz Kandiyoti, *Women, Islam and the State* (Philadelphia: Temple University Press, 1991); Inderpal Grewal and Caren Kaplan, eds., *Scattered Hegemonies: Postmodernity and Transnational Feminist Practices* (Minneapolis: University of Minnesota Press, 1994); Vrinda Narain, *Gender and Community: Muslim Women's Rights in India* (Toronto: University of Toronto Press, 2001); Katherine Franke, "Sexual Tensions of Post-Empire," Columbia Law School Pub. Law Research Paper No. 04–62, 2004, accessed August 22, 2011 http://papers.ssrn.com/s013/papers.cfm?abstract_id=491205.

44. Ironically, such gendered constructions of group identity may be shared by representatives of both minority and majority communities, as is demonstrated by the current debate over the hijab in France. See Shachar, "Religion, State, and the Problem of Gender."

45. For a critical discussion of the exit option, see Susan Moller Okin, "'Mistresses of Their Own Destiny': Group Rights, Gender and Realistic Rights of Exit," *Ethics* 112 (2002): 205; Phillips, *Multiculturalism without Culture*, 133–57.

46. Shachar, *Multicultural Jurisdictions*, 117–45.

47. A similar observation regarding the transnational aspects of these dilemmas is made by Anne Phillips. See Phillips, *Multiculturalism without Culture*, 173–75.

48. See, e.g., Ayesha Hasan, "Islamic Family Law in the English Courts," *Family*

Law 100 (Feb. 1998); Lucy Carroll, "Muslim Women and 'Islamic Divorce' in England," *Journal of Muslim Minority Affairs* 17 (1997): 97.

49. On the *mahr* situation in the United States, see generally Ghada G. Qaisi, "Religious Marriage Contracts: Judicial Enforcement of "Mahr" Agreements in American Courts," *Journal of Law and Religion* 15 (2001): 67; in comparative perspective, see generally Pascale Fournier, Canadian Council of Muslim Women Sharia/Muslim Law Project, "The Reception of Muslim Family Law in a Western Liberal State" (2004). On Islamic marriage and divorce, see generally Dawoud Sudqi El Alami, *The Marriage Contract in Islamic Law in the Shari'ah and Personal Status Laws of Egypt and Morocco* (London: Graham & Trotman, 1992); Jamal J. Nasir, *The Islamic Law of Personal Status* (New York: Kluwer Law International, 2002); John L. Esposito and Natana J. DeLong-Basic, *Women in Muslim Family Law* (Syracuse, NY: Syracuse University Press, 2001).

50. Bruker v. Marcovitz, [2007] S.C.C. 54.

51. *Id.* paras. 3–9.

52. *Id.* para. 12.

53. *Id.* In light of the decision's minority opinion, which did not even permit the damages remedy, it is fair to assess that any claim to make pronouncement on religious precepts or to appear before a religious authority would have likely been rendered by the court as an impermissible breach of the husband's constitutionally protected freedom of religion. See *id.* paras. 101–85 (Deschamps & Charron, JJ., dissenting).

54. [2003] R.J.Q. 1189, para. 30.

55. [2005] R.J.Q. 2482, para. 76.

56. *Marcovitz,* paras. 3, 92.

57. This is in line with national and provincial legislation that gives courts discretionary authority to rebuff a spouse in civil proceedings who obstructs religious remarriage. See Divorce Act, R.S.C., ch. 3, § 21(1) (Supp. II 1985) (Can.); Family Law Act, R.S.O., ch. F-3, §§ 2(4)-(7), 56(5)-(7) (1990) (Ont.). As the court notes in *Marcovitz,* these provisions were fully endorsed by the Jewish community's representatives, to discourage the serious harms caused to women by recalcitrant husbands. *Marcovitz,* paras. 8, 80, 92.

58. See generally Mnookin and Kornhauser, "Bargaining in the Shadow of the Law."

59. See Mathew D. McCubbins and Thomas Schwartz, "Congressional Oversight Overlooked: Police Patrols Versus Fire Alarms," *American Journal of Political Science* 28 (1984): 165.

60. Ibid., 165–67.

61. Arbitration Act, 1991 S.O., ch. 17, §§ 6, 19, 45–47.

62. See Marion Boyd, "Dispute Resolution in Family Law: Protecting Choice, Promoting Inclusion," Ministry of the Attorney General of Ontario, December 20, 2004, accessed August 23, 2011, http://www.attorneygeneral.jus.gov.on.ca/english/about/pubs/boyd/fullreport.pdf ("the Boyd Report").

63. The government's commissioned report held that beyond these recommended regulatory reforms, or what I have called the shift from ex post to ex ante regulation, as well as extensive educational outreach programs by the government, the Arbitration Act's status quo — namely, the *non*-prohibition of religious family dispute resolution — be left in place.

64. See Family Arbitration, R.O. 134/07. The regulation clarifies that, among other things, family arbitrators shall be subject to a licensing-like training process. This amounts to a much tighter regulation of phase 1 arbitration, making it conceptually closer to a standard, public-court-like proceeding, here responding to the claims of those who advocated a phase 0 type of resolution.

65. Shachar, *Multicultural Jurisdictions*, 117–45.

66. Such a result is unattractive for the religious tribunal, which strives on providing distinct legal services that no other agency can offer, as well as for the individual who had turned to this specialized forum in order to bring closure to a charged marital or family dispute that bears a religious aspect that simply cannot be fully addressed by the secular court system.

67. See "Review of the Arbitration Process in Ontario: Submission by B'nai Brith Canada to the Ontario Ministry of the Attorney General," B'nai Brith Canada, 2004, accessed August 23, 2011, http://www.bnaibrith.ca/briefs/sharia/sharia040908.pdf.

68. I discuss the distinction between family law's demarcating and distributive aspects in Shachar, *Multicultural Jurisdictions*, 49–55.

69. See Family Arbitration, R.O. 134/07.

70. The *Hartshorne* decision, which emphasized the legitimacy of using secular contractual mechanisms (known as "domestic contracts") to reach unequal separation agreements, is a case in point. See note 36.

71. See Arbitration Act, 2006 S.O., ch. 1, § 1(2) (incorporated into section 2.2 of the 1991 Arbitration Act).

72. England is a case in point: it is reported that the majority of requests for help to resolve matrimonial disputes received by the Muslim Law (Shariah) Council were made by Muslim women who applied for assistance in obtaining religious-sanctioned divorce — often after they had obtained a civil divorce in accordance with secular law. See Williams, "Islam in English Law."

LINDA C. MCCLAIN

Chapter Three Marriage Pluralism, Family Law Jurisdiction, and Sex Equality in the United States

Introduction

Gender justice remains unfinished business. How is family law, in particular the relationship between civil and religious family law, relevant to the challenge of securing gender justice both in the United States and around the globe? This question has received comparatively little attention when measured against the by-now voluminous literature on whether multiculturalism and feminism (and sex equality) are in conflict, as well as on how constitutional democracies should accommodate members of minority groups, including religious minorities, within their borders. It should receive more, for as some feminist contributors to this literature explain, family life and family law are arenas in which women may experience special vulnerabilities and where commitments to religious freedom and to sex equality may conflict.[1] How do constitutional democracies regulate family life and allocate jurisdiction over family law in a way that honors important public values and shows respect for citizens — and other members of the polity — who have multiple sources of affiliation, including to religious communities whose norms shape family life?[2]

In recent years, controversies over veiling are perhaps the most visible example of an evident clash between religious norms and civil norms of sex equality. What is at stake, for example, when women and girls in constitutional democracies are barred, in the name of constitutional values and democratic principles such as secularism, neutrality, and gender equality, from wearing the veil in certain public settings? What happens when such restrictions seem to disregard women's agency and conscientious religious practice? Barring women from veiling contrasts with another potent example of the apparent clash between sex equality and religion: the specter, in some Islamic countries, of forced veiling and punishments exacted on women for not veiling or violating norms of modesty.

The multiple meanings of the veil continue to engender political and scholarly debate.[3] The most dramatic recent examples of the apparent clash between sex equality as a political value and veiling as a religious commitment come from France. As Joan Scott, in her study of the veiling controversy in France, observed, one prominent rationale for targeting the veil is its symbolic clash with sex equality: in "removing *the* sign of women's inequality from the classroom," French lawmakers were "declaring that the equality of women and men is the first principle of the Republic."[4] One notable news story was of the denial of citizenship to a veiled Muslim woman, Faiza Silmi, on the grounds of "insufficient" assimilation to French values.[5] Mary Anne Case points out, however, that although the press reports made it seem as though the mere fact of Silmi's wearing a niqab barred her from citizenship, and her lawyers framed the issue as a clash between her religious practices and the French value of *laicite*, "the record highlights 'in particular the equality of the sexes' as one of 'the essential values of the French community' she had failed 'to make her own.'"[6]

In June of 2009, in a remarkable "state of the nation" speech, President Sarkozy, in effect, declared war on the burka, asserting that "in our country we cannot accept that women be prisoners behind a screen, cut off from all social life, deprived of all identity."[7] Again, the symbol itself seemed an affront to French values: "The burka is not a religious sign. . . . It is a sign of subservience, a sign of debasement. It will not be welcome on the territory of the French republic."[8] Somewhat contradictorily, he also called for a "debate" on the issue in which "[a]ll views must be expressed," while admonishing Parliament that "we must not be ashamed of our values, we must not be afraid of defending them."[9] Closer to home here in North America, a stated concern both with loss — or concealment — of identity and with the evident clash between veiling and a message of equality between women and men featured in the recent call by the Canadian Muslim Congress for the Ottawan government to ban women wearing the burka and niqab in public. The Congress further contended that such practices are rooted in culture, rather than religion.[10]

Another arena of evident conflict between religious law and practice and civic norms of sex equality is the relationship between religious and civil family law, even though it less frequently spills into news headlines. This is the subject of my chapter. Pressing questions include the respective jurisdiction of religious and civil courts, whether religious law should be accommodated in civil courts, and how pluralistic or multicultural a society should be when it comes to regulating the family. One area of tension is between terms of religious family law that seem to be patriarchal and diverge from secular family law's principles of gender neutrality and equal spousal and parental rights and responsibilities. As with the veiling controversy, religious family law can take on symbolic importance as an arena of troubling sex inequality. So, too, with the contrast between restricting versus compelling veiling, women's agency may be at stake both in civil rules, on the one hand, that bar them from resorting to religious tribunals or seeking civil enforcement of religious family law and, on the other, that consign them to such tribunals at the expense of access to civil courts and the remedies afforded by civil family law.[11]

The challenging question of the relationship between religious and civil family law received international attention when, on February 7, 2008, the archbishop of Canterbury gave what proved to be a controversial lecture on civil and religious law in England. He explained that his aim was "to tease out some of the broader issues around the rights of religious groups within a secular state, with a few thought[s] about what might be entailed in crafting a just and constructive relationship between Islamic law and the statutory law of the United Kingdom."[12] In this lecture, he explained that within Britain, there are communities "which, while no less law-abiding than the rest of the population, relate to something other than the British legal system alone." Noting that this issue is not peculiar to Islam, but also about other faith groups, he used the example of the place of Muslims in British society as a way to open up the discussion to wider issues about the uncertainty over "what degree of accommodation the law of the land can and should give to minority communities with their own strongly entrenched legal and moral codes."[13]

Other contributors to this volume make reference to the archbishop's lecture. I note it here, as they do, to suggest the prominence given in recent years to the question of the relationship between civil and religious law. It also usefully presents in a highly public — and publicized — way how this relationship raises issues about the meaning, rights, and protections of citizenship, especially women's equal citizenship, and the meaning of and sources constituting individual and group identity. The swift reaction to the archbishop's remarks — including calls for his resignation — suggests how fraught these issues are and how readily fears of "extreme applications of Shariah . . . in some Muslim countries"[14] make serious conversation about accommodation and legal pluralism difficult.

After the archbishop's speech, press coverage in the United States opened, as it were, a window for readers into a world of "Islamic justice," in which Islamic tribunals or councils hear divorce cases.[15] One news story details that Islamic councils in Britain have expanded significantly and seen a large increase in cases and that "almost all of the cases involved women asking for divorce." Women's success in their cases is tempered by expression of concerns about their vulnerability under this system. Critics "point to cases of domestic violence in which Islamic scholars have tried to keep marriages together by ordering husbands to take classes in anger management, leaving the wives so intimidated that they have withdrawn their complaints from the police."[16] A founding director of a women's help group, Fatima Women's Network, charges that such women are "hostages to fortune" and says of the courts, "There is no outside monitoring, no protection, no records kept, no guarantee that justice will prevail."[17] That one source of protection is the woman's father seems, from a feminist point of view, simply to highlight this vulnerability.

This news story reveals a form of legal pluralism — side by side civil courts, there are religious courts in Britain granting religious divorce. It also raises the issue of religious women's agency and vulnerability. Increasingly, women seek out these courts to obtain a religious divorce when their husbands do not want one; and yet, the patriarchal aspects of this system are evident in descriptions of the greater weight given to the women's father's testimony than hers and the fact that it is (apparently) solely male scholars who sit in these councils or tribunals. Moreover, there are glimpses of ways in which religious law itself favors men over women. Women's very recourse to these tribunals stems from the fact that a "woman needs the blessing of a scholar of Islamic jurisprudence to be divorced, while a man can simply say three times that he is divorcing his wife."[18]

Finally, the news story introduces the complicated issue of the relationship between civil and religious authority: religious divorces are not civil divorces, and "most of the [Islamic] courts' judgments have no standing under British civil law." This does not mean that all religious tribunals in Britain lack capacity to issue rulings with civilly binding effects. Longstanding are ecclesiastical courts of the Church of England and *beth din* courts for British Jews. Because they comply with Britain's arbitration law, the latter courts can function as an "official court of arbitration in the consensual resolution of other civil disputes, like inheritance or business conflicts." The story implies that Islamic councils could do the same thing but notes the potential for a clash between principles of civil law and religious law and the supremacy of British law in such a conflict. Thus, the British justice minister explains this latitude: "There is nothing whatever in English law that prevents people abiding by Shariah principles if they wish to, provided they do not come into conflict with English law;" but British law would "always remain supreme." He further states, "Regardless of religious belief, we are all equal before the law."[19]

As these stories from France and Britain illustrate, this issue of family law jurisdiction lends itself to many different framings of what is at stake in these conflicts. One is the struggle of minority communities to preserve, identify, and live according to their values. Another is a clash between religious and civil norms about family life and the status of men and women in the family and broader community. Another framing stresses the meaning of legal pluralism: How much sovereignty and authority should religious courts have in a society with a secular legal system? Should civil courts give civil effects to rulings of religious courts? Do civil courts have authority to adjudicate the terms of a religious marriage contract? What happens when civil rules about family dissolution conflict with those of religious law? Does, or should, secular law — and its commitments to equality — "reign supreme"?

For the last few years, I have participated in an interdisciplinary scholarly conversation (called "The Multi-tiered Marriage Project") about whether the United States should move toward a more robustly pluralistic system of family law, in which civil courts more readily share jurisdiction with religious courts.[20] A basic premise of that project is that the United States could find many instructive examples of such pluralism in other legal systems. While I do not deny the value of learning from other legal systems, I argue that a substantial body of feminist work on those very legal systems urges caution about transporting such models to the United States. In this chapter, I examine the lure of pluralism and situate the call for more pluralism in the context of the current system of U.S. family law. It may not be evident that, in the United States, there is already a notable degree of intermingling of religious and civil family law. I illustrate this by examining the interplay of civil and religious marriage in the ongoing controversy over same-sex marriage. I also canvass some of the ways that courts in the United States already do enforce religious rulings and the terms of religious marriage contracts. At the same time, core commitments of civil family law, including to sex equality, limit the extent of such accommodation. To use the terms introduced in Martha Minow's contribution to this volume, sometimes there is "convergence" between secular and religious norms, and no evident "compromise" of principles.[21] But sometimes, courts must limit accommodation because they cannot compromise on core family law principles. I conclude that a call for legal pluralism in the form of a modern millet system in the United States clashes with basic political and family law norms of sex equality.

The Call for More Pluralism and Shared Jurisdiction in U.S. Family Law

As Brian Tamanaha observes, "Legal pluralism is everywhere."[22] Not only is there, "in every social arena one examines, a seeming multiplicity of legal orders, from the lowest local level to the most expansive global level," but in the last few decades, legal pluralism itself "has become a major topic in legal anthropology, legal sociology, comparative, law, international law, and socio-legal studies."[23] But problems with defining and understanding legal pluralism continue to "plague" its study.[24]

What of legal pluralism in family law? A common observation is that family law — and family law practice — in the United States have become global due to "the globalization of the family."[25] As people who form families cross geographic and national boundaries, lawyers and courts routinely must deal with complex questions of jurisdiction and comity with respect to marriage, divorce, child custody, and the like.

Has the time come, at the normative level, to embrace more legal pluralism in family law within the United States? If so, what form should it take? To answer these questions, clarifying what is meant by "legal pluralism" in family law is crucial. Broadly defined, legal pluralism acknowledges that there are multiple sources of normative ordering in every society. Such sources include not only the "official" legal system, embodied in civil cases, statutes, and constitutions, but also, as Ann Estin describes, the "unofficial family law" of religious tribunals, rules, customs, and the like.[26] This "unofficial family law" has a formative effect on persons and communities even if it is not buttressed by binding state authority.

More narrowly defined, *legal* pluralism refers not to this broader *normative* pluralism but to questions of jurisdiction and juridical power.[27] Sally Engle Merry explains that "state law" is "fundamentally different" than non-state forms of ordering because "it exercises the coercive power of the state and monopolizes the symbolic power associated with state authority." She urges that the study of legal pluralism attend to the interaction of state law with these other forms of ordering.[28]

The Multi-tiered Marriage Project calls for a national conversation on this interaction between state and non-state power with respect to jurisdiction over marriage and divorce. To the "ought" question about whether there should be more jurisdictional pluralism, it answers "yes." Project convenor Professor Joel Nichols, of St. Thomas University, proposes that, in the United States, "civil government should consider ceding some of its jurisdictional authority over marriage and divorce law to religious communities that are competent and capable of adjudicating the marital rites and rights of their respective adherents."[29] He finds, already within the United States, some forms of a multi-tiered system: covenant marriage, available in three states, and New York's *get* statutes.[30] In Louisiana, for example, key proponents of covenant marriage self-consciously sought to instantiate a covenant model of marriage in keeping with "God's intended purpose for marriage."[31]

To usher in more legal pluralism in the United States, Nichols proposes to learn from other legal systems. He spins the globe and finds many instructive ways to share jurisdiction over marriage and divorce law, such as multiple systems of personal law, in which religious tribunals have jurisdiction (as in India, Kenya, and Israel); legal recognition of customary marriage (as in South Africa); and allowing religious bodies to arbitrate family law matters (an issue of recent controversy in Ontario, Canada).[32]

What form would a new jurisdictional pluralism in U.S. family law take? Nichols proposes a "more robust millet system."[33] The analogy is to the Ottoman Empire's millet system, in which personal law (including marriage) was administered by religious tribunals, a system still operating to varying degrees in some countries that Nichols canvasses. His model, which envisions "semi-autonomous" religious entities and the state acting as the overarching sovereign that intervenes only when basic minimum guidelines are not met, seems to reject a model of complete autonomy of religious tribunals. However, the reference to "basic minimum guidelines" suggests a thin supervisory role for the state.

In this chapter, I will concede the descriptive point that "legal pluralism is everywhere" and challenge — or at least raise cautions about — the normative claim that there should be more of it in U.S. family law. An exercise in comparative law readily *does* reveal many different ways of allocating jurisdiction over family law. This does not, however, answer the normative question of whether these are good models for U.S. family law.

One normative concern over civil law ceding authority to religious and other tribunals to regulate marriage and divorce regards the place of key commitments, values, and functions of civil family law. What authority will civil government have in the modified system to advance family law's functions of protecting the best interests of children and other vulnerable parties? What will happen if its model of marriage as an equal partnership premised on gender-neutral and reciprocal (rather than complementary and hierarchical) rights and duties conflicts with religious models? What will happen if there is a gap between religious law on marital dissolution and civil law's norm of equitable distribution of marital property and rationales for spousal support?

Another pressing concern is whether such a millet system can adequately protect the equal citizenship of women. I am skeptical that it can, for reasons I elaborate below. Nearly every foreign example that Nichols offers of jurisdictional pluralism concerning family law raises troubling question about how to reconcile sex equality with religious freedom.[34] Feminist scholars highlight the importance of "encultured women's" claims of national and constitutional citizenship — or "public citizenship" — as a strategy for redressing sex inequality, even as such women affirm the value of membership in religious and cultural groups.[35] Will a new jurisdictional pluralism accommodate this dual membership? Training a gender lens on the question of jurisdictional pluralism would better inform a national conversation on the subject.

Nichols assures readers that "[m]oving toward multi-tiered marriage" system is compatible with family law's protective functions and with "core values of equality."[36] But his international examples contradict this reassurance. They call into question whether the proper model should be "ceding" authority or recognizing plural forms of authority, but only subject to constitutional and civil limiting principles. When government forms a partnership with religion, we might contrast two competing models of this relationship: unleashing, in the sense of turning loose or freeing; versus harnessing, in the sense of utilizing by yoking or restricting in light of important constitutional and public values.[37] This distinction between unleashing and harnessing may prove useful when considering calls for shared, or multiple, jurisdiction.

Family law, to be sure, already allows persons to opt out, to some extent, from its protective "default rules" through private ordering (such as premarital agreements and arbitration). Thus, in assessing the demand for jurisdictional pluralism, it is important to consider the place family law already accords to individual choice and freedom of contract.

This chapter first asks precisely what form of marriage pluralism in the United States is sought and what might be motivating this demand. It examines differing views about the relationship between religious and civil marriage and notes how public norms of sex equality in the family may be in tension with religious traditions. It then examines some of the case law in which state courts within the United States have dealt with religious and foreign family law in resolving civil disputes about marriage and divorce. It asks what this case law suggests about the prospects for a multi-tiered marriage law in the United States and what tension points might arise. Finally, it concludes by asking what lessons this might teach about the possibilities for more pluralism in U.S. family law.

Whither the Demand for More Marriage Pluralism in the United States?

AN INITIAL QUESTION: SHOULD RELIGIOUS AND CIVIL FAMILY LAW BE CONGRUENT?

Is there a demand, within the United States, for "multi-tiered marriage"? It may clarify matters to distinguish two types of demands for more legal pluralism: First, particular religious communities might challenge the authority of the state to regulate marriage and argue either for sole or shared authority. This demand could arise either from religious communities that are long-established within the United States or, as a part of multicultural accommodation, from newer immigrant religious communities. A solution that Nichols floats is a millet system in which religious tribunals have jurisdictional autonomy with minimal state oversight. Second, religious communities might express discontent with the substance of civil marriage law and desire to instantiate, with more binding force *in civil law*, religious understandings of marriage so that the two are congruent. If this latter strategy is preferred, the question arises: which religious understandings? That of majority religious institutions? What place will there be for the many minority religions practiced in America? And for minority views within the respective religious traditions?

The political and legal battles over same-sex marriage seem to be one motivating factor in the demand for both forms of legal pluralism. One response to the prospect of states redefining civil marriage to permit same-sex couples to marry (as Massachusetts and now five other states have done) is to propose that the state "get out of the marriage business" and leave it to religious institutions to define and regulate marriage. Offering a "Judeo-Christian" argument for "privatizing marriage," legal scholar Daniel Crane proposes that civil law permit couples to make civil contracts assigning jurisdiction over their marriage to religious authorities.[38] That way, religious believers and institutions would not cede the power to define marriage to the state. Edward Zelinsky offers a different "pro-marriage case" for abolishing civil marriage: government should shed its monopoly on marriage in favor of a "market for marriage" in which civil marriage competes with other models of marriage offered by religious and other sponsoring institutions.[39]

Given the role of religious understandings of marriage in opposition to extending civil marriage to same-sex couples, another way to clarify that religious and civil marriage are distinct would be for states to cede the term "marriage" to religious traditions and replace it with a new status like civil unions or civil partnerships to which would attach various benefits and obligations now linked to civil marriage.[40] More typically, religious opponents of same-sex marriage seek *congruence* between religious and civil law. Appeals to religious tradition have animated efforts by religious institutions and lawmakers to "defend" marriage by enshrining in state and federal constitutions a definition of marriage as one man and one woman. The argument for congruence is that if the legal definition of marriage is so altered that it no longer recognizes the goods and purposes of marriage as understood in religious traditions, marriage law will not rest on a true conception of marriage.[41] A comparative example may be found in Canada. After Parliament passed a law redefining marriage as being "between two persons," a group of religious leaders issued a "Declaration on Marriage" urging members of Parliament and Canadian citizens to reconsider such redefinition because it severed marriage from its "nature and purpose," and faith communities could not promote an institution "when the identifying language has been stripped of its real meaning."[42] These opponents of redefining marriage seek greater congruence between religious and civil marriage, *not* marriage pluralism.

Covenant marriage also reflects a congruence strategy: it harnesses state power to instantiate an ideal of marriage in keeping with Christian traditions about permanence and mutual sacrifice.[43] An architect of Louisiana's law, Katherine Shaw Spaht, describes covenant marriage as a step toward a "robust pluralism" in marriage and divorce law but also acknowledges that advocates of covenant marriage statutes envisioned that if couples widely embraced it, the paradigm would shift from no-fault to covenant marriage.[44] (For this reason, Spaht and some proponents of covenant marriage express disappointment that religious authorities have not embraced it and required members to enter into this model of marriage.)[45] Moreover, requiring premarital counseling and specifying that it may be performed by religious functionaries draw attention to the unique capacity of religious communities to preserve marriages.[46] Congruence is evident in Spaht's argument that conceding a difference between civil and religious marriage fails to recognize that "[n]atural moral law applies equally to the religious and non-religious alike" and is accessible through the exercise of reason.[47]

If covenant marriage is a way for religion to harness state power, the state also harnesses — and does not simply unleash — religion. *Civil* officials issue marriage licenses, and *civil* courts adjudicate divorces and rule on custody, property distribution, and the like. Covenant marriage proponents are not making the argument that the state should cede this authority to religious tribunals so that civil courts no longer have jurisdiction in such matters.

In the U.S. family law system, civil and religious authorities already share jurisdiction over marriage to a degree. In contrast to some legal systems (like France or the Netherlands), in the United States, religious leaders may perform marriage ceremonies that will be recognized as civil marriages provided the couples comply with civil formalities. Through this "simultaneously . . . secular and . . . religious event," which incorporates "unofficial law and norms into the civil rite" and "reinforces the solemnity of the occasion," the state might be said to harness religious power for its own ends.[48] On the other hand, if religious leaders or couples do not comply with these civil formalities, the resulting religious marriage generally will not have civil effects.[49] This highlights the status of religious marriage as independent of the secular government but also carries risk for the participants in such a marriage. It shuts them off from the protections of civil family law with respect to the incidents of marriage and procedures for marital dissolution, property distribution, spousal support, and the like.[50]

Within the United States, certain religious faiths (for example, Catholicism, Judaism, and Islam, but notably not the Protestant traditions) have their own system of courts that handle certain family matters.[51] Parties to such proceedings already ask civil courts to enforce or decline to enforce religious marriage contracts, divorce orders, arbitration agreements, and custody and support orders.[52] One motivating factor for the demand for "multi-tiered marriage" might be the perception that such courts are failing at this task, either out of a lack of understanding of the particular religious tradition at issue or out of an overzealous view of separation of church and state. Some Islamic scholars, for example, critique civil courts in the United States and Canada for ignorance about Islamic traditions and for failure to adjudicate properly claims arising from Islamic marriage contracts.[53] But these analyses generally call for civil courts to do a better job when they confront Islamic family law, rather than to cede authority to religious courts and cease exercising jurisdiction over family law.[54] Thus, a participant in the Multi-tiered Marriage Project, Mohammad Fadel, asserts that Muslims have a "keen interest" in a pluralistic system of family law but concludes that "orthodox Muslims' interests in family law pluralism are better served through marginal reforms to the current family law regime" than by "more robust proposals that would award religious institutions greater jurisdiction over family life."[55] Notably, in the recent controversy in Ontario over so-called "Sharia arbitration" of family law, many Muslim groups stressed the religious obligation of Muslims to obey civil authority and urged that any religious arbitration should be subject to proper civil law norms.[56]

The demand for a more "robust" millet system in the United States, therefore, is not evident. What is evident is that some religious groups seek greater congruence between civil and religious family law. Others seek greater accommodation of or at least appreciation by civil courts of religious law.

A complicating factor in considering calls for congruence between civil and religious marriage is that although *civil* marriage, as distinct from religious marriage, is in a sense a creature of state law and regulation,[57] America's history reveals the strong influence of Christian conceptions of marriage on the secular law.[58] As the late Lee Teitelbaum observed, "For most of American history, . . . the law of marriage was consistent with and supported — if not created — by the views of dominant religious communities."[59] The incompatibility of polygamy with Western, Christian understandings of marriage animated governmental campaigns against Mormons and Native Americans. Thus, "to the extent that the majority faith communities were oppositional, it was to value sets that argued for change in the formation of families," whether it be polygamy in the nineteenth century or, in the late twentieth, the values of secular humanism.[60] Even today, as Estin observes, although U.S. family law is thought to be secular and universal, traces of its religious roots are apparent in aspects of the law of marriage and divorce, which may look Christian, exclusive, or sectarian to people of other faiths.[61]

Once again, the issue of same-sex marriage is a crucible for sorting out marriage's dual status. Some religious authorities and lawmakers oppose extending marriage to same-sex couples because such a redefinition would be contrary to "millennia" of cultural and religious tradition as well as to the created order.[62] However, a dissenting theological view is that insisting on congruence by calling for a national definition of marriage risks "reifying marriage as a legal, rather than religious, construct" and concedes to the state — rather than religious traditions — the power to say what marriage *is*.[63]

I will not attempt to resolve this theological debate about congruence. I believe that, notwithstanding the religious roots of contemporary civil law, distinguishing religious and civil marriage is necessary to clarify government's interest in recognizing and regulating marriage. Indeed, state legislatures and governors that have opened up civil marriage to same-sex couples stress this distinction as they declare support both for equality in — that is, equal access to — civil marriage and for protecting religious freedom.[64] Making this distinction follows from constitutional principles and from liberal political principles about the fact of reasonable moral pluralism and toleration of religious difference.[65] Furthermore, the nature of civil marriage has evolved over time. As Case observes, what "marriage licenses" today is quite different from what it licensed in an earlier era, when marriage entailed a hierarchical set of rights and duties of husband and wife (*baron* and *feme*) and the criminal law prohibited non-marital, non-procreative, and non-heterosexual sexual expression.[66] Today, much of that criminal law has given way to understandings of a realm of constitutionally protected liberty and privacy. And, pursuant to the transformation of family law spurred by the Supreme Court's series of Equal Protection rulings, the rights and obligations of civil marriage are stated in gender-neutral terms. Spouses are much freer to choose how to live their marital life, and the rules of exit are far less strict.[67]

TENSIONS BETWEEN CIVIL AND RELIGIOUS LAW: GENDER ROLES AND GENDER EQUALITY

What civil marriage licenses is at odds with at least *some* religious conceptions of marriage. Considerations of a more pluralistic approach to legal regulation should attend to these possible tension points. One example is sex equality and gender roles in the family. Contemporary family law rejects the common law's model of husbandly rule and wifely obedience. Sex equality is also an important political value and constitutional principle.[68] Civil family law's model of equal spousal and parental rights and responsibilities may be in tension with religious conceptions of proper gender ordering.

In the book *American Religions and the Family: How Faith Traditions Cope With Modernization and Democracy*,[69] nearly every religious tradition examined includes a tenet that men are to exercise authority and leadership in the home (and, often, in the broader society) and that women have special duties in the home including (in some traditions) submission to or respect for male authority. In coping with modernization, religious leaders and adherents confront how to reconcile such traditional religious beliefs with contemporary American values about equality of the sexes and marriage as a partnership.[70] Similarly, another recent book, *Muslim Women in America: The Challenge of Islamic Identity Today*, identifies a central tension between support in Muslim cultural and religious traditions for male authority in the home and in society and "the general climate of American discourse about equality and justice between the sexes," including equal responsibility and decision making in the family.[71] (The fact that American social practice may vary from these ideals is not the point; the discourse and public attitudes themselves serve as identifiable contrasts to religious and cultural traditions.)

Religious communities have diverse responses to this challenge. Some religious traditions (for example, mainline Protestantism) have moved away from teachings about male dominance and female submission, fixed gender roles, and the marital, nuclear family to more egalitarian and pluralistic visions of marriage and family forms.[72] In various religions, women — and men — have engaged in efforts to generate less patriarchal interpretations of religious texts and to critique subordinating practices that have been justified by religious teaching. By contrast, some religious groups embrace traditional gender roles as part of an "oppositional" stance to American culture and the perceived weakening of family values.[73] Various immigrant communities contrast the morals and family values of their own societies of origin favorably with perceived American values, similar to how many religious conservatives in America view feminism and challenges to traditional gender roles as part of a longer litany of forces (for example, individualism and secularism) that threaten strong families.[74]

Muslim communities in America illustrate this diversity of responses to ideals of equality. On the one hand, "[m]uch of the contemporary discourse, joined by both men and women, portrays the liberal Western model of 'equality' between the sexes as unrealistic, unnatural and leading ultimately to many Western women trying to raise children alone and below the poverty level."[75] On the other, women and men attempt to "reinterpret Qur'anic texts that seem to support male dominance over women, trying to argue that the justice of God affirmed in the holy text cannot allow women to be subordinated in any way to men."[76] Generational differences are also a relevant factor. One study reports that "[y]oung Muslims in America struggle both to respect the honor of the family and to break free of expectations it imposes on them. Muslim girls are becoming more articulate about their own frustrations at the double standards that their parents seem to apply to the girls and their brothers."[77]

This diversity of views and these generational tensions are pertinent to the proposal for multi-tiered marriage. They raise questions about how to define and interpret religious family law and whose voice will prevail if there are conflicting interpretations.

Pluralism in U.S. Family Law: Jurisdiction, Location, and Citizenship

Some likely tension points in moving to a multi-tiered marriage system may be evident from reasoning by analogy from case law in the United States in which courts already consider the relationship between civil and religious family law and are asked to enforce terms of a religious marriage contract, recognize a foreign or religious marriage or divorce, or assume jurisdiction over child custody disputes. The case law suggests a certain capaciousness already at work as courts have embraced pluralism to a degree. But it also suggests important limiting principles about when courts will not and should not cede authority to religious or foreign courts or apply religious family law. At issue also are questions of how to relate membership and location in particular communities to citizenship.[78] In this chapter, I can discuss only a handful of illustrative cases about marriage and divorce and must direct readers elsewhere for a more complete survey of this body of multicultural family law.[79]

Finding multiculturalism in the context of civil family law may come as a surprise, even though, as Estin observes, it should not, given the religious heterogeneity within the United States and the migration of people across national borders.[80] This "growing body of multicultural family law," she concludes, demonstrates the potential to embrace both "a number of fundamentally different family law traditions" and "deeper values that structure and constrain the process of accommodation," such as "principles of due process, nondiscrimination, and religious freedom" as well as family law's "protective policies."[81] Estin calls for courts and lawmakers to develop a framework for a multicultural family law that would "allow individuals greater freedom to express their cultural or religious identity and negotiate the consequences of these commitments," but also "protect the rights of individuals to full membership and participation in the larger political community."[82]

This twin focus on expressing identity and safeguarding rights captures an important challenge posed to legal pluralism: how to provide space for living according to and negotiating within the framework of religious law while also ensuring that membership in the political community is a source of entitlement and obligation that coexists with, and may put constraints on, other forms of affiliation. Bringing a feminist perspective — indeed a multicultural feminist perspective[83] — to bear on this challenge may fortify analysis.

Because Nichols proposes a robust millet system of religious courts with civil government, upholding basic minimal guidelines, what civil courts have done may not be a useful model for what religious tribunals would do. But this case law is instructive on how civil family law's concerns for procedural and substantive fairness shape the accommodation now afforded to religious law. Religious family law often has gender asymmetries in the rights and duties of husbands and wives (including the power to initiate a divorce) and of fathers and mothers. Rules concerning the economic consequences of marriage and divorce also differ from the economic partnership model of civil family law. How have civil courts handled these tensions between civil and religious law?

CIVIL ENFORCEMENT OF RELIGIOUS MARRIAGE CONTRACTS AND RELIGIOUS ARBITRATION

Courts are sometimes asked to enforce — or to decline to enforce — terms of marriage contracts entered into pursuant to Jewish or Islamic marriages. In the instance of Jewish marriage contracts, these cases generally involve seeking to enforce an agreement to submit to religious arbitration.[84] This case law should be put in context of a general trend in family law away from hostility to premarital agreements about property distribution in the event of divorce — on the public policy ground that such agreements encourage divorce — to permitting parties to a marriage to make contracts with each other, that is, to engage in private ordering. At the same time, these Jewish and Islamic marriage contracts are not *pre*marital agreements, although courts sometimes mistakenly treat them as such.[85]

Another relevant trend in family law is to allow, and sometimes require, arbitration and other alternatives to divorce litigation. However, there are limits to private ordering, rooted in process concerns and in substantive concerns about fairness or protection of vulnerable or dependent parties. When private ordering also entails religious law, courts face additional questions about whether enforcing such agreements excessively entangles a civil court with religion, in contravention of the First Amendment.

Religious Marriage Contracts, Religious Arbitration, and the *Get* Statutes

A leading case for the proposition that a civil court may properly exercise jurisdiction in an action arising out of a religious marriage contract is *Avitzur v. Avitzur.*[86] In that case, New York's highest court held that secular terms of a religious marriage contract, the Jewish *ketubah*, may be enforceable as a contractual obligation. Relying on U.S. Supreme Court precedents, the court said it could apply "neutral principles of contract law" and need not consider religious doctrine.[87] The specific contract term was an agreement to appear before the *beth din*, a Jewish religious tribunal, to allow it to "advise and counsel the parties" in matters concerning their marriage. The wife had already obtained a civil divorce but, under Jewish law, would not be religiously divorced and thus able to remarry and have legitimate children until her husband granted her a Jewish divorce decree, a *get.*[88]

Jewish tradition refers to women whose husbands do not give them a *get* as *agunah*, "a chained woman" (chained to the dead marriage).[89] Jewish tradition has developed ways to address this problem, such as putting a clause in the *ketubah* to agree to arbitration. *Avitzur* rationalized enforcing such an agreement as simply compelling a husband "to perform a secular obligation to which he contractually bound himself."[90] The New York legislature subsequently enacted two statutes aimed at addressing the plight of the *agunah.*[91]

Nichols offers the *get* statutes as an example of multi-tiered marriage,[92] but I think *Avitzur* and these statutes could better be understood as an attempt by civil government to remedy a disadvantage arising out of gender asymmetry in religious law that disproportionately affects religious women and has troubling spillover effects in the civil realm, such as unequal bargaining power and one-sided settlements.[93] Broyde suggests that these statutes seek to harmonize civil and religious divorce law, with the encouragement of religious leaders, based on advancing the "purpose and function of the secular divorce law" — "ensuring that all of [New York's] citizens are in fact free to remarry after they receive a civil divorce."[94]

Thus, civil law's attempt to solve the *get* problem seems less an argument for civil government ceding more authority to religious tribunals than for shared or cooperative jurisdiction: religious and secular authorities cooperate to solve a problem that neither can solve entirely on its own.[95] In this volume, Minow argues that though some may see these statutes as an objectionable compromise because New York acknowledges the parallel existence of a religious legal system, New York actually aligns the two systems by extending protection for religious women while holding fast to "its gender equality norm."[96] Lisa Fishbayn Joffe's analysis of Canada's *get* statutes finds a similar concern on the part of civil authority both to ameliorate disadvantages for religious women and to cooperate with religious authorities to solve the problem.[97]

Adjudication of Islamic Marriage Contracts: The *Mahr*

Scholars of Islamic family law describe the marriage contract as a protective mechanism that affords a Muslim woman a chance to customize her marriage through provisions that guarantee her rights with regard to her spouse (for example, to work outside the home without her husband's permission, to initiate divorce, or not to clean the house). Many Muslim women, unaware of their rights, underutilize this protective device.[98]

Some state courts (among them, New York) have enforced a wife's right in Islamic marriage contracts to *mahr*, a bridal gift or dower.[99] Islamic traditions regarding whether a woman is entitled to *mahr* at divorce are complex and differ based on who initiates divorce, the type of divorce at issue, and the school of interpretation.[100] Nonetheless, some civil courts have stated that the fact that these contracts were entered into in the context of Islamic religious ceremonies does not render them unenforceable.

An illustrative case is *Odatalla v. Odatalla*.[101] In this case, a New Jersey court rejected the husband's argument that the court could not order specific performance of his obligation to pay $10,000 in postponed dower because (1) the First Amendment doctrine of separation of church and state precluded a civil court's review of the agreement and (2) the agreement was not a valid contract under New Jersey law. Instead, the court ruled that it could specifically enforce terms of the agreement, which was entered into during an Islamic marriage ceremony. The court reasoned that the agreement could be enforced "based upon 'neutral principles of law' and not on religious policy or theories."[102] Applying those neutral principles, the court held that the agreement had the elements of a valid contract.[103] Rejecting the husband's argument that the term "postponed" made the contract too vague, the court found persuasive the wife's offer of testimony concerning Islamic custom in which the sum could be demanded by the wife at any time, although it usually is not unless there is a death of the husband or a divorce.[104] The court also suggests that interpreting the demands of the First Amendment requires attending to the contrast between the more religiously homogenous community of the late 1700s "when our Constitution was drafted" and the more religiously and ethnically diverse "community we live in today."[105]

A Florida appellate court, in *Akileh v. Elchahal*,[106] similarly looked to New York precedents and to testimony about Islamic law to uphold a husband's agreement in an Islamic marriage contract to pay his wife a "postponed dowry" of $50,000. The wife demanded payment in a divorce proceeding brought in civil court. The court concluded that the *sadaq*, the postponed dowry incorporated into the couple's marriage certificate when they married in Florida in a Moslem ceremony, could be enforced using principles of Florida contract law. The court heard four witnesses, including Islamic experts, as to the meaning of *sadaq*, and was persuaded that the parties understood the *sadaq*'s protective function and that the wife's right to receive it was not negated if she filed for divorce.

Some courts, by contrast, have declined to enforce the obligation to pay *mahr.* One ground has been that although in principle such an obligation could be enforced by a civil court, a particular contract failed to satisfy general contract principles such as stating the material terms of the agreement.[107] An alternate ground for nonenforcement, under contract principles, illustrated in a recent Ohio appellate decision, is that the husband "entered into the marriage contract as a result of overreaching or coercion." Analogizing to case law concerning when a prenuptial agreement will be invalid, the court noted that the husband did not have a chance to consult an attorney, was presented with the agreement just a few hours before the ceremony, and signed only because he was "embarrassed and stressed."[108]

A different ground is that the *mahr* agreement offends public policy because it provides an incentive for the wife to seek divorce. In *Dajani v. Dajani*,[109] the

California court declined, on public policy grounds, to enforce a foreign proxy marriage contract (entered into in Jordan) involving an Islamic dower agreement under which the husband was obliged to pay the balance of the wife's dowry either when the marriage was dissolved or the husband died. The court bypassed the conflicting expert testimony over whether or not the husband had an obligation to pay if the wife initiated the divorce and, analogizing the contract to a premarital agreement, ruled that it "clearly provided for [the] wife to profit by a divorce."[110]

The court found "apt" the rationale of the earlier California case, *In re the Marriage of Noghrey*,[111] in which the court declined on public policy grounds to enforce an agreement entered into before a Jewish religious ceremony that the husband would give his wife a house and $500,000 or "one-half of my assets, whichever is greater, in the event of a divorce." The *Dajani* court noted that, in *Noghrey*, the protective function of the *ketubah* — to discourage divorce by making it costly for the husband and to provide economic security for the wife because the husband "could apparently divorce his wife at will" — did not matter to the holding.[112] In effect, both the *ketubah* term in *Noghrey* and the Islamic dower agreement in *Dajani* encouraged divorce "by providing wife with cash and property in the event the marriage failed."[113]

These cases raise difficult questions about how civil courts should grapple with a religious tradition's protective devices adopted in light of vulnerabilities that women face due to gender asymmetry in religious law and broader cultural norms. For example, in *Noghreyi*, the wife testified that this economic protection was necessary because "it is hard for an Iranian woman to remarry after a divorce because she is no longer a virgin."[114] She testified that in return for the agreement, she gave the groom "assurances that she was a virgin and was medically examined for that purpose."[115] Like Estin, I wonder if the courts in these cases were too inattentive to this protective function and whether they couldn't find an analogy to protective measures of U.S. divorce law. [116] Furthermore, as some Muslim scholars point out, had the *Dajani* court not taken such a "superficial" approach to Islamic law, it might have recognized that its "profiteering" assumptions about *mahr* did not apply uniformly to the rules about the wife's entitlement to *mahr.*[117]

In some recent cases, judges seem comfortable handling claims based on Islamic marriage contracts and capable of making fine distinctions when necessary. For example, in a Texas case, *Ahmed v. Ahmed*, an appellate court considered a trial court ruling that the husband's agreement, in a *nikah nama*, Islamic marriage certificate, to pay a deferred *mahr* of $50,000 was a martial contract executed in contemplation of a forthcoming marriage and was a "valid, binding, and enforceable contract" under the Texas statutory law governing premarital agreements.[118] On appeal, the husband argued that the *mahr* agreement could not be enforced as a *premarital* agreement because the parties were already married in a civil ceremony six months *before* the religious ceremony and "the terms of the *mahr* agreement are too vague and uncertain to be enforced," because he could not understand his obligation under the contract. The appellate court agreed with his first argument and rejected the wife's argument that the date of the religious ceremony controlled: "if the legal requirements for a ceremonial marriage are satisfied, Texas does not distinguish between civil and religious marriage ceremonies." Thus, the parties were spouses, not "prospective spouses," at the time they signed the *mahr* agreement.[119] The former wife argued in the alternative that the *mahr* agreement could be enforced as a "postmarital partition and exchange agreement" under other provisions of Texas's family law statutes.

The court rejected the husband's second argument, finding that the agreement was "sufficiently specific." It looked to "the relationship between the parties and the circumstances surrounding the contract" on this question. Both parties "were raised in the Islamic faith"; the former wife testified that "the *mahr* agreement is a contract based on Islamic custom and religious principles," a promise of an amount to be paid to the bride and must be paid at the time of a divorce, if not given before. Husband offered no testimony, and the reviewing court noted that if wife's testimony were credited by the trial court, then the evidence established that the parties understood the agreement and that the terms were sufficiently specific enough to be enforced.[120] However, wife faced a further hurdle because of failure to meet other statutory requirements for a partition and exchange agreement. Nonetheless, the court exercised its "broad discretion" to remand because "it serves the interest of justice to allow [the wife] another opportunity on remand to prove that the *mahr* agreement is enforceable on grounds other than as a premarital agreement, be it a partition and exchange agreement or otherwise" — theories of enforcement not fully explored in the earlier proceedings.[121]

Another interesting feature of some recent case law is that it is not always the husband who seeks to thwart the relief a wife obtains in civil court. Nor, in the case of a migratory couple, is it always the husband who is more acclimated and economically successful in the United States. For example, in *Mir v. Birjandi*, an Ohio appellate court considered the wife's argument that the trial court lacked jurisdiction to issue a divorce because, while the civil case, initiated by the husband, was pending in Ohio, she obtained a divorce in an Iranian court.[122] She argued that the Ohio court erred in awarding her husband spousal support, challenged the court's division of marital assets, and argued that it abused its discretion in "ordering her to return the $17,000 *mahr* that [husband] paid to her in order to obtain a release from Iran," where he was allegedly detained (after traveling there) due to the wife's divorce proceedings initiated in Iran.

The couple married in Iran in 1982 but soon immigrated to the United States. The wife earned a PhD in engineering and worked for a military technology institute. The husband, an agriculture engineer in Iran, had difficulty finding work in his field in the United States, due to his poor English skills. He worked as a tow truck driver and taxi driver to support the family. By the time of divorce, the wife earned "substantially more income."[123]

The appellate court affirmed the trial court's ruling that the Iranian divorce decree was not binding on the court. The wife argued, with respect to the order that she pay her ex-husband spousal support for ten years, that the court wrongly imputed income to her based on her prior income although she quit her job during the course of the trial. Testimony suggested she would not have been renewed in her current job because of poor performance and difficulty getting security clearance due to her dual citizenship. The trial court did not elaborate reasons for the award but apparently based it on the fact that the husband's income was $18,200 per year, while the wife's was $118,000–120,000. It did not credit her testimony that medical conditions prevented her from working. On appeal, the court concluded that the trial court could reasonably have concluded that the husband, who soon after filing for divorce had moved to a new city, was "not capable of earning substantially more income," while the wife "was capable of finding another engineering position" in which she would have earnings comparable to her previous job.

With respect to the issue of *mahr*, the court noted, "In Iran, *mahr* is money paid to the bride by the groom or his family for the financial protection of the bride in case of divorce."[124] The court noted the husband's testimony that he paid the *mahr* in Iran (using his credit cards) because he was not allowed to leave the country unless he did so. The reviewing court found no error in crediting the husband for this payment as part of the division of marital assets.

Notably, the reviewing court upheld the ruling that the wife pay the husband's attorney's fees and costs, stressing the inequality of their economic positions and her misconduct in the litigation process. She had all the marital assets in her name; during the divorce process, he "was forced to live on credit cards, low-wage employment, and charity." Implicitly, the court was critical of her resort to the Iranian forum, which required him to incur credit card debt to secure release from Iran.[125]

RESOLVING CONFLICTS BETWEEN CIVIL AND RELIGIOUS DIVORCE LAW: TWO CONTRASTING CASES

How would a modern millet system handle clashes between civil and religious laws concerning the process due when spouses seek to divorce each other? Or concerning whether divorcing spouses have a right to support or to equitable distribution of property? Would civil family law's protective rules be part of a "minimum" insisted upon by civil law, or would private ordering prevail? For example, in Islamic family law, husband and wife generally maintain their separate property, and unless the contract specifies, there is no presumption of property division.[126] This contrasts with notions in civil family law either of community property during marriage and equal or equitable division of such property at divorce (in community property states) or, in common law states, of deferred community property in the form of equitable distribution at divorce.

To explore these questions and to illustrate how challenging questions about the interplay of religious and civil law intertwine with geographical location, family mobility, and citizenship, I will discuss two contrasting cases. In *Chaudry v. Chaudry*,[127] the wife filed suit in a New Jersey civil court for separate maintenance and child support, alleging unjustified abandonment by her husband. The husband's defense was that he had obtained a valid divorce in Pakistan in accordance with Pakistani law. Both husband and wife were Pakistani citizens; the wife and children resided in Pakistan (but had lived in the United States for a few years early in the marriage), and the husband resided and practiced medicine in New Jersey.

The appellate court held there was not an "adequate nexus" between the marriage and the state of New Jersey to justify a New Jersey court awarding the wife alimony or equitable distribution. Second, it saw "no reason of public policy" not to interpret and enforce the marriage contract in accordance with the law of Pakistan, "where it was freely negotiated and the marriage took place."[128] Expert testimony established that alimony "does not exist under Pakistan law" and that providing for it by contract is "void as a matter of law" in Pakistan. Conversely, the agreement could have given the wife an interest in her husband's property, but it did not.

Had there been a sufficient nexus, the court observed, a New Jersey court could consider a claim for alimony or equitable distribution, even though such relief could not be obtained in the state or country granting a divorce. Location is of obvious significance for jurisdiction. The wife's insufficient connection to the state of New Jersey (evidently due in part to husband's conduct) barred relief. Husband and wife remained citizens of Pakistan, and expert testimony indicated that such citizenship was a "sufficient basis" for a divorce judgment in Pakistan. In concluding that the lower court should have applied comity to recognize the decree, the reviewing court stressed, "The need for predictability and stability in status relationships requires no less."[129]

An instructive example of when such a nexus *does* exist, also involving the law of Pakistan and a mobile family, is *Aleem v. Aleem.*[130] There, a Maryland appellate court upheld a lower court's ruling that it need not give comity to a Pakistani *talaq* divorce and was not barred from ruling that a wife receive equitable distribution of her husband's pension. The appellate ruling was affirmed by Maryland's highest court. This case illustrates how migration gives rise to jurisdictional questions and the possibility of forum shopping. The husband, at age twenty-nine, and wife, eighteen, married in Pakistan after their families arranged a meeting. They never lived together in Pakistan and had been living in Maryland over twenty years at the time the wife initiated a civil divorce proceeding. They had two children, both born in the United States and U.S. citizens.

When the wife filed for divorce, the husband moved to dismiss on the ground that "all issues have already been decided in Pakistan." He referred to the parties' marriage contract, entered into in Pakistan, which called for a deferred dowry of about $2,500 U.S. dollars. He also informed the court that subsequent to the wife filing her action, he obtained a *talaq* divorce at the

Pakistani Embassy in Washington, D.C., by pronouncing three times that he divorced his wife. The wife was served with the "Divorce Decree" and an attached notice from the "Union Council" about whether the parties wanted to reconcile.

The lower court declined to give comity to the divorce, stating that it "offends the notions of this Court in terms of how a divorce is granted."[131] On appeal, Maryland's highest court (the Court of Appeals of Maryland) invoked Maryland's Equal Rights Amendment to indicate that "a foreign *talaq* divorce provision, . . . where only the male, i.e., husband, has an independent right to utilize *talaq* and the wife may utilize it only with the husband's permission, is contrary to Maryland's constitutional provisions and . . . to the public policy of Maryland."[132] Moreover, allowing such strategic forum shopping by the husband would defeat civil law's protective purposes if the process to which a wife would be entitled under state law would be denied to her:

> A husband who is a citizen of any country in which Islamic law, *adopted as the civil law*, prevails could go to the embassy of that country and perform *talaq*, and divorce her (without prior notice to her) long before she would have any opportunity to fully litigate, under Maryland law, the circumstances of the parties' dissolution of their marriage.[133]

Thus, public policy — including concern for due process — justified denial of comity to the foreign divorce.

The conflict between Maryland's and Pakistan's rules concerning post-divorce property distribution afforded the ground for a second ruling: that, as a form of spousal support, the husband must pay his wife 50 percent of his monthly pension benefit until the death of either party. The husband argued that by virtue of the marriage contract and governing Pakistani law, his wife was not entitled to any portion of his pension. Both reviewing courts upheld the pension award and concluded that because Pakistani statutes were in conflict with Maryland's public policy about property distribution, comity should be denied.[134] Under Pakistani law, the "default" was that the wife had no rights to property titled in husband's name, while under Maryland law, the "default" is that she has such rights.[135] The Court of Special Appeals also cautioned against equating the Pakistani marriage contract with "a premarital or post-marital agreement that validly relinquished, under Maryland law, rights in marital property."[136]

The location of the family anchored the judicial assertion that "it is clear that this State has a sufficient nexus with the marriage to effect an equitable distribution of marital property."[137] By contrast to the facts in *Chaudry*, in *Aleem* the court noted the couple's long residence in Maryland, the birth and rearing of their children in Maryland, and the permanent resident status of the wife, who sought the equitable distribution. Nor was there any plausible basis for Pakistani personal jurisdiction over the wife with respect to the *talaq* divorce. The decisions in *Aleem* express a public policy against strategic forum shopping, which would allow a domiciliary, while continuing that domicile, to seek to "'avoid the incidents of his domiciliary law and to deprive the other party to the marriage of her rights under that law'" and of due process by traveling elsewhere to invoke another state's jurisdiction.[138]

This point about the link between the protections, benefits, and obligations of civil marriage and domicile seems important to a consideration of marriage pluralism in which a religious tribunal might not be in another country, but within the territorial boundaries of the state of which the party is a resident. How might this concern for strategic exploitation of nationality and of favorable religious law apply in a millet system within the United States? Would a new system of personal law mean that persons, no matter where they were located as citizens or resident aliens, would carry on their backs the religious law applicable to them? Would this regime resemble the legal pluralism of an earlier Europe, of which a ninth-century bishop observed that "[i]t often happened that five men were present or setting together, and not one of them had the same law as another"?[139]

One criticism of the traditional millet system and of its contemporary vestiges is the lack of choice in jurisdiction. One's religious affiliation determines the religious court to which one may go. In a more contemporary system of legal pluralism, to what extent would people who are members of religious communities have rights, in terms of being free to leave that community or to stay but seek the protection of civil law? When adults exercise those exit rights, what is the impact on the rights of their children? Thus, one critical question is how robust legal pluralism would reconcile civil law's commitments to equal parental rights and responsibilities with religious law systems that have asymmetrical treatment of the rights of fathers and mothers. Shachar proposes that what is needed is a form of multiple jurisdiction that attempts to respect membership in religious communities as well as rights of citizenship and resists affording religious tribunals a monopoly.[140] These concerns indicate the challenges of finding a useful model of contemporary legal pluralism.

International Models? Assessing Jurisdictional Pluralism through a Gender Equality Lens

Training a gender lens on the comparative enterprise the Multi-tiered Marriage Project proposes would better inform the national conversation it invites. A significant body of feminist work identifies problems of gender inequality and discrimination in legal systems that cede jurisdiction to religious tribunals or apply religious and customary family law. As Helen Irving's comparative study of constitutional design concludes, when women have participated in the process of constitution making in societies adopting new constitutions, they have "consistently asked" for constitutional equality and full citizenship, including "the supremacy of the constitution over tradition and custom, including over customary laws that perpetuate subordination."[141] In another comparative work on gender and constitutions, Beverley Baines and Ruth Rubio-Marin, speaking of Israel, India, and South Africa (three of Nichols's examples), note that governmental decisions "to recognize customary or religious jurisdiction over certain relationships, often including those which are the most intimate and intense, such as marriage, divorce, custody, property, and succession," have been of particular concern to feminists.[142] In that volume, Shachar and comparative constitutional law scholar Ran Hirschl argue, "A major obstacle to establishing women's full participation as equals in all spheres of life in Israel . . . continues to be the intersection of gender and religious/national tensions."[143] Israel's contemporary millet system, they contend elsewhere, grants religious communities "a license to maintain intragroup practices that disproportionately injure vulnerable group members, such as women," for example, through "gender discrimination in the religious divorce process."[144] To afford redress, Israel has made recent efforts "to enforce secular and gender egalitarian norms over the exercise of religious tribunals."[145] In the constitution-building process of various nations, bringing constitutional commitments to sex equality to bear on family law has been viewed as a sign of progressive change.[146] Frances

Raday argues that human rights norms of women's equality are translated into a "normative paradigm," within states, in such constitutional law, although there is often a clash between these norms and "traditionalist religion and culture, especially as they bear on family law."[147]

As the ongoing debate about accommodation of multiculturalism reveals, "the status of women in distinct cultural communities" is often at stake because "[w]omen and their bodies are the symbolic-cultural site upon which human societies inscript their moral bodies."[148] Calls to preserve religious or cultural autonomy often target the family and women's roles as core features that must be preserved, even as other aspects of religion and culture adapt to modernization.[149] In response, some women and women's groups (such as Women Living under Muslim Laws) contest patriarchal interpretations of culture and religion and reveal the actual diversity of religious laws and customs and the possibility for greater equality within particular traditions.[150]

If civil government is to cede authority to religious tribunals, who within the religious tradition has authority to say what constitutes religious law, and what room will there be for dissenting voices that contest the most patriarchal interpretations of religious family law?[151] A millet system that relegates religious women to the primary or exclusive jurisdiction of religious tribunals is not likely to facilitate such dissent, by contrast to a jurisdictional model that attempts to secure women's rights both as members of religious communities and as citizens. Shachar proposes a form of "multicultural feminism" that "treats women as *both* culture-bearers and rights-bearers."[152] It is attentive to the risks to women's rights to equality and full citizenship that arise both from privatizing family law (e.g., through such devices as private arbitration) and from granting public and binding authority to religious codes. These risks inform my own concerns about developing a millet system in the United States.

Conclusion

In this chapter, I have argued for greater attention to how the interplay between civil and religious jurisdiction over family law bears on women's equality. I have contrasted two possible strategies for giving more voice to religious models of marriage: securing congruence between religious and civil law by instantiating religious law in civil law or recognizing the binding authority of religious tribunals to adjudicate family law. I have concluded that the call for multi-tiered marriage, or a "robust" modern millet system, in the United States should be resisted. Normative pluralism is indeed everywhere, including in the "unofficial" family law that shapes many people's lives. Translating this into more legal pluralism, however, warrants concern. U.S. courts already give official, or civil, effect to certain aspects of religious family law. But they also decline to do so based on certain limiting principles rooted in concerns for due process and for the substance of civil family law's commitments and to broader legal and political principles of sex equality.

Civil law's concerns for gender equality and for protecting vulnerable parties are salient reasons to be cautious about new forms of legal pluralism. Any system of "multi-tiered marriage" that does not attend adequately to the equal protection and equal citizenship of women as well as men conflicts with the commitments of the U.S. family law system and constitutional principles. Moreover, lending the state's imprimatur to models of family based on male authority and female submission or on other forms of gender privilege and preference may educate children as to the legitimacy of those models in broader society. This implicates the state's interest in children as future citizens. What is needed is a model of legal pluralism that holds fast both to the value of religious membership and to the rights and duties of equal citizenship.

Acknowledgments

This chapter benefitted from helpful comments that I received in presenting it at conferences at the Hadassah-Brandeis Institute, the University of St. Thomas School of Law, and the University of Maryland, and at faculty workshops at the University of Toronto and the University of Notre Dame. Thanks for help with research to Boston University students Erica Cadez, Jennifer Dixon, and Melissa Sullivan, and head of reference at the Pappas Law Library Stefanie Weigmann. A summer research grant from Boston University School of Law funded this project.

Notes

An earlier version of this chapter was first published in *Marriage and Divorce in a Multi-Cultural Context: Multi-Tiered Marriage and the Boundaries of Civil Law and Religion* (Joel A. Nichols, ed., Cambridge University Press, 2011) as "Marriage Pluralism in the United States: On Civil and Religious Jurisdiction and the Demands of Equal Citizenship." A revised and updated version is reprinted here by permission of the publisher.

1. For example, Ayelet Shachar, *Multicultural Jurisdictions: Cultural Differences and Women's Rights* (Cambridge: Cambridge University Press, 2001).

2. Ayelet Shachar, "Privatizing Diversity: A Cautionary Tale from Religious Arbitration in Family Law," *Theoretical Inquiries in Law* 9 (2008): 573.

3. See Lila Abu-Lughod, "Do Muslim Women Really Need Saving?" *American Anthropologist* 104 (2002): 783.

4. Joan Scott, *The Politics of the Veil* (Princeton, NJ: Princeton University Press, 2007): 131; see also a review of Scott's work, in Anita L. Allen, "Undressing Difference: The Hijab in the West," *Berkeley Journal of Gender Law & Justice* 23 (2008): 208, 221.

5. Mary Anne Case, "Feminist Fundamentalism and Constitutional Citizenship," in *Gender Equality: Dimensions of Women's Equal Citizenship*, ed. Linda McClain and Joanna L. Grossman (Cambridge: Cambridge University Press, 2009): 114 (citing the Conseil d'Etat Decision in the case of Mme. M., 286798, delivered June 27, 2008).

6. Ibid., 114 (quoting from Case's own translation of the official French version of the conclusions of Government Commissioner Mme. Prada Bordenave, adopted by the Counseil d'Etat, available at http://www.conseil-tat.fr/ce/jurispd/conclusions/conclusions_286798.pdf). For an example of such media coverage, see Karen Bennhold, "A Veil Closes France's Door to Citizenship," *New York Times*, July 19, 2008, A1.

7. Charles Brenner, "Burka Makes Women Prisoners, says President Sarkozy," *Times Online*, June 23, 2009, accessed September 8, 2011, http://www.timesonline.co.uk/tol/news/world/europe/article2600320.ece.

8. Ibid.

9. Ibid.

10. See "Canadian Muslim Group Calls for Burka Ban," accessed October 22, 2011, http://www.alarabiya.net/save_print.php?print=1&cont_id=87402&lang=en; "Muslim Group Calls for Burka Ban," CBC News, accessed

October 29, 2009, www.cbc.ca/canada/story/2009/10/08/canada-muslim-burka-niqb-ban-government.html.

11. Contributors to this volume detail the controversy over religious arbitration of family law disputes in Ontario.

12. Rowan Williams, "Archbishop's Lecture — Civil and Religious Law in England: A Religious Perspective," February 7, 2008, accessed September 8, 2011, http://www.archbishopofcanterbury.org/articles.php/1137/archbishops-lecture-civil-and-religious-law-in-england-a-religious-perspective.

13. Ibid.

14. John F. Burns, "Top Anglicans Rally to Besieged Archbishop," *New York Times*, Feb. 12, 2008, A7.

15. Elaine Sciolino, "Britain Grapples with Role for Islamic Justice," *New York Times*, Nov. 19, 2008, A6. I use these news items to illustrate the framing of these jurisdictional tensions in the press, not for the truth of the matter.

16. Ibid.

17. Ibid.

18. Ibid.

19. Ibid.

20. The result of that conversation is a book, Joel A. Nichols, ed., *Marriage and Divorce in a Multicultural Context: Multi-Tiered Marriage and the Boundaries of Civil Law and Religion* (Cambridge: Cambridge University Press, 2011). My contribution to that volume, on which this chapter draws, is entitled "Marriage Pluralism in the United States: On Civil and Religious Jurisdiction and the Demands of Equal Citizenship."

21. Martha Minow, "Principles or Compromises: Accommodating Gender Equality and Religious Freedom in Multicultural Societies," chapter 1 in this volume.

22. Brian Z. Tamanaha, "Understanding Legal Pluralism: Past to Present, Local to Global," *Sydney Law Review* 29 (2007).

23. Ibid.

24. Ibid.

25. Ann Laquer Estin and Barbara Stark, *Global Issues in Family Law* (St. Thompson, MN: Thompson/West, 2007): 1, 14.

26. Ann Laquer Estin, "Unofficial Family Law," in Nichols, *Marriage and Divorce in a Multicultural Context*, 92.

27. Tamanaha, "Understanding Legal Pluralism."

28. Sally Engle Merry, "Legal Pluralism," *Law and Society Review* 22 (1988): 869.

29. Joel A. Nichols, "Multi-tiered Marriage: Ideas and Influences from New York and Louisiana to the International Community," *Vanderbilt Journal of Transnational Law* 40 (2007): 135.

30. Ibid., 148. The three states are Arkansas, Arizona, and Louisiana.

31. Katherine Shaw Spaht, "Covenant Marriage: An Achievable Legal Response to the Inherent Nature of Marriage and Its Various Goods," *Ave Maria Law Review* 4 (2006): 467.

32. Nichols, "Multi-tiered Marriage,"164–95.

33. Ibid., 164.

34. On clashes between religious liberty and sex equality in India, see Martha C. Nussbaum, *Women and Human Development: The Capabilities Approach* (Cambridge: Cambridge University Press, 2000): 167–240. For a critical evaluation of the millet systems in Canada, India, Israel, and Kenya, see Shachar, *Multicultural Jurisdictions*.

35. See Audrey Macklin, "Particularized Citizenship," in *Migrations and Mobilities: Gender, Citizenship, and Borders*, ed. Seyla Benhabib and Judith Resnik (New York: New York University Press, 2009): 276, 284–92.

36. Nichols, "Multi-tiered Marriage," 195.

37. Linda C. McClain, "Unleashing or Harnessing 'Armies of Compassion'? Reflections on the Faith-Based Initiative," *Loyola University Chicago Law Journal* 39 (2008): 361.

38. See Daniel A. Crane, "A 'Judeo-Christian' Argument for Privatizing Marriage," *Cardozo Law Review* 27 (2006): 1221.

39. Edward A. Zelinksy, "Deregulating Marriage: The Pro-Marriage Case for Abolishing Civil Marriage," *Cardozo Law Review* 27 (2006): 1164.

40. This was considered but rejected in the Law Commission of Canada's report, *Beyond Conjugality*, 2001, available at Equal Marriage for Same Sex Couples, accessed September 8, 2011, http://www.samesexmarriage.ca/docs/beyond_conjugality.pdf.

41. See, e.g., The Witherspoon Institute, *Marriage and the Public Good: Ten Principles*, 2006, accessed September 8, 2011, http://www.w.inst.org/family_marriage_and_democracy/WI_Marriage.pdf.

42. "Declaration on Marriage" (November 9, 2006), accessed September 8, 2011, http://www.cccb.ca/site/Files/Declaration_Marriage_En.pdf.

43. See Spaht, "Covenant Marriage" (discussing how covenant marriage is closer to God's purpose for marriage). Spaht reports that the Catholic Bishops of Louisiana, while agreeing with the ideal of permanence, disagreed with the law's allowance of divorce. Katherine Shaw Spaht, "Louisiana's Covenant

Marriage: Social Analysis and Legal Implications," *Louisiana Law Review* 59 (1998): 63.

44. Spaht, "Covenant Marriage."

45. Ibid.

46. Spaht, "Louisiana's Covenant Marriage," 75–77.

47. Spaht, "Covenant Marriage."

48. Estin, "Unofficial Family Law."

49. I say "generally" because some states are lenient if the parties have a good faith belief they were complying. Some states also will forgive failure to get a license as long as there was solemnization. See, e.g., Estate of Cygniel, 2006 N.Y. Misc. LEXIS 4145, 237 N.Y.L.J. 9 (Surr. Ct., Kings County, 2006) ("as long as a facially valid religious ceremony was performed by a clergyman, the marriage is a valid one"; applying this rule to uphold marriage performed in accordance with Orthodox Jewish ritual by someone authorized to solemnize a marriage, but without a marriage license); Estate of Harold H. Whitney, 2007 N.Y. Misc. LEXIS 5497 (Surr. Ct., N.Y. County 2007) ("although persons who intend to be married in New York State must secure a marriage license from a town or city clerk in the state . . . , a failure to procure such a license will not render a duly solemnized marriage void"; upholding civil effect of Orthodox Jewish ceremony). Other states are stricter in treating a religious marriage performed without a license as void. See, e.g., Yaghoubinejad v. Haghighi, 384 N.J. Super. 339, 894 A.2d 1173 (Sup. Ct., App. Div., N.J. 2006) (holding marriage "absolutely void" where ceremony was "performed in accordance with the Islam religion" and was solemnized but "the parties never obtained a marriage license"); In re Kulmiye & Ismail, Opinion Letter (Cir. Ct. Fairfax County, VA Aug. 26, 2008) (Roush, J.) (denying petition to affirm a marriage because, although parties were married in an Islamic ceremony by a religious official authorized in the county to perform marriages, they "did not obtain a marriage license").

50. See Lynn Welchman, ed., *Women's Rights and Islamic Family Law: Perspectives on Reform* (London: Zed Books, 2004), 188.

51. See Ann Laquer Estin, "Embracing Tradition: Pluralism in American Family Law," *Maryland Law Review* 63 (2004): 540.

52. Ibid.

53. See Pascale Fournier, "The Erasure of Islamic Difference in Canadian and American Family Law Adjudication," *Journal of Law & Policy* 10 (2001): 51 (critiquing Kaddoura v. Hammond, 168 D.L.R. [4th] 503 [Ont. Gen. Div., 1999]); see also Asifa Quraishi and Najeeba Syeed-Miller, "The Muslim Family in the USA: Law in Practice," in Lynn Welchman, *Women's Rights and Islamic Family Law*

(London: Zed Books, 2004), 199–212 (offering praise and criticism of how civil courts in the United States have handled Islamic family law).

54. Quraishi and Syeed-Miller, "The Muslim Family in the USA," 199–212.

55. Mohammad H. Fadel, "Political Liberalism, Islamic Family Law, and Family Law Pluralism," in Nichols, *Marriage and Divorce in a Multicultural Context*, 164, 197.

56. Marion Boyd, *Dispute Resolution in Family Law: Protecting Choice, Promoting Inclusion* (Toronto: Ministry of the Attorney General, 2004).

57. Most vividly, Goodridge v. Dept. of Public Health, 798 N.E.2d 941 (Mass. 2003), repeatedly refers to "civil marriage" and describes it as a "wholly secular institution." For a critique of *Goodridge* on this point, see Perry Dane, "A Holy Secular Institution," *Emory Law Journal* 58 (2009).

58. See John Witte, Jr., *From Sacrament to Contract: Marriage, Religion, and Law in the Western Tradition* (Louisville: Westminster John Knox Press, 1997).

59. Lee E. Teitelbaum, "Religion and Modernity in American Family Law," in *American Religions and the Family: How Faith Traditions Cope with Modernization and Democracy*, ed. Don S. Browning and David A. Clairmont (New York: Columbia University Press, 2007), 227, 229.

60. Ibid., 229–30.

61. Estin, "Embracing Tradition," 543–46.

62. See Linda C. McClain, "'God's Created Order,' Gender Complementarity, and the Federal Marriage Amendment," *Brigham Young University Journal of Public Law* 20 (2006): 313.

63. Crane, "A 'Judeo-Christian' Argument for Privatizing Marriage," 1221–22.

64. Examples include New Hampshire, New York, Vermont, Washington, and the District of Columbia.

65. On these tenets of political liberalism, see John Rawls, *Political Liberalism* (New York: Columbia University Press, 1993).

66. Mary Anne Case, "Marriage Licenses," *Minnesota Law Review* 89 (2005): 1758, 1765–68.

67. Indeed, some argue that these legal changes create a "vacuum . . . of legally mandated meaning" of marriage precisely because individuals have more latitude to decide or negotiate the content of marriage." Martha Albertson Fineman, *The Autonomy Myth: A Theory of Dependency* (New York: New Press, 2004), 99.

68. Linda C. McClain, *The Place of Families: Fostering Capacity, Equality, and Responsibility* (Cambridge, MA: Harvard University Press, 2006).

69. Browning and Clairmont, eds., *American Religions and the Family*.

70. Examples of this tension found are found in Browning and Clairmont, eds.,

American Religions and the Family, in the chapters on mainline Protestantism, evangelical Christianity, Hinduism, Islam, Confucianism, and Buddhism.

71. Yvonne Yazbeck Haddad, Jane I. Smith, and Kathleeen M. Moore, *Muslim Women in America: The Challenge of Islamic Identity Today* (New York: Oxford University Press, 2006): 90–91.

72. See W. Bradford Wilcox and Elizabeth Williamson, "The Cultural Contradictions of Mainline Family Ideology and Practice," in *American Religions and the Family*, ed. Browning and Clairmont, 37, 42.

73. See Paul D. Numrich, "Immigrant American Religions and the Family," in *American Religions and the Family*, ed. Browning and Clairmont, 20–34; Margaret Bendroth, "Evangelicals, Family, and Modernity," in *American Religions and the Family*, ed. Browning and Clairmont, 56–69.

74. Numrich, "Immigrant American Religions and the Family," 27.

75. Haddad et al., *Muslim Women in America*, 91.

76. Ibid.

77. Jane I. Smith, "Islam and the Family in North America," in *American Religions and the Family*, ed. Browning and Clairmont, 211, 215.

78. On tensions between group membership and national citizenship, see Shachar, *Multicultural Jurisdictions.*

79. See, e.g., Estin, "Embracing Tradition"; Quraishi and Syeed-Miller, "The Muslim Family in the USA," 199–212. One important area of law that I omit is the care, custody, and support of children. I also do not discuss the most familiar instance in which civil family law within the United States is not accommodating of religious law or of conduct justified by appeal to religious teaching: its steadfast refusal to allow or to recognize polygamous marriages.

80. Estin, "Embracing Tradition," 540.

81. Ibid., 603–4.

82. Ibid., 542.

83. Ayelet Shachar, "Feminism and Multiculturalism: Mapping the Terrain," in *Multiculturalism and Political Theory*, ed. Anthony Simon Laden and David Owen (Cambridge, UK: Cambridge University Press, 2007).

84. See Michael J. Broyde, "New York's Regulation of Jewish Marriage: Covenant, Contract or Statute?" in Nichols, *Marriage and Divorce in a Multicultural Context*, 138, 146-48.

85. Quraishi and Syeed-Miller, "The Muslim Family in the USA," 202 (critiquing Dajani v. Dajani, 204 Cal. App. 3d 1387 [Cal. App. 4th Dist. 1988]).

86. 446 N.E.2d 136 (N.Y. 1983).

87. Ibid., 138 (citing to Jones v. Wolf, 443 U.S. 595, 602 [1979]).

88. Ibid.

89. Estin, "Unofficial Family Law," 104–5 (giving sources).

90. *Avitzur*, 446 N.E.2d at 139.

91. Removal of Barriers to Marriage, N.Y. Dom. Rel. L. § 253(6), *McKinney's Consolidated Laws of New York Annotated* (2008); Special Controlling Provisions; Prior Actions or Proceedings; New Actions or Proceedings, N.Y. Dom. Rel. L. § 236(6)(d), *McKinney's Consolidated Laws of New York Annotated* (2008).

92. Nichols, "Multi-Tiered Marriage," 163.

93. Estin, "Embracing Tradition," 583–84 (discussing cases).

94. Broyde, "New York's Regulation of Jewish Marriage," 158.

95. Ibid, 158-59.

96. Minow, "Principles or Compromises."

97. Lisa Fishbayn, "Gender, Multiculturalism and Dialogue: The Case of Jewish Divorce," *Canadian Journal of Law and Jurisprudence* 21 (2008): 71. The Supreme Court of Canada has spoken of how the *get* problem impinged on the dignity and equality interests of religious Jewish Canadian women. Marcovitz v. Bruker, 2007 SCC 54.

98. Haddad et al., *Muslim Women in America*, 114 (discussing the work of Azizah al-Hibri and her organization, KARAMAH: Muslim Women Lawyers for Human Rights, in educating women about marriage contracts).

99. Aziz v. Aziz, 488 N.Y.S.2d 123 (Sup. Ct. Queens County 1985). In the case law I discuss, courts sometime refer to *mahr* as "dowry" or "postponed dowry," rather than "dower."

100. See Pascale Fournier, "In the (Canadian) Shadow of Islamic Law: Translating *Mahr* as a Bargaining Endowment, "*Osgoode Hall Law Journal* 44 (2006): 649.

101. 810 A.2d 93 (N.J. Super. 2002).

102. *Id.* at 95–96, citing Jones v. Wolf, 443 U.S. 595 (1979).

103. *Id.* at 97.

104. *Id.* at 97–98.

105. *Id.* at 96.

106. 666 So. 2d 246 (Fla. Dist. App. 1996).

107. See, e.g., Habibi-Fahnrich v. Fahnrich, 1995 WL 507388 (Sup. Ct. Kings County 1995) (not reported in N.Y.S.2d).

108. Zawahiri v. Alwattar, 2008 3474; 2008 Ohio App. LEXIS 2928 (Ct. App. Ohio, 10th App. Dist. 2008).

109. 251 Cal. Rptr. 871 (Cal. App. 4th Dist. 1988).

110. *Id.* at 872.

111. 215 Cal. Rptr. 153 (Cal. App. 6th Dist. 1985).

112. *Dajani*, 251 Cal. Rptr. at 872.

113. *Id.*

114. *Noghrey*, 215 Cal. Rptr. at 154.

115. *Id.* at 154–55.

116. Estin, "Embracing Tradition," 584–85.

117. Quraishi and Syeed-Miller, "The Muslim Family in the USA," 202.

118. Ahmed v. Ahmed, 261 S.W.3d 190, 2008 Tex. App LEXIS 4660 (Ct. App., 14th Dist., Tex, 2008).

119. *Id.* at *6.

120. *Id.* at *8–*9.

121. *Id.* at *10–*11.

122. Mir v. Birjandi, 2007 Ohio 6266; 2007 Ohio App. LEXIS 5517 (Ct. App. Ohio, 2nd App. Dist., 2007).

123. *Id.* at **3.

124. *Id.* at **19.

125. *Id.* at **22.

126. See Fadel, "Political Liberalism, Islamic Family Law, and Family Law Pluralism," 188–90.

127. 388 A.2d 1000 (N.J. Super. App. Div. 1978).

128. *Id.* at 1006.

129. *Id.* at 1005.

130. 931 A.2d 1123 (Md. Spec. App. 2007), *aff'd*, 947 A.2d 489 (Md. 2008).

131. *Aleem*, 931 A.2d at 1127.

132. *Aleem*, 947 A.2d at 500–501.

133. *Id.* at 501.

134. 931 A.2d at 1130; 947 A.2d at 502.

135. *Id.* at 1134.

136. *Aleem*, 931 A.2d at 1134. Another case illustrating how a U.S. civil court will affirm a state's public policy favoring equitable distribution of property when a party attempts to avoid those rules by asserting a religious marriage contract is *In re Marriage of Altayar*, 2007 Wash. App. LEXIS 2102 (Ct. App. 2007). The couple's marriage was arranged by their families in Iraq and took place in Jordan in 2000. The husband had lived in the United States since 1982, and the wife joined him after the marriage. The religious marriage contract specified a dowry of "one Quran and a payment of 19 grams of 21 karat gold due in the event of divorce of death." The dowry was accepted by the bride's brother. The couples divorced pursuant to a *talaq* divorce and then pursuant to a civil dissolution in Washington. The

husband asserted that Washington's community property laws should not apply because his wife's recovery was limited to her dowry. The wife countered that the Islamic marriage contract was enforceable under Islamic law but "does not limit her community property rights under Washington law." In the alternative, she argued that even if her Islamic marriage contract was a premarital agreement, it was "economically unfair" and a result of unequal bargaining power. The court held for the wife on both her substantive and procedural fairness arguments: "on its face, the exchange of 19 pieces of gold for equitable property rights under Washington is not fair"; and the wife also had no independent legal advice about the agreement. *Id.* at *7–8.

137. *Aleem*, 931 A.2d at 1131.

138. *Id.* at 1135.

139. Tamanaha, "Understanding Legal Pluralism," 6 (quoting Bishop Agobard of Lyons as quoted in John B. Morrall, *Political Thought in Medieval Times* [Toronto: University of Toronto Press, 1980]).

140. Shachar, *Multicultural Jurisdictions.*

141. See Helen Irving, *Gender and the Constitution: Equity and Agency in Comparative Constitutional Design* (Cambridge, UK: Cambridge University Press, 2008), 21.

142. Beverley Baines and Ruth Rubio-Marin, "Introduction: Toward a Feminist Constitutional Agenda," in *The Gender of Constitutional Jurisprudence*, ed. Beverley Baines and Ruth Rubio-Marin (Cambridge, UK: Cambridge University Press, 2005), 1.

143. Ran Hirschl and Ayelet Shachar, "Constitutional Transformation, Gender Equality, and Religious/National Conflict in Israel: Tentative Progress through the Obstacle Course," in *The Gender of Constitutional Jurisprudence* , ed. Beverley Baines Martha Rubio-Marin (Cambridge: Cambridge University Press, 2004), 205, 220.

144. Ran Hirschl, "Constitutional Courts vs. Religious Fundamentalism: Three Middle Eastern Tales," *Texas Law Review* 82 (2004): 1819, 1840 (citing Shachar, *Multicultural Jurisdictions*, 57–60).

145. Shachar, "Feminism and Multiculturalism,"134.

146. Linda C. McClain and James E. Fleming, "Constitutionalism, Judicial Review, and Progressive Change," *Texas Law Review* 84 (2005): 433, reviewing Ran Hirschl, *Towards Juristocracy: The Origins and Consequences of the New Constitutionalism* (Cambridge, MA: Harvard University Press, 2004).

147. Frances Raday, "Traditionalist Religious and Cultural Challenges — International and Constitutional Human Rights Responses," *Israel*

Law Review (2008): 596 (offering examples from many countries, including Israel and India). She would resolve this clash by asserting the hierarchy of rights to equality.

148. Seyla Benhabib, *The Claims of Culture: Equality and Diversity in the Global Era* (Princeton: Princeton University Press, 2002), 83.

149. See Uma Narayan, *Dislocating Cultures: Identities, Traditions, and Third World Feminism* (New York: Routledge, 1997); Shachar, *Multicultural Jurisdictions.*

150. Linda C. McClain, "Negotiating Gender and (Free and Equal) Citizenship: The Place of Associations," *Fordham Law Review* 72 (2004): 1569; Madhavi Sunder, "Piercing the Veil," *Yale Law Journal* 112 (2003): 1399.

151. Sunder, "Piercing the Veil."

152. Shachar, "Feminism and Multiculturalism: Mapping the Terrain," 115.

Part Two
Exploring the Intersections of Civil and Religious Laws

SUSAN WEISS

Chapter Four From Religious "Right" to Civil "Wrong"

Using Israeli Tort Law to Unravel the Knots of Gender, Equality, and Jewish Divorce

"Legal discourse . . . is the divine word . . . [it] creates what it states." —*Pierre Bourdieu*[1]

The purpose of this paper is to describe how Israeli cause lawyers[2] are using tort law to untie the knots between gender, equality, and Jewish divorce law. To that end, I will give a brief overview of Israel's family law regime and its gender quagmire, explain how the tort of "*get*-refusal" is being constructed in response, present some preliminary statistics from the trenches, and outline some of the practical and theoretical implications of these new tort cases.

I will posit that using tort law is a creative way to reframe the gender problems posed by Jewish law and to "bring the state back in" to help resolve them. Tort law turns a Jewish husband's religious "right" to give a divorce at his "uncoerced behest"[3] into a civil "wrong" that harms his wife and entitles her to damages. This reframing delineates and distinguishes the harm being done to women, raises consciousness, demystifies the power relations that undergird Jewish divorce law, strips away the religious aura of a cruel act, and forces a dialogue of change.

Background: The Millet System

On or about its founding, the State of Israel incorporated the millet system (*millet* means "religious community") of the Ottoman Empire into its laws of personal status. In the spirit of religious pluralism, this system categorizes citizens in accordance with their religious affiliations, ceding jurisdiction over matters of marriage and divorce to religious courts. The millet system effectively subjects citizens of the same state to different rules of divorce, depending on their particular religious affiliation and irrespective of their religious beliefs. Secular, religious, traditional, ultra-Orthodox, atheist, agnostic, and fundamentalist Catholics, Muslims, and Jews of the State of Israel who get married or divorced must submit to the rules of canon law, the Sharia, and the halakhah,[4] respectively, whether they want to or not.

Marriage and divorce is the only area of law in which Israel defers exclusively to religious law and the religious courts.[5] In all other matters, civil law and civil courts, inspired by Western notions of liberalism and democracy, determine the outcome of disputes between Israeli citizens. In all other areas except family law, Israel empowers its women.[6] While the rabbinic courts might have risen to the challenge of interpreting the long and venerable tradition of Jewish law so that it responded to the needs of a modern democratic state and to the idea of gender equality, the rabbinic courts have fallen far short of such expectations.

Rabbinic courts apply Jewish law (halakhah) to determine whether or not a person is married or divorced. According to the halakhah, a divorce occurs only when a man delivers a bill of divorce (a *get*) to his wife[7] of his own free will.[8] A bill of divorce delivered by a man against his will is invalid (a *get meuseh* or a "forced divorce").[9] If a man is missing, is incapacitated, or simply refuses to give his wife a *get*, she remains married to him forever (an *agunah*, literally an "anchored woman"). The halakhah penalizes women who conduct extramarital relationships with men who are not their husbands, stigmatizing children born of such relationships as *mamzerim*. A *mamzer* and all the progeny of the *mamzer* for generations are banned from marrying other Jews.[10]

Only Orthodox Jewish men preside as Israeli rabbinic court judges. No Jewish woman of any religious affiliation and no Jewish man who is not of Orthodox persuasion can, by law,[11] sit on a rabbinic tribunal. Israeli rabbinic judges do not run a divorce court in any way similar to what a reader living outside of Israel may imagine. In determining whether a husband should divorce his wife, the rabbis are not informed by notions of fault or no-fault. Instead, the rule against the "forced divorce" (the *get meuseh*) holds sway, with the rabbis favoring tactics of delay and extortion. If the rabbis refrain from making decisions, wives may remain trapped in failed marriages, but the sacred rule against the forced divorce is not compromised. Similarly, if wives yield to extortion and pay for their freedom, the rabbis would not have to apply any pressure on husbands to give the divorce. The tactics of delay and extortion ensure that no invalid force is brought to bear upon husbands. Only when delay and extortion prove ineffective do the rabbis exercise the limited authority that Jewish law gives them to influence husbands to divorce their wives.[12]

Remedy of Desperation: The Tort of *Get* Refusal

In 1999, Hanna was thirty-six years old. An ultra-Orthodox woman, Hanna was the mother of six children and had lived apart from her husband for the last ten years when she came to my office for advice. Though she desperately wanted a *get*, Hanna had not set foot in a rabbinic court since 1994. At her last hearing, the tribunal tried to persuade her to surrender her half of the family home and to waive her entire child support award, past and future, in exchange for the *get*. These were her husband's conditions for the *get*, and they were, to say the least, not acceptable to Hanna. When she rejected those terms, the tribunal blamed Hanna for her state of marital limbo. She absolutely refused to go back to the rabbis for help. And meanwhile, she had used up the conventional and not very effective arsenal[13] available to Israeli divorce attorneys to try and convince her husband to give her a *get*, of his own free will of course.

I suggested to Hanna that she sue her husband in tort. Academics had for some time raised the possibility of recovery in tort for *get* refusal.[14] But in 1999, there had been no successful attempt to do so, whether inside of Israel or outside of the country, except in France.[15] Hanna, however, had nothing left to lose, and I, as a cause lawyer for an NGO (non-governmental organization), had been waiting for her case.

A "tort" is a wrongful act that causes injury for which the law awards monetary damages (*tort* comes from the Latin word for "twisted, dubious"). The Tort Ordinance of the State of Israel defines what acts are torts for purposes of the Israeli civil courts. This list includes traditional, as well as more modern conceptions of what is a "wrongful act" worthy of compensation, including threatening violence or intentionally inflicting physical harm (assault and battery), imprisoning someone against her will (false imprisonment), or doing something that is expressly prohibited by law and causes harm. It does not include "*get* refusal."

In 2000 Hanna filed a claim for damages against her husband for *get* refusal. She argued that her husband's refusal to divorce her caused emotional harm and infringed on her basic rights to marry and have children. In December 2001, on the same day that Hanna's husband agreed to give her a *get* in exchange for the dismissal of her petition, the Hon. Judge Ben-Zion Greenberger of the Jerusalem Family Court denied a motion to dismiss the complaint.[16] He held that *get* refusal is a tort because it violates a woman's *personal autonomy* protected under the Basic Law: Human Dignity and Freedom. Similar lawsuits followed. A few months later, Judge Philip Marcus ruled that *get* refusal is a tort because it breaches the *statutory duty to obey court decisions* under section 287 (a) of the Criminal Law Ordinance.[17] Like Greenberger, Marcus did not need to quantify the amount of damages that the husband owed his wife. Here too the husband gave his wife a *get* in exchange for the dismissal of her damage claim.

In December 2004, Judge Menachem HaCohen ruled on the merits of a case, awarding a wife 325,000 NIS in damages, and another 100,000 NIS in aggravated damages (about $120,000 in total).[18] HaCohen held that *get* refusal was a tort because it was *unreasonable* behavior that fell under the rubric of *negligence*, section 35 of the Tort Ordinance. And in 2006, Judge Tzvi Weitzman, following the logic of Judge HaCohen, ordered the estate of a man to pay his estranged wife 711,000 NIS in damages (about $180,000).[19] Most cases rendered since 2008 place the tort under the rubric of "negligence," with a growing number also arguing that it is a violation of the statutory duties embodied in the Basic Law: Human Dignity and Freedom.[20]

The Cases

For this article, I examined twenty-five tort cases that were filed between the years 2000 and 2008 against recalcitrant husbands.[21] Of the plaintiffs, 63 percent were religious women (42 percent ultra-Orthodox and 21 percent religious-Zionists), 33 percent were not religious (8 percent secular and 25 percent traditional), and 4 percent are unknown. These women waited or have been waiting an average of ten years for their *get*.

Of the twenty-five women in the sample who sued for *get* refusal, the *longest* amount of time a woman waited for a *get* was twenty-nine years (her husband died). Seventeen (the vast majority) of the women waited or have been waiting between seven and eleven years for the *get*.

Twelve of the twenty-five women "closed" their tort cases before the family courts could render a decision in them. Ten of the women who "closed" their cases agreed to dismiss their cases *with prejudice* (they can't reopen the cases) in exchange for the *get*. Nine of the ten husbands gave the *get*. One husband reneged on his promise.[22] The nine women who received their *get* had lived an average of eight years apart from her husbands; but they waited an average of only *fourteen months* for the *get* from the time that they filed for damages. Two of the women who "closed" their cases agreed to dismiss their cases *without prejudice* (they can reopen their cases). In these cases, the wives closed their files in response to pressure from the rabbinic judges.[23]

Since 2000, family court judges all over Israel have rendered awards of damages for *get* refusal.[24] As mentioned, in 2004, J. HaCohen awarded 425,000 NIS (about $120,000) to a *haredi* woman. The court transferred the rights to the marital home to the wife in execution of the judgment, but her husband has still not given her *get*. They have been living apart for seventeen years. In 2006, J. Weizman awarded 711,000 NIS (about $200,000) to a secular woman. She had been living apart from her husband for twenty-nine years when he died without having given her a *get* or leaving her any money. She sued her husband's estate and collected damages. From 2008 to 2010, family court judges rendered decisions awarding damages ranging from 108,000 to 700,000 NIS (between $30,000 and $200,000).[25] These decisions have expanded on HaCohen's 2004 decision, holding that get refusal is not contingent on a rabbinic court decision that orders a husband to give a *get* (Greenberger 2008); and can be awarded to a woman even after she has received her *get* (Marcus 2010).

New cases are being brought on a regular basis. At the time of final editing of this chapter, at least seventeen rulings have been rendered in family courts all over the country (including preliminary decisions and final judgments) upholding these cases, and more judgments are pending. One judgment was upheld in the Tel Aviv District Court and has been turned down for appeal by the Supreme Court.[26]

Some preliminary observations regarding the above rudimentary statistics:

1. Most of the men who are sued for damages for *get* refusal give their wives a *get* in exchange for the waiver of the damage claims.

2. All the men who gave their wives a *get* after having been sued for damages for *get* refusal did so within two years.

3. Not all the men who were sued for damages for *get* refusal agreed to give a *get*. One man refused to give the *get* even after the court ordered him to pay substantial damages and even after the wife transferred his rights in the marital home onto her name. Tort is not a complete, systemic solution to the problem of Jewish women and divorce.

4. Religious women are more likely to sue for damages for *get* refusal than are secular women.

It seems reasonable to speculate that religious women are more likely to sue for damages than are secular women because their freedom is more drastically affected by their husband's refusal to give them a *get*. The two most extreme cases in this study are those of secular women who waited more than twenty years for a divorce.[27] It cannot be determined from this study that religious Israeli men are more likely than secular men to withhold a *get*, though it indeed might be the case.

Why Tort? Reframing

Tort law is an important tool in the hands of innovative cause-lawyers who want to reform Israeli divorce law and whose vision of a good Israeli society is one that is both Jewish and democratic. Tort law allows these cause lawyers to articulate and reframe the problem of Jewish women and divorce in a manner that makes room for such vision. Such reframing is far-reaching in its goals and theoretical underpinnings.

Reframing is an act of translation in which an interpretive code ("schema") is transposed from one setting to another. This act of translation and renaming allows the legitimacy of the familiar (harms should be redressed) to be attached to the strange (a Jewish husband gives a divorce of his free will).[28] Translation is a creative but difficult balancing act in which the translator–cause lawyer must maneuver adroitly between tradition and change, politics and justice, words and visions. The translator must try to resonate with existing laws and customs and at the same challenge them. At any given moment, she must decide to what extent she can openly challenge existing ways of thinking and to what extent she must conceal her radical ideas.[29] Cause lawyers who reframe a Jewish husband's "right" to deliver a *get* at will into a civil "wrong" translate simultaneously in more than one direction. They reframe tort law to include *get* refusal, and they reframe religious law to recognize the forced divorce as an actionable injurious act. They translate transnational human rights principles (women have the right to divorce[30]) *down* into civil tort claims, and they translate local religious customs (only the husband can give the *get*) *up* into tort violations.

I will posit that these delicate acts of translation and reframing allow the cause lawyer to improvise, invent, and create. Dubbing *get* refusal a "tort" allows cause lawyers to define and delineate the problem of Jewish women and divorce, rally consciousness and unite women, demystify an act of power, defrock a religious act, and bring the state back in to redress the harms inflicted on its citizens. Moreover, by constructing the tort of *get* refusal, cause lawyers draw attention to the conflict of values that are in issue and force a dialogue that the rabbinic courts would otherwise avoid.

DEFINES, DELINEATES, AND QUANTIFIES

For Jewish women whose husbands refuse to give them a divorce, the tort of *get* refusal gives them a voice. It breaks what Catherine MacKinnon would refer to as the "silence of a deep kind" — "the silence of being prevented from having anything to say."[31] Though rabbis have for years bemoaned the plight of the *agunah*, Orthodox rabbis — the only ones that count in Israel — have not articulated a satisfying response or a systemic solution to the problem of Jewish women and divorce. Nor have these Orthodox rabbis listened to women. They have consistently held that women cannot act as judges and cannot write reponsa. They have even refused to allow women to attend conferences scheduled to discuss the problems of Jewish women and divorce. In short, they have effectively "prevented women from having anything to say." By suing husbands (and rabbis[32]) for damages, women are forcing the rabbis to listen. Women, not the rabbis, are defining and delineating what is happening to them: it's a tort, a twisted and distorted act that causes harm. What's more, it is a harm that Judge HaCohen has quantified in the amount of $150 a day. Cause lawyers use his evaluation as a benchmark when suing.[33]

In my mind, *get* refusal is a tort that requires still further clarification. The term "*get* refusal" is one that I have adopted for purposes of this article, but it hardly does justice to the injustice. The judges in the Israeli family courts are still jostling for the privilege of naming the tort. One judge claims that *get* refusal is an infringement on personal *autonomy*. Another posits that it is an act of *negligence*. I would like the judges to declare that *get* refusal is a violation of the Law against Family Violence (1991), thus emphasizing the torts' intentional and harsh effects. Instead of *get* refusal, perhaps the act of causing harm to one's wife by refusing to give her a religious divorce should be referred to as the tort of "marital bondage" or "marital imprisonment."

RALLIES CONSCIOUSNESS AND UNITES

By articulating *get* refusal as a tort, women's groups and responsive family court judges have raised the consciousness of Jewish women. Leslie Bender, a feminist tort expert, explains, "Feminist consciousness-raising creates knowledge by exploring common experiences and patterns that emerge from shared telling of life events. What were experienced as personal hurts individually suffered reveal themselves as a collective experience of oppression."[34] The publicity given to damage cases for *get* refusal by the press, women's groups, and the family courts has allowed individual Jewish women to understand that their individual experience of *get* refusal is not unique and isolated, but a collective injustice.

DEMYSTIFIES RELATIONS OF POWER

To this very day the rabbis are more concerned with protecting the "right" of husbands to divorce their wives at their "uncoerced behest" and with monitoring the rule against the "forced divorce" (*get meuseh*) than they are in redressing the harms done to women who remain anchored to their recalcitrant husbands. Calling *get* refusal a "religious right to divorce your wife of your own free will" is like calling a terrorist a freedom fighter. The "forced divorce" is a euphemism that conceals the relations of domination that underlie *get* refusal.[35] *Get* refusal is an act of raw patriarchal power. Calling it a privilege of free will or a problem of the "forced divorce" masks its relations of domination. Tort law demystifies the language that dissimulates the relations of domination and reveals them.

DEFROCKS

Similarly, calling *get* refusal a tort avoids any attempt to sanctify it and place it under the protective aegis of religion. Using the civil tort laws of the state, Israeli women reframe a husband's exercise of a *religious* "right" to refuse to give his wife a *get* into a *civil* "wrong" that entitles her to damages. Instead of an act of religious conscience, *get* refusal becomes a secular tort that the liberal state — in particular a state like Israel where there is no separation of church and state — is more willing to remedy under routine civil law. By calling it a tort, the law can more easily "bring the state back in" to redress what is happening.[36] Calling *get* refusal a tort counterbalances confusing "religious" language that places the husband's behavior beyond the reach of civil law.

What's more, it is clear from the cases described that awarding damages for *get* refusal does *not* in fact interfere with a religious act at all. Husbands can, and do, continue to exercise their "right" to refuse to give their wives a *get* just as they always have before the introduction of tort law. If women had the choice, they would probably choose both the *get* as well as the damages for their lost years. In my opinion, the fact that most defendant-husbands manage to convince their wives to give up their tort claims in return for the *get* just proves that the power to give or take the *get* still remains strongly lodged in the hands of Jewish men.

Dialogues

Calling *get* refusal a tort provokes a direct confrontation between religious values and modern ones. *Get* refusal is about male dominion over women. Equal power to sue for divorce is about liberty, autonomy, and equality for women. It is a modern notion. The tort of *get* refusal forces the rabbinic court to confront modernity and to conduct a dialogue, whether they want to or not, with women.

It was and remains the hope of Israeli cause lawyers that this dialogue and confrontation would yield a transformative response from the rabbinic court and religious communities that will untie the knots between gender, equality, and Jewish divorce law. Various transformative responses are imaginable, some more radical than others, all of which are possible: (1) The rabbinic courts could embrace the tort of *get* refusal as a way to help them resolve difficult cases; theoretically at least, the rabbis could encourage women to sue for damages in the civil court as a way of warning husbands against recalcitrance; (2) rabbinic leaders might be encouraged to find internal systemic halakhic solutions to the problem of religious divorce; (3) alternative Israeli Orthodox rabbis could break with existing rabbinic judges to form more modern rabbinic courts; and (4) an increasing rift may develop between the secular and religious courts that would pave the way for the legislation of secular marriage and divorce in Israel.

Rabbinic Supreme Court Responds to Tort Claims: March 11, 2008

Despite the effectiveness of the tort law in solving long-standing cases in the rabbinic court (not to mention doing justice), the Israeli rabbinic courts have not embraced tort as a solution or as a way of ameliorating the problem of *get* refusal. On the contrary, as more and more women have been suing for damages for *get* refusal, the rabbinic court has been expressing more and more opposition to those cases on religious grounds, arguing that these cases violate the rule against the forced divorce (*get meuseh*). The rabbis claim that husbands who give the *get* after they've been sued in tort are not giving the divorce freely, but in response to the tort cases.

On March 11, 2008, the Supreme Rabbinic Court[37] issued a twenty-six-page decision (all *obiter dictum*) in which it held as follows:

> All petitions filed outside the rabbinic court — like petitions to civil courts for damages — that relate to *get* refusal, whose practical consequence is to accelerate the delivery of the *get*, are an interference with the laws of the Torah regarding divorce, and effectively preclude the possibility of the execution of a [kosher] *get*. . . .

> Attorneys who deal in family law should be advised to weigh carefully their recommendations to clients to file damage claims in the family court for *get* refusal. Such recommendations are tantamount to malpractice, and I doubt that attorneys could avoid such claims [of malpractice], even it if they were to sign their clients on waivers to that affect. It can be assumed that clients are not aware and cannot possibly foresee what serious consequences and delays can occur in the delivery of the *get*, even after the husband has agreed to give the *get*, if the husband's agreement [to give the *get*] was given subsequent to a petition for damages for *get* refusal (J. Algrabli).

In short, the rabbinic court declared in no uncertain terms that it would not yield to outside attempts to reform its failings and wielded, once again, the immutable rule against the "forced divorce" (*get meuseh*), thus rewinding the knot of religion that had for a moment loosened. Recent rabbinic court cases have reconfirmed this stand.[38]

In Conclusion

The tort of *get* refusal is delineating, distinguishing, demystifying, and defrocking the knots that bind gender, equality, and Jewish divorce law. The tort has prompted an important dialogue/confrontation in the Israeli courts between modernity and tradition, between liberal principles and religious values. It remains to be seen how this encounter will play itself out and if the knots that bind Israeli Jewish women unremittingly to their husbands will somehow be undone. It could be that women will lose patience in their attempt to unravel these knots and will simply cut them in order to escape entanglement.

Appendix: The Tort of Get Refusal (in alphabetical order, according to judge)

FAMILY COURT CASES

Bergman, J. Rachel (2010) (Haifa, File 12200/08) (awards 108,000 NIS to woman for *get* refusal)

Buhadana, Esther (2012) (Tiberius, File 15377-09-10) (awards 180,000 NIS damages to woman for *get* refusal that is not contingent upon rabbinic court order against husband)

Elbaz, J. Shlomo (2001) (Jerusalem, File 12130/03, Motion 50576/04) (denies motion to dismiss claim for damages for *get* refusal)

Felix, Nimrod (2011) (Jerusalem File 44248-05-10) (awards 164,000 NIS — 4,000 NIS a month from the day the wife left the marital home)

Greenberger, J. Ben-Zion (2001) (Jerusalem, File 3950/00) (denies motion to dismiss claim for damages for *get refusal)*

——— (2008) (Jerusalem, File 006743/02) (awards 550,000 NIS damages to woman for *get* refusal that is not contingent upon rabbinic court order against husband)

HaCohen, J. Menahem (2004) (Jerusalem, File 19270/03) (awards 425,000 NIS damages to women for *get* refusal, first instance)

——— (2007) (Jerusalem, File 022158/97, Motion 056986/07) (declares that there is claim for damages for *get* refusal independent of rabbinic court order)

——— (2010) (Jerusalem, File 021162/07) (awards 53,333 NIS damages to man whose wife refuses to accept *get*)

Katz, J. Itai (2010) (Jerusalem, File 18561/07) (awards damages of 400,000 plus 4,000 NIS a month to man whose wife refuses to accept *get*) (lowered on appeal)

Kitsis, J. Yehudit (2008) (Rishon Le'Tzion, File 030560/07) (awards 377,200 NIS damages to woman for *get* refusal and declares that *get* refusal is violation of Basic Law: Human Dignity and Freedom)

Maimon, J. Nili (2008) (Jerusalem, File 022061/07, Motion 054445/08) (denies motion to dismiss claim for damages for *get* refusal filed against husband's family)

——— (2004) (Jerusalem, File 20673/04) (awards damages to woman who was victim of abuse, including *get* refusal; amount increased on appeal)

Marcus, J. Philip (2001) (Jerusalem, File 9101/00, Motion 054233/01) (denies motion to dismiss claim for damages for *get* refusal)

——— (2009) (Jerusalem, File 22511/08, Motion 059740/08) (denies motion to dismiss claim for damages for *get* refusal, husband claiming that rabbinic court did not order him to give *get*)

——— (2010) (Jerusalem, File 9189/01) (awards 600,000 NIS damages to woman at rate of 100,000 NIS a year who sued for damages *after* she had already received her her *get*)

Sivan, J. Tova (2008) (Tel Aviv, File 24782/98) (awards 700,000 NIS to woman for *get* refusal)

——— (2011) (Tel Aviv, File 10-02-35371) (awards 400,000 NIS to ultra-Orthodox husband who received dispensation from rabbinic court to take a second wife, but whose first wife still refused to accept a *get*)

Stein, Yaffa (2011) (Rishon Le'Zion File 9877/02) (awards 680,000 NIS to woman even though rabbinic court rescinded order issued against husband to give a *get*)

Weitzman, J. Tzvi (2006) (Kfar Saba, File 19480/05) (awards 770,00 NIS to woman for *get* refusal against estate of husband)

DISTRICT COURT

Kovo, J. Esther, with J. Michal Rubensteing and J. Ofra Cherniak (2011) (Tel Aviv 1020/09) (affirming decision of Tova Sivan, Tel Aviv, File 24782/98)
Rachel Avraham TA file 43840/07

Acknowledgments

Susan Weiss initiated the tort cases described in this paper. My thanks to Susan Aranoff for her cogent comments and editing.

Notes

1. Pierre Bourdieu, *Language and Symbolic Power* (Cambridge, MA: Harvard University Press, 1991), 42.

2. Stuart Scheingold and Austin Sarat, *Something to Believe In: Politics, Professionalism, and Cause Lawyering* (Stanford: Stanford Law and Politics, 2004), 2. ("For cause lawyers, . . . [l]awyering . . . is a deeply moral or political activity, a kind of work that encourages pursuit of their vision of the right, the good, or the just.")

3. J. David Bleich, "Modern-Day Agunot: A Proposed Remedy," *Jewish Law Annual* 4 (1981): 167, 171. ("*Halakhah* requires that the *get* be drafted at the uncoerced behest of the husband. Free will on the part of the husband is a necessary condition of validity.")

4. Israeli Rabbinic Courts Jurisdiction (Marriage and Divorce) Law of 1953. See generally Irving A. Breitowitz, *Between Civil and Religious Law: The Plight of the Agunah in American Society* (Westport, CT: Greenwood Press, 1993), setting forth a thorough overview of the structure of halakhah (Appendixes E and F, pp. 307–20).

5. Under certain circumstances, and with respect to certain matters that are ancillary to the divorce process like child support, custody, and marital property, the family courts of Israel have parallel jurisdiction with the rabbinic courts. However, only the rabbinic courts can decide if an Israeli Jew is married or divorced. In matters of personal status, Israel is a theocracy (defers to the laws of God), not a democracy (defers to the laws of men).

6. Valerie Moghadam, *From Patriarchy to Empowerment: Women's Participation, Movements, and Rights in the Middle East, North Africa, and South Asia* (Syracuse: Syracuse University Press, 2007), 353–64. Of the six variables by which the sociologist assesses a states' empowerment of women, family law is the only one in which Israel fails its women.

7. Deuteronomy 24:1(cited as the proof text for this principle).

8. Talmud Bavli, Yevamot 112b.

9. Talmud Bavli, Gittin 88b.

10. Shulhan Arukh, Even Ha'Ezer 4:1, 13, 22.

11. See, e.g., "Convention on the Elimination of All Forms of Discrimination against Women," United Nations Division for the Advancement of Women, accessed September 21, 2011, http://www.un.org/womenwatch/daw/cedaw/cedaw.htm. (Israel expressly notes its reservations to section 7[b] of the law stating: "1. The State of Israel hereby expresses its reservation with regard to article 7 [b] of the Convention concerning the appointment of women to serve as judges of religious courts where this is prohibited by the laws of any of the religious communities in Israel. Otherwise, the said article is fully implemented in Israel, in view of the fact that women take a prominent part in all aspect of public life." See "Declarations, Reservations, and Objections to CEDAW," United Nations Division for the Advancement of Women, accessed September 21, 2011, http://www.un.org/womenwatch/daw/cedaw/reservations-country.htm.)

12. Susan Weiss, "The 3 Methods of Jewish Divorce Resolution: Fundamentalism, Extortion and Violence" (in Hebrew), *Eretz Aheret* 13 (2002): 42–47.

13. Israeli couples can divorce by agreement with no waiting period. In cases of contested divorces, most divorce attorneys who represent wives "race" to the family courthouse to sue for matters ancillary to the divorce. They hope to obtain financial

advantage in the family court with which they can leverage their clients' freedom. Hanna, an Orthodox woman, had sued in the rabbinic court. Moreover, she had offset her husband's child support debt against his half of the marital home. He still refused to give her a *get*.

14. Barbara J. Redman, "Jewish Divorce: 'What Can Be Done in Secular Courts to Aid the Jewish Woman?'" *Georgia Law Review* 19 (1984–85): 389; David M. Cobin, "Jewish Divorce and the Recalcitrant Husband — Refusal to Give a Get as Intentional Infliction of Emotional Distress," *Journal of Law and Religion* 4 (1986): 405; Breitowitz, *Between Civil and Religious Law*, 239–49.

15. Jews who feel bound by Jewish law, irrespective of where they live, will not feel free to remarry until their marriage is terminated with a *get*. In France, Jewish women successfully sued their husbands for damages when they refused to give them a religious divorce after they had been civilly divorced. See, J. C. Nidas, "The Position of French Civil Courts with Regard to Claims Filed against Jewish Husbands for the Delivery of a Get" (in Hebrew), *Dinei Israel* 20–21 (2000–1) (reviewing and translating French court cases that addressed the claims of wives for damages against their recalcitrant husbands).

16. J. Greenberger (2001), Jerusalem File 3950/ 00. (All Israeli family court cases are anonymous. They do not refer to the name of the parties. Most of the cases cited here were not published but can be found on Israeli legal websites. Some can be read on CWJ website at http://cwj.org.il/our-projects/torts [English] and http://sites.google.com/site/cwjhebrew/tort-of-get-refusal [Hebrew].)

17. J. Marcus (2001), Jerusalem File 9101/00.

18. J. HaCohen (2004), Jerusalem File 19270/03.

19. J. Weizman (2006), Kfar Sava File 19480/05.

20. See Judge Kitsis (2008), Rishon Le'Tzion File 030560/07; and Judge Katz (2010), Jerusalem File 18561/07 (placing the tort squarely under the Basic Law).

21. These were all the cases that I know of. Since 2008, at least another fifteen cases have been filed. Statistics gleaned from those additional cases are similar to the ones set forth in this article. Most of the cases have been brought by the Center for Women's Justice, an NGO that I founded and stand at the head of. I think it fair to say that all the cases filed were inspired by our work, and all were bent on expanding the tort to cover all cases of *get* abuse, irrespective of rabbinic court order. I have listed all the decisions that I know of in the appendix.

22. This client alleged that she was fraudulently induced to agree to dismiss her case with prejudice, and she moved to reopen her case. A trial was conducted, and as of January 2011, the decision in the matter is still pending.

23. In 2007, the rabbinic court put one of the husbands into prison (and on

alternative weeks into solitary confinement) for refusing to give a *get*. As of 2010, he has yet to give the get, even though he has been in jail for close to four years. Rabbi Levi Brackman and Rivkah Lubitch, "Rabbinical Court Send Divorce Recalcitrant to Solitary Confinement," *Jewish World*, accessed January 25, 2010, http://www.ynetnews.com/articles/0,7340,L-3523781,00.html. In the second case, the rabbinic court first ordered the husband to give a *get* in 2009. In December 2010, the rabbinic court agreed to incarcerate the husband. After a week in jail, he agreed to give the *get*. Both women had been living apart from their husbands for over ten years. They are both in their late thirties.

24. See comprehensive list in the appendix. Note that this includes cases that award damages to men. In 2010, Judge HaCohen (Jerusalem File 21162/07) and Judge Katz (Jerusalem File 18561/07) also awarded damages of 533,333 NIS and 400,000 + 4,000 NIS each month, respectively, to men whose wives refused to accept a *get*.

25. See appendix.

26. The appeal was decided on January 25, 2011, upholding Tel Aviv District Court award of 700,000 NIS (almost $200,000) issued by J. Sivan in 2008 (Appeal 1020/09). On February 15, 2012, Judge Neal Hendel denied the husband the right to a second appeal (Motion for Appeal 2374/11).

27. In both those cases, an outside event triggered their tort claims. Another secular woman who withdrew her tort case (she is exploring other avenues) is also waiting more than twenty years for a divorce.

28. See Patrick Ewick and Susan S. Silbey, *The Common Place of Law: Stories from Everyday Life* (Chicago: University of Chicago Press, 1998); Austin Sarat and Stuart Scheingold, *The Worlds Cause Lawyers Make: Structure and Agency in Legal Practice* (Stanford: Stanford Law and Politics, 2005) (discussing how lawyers use schemas creatively).

29. Sally Engle Merry, "Transnational Human Rights and Local Activism: Mapping the Middle," *American Anthropologist* 108:1 (2006) (explaining how social movement activists and NGO participants translate ideas from the global arena down and from the local arena up).

30. See generally Convention for the Elimination of Discrimination against Women (CEDAW).

31. Catherine MacKinnon, *Feminism Unmodified: Discourses on Life and Law* (Cambridge, MA: Harvard University Press, 1987), 39. ("When you are powerless, you don't just speak differently. A lot, you don't speak. Your speech is not just differently articulated, it is silenced, eliminated, gone. . . . Not being heard is not just a function of lack of recognition, not just that no one knows how to listen

to you, although it is that; it is also silence of the deep kind, the silence of being prevented from having anything to say. Sometimes it is permanent.")

32. For example, Rachel Avraham (Tel Aviv File 43840/07) (sued the state for negligent supervision of rabbinic court judges that allowed case to drag on for almost nineteen years).

33. Though awards have been averaging between 40,000 and 60,000 NIS per year of refusal (between $12,000 and $16,000 a year.) See appendix.

34. Leslie Bender, "A Lawyer's Primer on Feminist Theory and Tort," *Journal of Legal Education* 39 (1988): 3, 9.

35. John B. Thompson, *Ideology and Modern Culture: Critical Social Theory in the Era of Mass Communication* (Stanford: Stanford University Press, 1990) (how meaning sustains relations of domination).

36. Compare Cass Sunstein, "Should Sex Equality Law Apply to Religious Institutions?" in *Is Multiculturalism Bad for Women?* ed. Susan Muller Okin et al. (Princeton: Princeton University Press, 1999).

37. File 7041-21-1.

38. See also Tel Aviv District Rabbinic Court File No. 8455-64-1; and Netanya District Rabbinic Court File 272088/6, (calling on rabbinic courts to refrain from deciding divorce cases or issuing *gittin* subsequent to the filing of tort claims and claiming that the filing of a tort claim renders any future *get* invalid). Despite these decisions, at least three CWJ clients have received a *get* after the filing of the tort claims and with the full knowledge of and cooperation of the rabbinic courts. Despite these decisions, I know of no occasion in which a *get*, once rendered, was declared invalid because of a tort claim for damages for *get* refusal.

PASCALE FOURNIER

Chapter Five Flirting with God in Western Secular Courts *Mahr* in the West

Introduction

If liberalism is committed to the individual and individual choice, it is also conventionally taken to be committed to freedom and equality. Giving effects to such principles often creates tensions: the "free" acts of individuals will sometimes produce inequality, and state enforcement of equality will likely reduce individual freedom. Moreover, when faced with the claims of subordinated groups, liberalism is asked to make concessions in which these collisions intensify and multiply. In fact, if the mandate to address the rights or interests of groups is not perfectly consistent with liberalism's commitment to individuals, such group accommodation may, however, be necessary if individuals in those groups are to be treated liberally — that is, accorded liberty or equality. And the mandate to address the subordination of groups generates new collisions between liberty and equality: de facto freedom for subordinated groups may require their specific regulation, while equality of their members may require active distributions in their favor. The "politics of recognition" invoked by subordinated groups within liberalism is thus an inherently contradictory project, exposing in practice the ideals of liberty and equality as fundamentally paradoxical. This analysis welcomes such contradictions, as they operate in the specific context of the politics of recognition invoked by Muslim groups in Canada, the United States, France, and Germany.

Through the journey of one symbolic legal institution — *mahr* (a form of dowry) — I will follow the ways in which Islamic marriage travels, offering a panoply of conflicting images, contradictions, and distributive endowments in the transit from Islamic family law to Western adjudication. I insist that *distributive* consequences rather than recognition occupy central place in the assessment of the legal options available to Muslim women in Western courts. In family law matters, the enforcement of *mahr* by Western courts carries considerable distributive power, although *mahr* is often treated as a mere expression of religious recognition by the judiciary. Moreover, the distributional impact is far from homogeneous and predictable. At times, the *mahr* that is being institutionally transferred by Western courts unfolds as an exceptional penalty imposed on the Muslim husband (courts add the amount of *mahr* to the division of family assets and to spousal support), whereas sometimes it becomes an exceptional penalty for the Muslim wife (through conflict of laws, *mahr* replaces alimony and equitable division of property). Still at other times, the unenforceability of *mahr* for an economically dependent wife leads to an exceptional bonus (through conflict of laws, *mahr* is rejected as against "public order" and Western equity standards are applied instead).

To represent this distributive framework, I will introduce several short scripts in which a fictional Leila embarks in a bargaining tactic with her husband Samir upon divorce and uses *mahr* as its central object. In offering the many conflicting faces of *mahr* as bonus and penalty, I will assess the interaction between Islamic law and Western law, as well as the subjective gains and losses predicted by Leila in relation to the enforceability of *mahr*. What does it mean, concretely and legally, to be flirting with God in Western secular courts? Can the current public policy debate, assembled around the perfect dichotomies of the secular/religious, the Us/Them, the public/private, the Western/Islamic, grasp any of the gray zones? What is it that we can't see? This chapter will implicitly address the stakes of conceiving *mahr* as an autonomous legal institution, rather than as a dynamic part in a larger marital web of rights and duties. Ultimately, I will claim that the stakes are the constitution of a romantic subject in the former (the husband offers a gift to the wife upon marriage to express his love for her and his respect for God; this gift must travel as a legal transplant to Western states) and a calculating subject in the latter (*mahr*, inherently plural, is used by the parties to gain something from the other; this institution is always-already resisting claims of "true" and "authentic" Islamic law). A distributional analysis of *mahr* is crucial, I will argue, because *mahr* is encountered by actual parties and often used by them as a tool of relative bargaining power in the negotiation of contractual obligations related to the family. Moreover, Islamic law travels with a multiplicity of voices, and it is this complex hybridity that will be mediated through Western law upon adjudication.

The Place of Departure: *Mahr*'s Internal Pluralism

Mahr, meaning "reward" (*ajr*) or "nuptial gift" (also designated as *sadaqa* or *faridah*), is the expression used in Islamic family law to describe the "payment that the wife is entitled to receive from the husband in consideration of the marriage."[1] *Mahr* is usually divided into two parts: that which is paid at the time of marriage is called prompt *mahr* (*muajjal*), and that which is paid only upon the dissolution of the marriage by death or divorce or other agreed events is called deferred *mahr* (*muwajjal*).

Three forms of Islamic divorce (*talaq*, *khul*, and *faskh*) can be used by the parties involved in a marital relationship. Islamic family law determines the degree to which the husband and wife may or may not initiate divorce and the different costs associated with each form of divorce.[2] *Talaq* (repudiation) is a unilateral act that dissolves the marriage contract through the declaration of the husband only.[3] What comes with this unlimited "freedom" of the husband to divorce at will and on any grounds is the (costly) obligation to pay *mahr* in full as soon as the third talaq has been pronounced.[4] In this regulatory regime, there is no shortcut for a wife who wants to obtain a divorce but who cannot obtain the consent of her husband. A wife may unilaterally terminate her marriage without cause only when such power has been explicitly delegated to her by her husband in the marriage contract.[5] Otherwise, she may apply to the courts either for a *khul* or a *faskh* divorce. *Khul* divorce can be initiated by the wife with the husband's prior consent; however, the court (*qadi*) must grant it, and divorce by this method dissolves the husband's duty to pay the deferred *mahr*.[6] In the case of a *faskh* divorce, a fault-based divorce initiated by the wife, she must demonstrate to the court that her case meets the limited grounds under which divorce can be granted,[7] in which case she will be entitled to *mahr*. This description of classical Islamic family law, however, is expressed differently in contemporary jurisprudence.

The Place of Arrival: *Mahr*'s External Pluralism

My analysis of how the law captures claims based on identity within the liberal framework suggests that in adjudicating *mahr*, courts have characterized this Islamic institution in three different ways: the legal pluralist approach, the formal equality approach, and the substantive equality approach.[8] I decided to classify these three disciplinary discourses within the wider expression of liberalism because they all share, in both their normative and descriptive dimensions, the same commitment to autonomy and liberty of the individual. Along this spectrum of ideology, *mahr* has been the subject of competing aesthetic and political representations, from a form of religious family affiliation under legal pluralism, to a space of mere secular contract under formal equality, and finally to the projection of a gendered symbol under substantive equality. The reason I focus on the locus of the state, on adjudication, and on case law is that courts present themselves as invested in the technical enterprise of applying the law in a non-ideological manner. In the table on pages 140 and 141, I briefly introduce the three forms of adjudication.

A Legal Realist Shift: *Mahr* as Contradictions

In this section, I perform a legal realist shift to expose the contradictory nature of the adjudicative process. Through a case law analysis, I reveal the existence of two contradictions that have accompanied much of *mahr*'s journey to Western liberal courts. The first is the "doctrine-outcome contradiction": as the legal doctrine adopted by the court projects the mandate to recognize or the mandate not to recognize, the resulting outcome from that recognition does not follow the doctrine as would logically be expected; instead, it often reverses it. The second is the "ends/means perversity contradiction": the probability that the legal means available to judges to achieve a given end cannot, in a globalized context of rules, produce the anticipated result. Moreover, the parties involved in the dispute over the enforcement of *mahr* act out this contradiction, individually, relationally, in related but somewhat different terms. The aim of this section is to complexify and attempt to transcend the ruling binaries that have organized the disciplinary fields in which *mahr* is projected and produced.

THE DOCTRINE-OUTCOME CONTRADICTION

The doctrine-outcome[9] contradiction may well be the effect of the deeply contradictory nature of law in general and adjudication in particular.[10] This

Summary of Forms of Adjudication

	LEGAL PLURALISM	FORMAL EQUALITY	SUBSTANTIVE EQUALITY
Mahr as . . .	Western state views *mahr* under the umbrella of Islamic family law The Western judge welcomes the imam as an expert witness: multiculturalist understanding of *mahr* *Mahr* is the expression of religious identity	Western state views *mahr* under the umbrella of Western contract law The Western judge pictures the legal system as devoid of representative role for the minorities: secular understanding of *mahr* *Mahr* is a contract irrespective of race, gender, or religion	Western state views *mahr* under the umbrella of Western family law The Western judge engages in sexual identity politics: gendered understanding of *mahr* *Mahr* is a religious custom that has an effect on substantive equality
Mahr is . . .	*Mahr* is enforceable as an Islamic custom. It is srecognized on the basis of: • Manifestation of identity (Canada) • Islamic custom (France and Germany) • Related to a *khul* divorce (Québec and U.S.) OR *Mahr* is not enforceable because it is too "foreign" to be adjudicated by a Western (non-Muslim) judge. It is not recognized on the basis of: • Being utterly foreign (Canada)	*Mahr* is enforceable as a contract. It is recognized on the basis of: • Marriage agreement (Canada) • Antenuptial agreement (U.S.) • Legal debt (Germany) • Contractual condition of marriage (France) OR *Mahr* is not enforceable because it speaks to contractual exceptions. It is not recognized on the basis of: • Vagueness (U.S.) • Lack of consent (U.S.) • Abstractness (Germany)	*Mahr* is enforceable, but its amount must respect Western family law rules of equity. It is recognized on the basis of: • Readjusted alimony (Germany) • Being due even though the wife initiated the divorce (Québec) OR *Mahr* is not enforceable because it violates gender equality: the equal division of community property upon dissolution of the spouses' marriage is applied. It is not recognized on the basis of: • Equity (Québec) • Unjust enrichment (Germany) • Substantial justice (Canada) • Public policy (France and U.S.)

	LEGAL PLURALISM	FORMAL EQUALITY	SUBSTANTIVE EQUALITY
Case Law	**Canada:** M.(N.M.) v. M.(N.S.) (2004); Nathoo v. Nathoo (1996); M.H.D. v. E.A. (1991); Kaddoura v. Hammoud (1998); I.(S.) v. E.(E.) (2005) **France:** Cour de Cassation, 1978-000137 (1978) **Germany:** OLG Bremen, Fam RZ 1980, 606; Kammer-gericht (Berlin), Fam RZ (1988, 296); OLG Koeln IPRAx (1983, 73) **United States:** Akileh v. Elchahal (1996); Dajani (1988)	**Canada:** Amlani v. Hirani (2000) **United States:** Odatalla v. Odatalla (2002); Akileh v. Elchahal (1996); Aziz v. Aziz (1985); Habibi-Fahnrich v. Fahnrich (1995); Shaban v. Shaban (2001) **Germany:** Hamm FamRz (1988, 516); Amtsgericht Buende, 7 F 555/03 (2004); IPRax 1988, 109-113, BGH (1987) **France:** Cour de Cassation, Dec.2, 1997 (Pourvoi)	**Germany:** IPRax, OLG Koeln (1983, 73); OLG Cell, FamRZ (1998, 374) **Canada:** M.H.D. v. E.A. (1991); M. F. c. MA. A. (2002); Vladi v. Vladi (1987) **France:** Arrêt de la Cour d'appel de Douai, January 8, 1976: N. 76-11-613 **United States:** Dajani (1988)

section tests the doctrine-outcome contradiction by using concrete cases. It will address the indeterminacy between the legal doctrine used by the judge, on the one hand, and the outcome of particular legal pluralist decisions as represented by the holding of the case, on the other. The legal pluralist camp exemplifies this contradiction as it frequently adopts the doctrine of Islamic law to interpret *mahr*, and yet other doctrines and policies held by judges block the causal relationship between doctrine and outcome. In order to study the doctrine-outcome contradiction, the Critical Legal Studies (CLS) indeterminacy thesis is invoked to capture the "spin" that the holding receives in relation to the doctrine. This thesis posits that the interpretation of legal doctrine by judges may, in a given case, support opposing outcomes.

IPRax (1983) is a German case that enforced *mahr* as an Islamic custom by showing an ideological commitment to legal pluralism. In the absence of any written or oral contract, the judge accepted the religious expert evidence arguing for the existence of an Islamic *mahr al-mithl* ("proper *mahr*"), to be determined by comparing "the *mahr* paid to other female members of the wife's family, for instance sisters, paternal aunts and female cousins."[11] The wife argued that given her privileged socioeconomic status, she should be awarded

75,000 euros plus 4 percent interest as *mahr al-mithl the Islamic way.* However, the judge recast *mahr al-mithl* against the backdrop of the national legal order (Germany), and more specifically the local legal regime (Hamburg). He awarded 10,000 euros as *mahr al-mithl the German way*, divided into monthly payments of 1000 euros, based on what a similarly situated German woman living in Hamburg should receive. For the Muslim woman, the distributive consequences of such shift of rules lower her claim dramatically. Could those specific material stakes have motivated the "spin" of legal doctrine and hence the outcome that flowed from it?

The second example, *Kaddoura*, exemplifies judges' choice of interpretation through policy analysis rather than through deductive legal reasoning. The Canadian court concluded that all the elements related to the definition and enforcement of a "domestic agreement" pursuant to s. 52(1) of Ontario's Family Law Act[12] were met; thus, *mahr* could predictably have been enforced as a simple "domestic agreement." Yet, somehow, the chain of causality between the legal doctrine and the holding was broken down by the introduction of another legal doctrine: the (American!) principle of the separation of church and state.[13] Justice Rutherford compared *mahr* to Christian marital commitments "to love, honour and cherish and to remain faithful"[14] and refused to enforce it on the basis that it constitutes a "religious" obligation, not a civil one.

The first contradiction, which has revealed the effect of judges' ideology on the "broken" relationship between doctrine and outcome, is intimately related to the second one, the ends/means perversity contradiction. This next section further explores the ways in which ideology manifests itself concretely in the framing of a legal problem. It will specifically address the limits and frustrations of *not* achieving the outcome that strategic behavior was expecting to produce in the process of ideological interpretation, due to the perverse relationship between ends and means in the adjudication of *mahr* in Western liberal courts.

THE ENDS/MEANS PERVERSITY CONTRADICTION

The frustration of the ends by means can be explained as follows: for any end that a court aims at achieving, ideologically, discursively, the available (Western) means to reach that end cannot achieve it. As a result, *mahr* cannot travel either through recognition or through non-recognition. For instance, if the end is to enforce *mahr* as a form of classical Islamic family law—*as if* it were situated in Egypt, let us imagine — the means of the Western court cannot be used to achieve it. In fact, the legal tools available to judges cannot reproduce Egyptian *mahr* — that is, the enforcement of *mahr* incorporating the background Islamic legal regime of *talaq*, *khul*, and *faskh* divorce. In this section, three parts of the contradiction are presented. The first one, "*Mahr* as a Culturally Transformed Legal Transplant?" will present the perverse relationship between ends and means as it operates against the backdrop of the legal pluralist approach and ultimately fails to reproduce *mahr* as a legal transplant. The second one, "*Mahr* as Projecting a 'Religious' Contractual Intention?" will highlight the mysterious dimensions of "religion" and "Islamic intentions" as they permeate the relationship between means (contract law as acknowledging contractual intentions) and ends (*mahr* as merely secular). The third one, "The Performance of the Contradiction by the Parties Themselves: Holmes's 'Bad Man' and 'Bad Woman,'" will emphasize the puzzling role of parties involved in the adjudication of *mahr* as they strategically behave, from opposite ends of the spectrum, in relation to means and ends.

Mahr as a Culturally Transformed Legal Transplant?

The legal pluralist cases have all attempted to legally transplant *mahr* — that is, to re-create it through many different routes of cultural recognition: as "a manifestation of identity" in Canada; as "an Islamic custom" in France and Germany; as "related to a *khul* divorce" in Québec and the United States — yet along the way of its transportation, Western courts transformed *mahr*.

Nathoo[15] and *M.(N.M.)*[16] exemplify the ends/means perversity contradiction. In both cases, courts advanced an image of religion as an organized, comprehensive, and organic entity: Muslim subjects *chose* to be Muslims, and one consequence of performing Muslim identity is the enforcement of *mahr* by the court. Ironically, the *mahr* that was institutionally transferred unfolded as an exceptional penalty imposed on the husband, a result that cannot be explained or legitimated from the point of view of the original Islamic milieu of departure. In *Nathoo*, the court required the Muslim husband to pay $37,747.17 to his former wife upon reapportionment of family assets *and* enforced *mahr* as an additional and separate amount of $20,000. This holding is extremely bizarre. In fact, had *only* Canadian family law applied, a "marriage agreement" would have supplanted the marital equitable regime; had Islamic family law *only* applied, Mrs. Nathoo would have obtained only *mahr* besides maintenance during the *iddah* period. To get to such an unusual outcome in *Nathoo* — the enforcement of *mahr plus* the unequal division of property under the statutory regime — the court had to frame the issue as a minority rights one: religion is an exceptional field, it generates its own conception of the good life, and fairness is only an extension of this particularized vision. Under the disciplinary effects of the legal pluralist approach, the court held that the same contractual principles that governed other secular contracts were not to govern Muslim marriage agreements and that under such exceptional treatment the *mahr* agreement in question would be valid. Such a holding is explained by the ends/means perversity contradiction: the (Western) means available to legally transplant *mahr* cannot and, in fact, did not achieve that end.

Similarly in *M.(N.M.)*, the British Columbia court added the "amount of $51,250 on account of the Maher"[17] to an amount of $101,911 due by the husband upon the division of family assets *and* to an additional $2,000 monthly in spousal support. Confronted with the particularities of the Canadian legal culture, *mahr* faces resistance as it moves from an Islamic regime of "you get *mahr* and only *mahr* in cases of *talaq* and *faskh* divorce," to a family law system applying doctrines of equitable division in British Columbia. Muslim parties have to accept multiculturalism's insistence on viewing them in absolute and homogeneous terms in order to function properly in the legal pluralist paradigm. The complex, contradictory, and shifting *mahr*, which exists as a bargaining endowment "in the shadow of the law," does not easily travel. *Mahr*, once a "provision for a rainy day"[18] conceived by classical Islamic jurists as a "powerful limitation"[19] on the possibly capricious exercise of *talaq* divorce by the husband as well as a form of "compensation"[20] to the wife once the marriage has been dissolved, becomes under the legal pluralist approach a multiculturalist feature that supposedly reflects Muslim identity, yet in fact distorts it. Can the formal equality cases, which attempt to formally reject notions of "religious identity" and "recognition," achieve such a desired end through the means of contract law doctrine?

Mahr as Projecting a "Religious" Contractual Intention?

The ends/means perversity contradiction also affects the formal equality cases. In following a mandate *not* to culturally recognize *mahr*, the judicial narratives embracing formal equality have attempted to secularize *mahr* and to correctly and merely give effect to "the intention of the parties." Yet the contract law doctrinal analysis, *as applied* to the specific context of *mahr* (e.g., Were the parties capable of contracting *mahr*? Was there a "meeting of the minds" between the two parties regarding prompt and deferred *mahr*? Was there consideration, even in cases where no amount was specified [*mahr al-mithl*]?), has carried a religious intention into the law, and in effect, although pretending not to, courts have opened the door to the existence of this "contractual/religious" intention of the parties.

Aziz, *Odatalla*, and *Akileh* have all denied this perverse relationship between means and ends. In fact, the three American decisions all insist on the fact that the religious character of *mahr* is irrelevant: "Why should a contract for the promise to pay money be less of a contract just because it was entered into at the time of an Islamic marriage ceremony?"[21] asks *Odatalla*. "Its secular terms are enforceable as a contractual obligation, notwithstanding that it was entered into as part of a religious ceremony,"[22] responds *Aziz*. After all, suggests *Akileh*, the *mahr* "agreement was an antenuptial contract."[23] Under the formal equality approach, secular *mahr* becomes an antenuptial agreement immediately enforceable as long as the conditions of contract law doctrine are met. The irony lies in the fact that, in interpreting *mahr*, the the secular promise to pay money in the form of an antenuptial agreement can only be understood, contractually, contextually, by referring to the religious intentions of the Muslim parties. By *a priori* rejecting the pertinence of the Islamic shadow behind which husband and wife negotiate, bargain and determine *mahr* and its amount, courts have paradoxically refused an appreciation of contract law that would account for the parties' particular, peculiar private ordering regime. What is blocked from view by the ends/means perversity contradiction in these cases?

In this apparent refusal by the courts to explore the religious role of contracts in the social order, the formal equality gaze in *Aziz*, *Odatalla*, and *Akileh* projected *mahr*-as-contract, but could not observe *mahr*-as-status: the complexity of "the will of the parties" under Islamic law. The fact that *mahr* was possibly understood by Mr. Aziz or Ms. Odatalla as being enforceable under a *talaq* or *faskh* divorce, but not so under a *khul* divorce, has been buried from the discourse of secular *mahr*. *Mahr* is portrayed under Islamic family law as a "mark of respect for the wife,"[24] a sign of "honour to the bride,"[25] a "free gift by the husband,"[26] "a manifestation of his love for the wife,"[27] and a symbol of the "prestige of the marriage contract."[28] But the primary effect of a deferred *mahr* during marriage is to delineate a bargaining structure that exists in the shadow of the law, one that hides and preserves a capital in the event of *some* forms of divorce or of death. The formal equality approach rather projects and imposes a liberal "consent" to a contractual obligation that did not necessarily originate in the intention of the (Muslim) parties themselves: in *Aziz*, *Odatalla*, and *Akileh*, *mahr* is dissociated from the Islamic social and legal meaning to which it was once attached and becomes enforceable in *all* cases (*talaq*/*khul*/*faskh*), so long as "the neutral principles of law"[29] are met and respected. These cases illustrate the perverse relationship between ends and means: the contradiction seems irresolvable. The next section investigates whether the Muslim parties involved in the interpretation and adjudication of *mahr* perform, in strategic and opposing terms, the ends/means perversity contradiction.

The Performance of the Contradiction by the Parties Themselves: Holmes's "Bad Man" and "Bad Woman"

In Holmes's "The Path of the Law,"[30] the legal system is depicted as "an instrument . . . of business" whose "prophecies" the lawyer attempts to rigorously predict and master. If adjudication is about judges' "duty of weighing considerations of social advantage," parties must know not only the adequate rules and precedents but also "the relative worth and importance of competing considerations" that are likely to affect judges. Emphasizing the existence of battles between individuals or/and groups, Holmes develops the famous "bad man" theory of the law, the individual who cares only about the material (and not the ethical) consequences of his act.[31]

Holmes's predictive theory of law and his advocacy of the bad-man perspective constitute powerful strategies undermining the misleading picture of law. In this section, I will add another internal dimension to the ends/means perversity contradiction: the agency and active role of the Muslim parties themselves in relation to each other, as well as in relation to the Western court. Because of their individual motives, the husband and wife are continually speaking both the mandate to recognize and the mandate not to recognize. They advocate or oppose the judicial enforcement of *mahr* depending on how their interests would be affected by its recognition. In the following two subsections, I will inquire into whether the Muslim husband arguing for the non-enforcement of *mahr* mainly on religious grounds is the equivalent of

Holmes's "bad man" and, incidentally, whether the Muslim wife arguing for the enforcement of *mahr* mainly on secular grounds personifies a Holmesian "bad woman."

The Muslim (Religious/Secular) Husband as the Bad Man? In most of the matrimonial disputes analyzed in this essay, Muslim parties made contradictory claims about Islam and the role of religion in a secular, Western state more generally. The Muslim husband typically argued that the obligations imposed by *mahr* arise solely from religious/Islamic law and can therefore be interpreted only by reference to religious dogma. Consequently, *mahr* is a matter touching upon purely religious doctrine that can be enforced only by religious authorities — its enforcement by a civil court would violate the principle of the separation of church and state, *laïcité*, etc. It is, quite ironically, *in the name of religion* that the Muslim husband argued for the non-enforcement of *mahr* — an outcome that would coercively disengage his financial responsibility. Such was the argumentation of the husband in *M.(N.M.)*,[32] *Kaddoura*,[33] *Aziz*,[34] and *Odatalla*.[35] At times, however, the prediction of economic sanctions will dictate to the Muslim husband to borrow from the secular rhetoric. How, if at all, did the cases on the adjudication of *mahr* speak to issues that interested Holmes?

Holmes's "bad man" theory offers interesting analytical insights into *Odatalla*, our 2002 New Jersey decision. With an apparent cynicism, Mr. Odatalla asked the court *not* to enforce *mahr* — alleging that, according to his religious faith, *mahr* could only be decided by an Islamic authority[36] — but, on the same account, requested "alimony and equitable distribution of certain jewelry, furniture, wedding gifts and marital debt,"[37] demands that he could *not* have made under Islamic family law. Mr. Odatalla's adjudicative strategy is that of Holmes's "bad man" in that he uses law as a strategy to gain the most advantageous economic outcomes and material consequences while undermining the importance of religious law (Holmes's morality).

In caring only about what the law might *do* to him, not what it *is* abstractly for him, Mr. Odatalla presented his argument to the court in such a way that he would be compelled to pay *the least* and consequently gain *the most*. Let us imagine his strategy assessment in this situation. Mr. Odatalla considered the possible, predictable sanctions that the law might impose on him. The recognition/non-recognition of Islam as a religion, of him as a believer, and of *mahr* as an Islamic institution was crucial in his calculation. Will the mandate to recognize pay off? he asked himself. Surely not — *mahr* might be declared unenforceable on the basis of the separation of church and state, but he might *also* be prevented from enjoying the equitable dissolution of family assets. Will the mandate not to recognize pay off? he may have further inquired. Surely not — he might be ordered to pay the sum of $10,000 as *mahr* on the basis of contractual antenuptial agreement doctrine *on top of* the division of family property. Considering these complex and highly material predictions, Mr. Odatalla assumed an efficient hybrid position, one in which he would concurrently wear the religious/secular hat, that is, the mandate to recognize/not to recognize: the non-enforcement of *mahr*, for religious reasons; and "alimony and equitable distribution of certain jewelry, furniture, wedding gifts and marital debt," on secular grounds. This represents, he probably thought, the maximization of outcomes.

In *Amlani*,[38] the "bad man" strategy served as a focus of inquiry in a context of rules re-created by the parties themselves prior to the adjudication of *mahr*. In 2000, Mr. Amlani asked the British Columbia Supreme Court for a declaration acknowledging that the marriage contract made during the religious wedding ceremony did not constitute a "marriage agreement" under s.61 of the Family Relations Act. Consequently, *mahr* should not be enforced. The marriage contract however specified that Mr. Amlani would "pay the agreed sum of money by way of Maher to my said wife. It shall be *in addition and without prejudice* to and not in substitution of all of my obligations provided for by the laws of the land."[39] Thus removed and repositioned in British Columbia, *mahr* is named by the husband himself as a different and surprising institution compared to what it is under Islamic family law, its native place of departure. In anticipation of (Western) adjudication, *mahr* is no longer attached to a regime of *talaq/khul/faskh* divorce. The transfer has already occurred across jurisdictions: *mahr* embraces the complexity and perversity of flirting with the "laws of the land." It adds *itself* to a well-established family law regime, one of no-fault divorce and equitable division of family assets. It accepts to define itself as an exceptional penalty for the husband; in this particular case, *mahr* becomes a debt of $51,000 *added* to the equitable division of family property. Along the road to Western liberal states, *mahr* lost its coherence in relation to the law of origin, Islamic family law.

Ironically, against this background of previous legal transplanting, Mr. Amlani presented himself to court as a religious man, claiming the existence of a purely religious *mahr*. The relationship between "Islamic law" — you will get *mahr* and only *mahr* if *I* divorce you — and "Canadian law" — *you* can divorce me *and* get *mahr and* benefit from the division of property — clearly delineates to the "bad man" the least profitable "path of the law." Indeed, Mr. Amlani chose the path that paid off the most for him: Islamic law divorced from the "laws of the land." Such a regime, in the specific circumstances of the case, would have meant that Mr. Amlani was required to pay zero. This is so because his wife embarked on what Islamic law classifies as a *khul* divorce, and she should therefore waive $51,000 and not claim alimony or division of property. Mr. Amlani thus argued that "the Mehr amount is a traditional custom of Muslim law that was intended to provide financial compensation for a wife and children in the event of a marriage break-up. Muslim religious law did not allow a wife to pursue support for herself and any children, nor any rights to property."[40]

The court rejected this sudden redesign, regarded as profoundly lacking in good faith.[41] Not only did Mr. Amlani virtually change his reading of the original contract for his personal, economic benefit, but he asked the court to judge his case on the rule that none of the "laws of the land" applied. Could the court reproduce the practical consciousness of Islamic *mahr*? Could it crystallize the cultural codes of conduct that surround Islamic *mahr*? Could it do so *despite* the marriage contract, as if it were somehow expressing false consciousness? In the eyes of the court, such an interpretation cannot be sustained: "Ms. Hirani has civil remedies available to her. If the payment of the Maher/Mehr Amount only applied in the absence of civil remedies, as suggested by Mr. Amlani in his Examination for Discovery, there would have been no reason for these parties to have entered into the Marriage Contract."[42]

Until now, only instances where the Muslim husband has performed Holmes's "bad man" have been analyzed. Can we imagine the Muslim wife behaving in the same fashion, alternatively drawing upon and occasionally transcending the secular/religious performance? Can the Muslim wife, in asking for the enforcement of *mahr* in Western courts, constitute a Holmesian "bad woman"?

The Muslim (Secular/Religious) Wife as the Bad Woman? In most of the matrimonial disputes studied in this essay, the Muslim wife claimed that nothing in law or public policy prevents judicial recognition and enforcement of the secular terms of *mahr*. After all, *mahr* is a contractual matter. It should be enforced and distributed to her. This was the argumentation put before the court in *M.(N.M.)*,[43] *Kaddoura*,[44] *Aziz*,[45] and *Odatalla*.[46] At times, however, in response to the Islamic argument that she should waive *mahr* because she is the one asking for divorce (*khul* divorce),[47] the Muslim wife borrowed the religious hat and presented a profoundly surprising description and analysis of Islamic law. To illustrate this point, the examples of *Akileh*,[48] *Dajani*,[49] *M.H.D. v. E.A.*,[50] *Arrêt de la Cour d'appel de Douai*,[51] and *Vladi*[52] are examined.

The key to understanding the performance of the "bad woman" is to measure the *predicted* economic gains and losses of advocating the enforcement or the non-enforcement of *mahr* in a given situation, in relation to both Islamic family law and Western law. In response to the "waiver rule" of *khul mahr*, the "bad woman" has two options: either pretend that the waiver rule is *not* part of Islamic family law (the religious route), or suggest that the waiver rule is so discriminatory that it should be regarded as inherently contrary to "public order" in relation to international private law rules (the secular route). I will address these options in order.

In *Akileh* and *Dajani*, the Muslim wife offered a unique and fascinating dimension of the legal transplantation of *mahr*, one that entirely disregards Islamic theory. In *Akileh*, the wife testified that a Muslim woman's right to receive the postponed portion of *mahr* was "absolute and not affected by the cause of a divorce" and suggested "the exception was that a wife would forfeit the dowry if she cheated on her husband."[53] She testified she was unaware of any other instance where deferred *mahr* would be forfeited. Moreover, the wife's father also testified that deferred *mahr* was "an absolute right of a wife to request from the husband whenever she wished and especially in the event of divorce."[54] Similarly in *Dajani*, the Muslim wife claimed she was entitled to *mahr* upon her husband's death or dissolution of the marriage — notwithstanding the form of divorce. Her expert on the subject was "an attorney admitted to practice in California and Egypt who testified the dowry provided for a cash payment to the wife in the event of death or dissolution of the marriage. In the latter case, the sum was due no matter which party initiated the dissolution proceedings."[55]

In *M.H.D. v. E.A.*, a Québec trial court decision, the Muslim wife embarked on a "secular" argumentation and convinced the court that Syrian Islamic law could not apply in Canada because its application would create a negative effect on Muslim wives availing themselves of the Divorce Act. The Muslim wife argued *khul mahr* as a legal institution violates substantive equality, in that it requires the Western state to punish a wife because *she* is the one initiating the divorce proceedings, an outcome that would not similarly apply to the husband. In the name of gender equality, which the conflict of laws held at the heart of the principle of *l'ordre public* ("public order"),[56] such discriminatory Islamic traditions should be formally and rigidly rejected by the host legal system, despite rules of international private law incorporating Syrian Islamic law: "With all due respect to the beliefs of the religious authority as well as to those of the husband, the court believes that such traditions, customs and doctrine put before us are not applicable to the wife, and that the court must consider the wedding present discussed above only with respect to the Québec Civil Code."[57] *Mahr* should therefore be viewed as a contractual donation.[58]

The same "public order" logic was successfully used by the Muslim wife in a 1976 French Court of Appeal decision[59], as well as in *Vladi v. Vladi,* a 1987 decision from Nova Scotia (Canada) in which the court refused to enforce *mahr* on the basis of "substantial justice." In *Vladi*, the court held: "To put it simply, I will not give effect to Iranian matrimonial law because it is archaic and repugnant to ideas of substantial justice in this province. (. . .) In Iran, a wife in the position of Mrs. Vladi would be entitled to minimal support and a nominal award in relation to a so-called 'mahr' or 'morning-gift.' Otherwise she would have no direct claim against assets standing in the name of her husband."[60]

In *M.H.D. v. E.A*, the route to the material maximization of outcomes implied the following claim on the part of the Muslim wife: the rejection of *khul mahr* (which amounts to zero), on the one hand, and the adoption of the equitable division of family patrimony *plus* the enforcement of *mahr* as a contractual donation, on the other. In *Arrêt de la Cour d'appel de Douai* and *Vladi*, the wives' strategies precisely produced this highly sympathetic economic result: conflict of laws rejected *khul mahr* (which amounts to zero), on the one hand, and adopted the equitable division of family patrimony, which in the case of *Vladi* meant a generous equalization payment of $246,500.[61]

Such an unusual view of Islamic family law in Western liberal courts (the non-enforcement of *khul mahr* attached only to circumstances of adultery;

the enforcement of *mahr* as an absolute right, thus denying the existence of the waiver rule; the rejection of *khul mahr* as inherently contrary to gender equality) certainly underlines the perverse relationship between means and ends. In what appears as the perfect equivalent of an attempt to materially obtain the most out of the interplay between Islamic law and Western law (desired end), the Muslim wife subversively re-created the scope of this comparative law encounter to *her* economic advantage (means). The distributive character of adjudication as applied to this specific example of *mahr* allows us to ask certain questions: Would the Muslim wife have performed the "bad woman" script had no money been connected to the postponed portion of *mahr?* Does the shift in where the enforcement should take place tell us something about how religious the woman is? Does it matter to us that she might be strategically shaping her religiosity to match a maximal outcome? Do we care whether she is really a believer and that we know that we can't know? Do we consider the possibility, as she insists on the big M (her as a Muslim; us as multiculturalists), that she only pretends to be devoted to Allah in order to get a devastating public revenge (e.g., make her husband pay, for instance, because he left her for her best friend; humiliating him in obtaining a secular *mahr* to which they had never agreed)?

The ends/means perversity contradiction has produced the "impossibility of legal transplants"[62] in relation to the legal pluralist cases, the unavoidability of a "religious/contractual" intention in relation to the formal equality cases, and the strategic postures of the "bad" (religious/secular) Muslim husband as well as the "bad" (secular/religious) Muslim wife in relation to legal pluralism and formal equality.

Mahr as Bonus and Penalty

In this section, I perform a distributive shift to argue that in the social life of Islamic marriages, *mahr* is not unitary and autonomous but rather a functional institution that produces a series of inconsistent characteristics that we can study. Through this distributive reading of *mahr*, my hope is to offer a narrative concerned primarily with the social effects created by the judiciary as it claims to merely translate *mahr* according to ideological preferences when in fact it produces *mahr* as bonus or penalty. In an attempt to underline the complexity of *mahr* as it moves from ideology to contradictions, I have deconstructed the "Muslim woman reacting to *mahr*" into many conflicting players, situated in a continuum spectrum along the bonus/penalty lines. In every subsection, I will present Leila in relation to her specific background rules and norms and situate how *mahr* could be employed and deployed by her in strategic terms given that location. These perspectives are fictional, although I drew partly upon existing characters from autobiographical books,[63] feminist manifestos,[64] best-selling books,[65] and so on. In so doing, I meant to show that my Leilas are in some ways connected to real people out there in the world. All of these scripts also reflect, directly or indirectly, the legal reasoning or outcome of real cases I have encountered and studied in my research.

THE ENFORCEMENT OF *MAHR*

Mahr as Penalty for Wife and Bonus for Husband: Leila, the German-Egyptian "Foreign Bride"

Leila[66] has been married to Samir for fifteen years. Although of Egyptian origin and citizenship, she lives in Kreuzberg, the Turkish Muslim suburb of Berlin. She rarely goes out and makes contact with her German neighbours more hesitantly than do her sons and her husband. At home, men often gather to talk politics, the war in Afghanistan, the disastrous state of Iraq, the integration of Turkey into the European Union, while women cook, assist, clean — a mute shadow, outsiders. In recent years, Leila has been exposed to the new wave of feminist critiques coming from German women of Muslim background, such as Seyran Ateş' "Great Journey into Fire" and Necla Kelek's "The Foreign Bride."[67] In their work, they both address the everyday violence of arranged marriages as well as the oppressive and sexist behavior of Muslim men in Germany. Leila was powerfully seduced by their critique and the promising and assertive voice they developed. She saw herself in the eyes of the "Foreign Bride," this young Muslim woman imported to Germany as a bride, who led a fully insular and subservient life as a wife and a mother. This book represented an ultimatum for Leila: she would either embrace women's rights (and other Western, German conceptions of freedom) or remain forever "a foreign bride" whose equality is constantly being jeopardized. Leila opted for the former. She left Samir, her sons, her home — with perfect irresponsibility.[68]

While contemplating divorce, Leila was obsessed by the memory of her sister in Egypt, Fatima, who had been left financially destitute after obtaining a *khul* divorce. Fatima's husband had been emotionally abusive to her, but not having the financial resources to prove the abuse in a *faskh* divorce, Fatima had opted for the quicker, less expensive *khul* divorce. The court ruled that Fatima lost the right to seek any maintenance or deferred *mahr* from her husband and she had to repay the prompt *mahr* she had received. Even now, five years later, Fatima was still heavily indebted to her ex-husband. She worked twelve hours a day as a cleaner, just to make payments on the debt and to maintain a small apartment for herself and her daughter in Cairo.

Despite Fatima's painful experience, Leila wasn't worried about suffering the same fate as her sister because she was seeking a divorce in Germany, where divorce law, she had been told, was much more favorable toward women. Faced with the impossibility of surviving with very limited economic resources, Leila reached the courthouse confident that state alimony and division-of-property laws in Germany would guarantee her generous benefits. How *wrong* were her predictions! Leila soon realized that, as a non-German citizen, Egyptian Islamic law would apply to her case. Since she had no claim under Egyptian law at the time to post-divorce alimony or to her share of the profits accruing to the marital property, the court held that *mahr* constituted a substitute for post-divorce maintenance and division of the surplus of marital profits. Furthermore, because Leila was the one seeking the divorce, the court held that she had given up her right to deferred *mahr* and was obligated to pay back the prompt *mahr* she had been given at her wedding.

Leila felt trapped in a complex and seemingly incomprehensible reality. Was Leila fooled into thinking that she, too, could embrace German conceptions of freedom, as the book so delightfully suggested? Is Leila forever condemned, by virtue of the application of private international law rules in Germany, of representing this tragic "Foreign Bride" that she so hoped to escape?

Mahr as Penalty for Husband and Bonus for Wife: Leila, the Canadian-Pakistani Journalist Writing as a Lesbian Refusenik

This subsection presents a reading of Leila[69] asserting herself as a lesbian refusenik living in British Columbia, Canada: "The good news is I knew I lived in a part of the world that permitted me to explore. Thanks to the freedom afforded me in the West — to think, search, speak, exchange, discuss, challenge, be challenged, and rethink — I was poised to judge my religion in a light that I couldn't have possibly conceived in the parochial Muslim microcosm of the madressa."[70] Leila married Samir at the age of eighteen years old, and he repudiated her three years later, as soon as she made her sexual preferences known to him: "I'm openly lesbian. I choose to be 'out' because, having matured in a miserable household under a father who despised joy, I'm not about to sabotage the consensual love that offers me joy as an adult. I met my first girlfriend in my twenties and, weeks afterwards, told my mother about the relationship."[71] Leila has infinite gratitude toward Canadian society, where one can become a lesbian and even marry, write radical and provocative essays against Islam,[72] and choose an alternative path of life against the wishes of one's parents.

Leila gets furious with proponents of multiculturalism who romanticize Islam and excuse brutality as a "cultural feature": "I have to be honest with you. Islam is on very thin ice with me. I'm hanging on by my fingernails, in anxiety over what's coming next from the self-appointed ambassadors of Allah. . . . When I speak publicly about our failings, the very Muslims who detect stereotyping at every turn label me as a sell-out. A sellout to what? To moral clarity? To common decency? To civilization? Yes, I'm blunt. You're just going to have to get used to it."[73] Leila is angry, embarrassed at the fact that she was once "in the closet," married to Samir, sleeping next to Samir, faking with Samir, because one cannot be "a Muslim and a Lesbian": "You may wonder who I am to talk to you this way. I am a Muslim Refusenik. That doesn't mean that I refuse to be a Muslim; it simply means I refuse to join an army of automatons in the name of Allah."[74] Leila is very angry. She decides to ask the secular court for the enforcement of *mahr*, in the amount of $50,000, as a calculated revenge. Given that "the parties chose to marry within the Muslim tradition,"[75] knowing "full well that provision for Maher was a condition of so doing,"[76] the court chooses to enforce *mahr.* Leila is happy. But something new and quite surprising will make Leila even happier: not only is *mahr* culturally recognized and financially due to her, but it is added to an amount of $37,747.17 owed by Samir to Leila as a result of the division of family assets. Leila will thus receive $87,747.17 on that very special day, an exceptional and costly penalty for Samir.

Mahr as Penalty for Wife and Bonus for Husband: Leila, the American "Terrorist" Convicted under the Patriot Act

On September 25, 2001, Leila[77] was arrested and detained on the basis of allegations that she constituted a threat to the security of the United States, by reason of her involvement in terrorist activities linked to Al-Qaeda. She was convicted soon after under the Patriot Act. Having recently married Samir, whom she had met a few months before being arrested, Leila remains in detention. In response to these unfounded suspicions linking her to terrorist groups, Leila finds peace in reading the Koran and in writing letters to Samir, her soul mate. For her, *mahr* symbolizes the beauty and purity of Samir's love, like "a bone in the upper part of the breast, or gristles of the ribs; or something presentable as a gift like a pearl."[78] Leila is a romantic. Last week, she received a letter informing her that Samir wishes to divorce her religiously, with no further explanation. Samir came on Sunday for his weekly visit and irrevocably pronounced the three *talaq*. Leila was repudiated. Heartbroken, she asked a Californian lawyer to represent her in a claim for the enforcement of deferred *mahr*, a symbolic amount of $1700. She was informed that the court could not enforce *mahr*. It held that the marriage contract must be considered as one designed to facilitate divorce, because with the exception of prompt *mahr* "the wife was not entitled to receive any of the agreed upon sum unless the marriage was dissolved or husband died. The contract clearly provided for wife to profit by divorce, and it cannot be enforced by a California court."[79] Leila is perplexed. How can *mahr* provide *her* to profit from divorce? And how can it *clearly* do so? It is Samir who religiously divorced her! The least she can ask for is the enforcement of deferred *mahr*, a condition of issuing *talaq* in the first place. By distorting *mahr*'s function, the court penalized Leila.

Mahr as Penalty for Husband and Bonus for Wife: Leila, the French Member of Ni Putes Ni Soumises

To envision the unenforceability of *mahr* as a penalty for the husband and a bonus for the wife, imagine Leila[80] who is attempting to break her marriage in order to escape a hostile domestic environment. At age nineteen, Leila could have never guessed where life would take her when she married in Malaysia

Samir, a family friend. At the time of the wedding, Leila was proud that she had garnered both a fairly high amount of *mas kahwin* (*mahr*) as a young, unmarried woman, as well as an additional substantial amount of promised *pemberian* (a customary form of dowry). The very idea of divorce seemed unthinkable at the time.

Leila and Samir moved to France seven years later so that Samir could pursue an advanced engineering degree. Bored with her life as a housewife, Leila decided to take night courses to become a secretary. She excelled in her course and blossomed in her new job working for a women's organization. Samir became more and more jealous and possessive after Leila started working. His physical abuse escalated and he started to make degrading remarks on how she became a "Western slut." Samir would also make persistent comments, especially in the presence of her immediate and extended family, about the fact that she has been "brainwashed" by the French corrupted secular society.

He was particularly incensed that Leila had been introduced by a colleague to the organization Ni Putes Ni Soumises (Neither Whores Nor Slaves),[81] a French feminist movement founded in 2002, which had already secured the recognition of the French press and parliament. With ambivalence at first (the slogan used by the movement is meant both to shock and mobilize), she became with time an active member and an engaged activist. She organized several conferences and publicly shared her experience of suffering with other Muslim women, especially those from her native Malaysia. In the home and out in the streets, she was no longer afraid. Leila knew too well that Samir would never pronounce the three *talaq*, and she did not even attempt to negotiate a *khul* divorce. One day, she simply walked away and never came back. She decided to reach the French court system, though, to claim the unenforceability of *mahr*. She argued that, precisely because she is "neither a whore nor a slave," she should never have been submitted to the unequal and degrading treatment that the promise of *mas kahwin* and *pemberian* represents. Undoubtedly, these foreign institutions should be declared contrary to *l'ordre public français* (French public order)! Leila won her case with pride.[82] Considering the *mas kahwin* and *pemberian* payments together, the court relied on conflict of laws principles to reject the application of *mahr* as against "public order," on the one hand, and apply Western equity standards, on the other, which meant a generous amount of $253,000 for Leila instead of $0 under Islamic family law.

Conclusion

While liberalism is one possible way of framing emancipatory claims made by minorities in Western societies, it has become, I have argued, the dominant approach underlying the way the legal system in Western liberal states deals with claims made by Muslims in general and Muslim women in particular. Liberalism, in its encounter with *mahr*, has offered the following spectrum of positions: the legal pluralist approach, the formal equality approach, and the substantive equality approach. These approaches all share some problematic underpinning assumptions: (1) they portray judges as "independent" actors, denying strategic behavior in achieving outcomes; (2) they deny ideology so as to present legal doctrine as a coherent, logical, and consistent body of knowledge; and (3) they pretend that the legal doctrine chosen to adjudicate *mahr* generates predictable outcomes. However, as this essay has demonstrated, liberal ideologies hide behind judicial lawmaking, yet *inconsistently* generate the enforcement or non-enforcement of *mahr* — subverting the very rule of law behind which they operate.

In this chapter, I have explored *mahr*'s internal and external pluralism from its place of departure under Islamic family law to its place of arrival under Western secular law. I have analyzed *mahr* as "adjudication" and "reception" by the Western liberal court, without inquiring into its subjective significance for the Muslim woman involved. I have also performed a legal realist and distributive shift to follow the way *mahr* operates in the distribution of power and desire between the Muslim husband and the Muslim wife, as well as in the constitution of their respective identities through law. In a fictional style that borrowed from concrete decisions, I have argued that *mahr* is disciplinary in that it incorporates norms and rules regarding the family, both in relation to the Islamic law regime as well as in relation to the Western legal system. Those function as the rules of the game in the conflict between the Muslim husband and the Muslim wife — before, during, and after the concrete adjudication of *mahr*.

In this essay, I attempted to bring back into focus what has been hidden by the adjudicative discourse of *mahr* as "recognition," as "equality," and as "fairness." My four Leilas, broken down into several subcategories, such as the "secular Muslim woman," the "religious feminist Muslim woman," the "rich professional Muslim woman," and "the poor head-of-household Muslim woman," have served to demonstrate that the legal enforcement of *mahr* as a legal rule can be deemed to have asymmetric economic effects among different groups of women. For one Leila, the enforcement of *mahr* is a bonus; for the other, it is a penalty. For a third one, the unenforceability of *mahr* is a penalty; for another one, it is a bonus. Every short script has put Leila's dilemma and negotiating strategies into different contexts, ranging from subversive uses of *mahr* as a moral victory, a personal revenge, or an act of liberation. Such complex itinerary travels along with *mahr* and reminds us too well that real women with real lives develop their own ways of flirting with God in Western secular courts. Can the structural nature of the law register this complexity; reproduce it?

Notes

This chapter was selected as the 2009 best law review article by the Québec Bar Foundation's legal contest prize. It was previously published in the *International Journal of Law, Policy and the Family* (2010) 24(1): 67–94 (©2010 Oxford University Press) and is reprinted here by permission of the publisher.

1. J. L. Esposito, with N. J. DeLong-Bas, *Women in Muslim Family Law* (Syracuse: Syracuse University Press, 2001), 23.

2. Pascale Fournier, "In the (Canadian) Shadow of Islamic Law: Translating *Mahr* as a Bargaining Endowment," *Osgoode Hall Law Journal* 44, no.4 (2006): 649–77.

3. Dawoud Sudqi El Alami and Doreen Hinchcliffe, *Islamic Marriage and Divorce Laws of the Arab World* (London: Kluwer Law International, 1996), 22.

4. A. A. A. Fyzee, *Outlines of Muhammadan Law* (Delhi: Oxford University Press, 1974), 133; Joseph Schacht, *An Introduction to Islamic Law* (Oxford: Clarendon Press, 1982), 167; N. J. Coulson, *A History of Islamic Law* (Edinburgh: University Press, 1964), 207; Esposito and DeLong-Bas, *Women in Muslim Family Law*, 36.

5. Muhammad Abu Zahra, "Family Law," in *Law in the Middle East*, ed. M. Khadduri and H. J. Liebesny (Washington, D.C.: The Middle East Institute, 1955), 140–41.

6. Judith Tucker, *Women in Nineteenth-Century Egypt* (Cambridge: Cambridge University Press, 1985), 54.

7. El Alami and Hinchcliffe, *Islamic Marriage and Divorce Laws of the Arab World*, 29.

8. For a detailed analysis of how legal pluralism, formal equality, and substantive equality play out in the enforcement of *mahr*, see Pascale Fournier, "Transit and Translation: Islamic Legal Transplants in North America and Western Europe," *Journal of Comparative Law* 4, no.1 (2009): 1–38.

9. In this section, I use the term "outcome" to refer to the case ruling in a given decision.

10. See Duncan Kennedy, *A Critique of Adjudication: Fin de Siècle* (Cambridge, Mass.: Harvard University Press, 1997).

11. David Pearl and Werner Menski, *Muslim Family Law* (London: Sweet and Maxwell, 998), 180.

12. Family Law Act, R.S.O. 1990, c.F.3 (ca.), part 1, s. 52(1).

13. Kaddoura v. Hammoud, [1998] O.J. No. 5054, 44 R.F.L. (4th) 228, 168 D.L.R. (4th) 503, 1998 Carswell Ont 4747, 83 O.T.C. 30 (Ont. Gen. Div.) at para. 26.

14. *Kaddoura*, above n. 13, at para. 25.

15. Nathoo v. Nathoo, [1996] B.C.J. No. 2720 (S.C.) (British Columbia Supreme Court).

16. M.(N.M.) v. M.(N.S.), 2004 CarswellBC 688; 2004 BCSC 346, 26 B.C.L.R. (4th) 80 (British Columbia Supreme Court).

17. *M.(N.M.)*, above n. 16, at para. 31.

18. Fyzee, *Outlines of Muhammadan Law*, 133.

19. Schacht, *An Introduction to Islamic Law*, 167.

20. Esposito and DeLong-Bas, *Women in Muslim Family Law*, 35.

21. Odatalla v. Odatalla, 810 A.2d 93, 309 (N.J. Super. Ct. Ch. Div. 2002).

22. Aziz v. Aziz, 127 Misc.2d 1013, 1013, 488 N.Y.S.2d 123 (Sup.Ct.1985).

23. Akileh v. Elchahal, 666 So.2d 246, 248 (Fla. Ct. App. 1996).

24. Pearl and Menski, *Muslim Family Law*, 179.

25. M. A. Wani, *The Islamic Law on Maintenance of Women, Children, Parents and Other Relative: Classical Principles and Modern Legislations in India and Muslim Countries* (Noonamy, Kashmir: Upright Study Home, 1995), 193.

26. Abdur Rahman I. Doi, *Shari'ah: The Islamic Law* (London: Ta Ha Publishers, 1984), 159.

27. Wani, *The Islamic Law on Maintenance*, 193.

28. Jamal J. Nasir, *The Status of Women under Islamic Law and Under Modern Islamic Legislation* (London: Graham & Trotman, 1994), 43.

29. See also Schwartz v. Schwartz, 153 Misc.2d 789, 583 N.Y.S.2d 716, 718 (Sup. Ct.1992).

30. Oliver Wendel Holmes, "The Path of the Law" (1897), in *American Legal Realism*, ed. William W. Fisher III, Morton J. Horwitz, and Thomas A. Reed (New York: Oxford University Press, 1993).

31. Ibid., 17.

32. *M.(N.M.)*, above n. 16.

33. *Kaddoura*, above n. 13.

34. *Aziz*, above n. 22

35. *Odatalla*, above n. 21.

36. *Odatalla*, above n. 21, at 95.

37. *Odatalla*, above n. 21, at 94.

38. Amlani v. Hirani, 2000 CarswellBC 2663.

39. *Amlani*, above n. 27, at para. 30 (the emphasis is mine).

40. *Amlani*, above n. 27, at para. 28.

41. *Amlani*, above n. 27, at para. 30.

42. *Amlani*, above n. 27, at para. 31.

43. *M.(N.M.*), above n. 16.

44. *Kaddoura*, above n. 13.

45. *Aziz*, above n. 22.

46. *Odatalla*, above n. 21.

47. *Mahr* is attached to a wider regime of Islamic family law dictating in which cases it will be enforced: under a *talaq* or *faskh* divorce, but not so under a *khul* divorce.

48. *Akileh*, above n. 23.

49. In re Marriage of Dajani, 204 Cal.App.3d 1387 (1988).

50. M.H.D. v. E.A, Droit de la famille — 1466, Québec Court of Appeal, 23 Septembre 1991, No 500–09–001296–896.

51. Arrêt de la Cour d'appel de Douai, January 8, 1976: N. 76–11–613.

52. Vladi v. Vladi, Nova Scotia Supreme Court, Trial Division, 1987 CarswellNS 72, 7 R.F.L. (3d) 337, 79 N.S.R. (2d) 356, 196 A.P.R. 356, 39 D.L.R. (4th) 563.

53. *Akileh*, above n. 23.

54. *Akileh*, above n. 23.

55. In re Marriage of Dajani, above n. 48.

56. *M.H.D.*, above n. 32, at para. 49.

57. *M.H.D.*, above n. 32, at para. 49 (translation by author).

58. In *M.H.D.*, the court ruled that gender equity principles should govern. Thus, the court enforced *mahr* as a simple donation despite the *khul* divorce.

59. *Douai*, above n. 51.

60. *Vladi*, above n. 52, at paras. 30 and 11.

61. *Vladi,* above n. 52, at paras. 46 and 70.

62. I borrow this expression from Pierre Legrand. Although I am sympathetic to the "law and society" perspective adopted by Legrand, my approach rejects the idea of an external, coherent, and real "culture," "society," or "religion" that exists in corresponding features to law. Pierre Legrand, "The Impossibility of Legal Transplants," *Maastricht Journal of European and Comparative Law* 4 (1997): 111.

63. See below, "Leila, the Canadian-Pakistani Journalist Writing as a Lesbian Refusenik."

64. See below, "Leila, the French Member of Ni Putes Ni Soumises."

65. See below, "Leila, the German-Egyptian 'Foreign Bride.'"

66. This script is partly based on *OLG Bremen*, FamRZ 1980, 606, a 1980 German decision from the Higher Regional Court of Bremen, and Necla Kelek, *Die fremde Braut: Ein Bericht aus dem Inneren des türkischen Lebens in Deutschland* (The Foreign Bride: A Report from the Inside of Turkish life in Germany) (Cologne: Kiepenheuer & Witsch, 2005).

67. In her book, Kelek strongly criticizes both the so-called fundamentalist Muslim society, for perpetuating a culture of female slavery, and the liberal German society, which in her opinion has adopted a hands-off approach based on tolerance.

68. I borrow this expression from Ralph Ellison's *Invisible Man* (New York: Random House, 1952), in which he argued that irresponsibility is, for subordinated groups, a consequence of their invisibility.

69. This script is partly based on Irshad Manji's autobiographical book *The Trouble with Islam: A Muslim's Call for Reform in her Faith* (New York: St. Martin's Press, 2003), an international best seller, which has been published in numerous countries (see http://www.muslim-refusenik.com). However, many of the facts that I have included in this story are purely fictional, including a first marriage with a man, and should not be interpreted as reflecting the life of Irshad Manji. I chose this perspective because I believe it does capture some of the anger of some Muslims who consider themselves as "Muslim refuseniks." I have also incorporated the outcome of two Canadian cases, namely *Nathoo*, above n. 15, and *M.(N.M.)*, above n. 16.

70. Manji, *The Trouble with Islam*, 19.

71. Ibid., 21.

72. Ibid., 35.

73. Ibid., 1.

74. Ibid., 3.

75. *Nathoo*, above n. 15, at para. 24.

76. *Nathoo*, above n. 15, at para. 24.

77. This script is partly based on In re Marriage of Dajani, above n. 48, an American appellate decision from California.

78. Wani, *The Islamic Law on Maintenance.*

79. In re Marriage of Dajani, above n. 49.

80. This script is partly based on the following French and Canadian decisions: *Douai*, above n. 51; and *Vladi,* above n. 52.

81. The French organization Ni Putes Ni Soumises has become a nationwide force in France. The movement expresses its anger at the "tolerance" of French society toward violence and stigmatization suffered by Muslim women in the name of Islamic tradition in the neglected French suburbs (http://www.niputesni soumises.com).

82. I refer specifically here to *Douai*, above n. 51.

RASHIDA MANJOO

Chapter Six Muslim Family Law in South Africa Conflating the Right to Religion with the Privileging of Religion?

Introduction

It is commonly accepted that the arena of family law is a tension-filled one; that the equality and nondiscrimination rights of women are violated through laws, policies, and practices; that despite both international and domestic obligations in regard to equality and nondiscrimination, impunity in this regard is the norm rather than the exception. The focus of this chapter will be limited to briefly highlighting issues around sex and gender equality and nondiscrimination, and religious freedom rights broadly manifested in laws, policies, and practices in South Africa, in relation to the Muslim community.

Bringing personal status laws into conformity with international and constitutional equal rights provisions is an imperative for the protection of women's equality and nondiscrimination rights. Many countries have family law systems, whether based on religion or custom, that violate the rights of individuals. Some states use the right of religious freedom to defend gender-based discrimination in the area of family law, while other states are reluctant to intervene, due to deferential attitudes in the area of religion (they avoid entanglement with religion). This is common among both states that implement religious laws and states that do not. In the struggle for equality and nondiscrimination rights, the right of freedom of religion very often overrides women's equality rights.

The incorporation of family laws can occur through multiple legal systems — for example, through a civil law system that codifies religious laws, through the reliance on uncodified laws that emanate from religious texts and practices, or through secular laws of marriage and divorce. The institutionalization of family laws can take place through secular courts, through religious tribunals or courts, or through both forums having concurrent and, very often, hierarchical jurisdictions.

The inclusion of the right of freedom of religion in many constitutions is usually not interpreted in the broader terms of equality and nondiscrimination, that is, in terms of both nondiscrimination against the religion/religious institutions and nondiscrimination by the religion/religious institutions. Thus the equitable treatment of other religious and belief systems and also the nondiscriminatory and equal treatment of women are violated through the use of the freedom of religion right. This is usually done through the state endorsement of a particular religion, the inequitable treatment of religions, or a state claiming exemption from the equality guarantee on the basis of freedom of religion. Religious exemptions from general laws may amount to preferential treatment and may also clash with the right to equality in some circumstances.

In their defense and justification for exemptions, states sometimes argue that women's equality rights are a private matter and not the legitimate concern of the state (which focuses on the public sphere). States also refuse to acknowledge that state endorsement of a particular religion is also a threat to the free exercise of religion and thus discriminatory and coercive. Many of these issues result in a non-interventionist approach because of respect for religious autonomy and a belief that the affected individual usually has the remedy of the "right of exit." In addition to general concerns around equality and nondiscrimination, additional challenges that occur, through both the process of incorporation and institutionalization of family laws, include issues of interpretation, legitimacy, vested interests, lack of uniformity, political manipulation, and the manifestation of power and privilege.

At the international level, all states have obligations as regards the promotion and protection of human rights. The articulation of this commitment was illustrated at the March 2008 Human Rights Council meeting in Geneva, where all states reaffirmed that human rights are universal, thus confirming their obligations to ensure a domestic system founded on the belief that women's rights are human rights. The problem is that such affirmations are rendered a mockery by the actions of states that defend discriminatory religious and cultural laws and practices as part of their free exercise of religious rights. The challenge is the translation of abstract notions of universal human rights into contextual guarantees in constitutions and laws.

The Constitution of South Africa Act 108 of 1996 (hereinafter the Constitution)[1] safeguards both the right to free exercise of religion and the right to substantive gender equality. The challenge facing South Africa is how to protect both these rights and how to address potential conflicts that may arise between these rights. As regards the current developments in respect of the recognition of Muslim marriages, the law reform efforts appear to be sponsoring one particular religion, in its attempt to accommodate religion. Furthermore, the proposed solution ignores the distinction between the state's duty to protect minority religions, rather than the privileging of any particular religion. Also the state refuses to acknowledge that there exists the real possibility that religious freedom arguments are being used as a smokescreen for gender discrimination.

This chapter identifies potential constitutional violations that may emerge in the law reform efforts that are currently taking place in South Africa. It explores, among other issues, the tensions between women's equality rights and religious rights, codification of religious personal status laws versus recognition of religious marriages, achieving equal access to justice for all women, and tensions arising between individual equality rights and group equality rights. This chapter starts with a brief discussion on legal pluralism and the accommodation of religion, a historical perspective of developments relating to the treatment of Muslim marriages, followed by an overview of legal obligations at the international, regional, and national levels. This is followed by law reform developments after 1994 and a critical overview of the proposed draft law.

Legal Pluralism and the Accommodation of Religion

The concepts of multiculturalism and legal pluralism have drawn significant scholarly attention and debate in the past and also more recently in Western societies. Such debates usually relate to legal pluralism in the family law arena. Multicultural states face a challenge in effectively and meaningfully guaranteeing the right to equality and the right to religion and culture. In contrast to many African and Asian systems of plural family law systems, most Western countries largely maintain unified family law, and persons of all religious, cultural, and ethnic backgrounds are subject to the same family law rules and institutions. Some countries, for example, Malaysia, South Africa, and India, follow an accommodationist model within which the state retains protective but benevolent neutrality toward religion. This sometimes results in preferential or more protective acts by the state in relation to a particular religion.

Legal scholar Ayelet Shachar describes a pluralist system as one that maintains the autonomy and sovereignty of different minority cultures.[2] She points out the benefits and the risks inherent in pluralist systems and argues that pluralist systems may put at risk the equality rights of vulnerable group members, while uniform systems might do a better job at protecting citizenship rights and ensuring equal treatment. Also, pluralist systems may deny the importance of particular cultural or religious norms and discriminate against minority groups whose traditions are distinct from those embedded within the dominant culture. In Shachar's view, one solution to achieving the protection and promotion of both individual and group rights is to have a joint governance system between the state and the cultural group.[3] In response it can be argued that a joint governance system presupposes internal reforms, real respect for diversity and difference, mechanisms and structures that can be both implemented and monitored, and a willingness to have women participate in such governance systems (at both the state and religious institutional level). Both the substantive and procedural challenges are huge, especially in contexts where interpretations of religious laws and practices remain unchanged (and also often unchallengeable).

In arguing for the accommodation of religion, religious institutions make both negative demands, that is, for privacy and non-intervention, and positive demands, that is, for autonomous control of their institutions. This then opens the door to potential violations of equality rights in general and women's equality rights in particular. One question that arises in the pursuit of legal pluralism and the accommodation of religion, is whether the state should have a greater interest in promoting sex equality rights and also in ensuring that this right trumps religious freedom rights.

Untying the Historical Knot

South Africa's past from 1652 onward is characterized by conflict, injustice, oppression, and exploitation. Colonization, first by the Dutch and then the British, was followed by White minority rule from 1910 until the entrenchment of a more formal legalized apartheid regime in 1948. The Nationalist Party government came into power in 1948 and ruled from 1948 to 1993. White supremacy was the principle on which the apartheid laws and policies were based and implemented. Most of the injustices and atrocities perpetrated by the state were committed in the name of national laws or under state orders, despite many of these acts being in violation of international human rights norms and laws. Using force against its opponents and oppressing civilians were the norm, in order to maintain a system of rigid segregation of the four official race groups at all levels, including political, social, and economic. South Africa's history of colonization and apartheid included discriminatory laws, policies, and practices based on factors including race, sex, gender, culture, and religion. The goal was to create a system of legal, social, and economic separation of the people of the country.

Under apartheid, despite the limited or nonrecognition of other forms of law by the state, there had been widespread observance of both religious as well as African Customary Law. During both the colonial and the apartheid eras, there was limited state recognition and codification of African Customary Law. As regards Islamic laws and jurisprudence, there was no recognition at all by the state. Marriages conducted by Muslim rites were refused legal recognition on the grounds that they are potentially polygamous (the correct term is polygynous), and hence repugnant to good public policy, as defined by the White minority ruling class.[4]

Muslims, who constitute approximately 1.5 percent of the population (numbering about six hundred thousand), have been present in South Africa for over three hundred years.[5] Their origins, interpretation of Islam, and daily practices are diverse. They do not constitute a homogenous group, with one approach to personal status or family issues within an Islamic framework. There is no uniform system of personal status laws, either at the formal state level or at the informal community level. In some Muslim communities, the judicial and social welfare divisions of the local Ulama Councils (Muslim clergy) informally provide services in the family law area. The dispute resolution function, which is performed by these Ulama Councils in the Muslim family law arena, is based on their own subjective interpretations of religious laws and jurisprudence. Thus, matters of marriage divorce, custody, succession, and so on are sometimes resolved by these bodies. There is no empirical research on how widespread the use of such forums has been and in which geographic region of the country such usage is most prevalent.

Since 1994, post-apartheid South Africa is a country where many diverse people coexist in harmony, despite differences based on culture, race, religion, etc. The Constitution is viewed by many as an ideal model for multicultural democratic contexts, wherein the right to equality exists with the right to culture, tradition, and religion. South Africa is described as a unitary, multicultural, secular democracy that protects individual liberty and freedom through a Bill of Rights, with applicability against both the state and against individuals. The mandate of the new Constitution is transformative justice, which requires positive measures to redress historical injustices and the consequences of past discriminatory laws and policies. The foundational values of the Constitution include non-sexism, non-racism, the right to dignity, and the right to substantive equality.

The current reality, as regards Muslim marriages, is one of denial of civil law status in terms of many laws, including, among others, the Marriage Act 25 of 1961, the Divorce Act 70 of 1979, the Intestate Succession Act 81 of 1987, and the Maintenance of Surviving Spouses Act 27 of 1990. The courts have been used by some people to seek relief against discrimination and disadvantage arising from the nonrecognition of their marriages. Cases that have been brought to court include claims for spousal benefits and support, inheritance claims, and actions relating to the determination of the legitimacy of children born of marriages conducted under Muslim rites. During the apartheid era, judgments rendered by the courts clearly reflect an intolerance of diversity and the imposition of values of the White minority ruling class on all South Africans. Post-1994, the courts are bound by the spirit, ethos, and values of the Constitution, which is based on human dignity, freedom, and equality. Hence, subsequent judgments reflect these new values and illustrate a rejection of the values articulated in the apartheid era judgments. But the courts have not recognized Muslim marriages as valid marriages in the numerous cases that have been brought. Furthermore, the legislature has not addressed the issue of recognition of Muslim marriages.

The right to equality has been widely explored by South Africa's courts. The Constitutional Court set out an equality test in *Harksen v. Lane NO and Others*,[6] which mandated that any discrimination on the grounds of gender, race, ethnic origin, religion, disability, and other grounds enumerated in section 9 of the Constitution, is considered to be unconstitutional. The court recognized both past historical discrimination women faced in marriages in South Africa and current experiences of women in relation to matrimonial property and the division of labor within the household, as well as how these factors compounded and further entrenched deep inequalities between women and men. The test developed in the Harksen case gives guidelines for determining absolute breaches of equality. In *Bhe and Others v the Magistrate, Khayelitsha and Others*,[7] the Constitutional Court resolved a conflict between African Customary Law and individual rights. In examining the rule of male primogeniture, which prohibited and discriminated against women's and girls' right to inherit property, the court held that the customary law of succession, based largely on primogeniture, discriminates unfairly against women and girls, both on the grounds of race and gender. This case supports the conclusion that when a conflict of rights arises, the right to gender equality takes precedence over cultural and religious rights.

South Africa's case law post-apartheid provides important direction on the legal treatment of Muslim marriages, the right to freedom of religion, and the right to gender equality. A few cases deal with the issue of Muslim marriages specifically and the right to marry generally. The pre-democracy era cases stand in sharp contrast to subsequent jurisprudence emanating from the courts. Under colonialism and apartheid, there was a refusal on the part of both the legislature and the courts to afford legal protection to parties in a Muslim marriage. The reason largely was that these marriages were viewed as potentially polygamous (polygynous) and thus *contra bonos mores* and hence were not regarded as legally valid. The views expressed in pre-democracy era cases were based on the dominant views on what religions and practices constituted civilized religious practices, what unions were considered an anathema to the dominant Christian norms, what marriages would not be reprobated by the majority of civilized peoples on grounds of morality and religion, what marriages were contrary to public policy, etc.[8]

Ryland v. Edros[9] is a seminal example of the different approach to Muslim marriages adopted by the courts when faced with an action for claims arising out of a marriage that was dissolved by Muslim Personal Laws. The court asserted that the Constitution's values prohibited the imposition of a dominant community's preferences and prejudices (in this case prejudice against Muslim polygynous marriages) in a plural society like South Africa.[10] The court held that the terms of an actually monogamous Muslim marriage contract were enforceable by civil courts. The *Ryland* case points toward the conclusion that the right to religious freedom emanates from the Constitution itself, and thus religious freedom cannot be pursued without due regard to other central constitutional values, such as individual and group equality rights.

Amod v. Multilateral Motor Vehicle Accident Fund[11] was a case related to compensation for the loss of support suffered as a consequence of the death of her husband in a car accident. The respondent had refused to pay compensation because Islamic marriages were not lawful at common law, since they were seen as contrary to good public policy, as they allowed for the practice of polygamy [polygyny].[12] The court, in giving recognition to the duty of support owed to the appellant, recognized the existence of a de facto monogamous Muslim marriage and granted the Muslim spouse the right to sue for survivor support.

In *Hassam v. Jacobs*[13] the court found that failure to accord inheritance rights on intestacy to a polygamous spouse violates individual and group rights to equality. In particular, the court found discrimination between civil and Muslim widows, monogamous and polygamous widows, and polygamous customary law unions versus polygamous Muslim unions. The remedy adopted was to read in "spouse or spouses" wherever the term occurs and to retroactively invalidate the impugned provision from the passage of the new Constitution.

In addition, the *Minister of Home Affairs and Another v. Fourie and Another*[14] decision on same-sex marriages asserted that the compass by which the "right to marry" cases are decided should be South Africa's modern equality jurisprudence — which has focused on the values of human dignity, equality, and freedom — rather than religious texts.[15] The court declared, "[I]t is one thing for the Court to acknowledge the important role that religion plays in our public life. It is quite another to use religious doctrine as a source for interpreting the Constitution. It would be out of order to employ the religious sentiments of some as a guide to the constitutional rights of others."[16] The *Fourie* case lends strong support to the contention that, in the marriage context, religious norms cannot outweigh the constitutionally protected right to equality, and hence the inability of parties to lawfully marry their same-sex partners constitutes discrimination.

The Constitutional Court has also faced another freedom of religion issue, that is, whether giving special recognition to one religious group is unfair to other religious groups that lack such special recognition. In *S v. Solberg*,[17] the majority held that state endorsement of a particular religion would not infringe on the right to freedom of religion as long as the endorsement did not have a coercive effect. However, Justice O'Regan strongly dissented and argued that any such endorsement would not be permitted in South Africa's new constitutional order.[18]

An important issue that *Solberg* raises in the Muslim marriages context is whether the SALRC draft bill creates "coercive effects." As will be outlined in the section below, one may well argue that the SALRC draft bill does this, insofar as it gives preferential treatment to some Islamic schools of interpretation over others and reinforces women's lesser socioeconomic status and autonomy, especially with regard to making religious and marital choices.

International, Regional, and National Law Obligations

From an international law perspective, there is strong support for individual and gender equality norms, and South African courts are expressly obliged to consider international law when interpreting the Bill of Rights. Section 39(1) of the Constitution states, "[W]hen interpreting the Bill of Rights, a court, tribunal or forum must promote the values that underlie an open and democratic society based on human dignity, equality and freedom . . . and must consider international law."[19] Among others, South Africa has ratified the International Covenant on Civil and Political Rights (ICCPR) in 1998; has signed (but not ratified) the International Covenant on Economic, Social and Cultural Rights (ICESCR) in 1994; has ratified the Convention on the Elimination of All Forms of Discrimination against Women (CEDAW) in 1995; and ratified the African Charter on Human and People's Rights (African Charter) in 1996. These documents all speak of the central place of equality norms in a democratic and pluralist society. Articles 18 and 26 of the ICCPR, in particular, promote both the individual's freedom of religion and the right to equality. Also, article 16 of CEDAW infuses this generalized language with much-appreciated specificity. It commands states parties to "ensure, on a basis of equality of men and women:

(a) The same right to enter into marriage;

(b) The same right freely to choose a spouse and to enter into marriage only with their free and full consent;

(c) The same rights and responsibilities during marriage and at its dissolution;

(d) The same rights and responsibilities as parents, irrespective of their marital status, in matters relating to their children; in all cases the interests of the children shall be paramount;

(e) The same rights to decide freely and responsibly on the number and spacing of their children and to have access to the information, education and means to enable them to exercise these rights;

(f) The same rights and responsibilities with regard to guardianship, wardship, trusteeship and adoption of children, or similar institutions where these concepts exist in national legislation; in all cases the interests of the children shall be paramount;

(g) The same personal rights as husband and wife, including the right to choose a family name, a profession and an occupation;

(h) The same rights for both spouses in respect of the ownership, acquisition, management, administration, enjoyment and disposition of property, whether free of charge or for a valuable consideration."[20]

At a regional level, the preamble of the African Charter on Human and Peoples' Rights sets out a duty for state members to achieve genuine equality and dignity for all people and to dismantle all forms of discrimination. It honors both the universalist aspirations of the UN Charter and the Universal Declaration of Human Rights and the traditions and values of Africa, which should "inspire and characterize their reflection on the concept of human and peoples' rights." Relevant articles include the following:

(a) Article 2 entitles every individual to the enjoyment of the rights and freedoms in the charter, without distinction of any kind such as race, ethnic group, color, sex, religion, etc.

(b) Article 3 states that every individual shall be equal before the law and be entitled to equal protection of the law.

(c) Article 8 guarantees freedom of conscience, profession, and free practice of religion.

(d) Article 17(2) and (3) states that "[e]very individual may freely take part in the cultural life of his [*sic*] community. The promotion and protection of morals and traditional values recognized by the community shall be the duty of the State."

(e) Article 18(3) requires states to eliminate "every discrimination against women" and to protect women's rights "as stipulated in international declarations and conventions." In this way, the African Charter emphasizes women's rights by referring to pertinent international law, such as the ICCPR and CEDAW.

(f) Article 19 states that "[a]ll peoples shall be equal; they shall enjoy the same respect and shall have the same rights. Nothing shall justify the domination of a people by another."

(g) Article 20 refers to the "unquestionable and inalienable right to self-determination." At first glance, the question that arises is whether the peoples referred to signify groups determined by nationality (e.g., South Africans) or race, ethnicity, culture, or religion (e.g., Muslims).

(h) Article 23, however, suggests that the former interpretation (i.e., national group) is closer to the truth when it says that "[a]ll peoples shall have the right to national and international peace and security."[21]

South Africa is one of fifteen nations that have ratified the Maputo Protocol, formally called the Protocol to the African Charter on Human and Peoples' Rights on the Rights of Women in Africa. The Maputo Protocol, which was adopted by the African Union in July 2003 and came into force on 25 November 2005, speaks most directly to the issues at hand. It comprehensively enumerates the rights of women, imposing obligations on the ratifying states to ensure maximum protection of women's rights, prevent discrimination, and undertake measures to ensure women are given appropriate space for development, equal opportunities, and full protection of social, economic, and civil rights. The preamble proclaims the rights of women to be "inalienable, interdependent and indivisible human rights" and states its determination to enable women to "enjoy fully all their human rights." The strength of this language is significant in trying to create a hierarchy of rights. Specifically, it compels the state to take positive action of both a legislative and a social, cultural, educational nature.

Relevant articles include the following:

> Article 2 states that "harmful cultural and traditional practices" are those that "are based on the idea of the inferiority or the superiority of either of the sexes, or on stereotyped roles for women and men."
>
> The above provision is strengthened by Article 17, which states that women "shall have the right to live in a positive cultural context and to participate at all levels in the determination of cultural policies." While there will certainly be disagreement over what constitutes a positive cultural context, the implication is that the cultural context is not and should not be static or fixed and that tradition is not inviolate if it is deemed not to be "positive" for women. The statement guaranteeing women the right to participate in the determination of cultural policies suggests that women should be, in large part, the ones deciding on what is positive for them. This suggests that tradition is not inviolate, and such change as is necessary to promote the free development of women's personalities is encouraged.
>
> Article 6 on marriage could scarcely be clearer in requiring states parties to "ensure that women and men enjoy equal rights and are regarded as equal partners in marriage." Article 6(c) states that "monogamy is encouraged as the preferred form of marriage and that the rights of women in marriage and family, including in polygamous marital relationship, are promoted and protected." The Maputo Protocol, while promoting monogamous marriages, recognizes the existence of polygamous marriages and the need for protection of the rights and interests of women in those marriages.
>
> Article 7 ensures protection of women's rights by law, requiring that all marriages must be annulled or divorced by judicial order. Article 7 states that "States Parties shall enact appropriate legislation to ensure that women and men enjoy the same rights in case of separation, divorce or annulment of marriage." This entails that they shall (1) have the same rights to seek separation, divorce, or annulment of a marriage; (2) have reciprocal rights and responsibilities toward their children; and (3) have the right to an equitable sharing of

the joint property deriving from the marriage. In short, these provisions are notable because they conflict with those found in both the SALRC and the CGE bills.

Article 8 requires reform of relevant discriminatory laws.[22]

Thus, these various provisions in the Maputo Protocol demonstrate — some more clearly than others — an ultimate recognition that where the individual rights of women collide with the cultural or religious rights of a group, it is the former that must be given special protection. The African Court on Human Rights, a judicial mechanism of the African Charter on Human and People's Rights, is also empowered to apply the African Charter and any other human rights treaty or convention ratified by the state parties. Thus provisions in both the Maputo Protocol and the African Charter enable both the domestic and the regional courts to draw on a broader pool of norms protecting human and, more particularly in this case, women's human rights.

At a national level, the South African Constitution mandates transformative justice, which requires positive measures to redress historical injustices and the consequences of past discriminatory laws and policies. The foundational values include non-sexism, non-racism, the right to dignity, and the right to substantive equality. The Constitution's remedial objective demands that it must be interpreted in light of its historical context and its attempt to remedy the effects of both racial and gender discrimination. This is embodied in the preamble, which states, "[T]he people of South Africa recognize the injustices of our past . . . adopt this Constitution as the supreme law of the Republic so as to: Heal the divisions of the past and establish a society based on democratic values, social justice and fundamental human rights [and] . . . [i]mprove the quality of life of all citizens and free the potential of each person."[23] This purpose can also be seen in the main text of the Constitution, especially the Bill of Rights. Chapter 1, section 1 sets out human dignity, equality, and non-sexism as foundational values. The constitutional guarantee of equality (section 9[1]) is the very first in the list of rights and as such enjoys a special prominence. It permeates and defines the very ethos upon which the Constitution is premised. Thus, in evaluating the proposed bill recognizing Muslim marriages, one should be keenly attuned to where they may heal some divisions and where they may instead create others. Moreover, one cannot rightfully ignore the problems of lingering patriarchal norms that sustain and idealize gender inequality and gender discrimination, either in theory or in practice, de jure or de facto.

Section 15 of the Bill of Rights provides that "[e]veryone has the right to freedom of conscience, religion, thought, belief, and opinion," adding in section 15(3)(a) that this does not prevent legislation recognizing marriages or systems of personal or family law under any tradition or religion, so long as such recognition is consistent with this and other provisions of the Constitution (section 15[3][b]).[24] This condition is significant. First, it suggests that such legislation may conflict with other provisions of the Bill of Rights. Second, if it does, it clarifies that such legislation is subject to all other rights, including the equality right.

Section 31 creates a similar limitation. It mandates that "[p]ersons belonging to a cultural, religious or linguistic community may not be denied the right, with other members of that community to . . . enjoy their culture, practice their religion and use their language." Despite this strong proclamation, the section goes on to state that these rights "may not be exercised in a manner inconsistent with any provision of the Bill of Rights." In contrast, the equality clauses contain no such internal limitation, or "but" clause.

The Promotion of Equality and Prevention of Unfair Discrimination Act is not simply relevant law, but also evidence of how the South African legislature interprets its own constitutional mandate. The guiding principle it stresses is the eradication of systemic racial and gender discrimination and inequality, which was injected into South African politics, economy, society, and psyche by an ill-famed triumvirate: colonialism, apartheid, and patriarchy. Chapter 2, section 8 of the act is devoted to clarifying the contours of gender discrimination. As such, it outlaws "any practice, including traditional, customary or religious practice, which impairs the dignity of women and undermines equality between women and men."[25]

Law Reform Efforts in Respect of Muslim Marriages

The South African Law Reform Commission (hereinafter SALRC) is a statutory body appointed by Parliament, which had in the 1980s and early 1990s considered the status of the Muslim Personal Law. In 1996 it reconsidered this project with a particular focus on the recognition of Muslim marriages. Due to concerns raised in the past about the representivity of the SALRC project committee on this issue and also the process followed, a new project committee was recommended and subsequently appointed by Parliament in 1999, following a more transparent process of nominations. The mandate of this project committee was to investigate Islamic marriages and related matters. An issue paper identifying the issues and problems in respect of Islamic marriages was published in May 2000. A discussion paper with a draft bill was published in December 2001. After responses were collated, a new bill was released in October 2002. The final report and a substantially amended draft Muslim Marriages Bill were released in July 2003, and this has been submitted to the minister of justice, but has not been tabled in Parliament as of 2012.

The proposed draft legislation — the Muslim Marriages Act (hereinafter referred to as the SALRC Bill) — in its preamble sets out the objectives it seeks to achieve.[26] These include the following, among others: to make provision for the recognition of Muslim marriages, to specify the requirements for a valid Muslim marriage, to regulate the registration of Muslim marriages, to recognise the status and capacity of spouses in Muslim marriages, to regulate the proprietary consequences of Muslim marriages, and to regulate the termination of Muslim marriages and the consequences thereof. Thus it addresses the registration of Muslim marriages, the dissolution of such marriages, custody of and access to minor children, and the issue of maintenance (both spousal and child support). Provision is also made for the regulation of polygynous marriages. According to the SALRC, adoption of the draft bill would go a long way in creating legal certainty regarding Muslim marriages, it would give effect to Muslim values, and it would afford better protection to women in those marriages, in accordance with both Islamic and South African constitutional tenets.

The SALRC draft bill codifies elements of Muslim Personal Laws, by outlining rules for a variety of marital situations. The SALRC justified the codification approach by seeking support both from the clergy and the Constitution. Section 15 of the Constitution opens the door by allowing for legislation recognizing systems of personal and family law under any tradition or adhered to by persons professing a particular religion — although any such legislation must be consistent with the rest of the Constitution. Also, the argument asserted in the SALRC Discussion Paper 101 was that Muslims currently had difficulty enforcing maintenance, termination of marriage, proprietary consequences, and custody rights arising from their marriages, and thus legislation must be specifically aimed at correcting these practical problems. The assertion was that women and children would be protected by specified substantive regulations. Thus, codification was asserted by the SALRC as a way to actively provide social protection in marital and family problems.

There has been widespread criticism, which included charges of preferential treatment being given to the clergy, by the SALRC. The project committee has asserted that the draft bill of 2003 is supported by the majority of the community. This assertion has been maintained despite the committee being notified that the consultation process was flawed, that many women are unaware that the bill codifies religious law (as opposed to just recognizing Muslim marriages), and that there is contestation over the schools of interpretation of Islamic law in many of the codified provisions.

As a consequence of receiving numerous concerns relating to the SALRC bill, which revolved around both constitutionality issues generally and women's right to equality in particular, the Parliamentary Office of the South African Commission for Gender Equality (CGE) drafted an alternative draft bill in October 2005. The CGE is one of the six state institutions established in chapter 9 of the Constitution, with the mandate of strengthening democracy. In terms of section 181 of the Constitution, these six state institutions are independent and subject only to the Constitution and the law. The Commission for Gender Equality Act No. 39 of 1996 is the enabling law that fleshes out the powers, functions, composition, and certain procedural aspects of the commission. These powers and functions are very wide and are set out in section 187 of the Constitution and also section 11 of the CGE Act. They include the promotion of respect for gender equality; the protection, development, and attainment of gender equality; and the power to monitor, investigate, research, educate, lobby, advise, and report on issues concerning gender equality.

The functioning of the CGE has focused broadly on the following: (1) monitoring and evaluating policies and practices of both private and public bodies, to establish whether they promote gender equality; (2) conducting information and education campaigns; (3) evaluating and making recommendations on existing and proposed acts of Parliament, and also proposing new laws; (4) investigating alleged violations of gender equality; (5) monitoring the implementation of international conventions; and (6) research.

One of the thematic areas of focus for the Parliamentary Office of the CGE has been the issue of recognition of Muslim marriages. The interrogation of this issue through monitoring, research, investigation, advocacy, and public education has been based on the notion of eliminating gender injustice and/or achieving gender justice. The development of a bill, called the Recognition of Religious Marriages Bill (hereinafter referred to as the CGE Bill), was produced with the assistance of the office of the state law advisor and was in fulfillment of the CGE's constitutional mandate. This is a secular bill, of general application, that provides for the recognition of all religious marriages and avoids issues of codification of specific religious tenets, so as to comply with both international and constitutional law imperatives. It also addresses the lacuna that exists with respect to the nonrecognition of other religious marriages.

The CGE Bill was discussed with the SALRC and then handed over to the relevant executive structures. The hope was that action around broad public consultations would be held by them, particularly by the Gender Directorate of the Department of Justice. But neither the Ministry of Justice nor the Ministry of Home Affairs has acceded to numerous requests for a meeting with the CGE, nor have they undertaken any public consultations on the CGE Bill. The CGE Bill will not be discussed in this article, as it does not form part of the current political and public discourse taking place as regards the recognition of Muslim marriages. This is an unfortunate development that does not bode well for a young democracy. The litigation before the Constitutional Court in July 2009, to challenge the unconstitutionality of nonrecognition of marriages conducted under Muslim laws, was dismissed, on the basis that the parties had to first seek a remedy in the lower courts.

Potential Constitutional Violations

The SALRC Bill raises many constitutional concerns, including the provisions relating to the codification of religious laws in a secular multicultural democracy; the scope of application of such a law; the potential violations of women's equality rights, both intergroup and intragroup; and issues relating to the achievement of both individual and group equality. The Constitution does not contain a provision that mandates strict separation of religion and state. As stated earlier, the Constitution guarantees freedom of religion and belief. The SALRC Bill violates this right both in terms of the interpretations of religious law as found within the codified provisions and in the provisions relating to state enforcement of such provisions. It is apparent that the bill represents a compromise to meet constitutional guarantees, and hence it includes provisions from the different schools of Islam. This is problematic for many, as it assumes a common understanding of Muslim Personal Laws and also assumes that the Muslim community in South Africa is a homogenous one. The imposition of one version of religious law to all Muslims is viewed by many as a violation of constitutional rights, as it empowers the state to enforce and control the manner in which people choose to practice their religion and express their faith and belief. Furthermore, the bill may also be viewed as undermining the autonomy of religious institutions.

In terms of equality between citizens of a nation-state, the codification of a religious system that privileges one religious group in a secular democracy may be viewed as violating the equality rights of other groups. This is particularly relevant to the South African context, where there are other religious groups whose marriages are not recognized. Furthermore, the provisions relating to the appointment of Muslim judges and assessors to hear disputes brought by Muslim litigants could also be interpreted as privileging one sector of society and be seen as a violation of the same standard of equality for all citizens and, worse still, as a divisive factor in a context with a history of divisions. The reality in South Africa is one where all judges are bound by the dictates of the Constitution and are expected to use that in their decision making, whether the litigants are of a different race, sex, or cultural or religious group.

Further, as regards intragroup equality norms, the bill advocates different rules and procedures for people bound by the SALRC Bill. It treats the proprietary consequences of marriage, divorce rules and procedures, maintenance of spouses, and custody of and access to children differently from those that are applicable to citizens using the civil law marriage system. One example of this relates to the fact that civil law marriages are automatically in community of property, while marriages under this bill will be automatically out of community of property. The consequences of a marriage out of community of property, excluding the accrual system, is that each party retains assets that they bring into the marriage and also assets that they acquire during the subsistence of the marriage. This effectively works to the disadvantage of the spouse who does not work outside of the home and who may also not inherit family assets because of biased gender equality rules and practices.

The provisions relating to divorce in the SALRC Bill reveal a lack of clarity, disparate levels of power granted to male spouses (i.e., the entrenchment of legal inequality), and a failure to pursue the substantive equality of women. For example, section 9(2) of the SALRC Bill provides that a court may terminate a Muslim marriage on any ground permitted by Islamic law. Yet, the bill fails to identify any of these grounds and thus opens the door to gender-biased interpretations of religious grounds. Also, in codifying different forms of divorce and post-divorce practices, the bill openly spells out and formalizes inequality in the law by giving the husband greater freedom to end the marriage. It also gives men the right to remarry immediately post-death or divorce, yet prohibits remarriage for women, for a mandatory waiting period of 130 days for a woman who is not pregnant and until the time of delivery for a woman who is pregnant (i.e., the *iddah* period). This is a violation of both domestic and international laws.

The process of dissolution of marriages under the SALRC Bill is another example of the different treatment in respect to divorce processes accorded to the Muslim community as compared to both civil law and customary law divorces. Compulsory mediation is the first step in the process of dispute resolution. This can be followed by arbitration and finally litigation if the matter is not resolved. Court proceedings will have to be presided over by a Muslim judge. Failing the existence of a Muslim judge in that court, the matter will have to be heard by a Muslim attorney (who would be designated as an acting judge). Courts would be assisted by two Muslim assessors who have specialized knowledge of Islamic laws. On appeal, the Supreme Court of Appeal would submit questions of Islamic law to two accredited Muslim institutions for guidance in its deliberations.

Numerous problems are evident in this approach. First, in court cases, the application of Islamic laws could introduce gender bias into both the procedure and substance of the case. Second, by creating a special role for Muslim judges and attorneys as judicial officers, the SALRC Bill may convey existing racial and gender judicial distributional problems into the courtroom. Third, because this bill mandates compulsory mediation, only Muslim people would be made to go through this additional procedural hoop in order to gain access to the formal justice system. This puts Muslims at a disadvantage vis-à-vis non-Muslims with regard to their constitutionally protected right to have access to both due process and effective justice. Fourth, because arbitration is a private process, there is concern that gender bias will proceed unchecked by public scrutiny. Studies have found that private bargaining in family law tends to yield inferior results for many women.[27] Compulsory mediation and arbitration are also viewed as problematic, based both on equality arguments as well as ignoring the reality of unequal power relations in many marriages. Furthermore, compulsory mediation is a contradiction in terms, as mediation by its very nature is a voluntary process that parties agree to, with them choosing a neutral third party as a mediator.

In terms of individual rights to gender equality, there are views that the current practice of Muslim Personal Laws cannot be reconciled with the constitutional guarantee of substantive gender equality. The SALRC Bill is seen as further entrenching the existing de facto inequalities that are faced by many Muslim women, due to the implementation and practices of Islamic law. This view is borne out by the provisions on issues relating to property, spousal support, *iddah* period, divorce rules and procedures, and polygyny. For example, the proviso relating to post-divorce/death waiting periods (*iddah*) is also viewed as a violation of gender equality, as it is a mandatory obligation imposed on Muslim women only. It is also viewed as illogical, as the practical purpose behind *iddah* is to ascertain the paternity of a child that may be born to her after the death of a husband or on the dissolution of a marriage. With technology today, this can be established in a fairly short time, and hence the specific time provision in the bill does not make sense. This a-contextual approach to codification of religious laws is seen as ignoring time, place, and scientific developments in the world today. It is also seen as conservative, backward looking, and harmful to both the individual and the religion.

Another example of potential violation of individual equality rights relates to provisions in the bill that recognize and sanction the practice of polygyny, while at the same time providing some legislative protective measures. This raises two crucial issues in the context of the entrenched right to equality, both in general terms as well as with regard to sexual equality. There is no provision in the bill for a woman's right to enter into multiple marriages, and this begs the question of whether the right to religion is overriding the right to equality in this instance. The bill also ignores economic factors and unequal power relationships that force women into polygynous marriages. By legislating to regulate polygyny through the courts, the inequality/discrimination defect is not necessarily cured. Further, there is no requirement for the wife's consent prior to her husband's entering into a subsequent marriage. Debates have ensued as to whether court regulation of polygyny is practically possible, in modern social and economic conditions, and whether men will follow the prescribed court process—particularly in a context where there is a lack of acceptance of the state's right to intervene in the religious domain.

Conclusion

In an ideal world, principles and institutions of constitutionalism, human rights, and citizenship would be the norm. The ideal constitutional provisions would guarantee both the right to equality and the right to freedom of religion, but with the right to equality interpreting the right of freedom of religion; prohibitions on discrimination based on religion; and a limitation on state endorsement of a particular religion. The ideal constitution would also include provisions for the creation of monitoring bodies to ensure effective implementation of such guarantees. The promotion of sex equality through the prohibition of discrimination within religious laws and institutions would not be off-limits—as sex equality guarantees serve a sufficiently important government purpose on many levels, be it ethical, moral, legal, political, social, economic, or developmental.

South Africa is a secular country, which has also constitutionally entrenched the right to freedom of religion, belief, conscience, and opinion. The protection of minority group rights whether based on religion or culture is constitutionally guaranteed in broad terms. The question of interpretation of such constitutional guarantees and the primacy of gender equality rights is also now clear after a seminal Constitutional Court case (the *Bhe* case). Generally, the cases post-1994 have articulated the preeminent values of equality and dignity in this new society. It is clear that the protection of minority group rights does not include a right to use a legal system that is in conflict with the Constitution and its fundamental protection of the principle and practice of equality of all citizens. Also, it is clear that an obligation to enforce an unconstitutional system, which violates individual rights, will not be sanctioned by the courts.

Eisgruber and Sager argue that "[w]e need to abandon the idea that it is the unique value of religious practices that sometimes entitle them to constitutional attention. What properly motivates constitutional solicitude for religious practices is their distinct vulnerability to discrimination, not their distinct value; and what is called for, in turn, is protection against discrimination, not privilege against legitimate governmental concerns. When we have replaced value with vulnerability, and the paradigm of privilege with that of protection, then it will be possible both to make sense of our constitutional past in this area and to chart an appealing constitutional future."[28]

In addition, Abdullahi Ahmed An-Na'im argues that one needs a secular state that facilitates the possibility of religious piety out of honest conviction (and not state coercion) and that the enactment and enforcement of religious laws result in the manifestation of the political will of the state and not the religious laws of Islam. Furthermore, valid concerns exist about the "ossification" that takes place when systems of laws and customs, which were fluid and accommodating, are codified and then imposed on groups who find this both alien and alienating.[29]

As stated earlier, section 15 of the Constitution opens the door by allowing for legislation recognizing systems of personal and family law under any tradition or adhered to by persons professing a particular religion — although any such legislation must be consistent with the rest of the Constitution. The codification approach utilized in the SALRC bill has put women and children at a greater disadvantage, both intergroups and intragroups. Many of these provisions are onerous in terms of a burden of proof, and they presuppose access to knowledge and an equal power of parties to negotiate mutually favorable terms. The codification of religious laws approach focuses on protecting the religious group, with the emphasis being on formalizing group norms and institutions, instead of protecting the rights of the religious individual, with the emphasis being on personal choice of forum. Because individuals, especially women, are often subjugated even within protected minority groups, and because the individual is the lowest common denominator of both individual and group rights, there is a greater imperative to protect individuals. Where foundational rights collide, the equality of women must take precedence.

The recognition of Muslim marriages on a par with all other religious marriages is not precluded. But cultural and religious rights, unlike equality rights, are subject to limitations, described above. Wayne van der Meide has argued,

"[A]lthough culture is practiced within and defined in reference to a group, in the Bill of Rights it is an individual, not a collective, right. Generally, therefore, the right to culture cannot be used to protect the interests of a group at the expense of the rights to equality, non-discrimination and inherent human dignity of individuals."[30] Hopefully, when appropriate draft legislation with regard to the recognition of Muslim marriages finally reaches the legislature, the substantive equality rights of women will trump the inclusion of archaic and discriminatory provisions that violate women's rights to sex/gender equality and religion.

Acknowledgments

Copyright of this article vests in the author. Materials used in this paper include information from the author's previous publications particularly the following: R. Manjoo (editor), Harvard Law School Human Rights Program Working Paper Series "The Recognition of Muslim Personal Laws in South Africa: Implications for Women's Human Rights" (July 2007); R. Manjoo (author), "Making Rights Real: Facing the Challenges of Recognition of Muslim Marriages in South Africa," in Miller du Toit Family Law Conference Compilation, Juta Publishers (2008); and R. Manjoo, "Tensions between Constitutional Guarantees of Equality and Family Laws" presentation made at the Musawah Global Meeting for Equality and Justice in the Muslim Family, Malaysia, in February 2009. I acknowledge the research and writing contribution of students, from the Human Rights Program, Harvard Law School, who worked with me on a larger research project on this topic.

Notes

1. "Constitution of the Republic of South Africa No. 108 of 1996," South African Government Information, accessed August 22, 2011, http://www.info.gov.za/documents/constitution/1996/a108–96.pdf.

2. Ayelet Shachar, *Multicultural Jurisdictions: Cultural Differences and Women's Rights* (Cambridge, UK: Cambridge University Press, 2001), 78.

3. Ibid., 131.

4. Ismail v. Ismail 1983 1 SA 1006 (A).

5. Ebrahim Moosa, "Prospects for Muslim Law in South Africa: A History and Recent Developments," in *Yearbook of Islamic and Middle Eastern Law* 3 (1996): 134–37.

6. Harksen v. Lane NO 1997 (11) BCLR 1489 (CC).

7. Bhe and Others v. Magistrate of Khayelitsha and others 2005 (1) BCLR 1 (CC)

8. See generally Bronn v. Fritz Bronn's Executors and others 1860 (3) Searle 313; Seedat's Executors v. The Master 1917 (A.D.); Kader v. Kader 1972 (3) SA 203 (A.D.); Ismail v. Ismail 1983 (1) SA 1006 (A.D.).

9. Ryland v. Edros 1997 (1) BCLR 77 (C).

10. *Id.* at 460

11. Amod v. Multilateral Motor Vehicle Accident Fund 1999 (4) SA 1319 (SCA).

12. Lourens Du Plessis, "Freedom of or Freedom from Religion?" *Brigham Young University Law Review* 439 (2001): 461.

13. Hassam v. Jacobs NO and Others (CCT83/08) [2009] ZACC 19; 2009 (11) BCLR 1148 (CC); 2009 (5) SA 572 (CC) (15 July 2009).

14. Minister of Home Affairs and Another v. Fourie and Another CCT 60/04.

15. *Id.* at para 48.

16. *Id.* at para 92.

17. S v. Solberg 1997 (10) BCLR 1348 (CC).

18. As stated in Paul Farlam, "The Ambit of the Right to Freedom of Religion: A Commentary on S v. Solberg," *South African Journal of Human Rights* 14 (1998): 301–2.

19. "Constitution of the Republic of South Africa," South African Government Information, accessed August 22, 2011, http://www.info.gov.za/documents/constitution/1996/a108–96.pdf.

20. "Convention on the Elimination of All Forms of Discrimination against Women (CEDAW)" adopted 18 Dec. 1979, G.A. Res. 34/180, U.N. Doc. A/34/46 (1980), accessed August 22, 2011, http://www.un.org/womenwatch/daw/cedaw/cedaw.htm.

21. "African (Banjul) Charter on Human and Peoples' Rights," University of Minnesota Human Rights Library, accessed August 22, 2011, http://www1.umn.edu/humanrts/instree/z1afchar.htm.

22. "Protocol to the African Charter on Human and Peoples' Rights on the Rights of Women in Africa" (informally called the "Maputo Protocol"), African Commission on Human and Peoples' Rights, accessed August 22, 2011, http://www.achpr.org/english/_info/women_en.html.

23. "Constitution: Preamble," South African Government Information, accessed

August 22, 2011, http://www.info.gov.za/documents/constitution/1996/96preamble.htm.

24. "Chapter 2 — Bill of Rights," South African Government Information, accessed August 22, 2011, http://www.info.gov.za/documents/constitution/1996/96cons2.htm#9.

25. "Promotion of Equality and Prevention of Unfair Discrimination Act" in *Republic of South Africa: Government Gazette,* 2000, accessed August 22, 2001, http://www.iwraw-ap.org/resources/pdf/South%20Africa_GE1.pdf.

26. "Muslim Marriages Bill," South African Government Information, accessed August 22, 2011, http://www.info.gov.za/view/DownloadFileAction?id=139895, 2.

27. Natasha Bakht, "Family Arbitration Using Sharia Law: Examining Ontario's Arbitration Act and Its Impact on Women," *Muslim World Journal of Human Rights* 1 (2004).

28. C. L. Eisgruber and L. G. Sager "Mediating Institutions beyond the Public/Private Distinction: The Vulnerability of Conscience; The Constitutional Basis for Protecting Religious Conduct," *Univerity of Chicago Law Review* 61 (1994): 1248.

29. Abdullahi Ahmed An-Na'im, *Islam and the Secular State: Negotiating the Future of Shari'a* (Cambridge, MA: Harvard University Press, 2008).

30. Wayne van der Meide, "Gender Equality v Right to Culture," *South African Law Journal* 116 (1999): 105.

Works Cited

Abdullah, Somaya (2002). "Multicultural Social Interventions and Nation-Building in South Africa: The Role of Islamic Counseling and Psychotherapy." Unpublished Phd dissertation, University of Cape Town, South Africa.

African Charter on Human and Peoples' Rights. Adopted 27 June 1981 and came into force in 1986. OAU Doc. CAB/LEG/67/3 rev.5, 21 ILM (1982) 58.

Amod v. Multilateral Motor Vehicle Accident Fund 1999 (4) SA 1319 (SCA).

Bhe and Others v. Magistrate of Khayelitsha and others 2005 (1) BCLR 1 (CC).

Bronn v. Fritz Bronn's Executors and others 1860 (3) Searle 313.

Cachalia, Feroz (1991). "Legal Pluralism and Constitutional Change in South Africa: The Special Case of Muslim Family Laws." Unpublished paper, University of Cape Town.

Daniels v. Campbell NO and others 2004 (7) BCLR 735 (CC).

Harksen v. Lane NO 1997 (11) BCLR 1489 (CC).

Ismail v. Ismail 1983 (1) SA 1006 (A.D.).

Kader v. Kader 1972 (3) SA 203 (A.D.).
Manjoo, Rashida (ed.) (2007). "The Recognition of Muslim Personal Laws in South Africa: Implications for Women's Human Rights." Human Rights Program at Harvard Law School Working Paper.
Manjoo, Rashida (2008). "Making Rights Real — Facing the Challenges of Recognising Muslim Marriages in South Africa." In Miller du Toit Family Law Conference Compilation, Juta Publishers, South Africa.
Manjoo, Rashida (2009). "Tensions between Constitutional Guarantees of Equality and Family Laws." Unpublished paper presented at Musawah Conference, Malaysia.
Minister of Home Affairs and Another v. Fourie and Another CCT 60/04.
Muslim Youth Movement Gender Desk (2003). "Response to the Proposed Draft Bill, Islamic Marriages Act . . . of 20. ." Unpublished paper.
Promotion of Equality and Prevention of Unfair Discrimination Act 4 of 2000.
Ryland v. Edros 1997 (1) BCLR 77 (CC).
S v. Solberg 1997 (10) BCLR 1348 (CC).
Seedat's Executors v. The Master 1917 A.D.
South African Law Reform Commission (2003). "Muslim Marriages Act . . . of 20— ." Published draft bill.
South African Law Reform Commission (2003). "Islamic Marriages and Related Matters." Project 106. Published report.
South African Law Reform Commission (2001). "Islamic Marriages and Related Matters." Discussion Paper 101, Project 59.

LIKHAPHA MBATHA AND LISA FISHBAYN JOFFE

Chapter Seven Recognition of Polygamous Marriages in the New South Africa

Introduction: Why Did Post-apartheid South Africa Recognize Polygamous Marriage?

> "On 03 July 2001 I gave birth to my first-born child. I went to Home Affairs to get her a birth certificate. When I got to Home Affairs I found out that my husband was married to another wife. When I got home, I asked him about what I had found out at Home Affairs but he denied it. I even called both families to discuss the matter. He also denied that he was married to another woman. Later, I found out that his mother knew about this other wife."[1]

In Setswana, the word for "polygyny" is *lefufa.* It also means "jealousy." *Mogadikane,* the word for "co-wife" is derived from the verb meaning "to rival, annoy, or cause a pain in the stomach."[2] Women complain that polygyny breeds insecurity, hostility, and witchcraft among those who find themselves in competition for their shared husband's scarce economic and emotional resources.[3] Polygyny brings with it both the humiliation of being supplanted in their husband's affections and anxiety over access to school fees and improved housing.[4] In many cases, women find themselves involved in a polygamous relationship without their knowledge or consent. Women outside polygyny reject it, and women in it hope that their children will avoid being party to it.[5] Eighty percent of South African women surveyed oppose the practice.[6]

The Universal Declaration of Human Rights,[7] the African Charter on Human and People's Rights,[8] and the International Covenant on Civil and Political Rights[9] all describe key rights in relation to marriage, which are honored to varying degrees by South African law.[10] They include the freedom to marry, the capacity to consent to marriage (and the correlative right to refuse marriage), the ability to have marriages registered (rendering rights annexed to marriage more readily enforceable), and the right to equality under substantive law during marriage and at its dissolution. The Convention on the Elimination of All Forms of Discrimination against Women (CEDAW) expands upon these rights to require that state parties "modify the social and cultural patterns of conduct of men and women, with the view to achieving the elimination of prejudices which are based on customary and all other practices that deal with the idea of the inferiority of either of the sexes or on stereotyped roles for men and women."[11] With regard to the practice of polygamy, the mandate of the International Covenant on Civil and Political Rights could not be more clear: "Polygamy violates the dignity of women. It is an inadmissible discrimination against women. Consequently it should be abolished wherever it continues to exist."[12]

South Africa is a signatory to these instruments and to many other international agreements on the human rights of women. However, when it reformed its marriage laws in 1998, South Africa granted legal recognition to polygamous marriages contracted under African Customary Law, for the first time.[13] This novel legislation was part of a concerted effort to bring the full range of South African laws in line with the mandates of the new, post-apartheid, Constitution, a document that identifies equality as one of its central values.[14] Why would a government committed to gender equality choose to do this? While a minority marital practice, polygamy occupies a disproportional space in public discourse about the dignity of African cultural values. The drafters of the new polygamy law faced the challenge of balancing competing obligations to comply with human rights norms, satisfy the political expectations of a newly empowered Black majority, and protect the interests of vulnerable members in existing polygamous families. The Recognition of Customary Marriages Act is the innovative, if imperfect, result of this balancing exercise.

A History of Polygamy in South Africa

African Customary Law permits polygyny. The number of wives that a man may marry is not subject to any formal limitation. The practice was already in decline by the early twentieth century[15] and is now quite rare.[16] It both reflected the high status of the husband and enhanced his status.[17] Additional wives enabled him to father more children and thus become a hallowed ancestor to a large clan.[18] Additional wives could also be a basis for increased landholdings, as a man would be allocated a supplementary piece of land for each wife to farm. A man might also take a further wife in situations where a couple had difficulties producing children.[19] Of course, polygamy also offered men the benefits of sexual novelty.

Speaking in the nineteenth century, Moshoeshoe, the king of Lesotho, summed up the various advantages of polygyny:

> Our women age rapidly and we cannot resist the temptation of taking younger ones. Among the older women there are some who become lazy, and they are the first to advise us to take one more wife, hoping to make a servant of her. For us chiefs, it is a means of contracting alliances with the heads of other nations, which helps to preserve peace. Moreover, we receive many travellers and strangers; how could we lodge them and what could we feed them, if we did not have several wives?[20]

The association of polygamy with prestige and the prerogatives of kings has enjoyed a resurgence in South Africa since Jacob Zuma assumed the presidency in 2009. Zuma has five wives married in accordance with Zulu customary law. His defense of his family life with reference to Zulu tradition is identified as one source of his enormous popularity, particularly in rural communities.[21] He invokes the history of colonial contempt for African values in defending his marriages: "When the British came to our country they said everything we are doing was barbaric, was wrong, inferior in whatever way. . . . I don't know why they are continuing thinking that their culture is more superior than others."[22]

The customary law scholar J. C. Bekker also sees echoes of the colonial project in efforts to reform customary family law to recognize women's rights: "The Bill of Rights has replaced Christianity, but the principle is still the same: things African are uncivilised, unconstitutional — un-Christian if you wish."[23]

Contemporary advocates for women's rights seeking to transform the institution of polygyny thus face a complex challenge, for their arguments indeed resonate with White supremacists' arguments made against it in the nineteenth century. Victorian campaigners against polygyny objected to the practice as an indignity to women because it was inconsistent with the Christian notion of marriage and because it reversed the perceived natural order of dependency between the sexes by making women work to support their husbands.

White objections to polygyny also had a material basis. Opponents were quite explicit that whatever its moral valence, the polygynous homestead family constituted an ideal working unit with which the White farmer could not effectively compete. In 1853, Governor Pine of Natal Province asked, "How can an Englishman with one pair of hands compete with a Native man with five to twenty slave wives?"[24] In this narrative, African men were portrayed as shiftless and unmotivated to work for European employers because they could rely on the labor of multiple wives to provide for their needs. The abolition of polygyny was called for in order to "force the Native man to work, and thus habituate him to labour."[25]

The decline in the popularity of formal polygny in South Africa has been ascribed to a number of causes. The active intervention of the state had a major effect. Changes in taxation policy based assessements on the number of huts within a homestead, so that increasing the number of wives would multiply a husband's tax liability. Limitations on the size of landholdings under individual tenure meant that new wives could not be given sufficient arable land to support a new household.[26] The apartheid state acted to break apart monogamous and polygamous families alike through the imposition of mobility controls. While migrant labor took men away from home for much of the year, their families were prevented by pass laws from joining them in urban areas. Thus, while formal polygamy has declined, de facto polygyny has become quite widespread. Many men have a partner or spouse in their rural home and other non-marital partners in the cities where they reside for work.[27]

In the past, women might enter into polygyny to gain status as married women, to secure economic support, or to gain access to land to use to support themselves. However, in contemporary South Africa, marriage no longer plays the role of sole gatekeeper to resources. Most of the land laws enacted during the constitutional dispensation period allow women to acquire land on an equitable basis with men.[28]

The legal status of polygyny in South African courts was already improving before the passage of the Recognition of Customary Marriages Act in 1998. The decision in *Rylands v. Edros* in 1997 was a watershed moment in this regard. The case turned on whether a marriage contracted solely under Islamic law constituted a valid contract under South African law. Until this point, South African courts refused to recognize Islamic marriages, because their potentially polygynous nature rendered them contrary to public policy.

However the *Rylands* case found that it was no longer tenable under the new constitutional dispensation to define public policy with reference only to the institution of Christian marriage at the expense of other marital traditions. Islamic marriage contracts, even potentially polygamous ones, could therefore give rise to enforceable claims in South African courts.[29] The recognition of actually polygamous marriages, solemnized under Islamic law and African Customary Law, was not far behind.[30]

History of the Reform of South African Customary Law

In discussing customary law, it is important to draw a distinction between *traditional law*, which may be defined as a speculative reconstruction of norms and practices in the distant past; *official customary law*, which is the system of laws, characterized as continuous with traditional norms, that is applied by state courts; and forms of *customary practice* with which families and individuals resolve disputes and organize their affairs in a fashion that they understand to be consistent with tradition.[31] There is a general consensus among scholars, practitioners, and courts in South Africa that emergent practices are an authoritative form of customary law.[32] Customary law may best be understood as the creation of dialectic processes involving the communities from which the law springs and official organs of the state by which it is interpreted and applied.[33]

This notion of contemporary customary law as a shifting, contested, and adaptive practice has been accepted by the Constitutional Court in affirming communal attempts to redefine customary law in line with constitutional norms.[34] In the 2005 case of *Bhe v. Magistrate Khayelitsha & Others*, the court rejected "official customary law" as a "poor reflection, if not a distortion of the true customary law" and held that "[t]rue customary law will be that which recognizes and acknowledges the changes which continually take place."[35] In the recent case of *Shilubana v. Nwamitwa*,[36] the court's preference for living customary law over official accounts was made even more clear. There the court had to evaluate a novel chieftainship policy adopted by the Valoyi traditional community that allowed a woman to be appointed chief. A rival male candidate, supported by the Congress of Traditional Leaders of South Africa, argued that this position failed to respect and apply customary law. The community had reinterpreted the customary law of chiefly succession through a resolution which stated, "[T]hough in the past it was not permissible by the Valoyis that a female child be heir, in terms of democracy and the new Republic of South Africa Constitution it is now permissible that a female child be heir since she is also equal to a male child."[37] The Constitutional Court found that this sort of transformative reinterpretation of customary law at the local level to bring it into conformity with the Constitution was a prime example of the "living law" and upheld the policy.[38]

South African courts now accept that the processes for the elaboration of customary law have been inflected by struggles over power within the customary law–observing community and between African communities and the colonial and apartheid state. In his classic work, the historian Martin Channock argued that the interpretation and enforcement of customary law by state courts transformed a fluid range of norms subject to negotiation into a more rigid system of rules in ways that disadvantaged women. While the embodiment of customary norms in rules had the advantage of certainty and coherence, it failed to capture the ways in which these rules were constantly changing. Women's successful negotiation of enhanced rights in practice was not reflected in rules that had been recorded at an earlier stage. Moreover, the rules themselves were defined against women's interests, as those drafting the codes of customary law relied upon the expert evidence of male elites. It was in the latter's interest to provide an account of customary law that privileged patriachal authority and diminished the claims of women and younger men.[39] Given this fraught history, Channock argued that there should be nothing to prevent communities from dismantling existing customary law norms or doctrines and developing and transmitting new ones.

The post-apartheid state has a complex relationship to this academic understanding of customary law. The Constitution of the Republic of South Africa provides protection for both gender equality and the right to participate in one's culture.[40] It permits the recognition of "systems of personal and family law under any tradition, or adhered to by persons professing a particular religion,"[41] and requires that African Customary Law be applied where appropriate.[42] The South African Constitution also allows legislation to be enacted recognizing religious and cultural marriages.[43] The Constitution seeks to solve the problem of the coexistence of equality and culture by prescribing that any cultural practice is protected only to the extent that it does not contravene other provisions in the Bill of Rights.[44]

Colonial and apartheid governments did not recognize customary marriages as valid legal marriages with legal consequences. The Black Administration Act defined marriage to exclude unions contracted "under Black law and custom."[45] When Black people did marry under civil law, their unions had different proprietary consequences than those contracted by Whites. Until 1988, civil marriages contracted by Black people were presumed to be out of community of property, while the default regime for White couples was in community of property.[46]

With the end of apartheid in 1994, the new regime made the improvement of the quality of life of Black South Africans one of its immediate objectives. Recognizing customary marriages was identified as one way of advancing that goal. What recognition of these marriages might actually entail was not properly mapped out.

The South African Law Reform Commission's Inquiry into Customary Marriage

The reform of the customary law of marriage in South Africa was part of a larger project to harmonize the common law and the indigenous laws of marriage under the Constitution. This, in turn, formed part of a broader agenda of extending equal civil rights in marriage that would come to embrace Islamic marriage, Hindu marriage, same-sex couples, and registered non-marital partnerships.[47] The coexistence of cultural and equality rights, together with the application of both customary law and human rights norms, were major concerns during the transition from the apartheid government to a democratic South Africa.

For decades, debate about the path for the reform for South African family law revolved around whether it was possible or appropriate to incorporate customary marriage practices into the civil law regime or whether a distinctive customary marriage law should be maintained but rendered more egalitarian. Channock, for example, advocated for multiple means of solemnizing marriage but for a single law regarding its financial, proprietary, and custodial consequences.[48] At the beginning of the investigation into customary marriages, the South African Law Commission (SALC) also favored the notion of enacting a single law of marriage containing elements of both the civil and customary regimes.[49]

The SALC analyzed the position of customary marriages in countries such as Tanzania, Botswana, Lesotho, Swaziland, and Zimbabwe. It showed that in some of these countries customary marriages were allowed to run parallel to civil marriages, while others had a single marriage code with provisions dealing with customary marriages. It also discussed the position in the Transkei (then a self-governing state in South Africa, now the Eastern Cape Province) where a single marriage law encompassing all the different types of marriage had been enacted.[50]

In its initial discussion paper, the Law Commission recommended that customary marriages should be fully recognized in order to correct past injustices[51] and to assist the country in overcoming historical divisions and inequalities. This generated twenty-seven written submissions providing overwhelming support for the recognition of customary unions as full legal marriages. Two main positions were evident: One group of responses supported the retention of a plural marriage regime, while another supported the creation of a single code of marriage for all. Support for the retention of plural regimes came from various provincial houses of traditional leaders, while women's groups pushed for a single marriage law.

We prepared the submissions on behalf of the Gender Research Project of the Centre for Applied Legal Studies (CALS) at the University of the Witwatersrand to the Law Commission. The Gender Research Project's work was motivated by the notion that law reform should be informed by the best current research about the operation of customary law on the ground. In collaboration with a leading South African women's group, the Rural Women's Movement (now the National Movement of Rural Women), CALS conducted extensive research on women's attitudes toward customary marriage. The CALS data was collected from Limpopo, the North West province, and Gauteng province, including both urban and rural areas. Two discussion groups were held in each of the areas mentioned to cross-check the information collected during the one-to-one interviews. The aim of the interviews was to identify customary cultural practices of marriage worthy of promotion and protection in line with the constitutional provisions.

CALS's findings informed the tone of these submissions. CALS concluded that very few people were still practicing polygyny. From the data collected during sixty interviews, only seven interviewees lived in polygynous relationships. Women said that polygyny forced women into endless strife over their husband and his resources. Polygamy presented a material threat to their prosperity because a husband might redistribute a woman's property to another wife or spread resources too thinly to adequately provide for multiple wives and children.[52] Women involved in such unions hoped that their children would not follow in their footsteps. They often stated that they felt that they were driven by circumstance to accept polygamy because they feared being stigmatized as "spinsters." The majority of women opposed its continuation.

The participants identified the problems of polygamy in different ways depending upon their age and whether they identified as a first or subsequent wife. Older women wanted the law to oblige their husbands to treat all wives equally. Some older women condemned their young co-wives for appropriating their husbands. They also accused the younger women of not being in love with their husbands but of being interested only in the property they had accumulated through the joint efforts of the spouses during the first marriage. Senior co-wives also felt vulnerable because they claimed that young women entering into polygyny sought to change the institution, the distribution of resources, and the role of men by dictating terms to their husbands.

Where the wives cohabited in the same household, young women claimed they were ill-treated by their senior co-wives by being relegated to the role of servants expected to discharge domestic chores. Although young women might possess the status of married women in the eyes of the outside world, and in instances where their husbands were well off, might be envied by their peers, these women complained of a lack of status within their marriages.

Polygamy was also problematic in the far more common situation in which wives did not cohabit. Many women sought to marry their husbands twice, under both the civil and customary regimes, in an attempt to secure the benefits available under both systems. While civil law might provide access to enforceable property rights, customary marriage was necessary for recognition of the validity of the marriage by the community.[53] One of the advantages of undergoing a civil ceremony was that it could, in theory, protect a wife from later becoming party to a polygamous union. However, their husbands' failure to disclose their true marital status at the time of marriage meant they often lost this protection. Both younger and older women in polygynous marriages argued that their husbands' misrepresentation had contributed to their problems in polygyny. Their husbands had led them to believe they were the only spouse or that the senior wives were long divorced. The prevalence of migrant labor often meant that wives of polygynists did not know of each other's existence.[54] Some women became involved in polygamous marriages when a migrant husband married under customary law to a wife in a rural area chose to marry another wife under civil law in the city without disclosing the existence of the other relationship to either woman. In the past, taking a subsequent wife might have been of benefit to the first wife because is provided her with someone to assist her with domestic chores and conferred the prestige of conspicuous wealth on the broader family.[55] Now, the older rural wife is more often merely thrown over for the new, urban wife and left to fend for herself.[56] A new customary practice has thus emerged that accommodates men's desire to take multiple wives while dispensing with their obligations to provide ongoing support for older wives.[57] It has also become clear that the abolition of formal polygamy has largely been replaced by such geographic de facto polygamy, as migrant workers keep a rural wife at home to mind their landholdings and a live-in girlfriend in town.[58]

The information collected by CALS suggested that it would be possible to bring customary law in line with the Constitution. CALS supported the Law Commission's recommendation for a unified law of marriage but emphasized the importance of synthesizing the positive elements from both legal systems. They urged that there be one law of marriage with a set of minimum requirements and consequences to accommodate the diversity of cultural and religious practices relating to marriage.[59]

Analysis of the CALS data showed that women in customary unions were not happy with the uncertainty of customary unions particularly with regard to women's rights to property during the marriage and in the event of divorce or death of the male spouse. Employed women may be particularly resentful that their wages are used to provide gifts, support, or brideprice for a new wife.[60] In practice a number of Black South Africans were already entering into marriages that were a hybrid of civil and customary law, for example, by contracting civil law marriages and paying *lobolo* (brideprice).

Given that both men and women sought to negotiate between the plural legal regimes to achieve their perceived advantage and that communities leading customary lives had *already* fused the requirements for both marriage laws in practice, CALS argued for a single marriage law for all South Africans.[61] A uniform system such as this would not simply treat civil law as the benchmark but would recognize the pervasiveness of this sort of hybrid legal life.

However, the Law Commission did not go down this road. It pointed to several factors that led to the rejection of consolidating the laws of marriage. Firstly, they cautioned that customary law could be lost in the unification process. Concerns were voiced with regard to the ideological impact of the assimilation of African customary family law into a single code of marriage.[62] The legacy of colonial and apartheid repudiation of African law could not be ameliorated by creating a single regime that rendered distinct African norms invisible. At least at this point in time, a dual regime was best able to express respect for the values of the newly empowered African majority.

Secondly, consolidation would not necessarily be the best approach to ameliorating the position of women and children already involved in polygamy. Because these marriages were not already recognized, the Law Commission did not have the option of simply grandfathering those marriages into the law and declaring that no polygamous marriages could be entered into in the future. Comprehensive legislation regulating past and future forms of polygyny was needed. The door was left open to full consolidation in the future, however, when material and ideological conditions might have changed.[63]

The Impact and Significance of the Recognition of the Customary Marriages Act

The resulting bill, the Recognition of Customary Marriages Act (RCMA), was passed in 1998 and came into full effect two years later. The RCMA gives legal recognition to both monogamous and polygamous customary marriages.[64] Its structure reflects recommendations CALS made based on its research findings. CALS suggested an approach that would permit polygyny but subject its most egregious effects to regulation. These regulatory impacts would kick in when a man sought to convert a monogamous union into a polygamous one. Polygamous members of the Rural Women's Movement had urged that the law make available a serial division of property. If a man sought to take a new wife, the first wife could elect to demand that the property of the existing marriage be divided before he could proceed. Thus, he could marry without dissipating her current entitlements although her rights in property acquired in the future would be diminished if she stayed in the marriage.

The RCMA makes clear that only men may have more than one spouse. Different rules and entitlements apply depending on whether these marriages existed prior to November 15, 2000, the date on which the act came into effect. Since 2000, when a man purports to enter into a polygamous marriage, he must submit to the review provisions of the act.[65] He must apply to a court for approval of his plan to take a second wife.[66] His current and prospective wives must be joined as parties to the application.[67] This provision requires the man and his existing wife/wives, as well as his intended wife, to draw up a contract setting out a division of property among all the wives, including the future wife. Where the first marriage was in community of property or the accrual system (where title remains separate but the value of family assets accrued over the course of the marriage are shared equally upon dissolution), the court is obligated to terminate this joint property regime and ensure an equitable division of property between the existing spouses before a new spouse can be allowed to enter the marriage. Some commentators have argued that while the act does not explicitly require the first wife or wives to consent to the marriage, their status as parties to this review means that they can frustrate or even veto the approval of a proprietary contract such that their consent to the marriage is implied.[68]

In theory, each spouse may own this share of the family property as separate property. This means that existing wives will not risk seeing their property rights redistributed to new partners to the marriage. The husband enters into his subsequent marriage with his share of the family property, and it is only this share that may be subject to community of property with the new wife. It is unclear what sort of arrangements the spouses might agree on in these contracts to regulate their polygamous marriage going forward. A wife who lacks the skill or resources to negotiate an initial marriage contract or who is dependent upon her husband's wages may bargain away her entitlements in this new contract for the polygamous marriage. The court has the power to amend the contract if fairness requires, but this discretion may be exercised by judges who share the patriarchal views embodied in traditional customary property norms.[69] The court also has the power to refuse the application on the basis that the contract does not sufficiently protect the interests of the other wives and family members.[70]

The act does not say what happens if the man fails to reapply. It also does not specify the consequences if the husband does not bother to apply for court approval at all. A recent judgment of the High Court in Gaunteng, however, has applied this provision to declare the second customary marriage invalid.[71] The court held that interpreting the Recognition of Customary Marriage Act in light of the equality guarantees of the Constitution meant that the first wife could not be made party to a polygamous marriage without her knowledge and acquiescence. Given the power disparities that might exist between husband and wife, the court rejected the notion that her failure to object to the new marriage could be taken as acquiescence. The court held that:

> An existing wife may very often be entirely dependent upon her husband together with her children, may be unaware of her rights, may be illiterate or too timid or impecunious to seek legal advice, and may suffer the economic and emotional deprivation brought about by a subsequent marriage long before a separation as a result of death or divorce. To rely on an absence of protest by a wife who may live in fear of rejection — not to mention the children born of an earlier union — would be to consign the issue of voidability to a most uncertain and indeed arbitrary test.[72]

In making this decision, Judge Bertelsmann acknowledged the hardship this ruling imposed upon the second wife. He suggested that she might have a basis to sue her husband or his estate for his deception. This failure of husbands to register their marriages can only be addressed by educating women, both existing wives and intending spouses, about their rights under the act and the implications if its provisions are not followed.[73]

Mothoka Mamashela and Marita Carnelley object that the new law should not entirely disenfranchise the second wife, but should restore her right to share in the entitlements that flow from a recognized marriage.[74] However, while a second wife who entered into such a marriage based on her husband's deceit might experience hardship, it is not at all clear why a woman who was indifferent or willfully ignorant of his marital status should be treated with the same concern. As women learn more about how this new conception of polygamy operates, they may be incentivized to learn more about their intended partner's marital history, preventing the creation of complex relations of dependence before they start.

Conclusion: The Future of South African Polygamy

Despite its adherence to international human rights instruments that would appear to require the contrary, South Africa has chosen to provide legal recognition to polygamous marriage. It made this choice for a range of pressing reasons in the era immediately after the end of apartheid. In symbolic repudiation of colonial and apartheid expressions of contempt for African cultural and legal norms, it recognized this distinctly African marital practice. As an aspect of political strategy, to avoid stigmatizing feminist reform with the taint of colonial reformist rhetoric, it chose to recognize this practice increasingly associated with Zulu nationalist ideology. As an instance of pragmatic law reform, it responded to the fact that abuses of power under formal polygamy now pale in comparison to the problems raised by the widespread practice of de facto geographic polygyny and abandonment of first families.

The impact of the recognition of polygamy in the RCMA is ambiguous. It has not undermined sexist conceptions that see men as family heads and women as subordinate in conventional representations of South African Customary Law. It may, in fact, have provided support for these notions.[75] However, this recognition has occurred in the context of dramatic enhancements to women's capacity to renegotiate their position under customary law. Constitutional litigation has become one of a number of tools in renegotiating gendered rights in customary marriage. The passage of the Constitution itself and the creation of a culture of rights have also increased women's capacity to bargain for greater equality under customary law. In addition to revised chieftainship policies like that confirmed in the *Shilubana* case, many local communities revised their policies on land allocation to allow women to hold land in their own right after 1994.[76]

The recognition of polygamy subject to regulation was not intended to eradicate polygamy or render it a fully egalitarian form of marriage. We suggest, rather, that it was meant to be a neutral placeholder that would ameliorate some of the worst abuses of the practice while allowing customary law norms to be revised around it. Polygamy, or at least its more exploitive forms, will only decline as women gain greater power to choose other marital arrangements under customary law. This view is supported by the position of the Law Commission itself. It concluded in its report:

> The Commission accepts the common point of these objections: that legislating a right for the first wife might create "paper law." . . . It should be noted that, if several other recommendations made in this Report are adopted, the position of the wife in a customary marriage will be stronger than before. Formal recognition of her equal proprietary, contractual and decision-making capacity and locus standi, the confirmation of her majority status and the removal of the marital power over her, should all conduce to the improvement of her bargaining position on major family issues. Education and economic empowerment above all else are the true emancipators, and where they exist they are infinitely more potent protections against practices such as polygyny than potentially unenforceable state laws.[77]

It is, therefore, wrong to place too much emphasis on the question of whether the Recognition of Customary Marriages Act has improved the position of women in polygamous customary marriages. Indeed, critics have rightly doubted the capacity of the act to improve the lives of parties to customary unions from its inception,[78] cautioning that the polygamy provisions will only be a "paper tiger."[79]

The recognition and regulation of polygyny by the RCMA was intended to allow this practice to develop in compliance with the Constitution. However, its effects cannot be seen in compliance with the terms of the act. Few customary marriages, whether monogamous or polygamous, have been registered under the act.[80] The act requires the high court to hear applications to take a second wife. In practice, men simply desert the first wife and cohabit or marry a second wife. Even if one were inclined to register, there are too few of these courts, and most are inaccessible because they are situated in urban areas.[81] Court personnel lack the expertise to deal with these cases, and potential litigants lack access to courts, legal literacy, and the conviction that they are entitled to equality in marriage that would enable them to pursue their cases.

The South African Law Commission had very modest expectations for these provisions on polygamy. The recognition of polygamy was intended to achieve the symbolic effect of affirming a distinctive South African Customary Law tradition, while awaiting changes in the legal and cultural context in which polygamy operated. While giving first wives a formal right of notice, if not consent, to their husbands' further unions, the commission admitted that the economic dependence of first wives on their husbands' resources and the social dependence upon marriage as a source of legitimate identity would vitiate most women's capacity to exercise this consent.[82] However, they stressed that this perhaps symbolic recognition of polygyny needed to be read in the context of the more wide-ranging changes in the status of women in customary marriage being wrought by other provisions of the RCMA and other legislative reform initiatives. The RCMA ended the legal minority of African women and created formal equality between men and women in terms of legal status and capacity.[83] It also granted women greatly enhanced property rights within marriage by making community of property the default regime for most marriages.[84] It is these advances and consequent changes in power relations that will bring an end to abusive forms of polygamy under South African customary family law.

Notes

1. Informant quoted in Mothokoa Mamashela and Thokozani Xaba, *The Practical Implications and Effects of the Recognition of Customary Marriages Act No. 120 of 1998* (Research Report No. 89, 2004).

2. Jean Comaroff and John Comaroff, *Of Revelation and Revolution: Christianity, Colonialism and Consciousness in South Africa*, vol. 1 (Chicago: University of Chicago Press, 1991), 133.

3. Alice Armstrong et al., "Uncovering Reality: Excavating Women's Rights in African Family Law," *International Journal of Law, Policy and the Family* 7, no. 3 (1993): 326.

4. Comments of participants, "Seminar on Customary Marriage and the Constitution," Transvaal Rural Action Committee, Johannesburg (1996).

5. Likhapha Mbatha, "How Black South Africans Marry" (1997), unpublished research report for the Centre for Applied Legal Studies, University of the Witswatersrand, Johannesburg, South Africa (on file with the authors).

6. Findings of a survey by the South African National Human Rights Trust, as cited in (*Project 90), The Harmonization of the Common Law and Indigenous Law: Report On Customary Marriages* (Pretoria: South African Law Commission, 1998), 84. The same study found that 70 percent of men support the practice.

7. Universal Declaration of Human Rights, G.A. res. 217A (III), U.N. Doc A/810 at 71 (1948), article 16.

8. African [Banjul] Charter on Human and Peoples' Rights, adopted June 27, 1981, OAU Doc. CAB/LEG/67/3 rev. 5, 21 I.L.M. 58 (1982), entered into force Oct. 21, 1986, article 18.

9. International Covenant on Civil and Political Rights, G.A. res. 2200A (XXI),

21 U.N. GAOR Supp. (No. 16) at 52, U.N. Doc. A/6316 (1966), 999 U.N.T.S. 171, entered into force Mar. 23, 1976, articles 18 and 19.

10. Section 23 of the Constitution of the Republic of South Africa, 1996, requires South African courts to interpret national law, including customary law, in line with the provisions of relevant international agreements.

11. Convention on the Elimination of All Forms of Discrimination against Women, G.A. res. 34/180, 34 U.N. GAOR Supp. (No. 46) at 193, U.N. Doc. A/34/46, entered into force Sept. 3, 1981, article 5. South Africa ratified CEDAW without reservation on the December 15, 1995.

12. "General Comment on the International Covenant on Civil and Political Rights," 28–29/03/2000.

13. Recognition of Customary Marriages Act, Republic of South Africa, 1998.

14. Ibid., section 9.

15. See, for example, Isaac Schapera, *A Handbook of Tswana Law and Custom*, 2nd ed. (Oxford: Oxford University Press, 1955); Sebastian Poulter, *Family Law and Litigation in Basotho Society* (Oxford: Clarendon Press, 1975), 69.

16. A recent study by the Community Agency for Social Enquiry (CASE) found that the rate of formal polygyny in even the most conservative rural areas of South Africa does not rise above 7 percent. However, the rate of those involved in informal plural relationships outside of marriage is much higher. Debbie Budlender, specialist researcher at CASE, personal communication, July 7, 2010.

17. Comaroff and Comaroff, *Of Revelation and Revolution*, 132.

18. Armstrong et al., *Uncovering Reality*, 15.

19. J. C. Bekker, *Seymour's Customary Law in Southern Africa* (Cape Town: Juta, 1989), 106–9. Anecdotal evidence suggests that where the husband was the one who was sterile, this may have been resolved clandestinely by arranging that another male family member impregnate the wife. Participant information from workshops organized by the Centre for Applied Legal Studies, Gender Research Project in Limpopo, North West, and Gauteng (1997). For a fictionalized account of such practices, see Lola Shoneyin, *The Secret Lives of Baba Segi's Wives* (London: Serpent's Tail, 2010).

20. Armstrong et al., *Uncovering Reality*, 23.

21. Miriam Koktvedgaard Zeitzen, "The Many Wives of Jacob Zuma," *Foreign Policy*, March 12, 2010.

22. Elizabaeth Diffin, "How Do Zulus Explain Polygamy?" BBC Online, http://news.bbc.co.uk/2/hi/uk_news/magazine/8549429.stm. Zuma characterizes such criticism as based on racial misunderstandings. However, criticism of his public romantic dramas, including fathering a child out of wedlock and undergoing a

healing ceremony with a wife who is expecting a child by another man, also comes from colleagues within the African National Congress. See R.W. Johnson, "Zuma's Marital Own Goal Blots World Cup," *The Sunday Times*, June 6, 2010, http://www.timesonline.co.uk/tol/news/world/africa/article7144830.ece

23. J. C. Bekker, "Recognition of Customary Marriages Act: An Evaluation," *South African Journal of Ethnology* 24, no. 2 (2001): 450.

24. H. J. Simons, *African Women: Their Legal Status In South Africa* (London: C. Hurst and Co., 1968), 21.

25. Belinda Bozzoli, "Marxism, Feminism and the South African State," *Journal of Southern African Studies* 9, no. 2 (April 1983): 158.

26. Simons, *African Women*, 79.

27. Beth Goldblatt, *Cohabitation and Gender in the South African Context: Implications for Law Reform* (Johannesburg: Gender Research Project of the Centre for Applied Legal Studies of the University of the Witwatersrand, November 2001), s. 1.4.1.

28. See, for example, the Restitution of Land Rights Act 22 of 1994, which provides for restitution of rights to those who were dispossessed of land through racially based policies of the apartheid government. Section 35(3) gives the Land Claims Court the power to impose conditions to ensure that all the dispossessed members of the community, including women, have access to the land or compensation on a nondiscriminatory basis.

29. See Rylands v. Edros 1997(2) SA 690 (C). See also Amod v. Multilateral Motor Vehicle Accident Fund 1999 (4) SA 1319 (SCA). For an extended discussion of the *Rylands* case, see Lisa Fishbayn, "Litigating the Right to Culture: Family Law in the New South Africa," *International Journal of Law, Policy and the Family* 13, no. 2 (1999): 160.

30. See Rashida Manjoo, "Muslim Family Law in South Africa: Conflating the Right to Religion with the Privileging of Religion?" in this volume, text accompanying footnotes 10–15.

31. Alice Armstrong, *Struggling over Scarce Resources: Women and Maintenance in South Africa* (Harare: University of Zimbabwe Publications, 1992), xi.

32. Ian Hamnett, *Chieftainship and Legitimacy: An Anthropological Study of Executive Law in Lesotho* (London: Routledge and Kegan Paul, 1975), 13.

33. T. W. Bennett, "Re-Introducing African Customary Law to the South African Legal System," *American Journal of Comparative Law* 57, no. 1 (2009): 28.

34. Catherine Albertyn, "'The Stubborn Persistence of Patriarchy'? Gender Equality and Cultural Diversity in South Africa," *Constitutional Court Review* 2 (2011) 165, text preceeding footnote 67.

35. Bhe v. Magistrate Khayelitsha & Others 2005 (1) BCLR 1 (CC), at paragraph 42.

36. Shilubana and Others v. Nwamitwa 2008 (9) BCLR 914 (CC).

37. *Shilubana*, paragraph 4.

38. *Shilubana*, paragraph 49.

39. Martin Channock, "Law, State and Culture: Thinking About 'Customary Law' after Apartheid," 1991 *Acta Juridica* 52, 71.

40. Constitution of the Republic of South Africa, sections 30 and 31.

41. Ibid., section 15.

42. Ibid., section 211

43. Ibid., section 15(3)(b).

44. Ibid., sections 30 and 31.

45. Ibid., section 35.

46. Marriage and Matrimonial Property Law Amendment Act 3 of 1988, repealing s. 22(6) of the Black Administration Act 38 of 1927.

47. See Michael Yarbrough, *South Africa's Wedding Jitters: Consolidation, Abolition, or Proliferation? Yale Journal of Law and Feminism* 18, no. 2 (2007): 497–521.

48. Channock, "Law, State and Culture," 65.

49. South African Law Commission, *(Project 90), The Harmonization of the Common Law and Indigenous Law (Customary Marriages)*, Issue Paper 3 (Pretoria: South African Law Commission, 1996).

50. See Transkei Marriage Act 21 of 1978.

51. South African Law Commission, *(Project 90) Harmonization of Customary and Indigenous Law (Customary Marriages)*, Discussion Paper 74 (Pretoria: South African Law Commission, 1997), paragraph 1.

52. Conflicts over school fees and housing were a source of widespread anxiety. Comments of participants, "Seminar on Customary Law and the Constitution," Transvall Rural Action Committee, Johannesburg (1996).

53. Gender Research Project, *Final Report on Gender, Citizenship and Governance Project* (Johannesburg: Centre for Applies Legal Studies, 2002), 18.

54. Armstrong et al., *Uncovering Reality*, 27.

55. Mamashela and Xaba, *The Practical Implications and Effects of the Recognition of Customary Marriages Act*, 24.

56. Ibid., 25.

57. Ibid., 27.

58. Comments of Lydia Kompe, MP, at the Rural Women's Movement Annual General Meeting, Johannesburg (1996).

59. South African Law Commission, *Report on Customary Marriages*, paragraph 2.1.2.

60. Thabile Mbatha, "In and Out of Polygyny: A Case of Black South African Women's Experiences of Marriage," *Agenda* 25, no. 1 (2011): 32.

61. Gender Research Project, *Gender, Citizenship and Governance*, 20.

62. South African Law Commission *Report on Customary Marriages*, paragraph 2.1.29.

63. Ibid., paragraph 2.1.28

64. Sections 2(1) and (2) of the Recognition of Customary Marriages Act. Section 2(1) provides that "marriages that are valid under customary law and existing at the commencement date of the Act are for all purposes recognised." Customary marriages that were entered into during the subsistence of a civil marriage were void *ab initio* under section 22 of the Black Administration Act 38 of 1927. See *Nkambula v. Linda* 1951(1) SA 377 (A). The RCMA repealed this provision, but its impact remains ambiguous. See, for example, E. Bonthuys and M. Pieterse, "Still Unclear: The Validity of Certain Customary Marriages," *Journal of Contemporary Roman-Dutch Law* 63, no. 4 (2000): 621; and I. P. Maithufi and G. M. B. Moloi, "The Need for the Protection of Rights of Partners to Invalid Marital Relationships: A Revisit of the 'Discarded Spouse' Debate," *De Jure* 38, no. 1 (2005): 144.

65. For an extended discussion of the operation of the RCMA, see the Centre for Appplied Legal Studies, *Customary Marriage Bench Book* (Pretoria: Justice College, Department of Justice and Constitutional Development, 2004).

66. Recognition of Customary Marriages Act, section 7(6).

67. Ibid., section 7(8).

68. Centre for Applied Legal Studies, *Customary Law Bench Book.*

69. Mamashela and Xaba, *The Practical Implications and Effects of the Recognition of Customary Marriages Act.*

70. Recognition of Customary Marriages Act, section 7(b)(iii).

71. MM v. MN 2010 (4) SA 286 (GNP). The first wife had been married in 1986; the second in 2008. The wives learned of the other's existence only upon the husband's death in 2009.

72. MM v. MN, paragraph 32.

73. MM v. MN, paragraph 34.

74. Mothokoa Mamashela and Marita Carnelley, "The Catch 22 Situation of Widows from Polygamous Marriages Being Discarded under Customary Law: *MM v. MN* 2010 (4) SA 286 (GNP) in a Historical Context," *Agenda* 25, no. 1 (2011): 112, 118–19.

75. Centre for Appplied Legal Studies, *Customary Marriage Bench Book*, 31.

76. Aninka Claassens and Sindiso Mnisi, "Rural Women Redefining Land Rights in the Context of Living Customary Law," *South African Journal of Human Rights* 3 (2009): 491, 493.

77. South African Law Commission, *Report on Customary Marriages*, paragraphs 6.1.19 and 6.1.20.

78. For example, Victoria Bronstein, "Confronting Custom in the New South African State: An Analysis of the *Recognition of the Customary Marriages Act 120 of 1998*," *South African Journal of Human Rights* 16 (2000): 558–75.

79. Mamashela and Xaba, *The Practical Implications and Effects of the Recognition of Customary Marriages Act*.

80. I. P. Maithufi and J. C. Bekker, "The Existence and Proof of Customary Marriages for Purposes of Road Accident Fund Claims," *Obiter* 30, no. 1 (2009): 164, 173.

81. Although draft legislation would amend the law to allow couples to register before the far more accessible magistrates courts. See Draft Recognition of Customary Marriages Bill, 2009.

82. South African Law Commission, *(Customary Marriages) Discussion Paper*, paragraphs 6.1.12.

83. Recognition of Customary Marriages Act, section 6.

84. The RCMA has provided a basis for other advances in the position of women under customary marriage law. Section 7 (2) makes all customary marriages contracted after 2000 subject to a community of property regime but section 7(1) held that marriages entered into prior to that point would continue to be governed by customary law. In the recent case of *Gumede v. President of the Republic of South Africa*, the wife challenged section 7(1) as a violation of her rights to gender equality under the Constitution. The effect in her case would have been to make her property rights subject to Zulu law, which granted her husband exclusive rights to the family's property and gave her no right to property upon divorce. The court agreed, finding that this version of customary law resulted in a "particularly crude and gendered form of inequality which left women and children singularly marginalized and destitute." The provision was thus declared unconstitutional and now all customary marriages, whenever contracted, are subject to community of property (at paragraphs 50–54).

Part Three
Narratives of Innovative Law Reform

IRIT KOREN

Chapter Eight Women, Resources, and Changing the Religious System A Case Study of the Orthodox Jewish Wedding Ritual

[W]omen even as subordinate players, always play an active part that goes beyond the dichotomy of victimization/acceptance, a dichotomy that flattens out a complex and ambiguous agency in which women accept, accommodate, ignore, resist, or protest sometimes all at the same time. —*Arlene Elowe MacLeod*[1]

For the last few years I have been researching a small, yet growing number of Modern Orthodox women in Israel who seek to challenge, resist, or adapt the Orthodox wedding ritual to transform it into an expression of their own identity, values, and ideals. These women identified themselves both as Orthodox and as feminists or having feminist consciousness, at least to some degree. These two identities are often at odds, since values embraced by feminism and Orthodoxy might be experienced as contradictory to each other. In my research, I have found that the wedding ritual is a prime context in which to examine the accommodation of these two identities, Orthodox and feminist.

For many Orthodox feminist women this ritual is a point of contention because, in halakhah, the wedding ritual marks the groom's acquisition of the sexual rights of the bride, and that legal action underlies many of the customs associated with the ritual itself as well as causes significant implications in case of divorce. The women I studied sought to modify the ritual and their approach to it in ways meant to put them on more of an equal footing with their husbands, both through visual performance and by confronting the ritual's legal construction.

The modifications and challenges the women did to their wedding ritual required them to negotiate extensively with their social environment: their husbands-to-be, parents, and rabbis.

The focus of this chapter is to identify and analyze what are the *resources* that the women found necessary in order to begin negotiating and changing parts of the wedding ritual. However, since these women chose not to leave the religious system but rather work from within it, they also needed to have resources that would enable them to remain in the system despite their criticism of it or when the changes they wished to do were not accepted. While one might argue that staying in a religious system in spite of one's criticism and objection is an act of weakness rather than an act of strength, I feel otherwise. Indeed there are instances in which staying in the religious system is a sign of weakness, but this is not the case with these brides. For these women, the option of the secular world is open and available. They can choose to leave their religious world at any time. Therefore it is my contention that in this case, choosing to maintain and work within the religious structure that sometimes contradicts some of their own values is an act of strength and requires social, emotional, and intellectual resources as well. This understanding of the resources these women have will finally lead me to the explanation of why it is this specific group of women who initiates this phenomenon of challenging the wedding ritual, thus the religious system, rather than other groups of women such as secular brides or ultra-Orthodox brides.

Background

The research methodology was qualitative and included interviews with twenty-five religious women for whom the wedding ritual was a point of contention. In order to further understand their social context, I also interviewed some of the mothers, fathers, and husbands as well as some of the rabbis who performed the weddings. In addition, I was a participant observer in many of these women's weddings.

When I started the research I was looking to interview women who defined themselves as religious[2] and who have tried to challenge their wedding rituals in different ways. I reached these women through the "snowball" method — each interviewee sending me to another woman who she thought would answer this definition. The women I studied composed a fairly homogeneous group. All were in their mid-twenties to mid-thirties at the time of their marriage, and all of the marriages took place within the past decade; all are well educated both in the religious and secular realm; and all lived in Jerusalem while single, specifically in the neighborhoods of Rehavia, Katamon, and Baka.[3] Many of them either were immigrants of English-speaking countries, came from families whose origins were English-speaking countries, or married English-speaking men. This, I believe, comes as no surprise, since feminism and specifically religious feminism was imported, at least initially, by feminist women who immigrated from the United States to Israel and brought with them these ideas of gender equality.[4]

Moreover, these women, who identify themselves as religious, feel constrained (to varying degrees) to abide by Jewish law (halakhah). Thus, they evinced a desire to have Orthodox weddings. They did not feel that they could take the path of some secular men and women who opt for egalitarian ceremonies that are not acknowledged by the Orthodox rabbinate, the only body authorized to register Jewish marriages in Israel. Such marriages can be registered only by means of a civil ceremony performed outside the country — a route followed by many secular Israelis in order to avoid the religious ceremony altogether.[5]

Although the women I interviewed are still a local vanguard, I believe this phenomenon is expanding and increasing its influence among the wider Orthodox community and within its discourse in Israel.

The transformative aims of the women's practices can be understood only in the context of the traditional wedding ritual as it is performed in Israel (and throughout the Orthodox Jewish world) today. That ritual comprises the following steps: Before the wedding ceremony, the groom signs the *ketubah*, a contract delineating his financial obligations toward his wife. Then he is led to the bride, who has been sitting in a chair awaiting him. Upon reaching her, he covers her face with a veil. He turns and walks to the huppah (marriage canopy), accompanied by the wedding guests, and awaits the bride there. The bride, similarly, proceeds to the huppah, and upon reaching it, in the Ashkenazi (European Jewish) custom, she circles the groom seven times, accompanied by her mother and mother-in-law to be. Only now does the formal two-part ritual begin. The first part is the *kiddushin* (acquisition) ceremony, in which, following recitation of the betrothal blessing and the blessing over wine, the man fulfills the active role of acquiring the woman by addressing her with the Hebrew words *Harei at mekudeshet li* ("You are hereby consecrated unto me") while giving her a ring. After this, the *ketubah* is read aloud, separating the two parts of the ritual. Now the second part begins — the *nisu'in* (marriage), in which the *sheva berakhot*, the traditional seven wedding blessings, are read by a man or several men. At the end of the ritual the groom shatters a glass by stomping on it.[6]

Numerous feminist critiques have been leveled against the traditional wedding ritual, specifically targeting the *kiddushin* as an act of acquisition (of the women's sexuality) and, therefore, one of oppression.[7] There are some harsh implications of this legal arrangement, which is still valid in the rabbinical courts in Israel as well as in the rest of the Orthodox Jewish world. Most importantly, a Jewish woman wed by the laws of the Torah can be divorced only by her husband's act of giving her a traditional bill of divorce (*get*). Should her husband stubbornly refuse or otherwise be unable to release her in this way, she will remain a *mesurevet get* or an *agunah*, unable to remarry.[8] In this matter, Jewish law discriminates openly and explicitly between men and women. A *mesurevet get* or *agunah* who chooses to live with another man pays a heavy price. Her children by that man are considered *mamzerim* (bastards), and under religious law neither they nor their offspring for the next ten generations are allowed to marry Jews. Because all marriages between Jews in Israel are governed by Orthodox religious law, such children and their descendants are unable to marry in the State of Israel. In contrast, a married man can have children by another woman without legal sanction.[9]

Critiques have also been leveled at other ritual acts or elements associated with the wedding: the covering of the bride with the veil has been interpreted as symbolically rendering her invisible; the circling of the groom strikes many as indicating that he is at the center, while the bride is at the margins; and the seven blessings, recited by men only, do not give women a voice in this part of the ceremony.

The changes put into place by the women I interviewed can be divided into two realms: the visual realm and the legal realm. The visual realm includes the following three strategies:

(a) Creating a parallel ritual act. The women who adopted this strategy initiated ritual acts that attempted to mirror the traditional male rites. By setting a female act opposite the male one, they endeavored to create a performance of equality without running afoul of halakhic prohibitions. An example of this is the bride's covering her groom with a *tallith* (prayer shawl) after she is veiled by him or the bride giving the groom a ring as well.

(b) Introducing variations on the ritual act. The women who used this strategy focused on creating a variation on a traditional act, such as circling each other instead of the bride circling the groom alone.

(c) Avoiding a particular ritual act. In this case, not performing the ritualistic act is in itself a performance of protest and objection. Examples of such actions are: avoiding the traditional act of circling the groom altogether or avoiding reading the *ketubah* out loud. [10]

As for the legal realm, the strategy typically does not involve a public performance under the huppah; rather it seeks to alter the acquisitional nature of the ritual. One way the brides did so was to draft and sign documents in the presence of an attorney, with the intention of diminishing the legal status of *kiddushin* as an act of acquisition. The core legal document employed in this strategy is the prenuptial agreement, called the "Agreement for Mutual Respect,"[11] which purports to supplement the *ketubah* by stipulating the exercise of economic pressure, in the form of increased alimony payments, in the case of a man refusing to give his wife her *get* (or of her refusing to receive it).[12]

Women, Religion, Agency, and Resources

The brides I have interviewed are unique in that they function as social agents of change in their religious system. Susan Sered, who writes about female agency in the context of religion, argues that when analyzing gender conflict in religious systems, it is crucial to understand that two ontologically different sets of issues are involved. The first set is "women" — female people who have varying degrees of agency within specific social situations. The second set is "Woman" — a symbolic construct mixing gender, sex, and sexuality. This construct is comprised of allegory, metaphor, fantasy, and (at least in male dominant religions) men's psychological projections."[13] Sered continues to argue that "'Woman' as a symbol is often associated with some of the deepest and most compelling theological and mythological structures in a religious tradition."[14] Therefore, these symbolic structures influence and shape women's behavior and attitudes. Hence the ability of women to enter a negotiation on changing the religious system depends on their own perception of themselves as "women" or as the "Woman." Sered thus concludes that "the more agency women have, the more control they have over the creation and interpretation of symbols. Where any particular group of women falls along the agent-symbol continuum, depends on their access to social resources."[15]

Sered then looks specifically at brides and argues that in the context of women's agency, brides seem to be a special group of women, since they embody powerful social forces such as sexuality and reproduction that are associated with women and are also performed ritually. Therefore, brides have almost no access to social resources. Moreover, they themselves are perceived by society as a social resource.[16]

The uniqueness of the group of women I have investigated is that they act as social agents of change within a religious system — an unusual thing in traditional societies, specifically for women. Moreover, the group of women in this research are characterized, as I will demonstrate later, by their access to many resources.

During my interviews with them, I have asked myself how these women live in this tension between modernity and tradition. I have tried to understand what are the social, personal, and intellectual resources that enable them to deal with the complex social location they choose to be in, specifically since they have the option to leave the religious world or, alternatively, to abandon feminist values altogether. I believe that part of the answer to these questions lies in understanding the resources these women possess.

Examining the resources of social groups is one way that the field of sociology uses in order to understand social processes. There is an understanding that people use the same resources in different ways to achieve different things. In this article I will look at the resources that these women use in order to maintain their acrobatic walk on a very thin rope. I have found five different recourses, or using an analogy — five different coins — these women use. Some brides use one side of the coin in one instance, while using the other side of the coin in a different instance. In other words, they use different sides of the coin either to achieve change in the wedding ritual or to accept the ritual and the religious system as it is.

As apposed to Sered's conclusion regarding the lack of resources of brides, the brides in my study did have access to many social resources. Therefore, they made themselves social agents who strived to challenge and change, if only in part, the religious symbols of the wedding ritual and, thus, impact the religious system as a whole. Their access to resources can be explained partially due to the fact that for the most part these brides were mature adults (in their late twenties or early thirties) as well as highly educated. Hence, since these brides were characterized as older and educated, they were able to "acquire more agency and lose their magnetism, as objects of symbolization."[17]

The Resources of the Brides

I categorized the resources utilized by the brides in my study into six groupings. These resources were used by the same women or by different women as a flexible currency at times in order to challenge and resist the wedding ritual, and at other times to accept the system as it is or, alternatively, to help them let go of their own wishes in times that the negotiation failed.

However, in addition to each one of these resources, which could be used in opposing ways, I found an additional resource that I view as an umbrella resource used by all the women in the same way. I see this resource, which I named "the ability to contain dissonance," as a personality trait that enabled these brides to enter these complex negotiations to begin with. These women's ability to embrace the tension in their life enabled them to engage in their multifaceted identity as religious and as modern and feminist women. On the surface, it seems that these women could have chosen a much easier path to end the identity dissonance they experienced. One way to do so is by crossing the line and moving to the secular world, defining themselves only as modern and feminist women. In this case, their motivation to identify and to justify the religious system would be lessened, and thus, if they still had chosen to get married in a traditional wedding they would most probably not feel the need to challenge it. Rather they could go through the ritualistic motions without expecting them to relate to their identity and values. Another option would have been to give up their feminist identity and focus mainly on their religious identity, thus having no motivation to challenge the wedding ritual and the religious system as a whole. However, none of these women chose either option and instead have chosen to live within this tension and negotiate their reality.

The ability of theses women to embrace their conflicting identities stands in opposition to some findings. According to different studies, individuals try to avoid painful cognitive dissonance, which is created from contradicting sets of beliefs, by adjusting one set of beliefs to the other in a way that protects them.[18] The need people have to diminish their cognitive dissonance is not a preference but rather a necessity. Therefore, they are driven to act in a certain way that will end the disharmony between their different cognitive representations.[19]

In the context of modern religious women, research found that the more women are expecting equality in different social contexts, the more the roles and the images that religious systems offer them are in discrepancy with their positive self-evaluation to which they are educated. Once again, although one might expect that this fact would encourage women to leave their religion, the findings point out that a high proportion of women choose not to do so.[20]

It seems that the aspirations of the brides in my research — to stay within the religious system and to work within it — relate to a deep identification they have with larger parts of this system. They do not feel estranged from the system; rather they wish to change the system specifically because they identify with it. Thus these two ideological stances: the religious and the modern are intertwined with each other and stem from each other. Tehila, one of my interviewees, describes this complexity:

> In my eyes to be religious is to listen. It is to implement the moral wishes of God in an authentic way every moment, and this wish is something that changes. When one reads the Bible and understands that it nurtures a patriarchic society, then it undermines the concept that the Torah was given from God, since how could it be that God encourages a patriarchic society? The theologian Tamar Ross solves this problem by saying that the revelation of God is a continuous one. In each time period, it reveals the moral message suited to meeting the challenges faced by that generation and advancing the world.[21]

Tehila thus recruits the feminist theological discourse to explain her double identity and hence transforms her feminist perception to something that is inherent to the religious system itself.

Rivki, an Israeli religious feminist activist, gives another example of this hybrid identity and her approach to this conflict when she says, "When it comes to being [a modern woman like] an attorney general, but you can not pray [like men], it results in a social blowing up with a lot of emotions involved. And then some women stop praying altogether, some women make peace with it, and some women create something new."

Indeed many women in my research made peace with this conflict of identity by creating something new, such as new and innovative interpretations and actions regarding the wedding ritual. They chose to change the system within but not to "stop praying altogether." These women roam between the different worlds, the religious and the modern, and decide in each social situation which structure of interpretation they accept — the feminist one or the traditional one.

First Resource: Knowledge of Torah — "And a Tree to Be Desired to Make One Wise"

The ideal of studying Torah was always a central value in the Jewish world. Boys were directed, from a very young age, to dedicate themselves to the study of Torah and to excel in it. At the same time, there were marginal groups who were not able to access this knowledge due to social or economic status, such as women. The prohibition to teach women Torah became, with time, an ideal in itself. This prohibition stems from the Talmudic saying of Rabbi Elieazer: "Every one who teaches his daughter Torah, these teach her folly [or, lasciviousness]" (Mishnah, Sotah 3:4). This saying, which was originally more a recommendation than a prohibition, became, with time, an all-encompassing ban and an impassable boundary for any woman who wished to study Torah.[22] In this sense Jewish society created a deliberate legacy of illiteracy for women by closing the gates of religious knowledge to them.[23]

In the context of Jewish women and religious literacy, Jewish girls were allowed to enter religious education through the Beis Yakov schools only in the nineteenth century. This occurred originally in order to teach these girls how to become better religious wives and mothers who could maintain and pass on the Jewish tradition to their children. Here, too, religious education had the unintended consequence of women undergoing personal and social changes that went beyond the scope of what was intended for them. Eventually by the twentieth century, women pushed the boundaries of learning and entered the world of Talmud, which until then had belonged to men only. This knowledge enabled them to start interpreting and negotiating the religious system in a way that wasn't done beforehand. From the moment women tasted the tree of knowledge, they discovered that there was no way back. This knowledge changed not only them, but also social norms and practices as well.[24] Thus the entrance of women to religious literacy has created a social revolution.[25]

Therefore, the most important resource, in my view, possessed by most of these women was an intellectual one — Jewish religious literacy. Here, the feminist saying "Knowledge is power" takes on real meaning. Many of my interviewees had a master's degree or were working on their PhD in Jewish studies specifically in the areas of Talmud and Jewish thought. Others have learned for a significant amount of time in one of the many *batei midrashot* (Torah houses of study) that are open to women and are spread throughout different parts of Israel, mainly Jerusalem. The relationship between the resource of knowledge and social change has been discussed extensively in research concerning literacy.[26] This perhaps can explain why their resource of religious knowledge enabled these women to start a negotiation vis-à-vis their social environment.

The women in my study, who had a strong command of religious knowledge, felt a certain sense of ownership of the religious texts,[27] and this enabled them to move on to the next stage of changing religious praxis. The fact that these women have access to religious texts — meaning they are able to locate the texts, understand them, and interpret them — also enabled these women to take issue with these texts and challenge conventional applications. However, having this literacy was not always a sufficient resource to allow these women to bring about change, in that religious authority figures, including rabbis, often did not view the women as legitimate partners in a discussion of how to interpret religious texts, precisely because they are women. Oshrat's story demonstrates this point very well. Oshrat, a learned Talmudic scholar herself, wanted women to read some of the seven blessings under her huppah. After she looked at the various sources from the Talmud, she concluded that there is no apparent prohibition to prevent this. Yet she still wanted to get a formal halakhic affirmation. Therefore she asked to meet the head of the religious court in Jerusalem. Oshrat describes this meeting as follows:

> I was in a dream world. I thought that if I will just ask someone what the halakhah is regarding this issue, it will all work out.... I went to ask him [the head of the religious court] and it was simply terrible. I left there crying. He treated me as if I am not part of the Jewish nation.... He yelled at me, "You are coming from the Diaspora and bringing with you all this feminism to Jewish ideas.... He didn't respond to my halakhic question at all....
>
> At first, I thought we were having a conversation, and I tried to tell him that this doesn't come from outside of Judaism. There is a source in the Talmud that talks about the ways the priests would let women participate, to some extent, in the sacrificing of animals' rituals [by allowing them to lay their hands on the animals' heads]. From there you can see that women wished to actively participate in the mitzvah [religious commandment]... so I tried to say that this aspect was always in our tradition, but this was not a conversation. He just kept yelling at me. It was terrible.

This story demonstrates how Oshrat's knowledge and religious arguments were irrelevant. Her knowledge and arguments were not taken into account in her negotiation with the rabbi.

There is a flip side to this coin. The resource of religious literacy was used by some of the women, not in opposition to religious leaders or religious law regarding the wedding ritual, but internally in order to enable them to remain within the system without challenging it. The ownership these women felt they have of the texts made it possible for them to reinterpret, reimagine, and even find feminist voices in the different wedding actions, which in turn enabled them to develop a discourse that could undermine the traditional patriarchal reading of the wedding ritual without making any actual changes.

Second Resource: Age— "When Will You Get Married Already?"

Similar to Sered's argument that the older and more educated the brides are, the more they acquire an ability to become social agents, in this case it also seems that the fact that these women married relatively late in life can help to explain, in part, their ability to challenge the religious tradition and establishment and to strive for change.

One might not understand why marrying in one's late twenties or mid-thirties should be a significant factor or resource for these women. However, the social context should be taken into consideration. In Orthodox society there is an expectation that women and men will get married in their early twenties. Moreover, since it is forbidden for men and women who date to have any physical contact, they are expected to make their decision relatively fast and get married a few months following their introduction. The phenomenon of "elderly bachelors" and single women is a new and modern phenomenon in the religious world, and many religious leaders see it as an illness spreading in the religious society.[28]

Due to this "elderly" singlehood, these women leave the traditional confines of their parents' homes and wander to Jerusalem, which attracts them because of the unique social scene there, which includes many single men and women and a relatively open religious environment. During this time they are exposed to the liberal, modern, pluralistic, and feminist discourse prevalent in many social circles in these neighborhoods. Living in these neighborhoods influences their identity and their religious conceptions. Their acquaintance with different synagogues, friends, and political and social movements exposes them, among other things, to egalitarian ideas that they have not been aware of or exposed to beforehand. These women thus arrive at their weddings after living away from their parents for a while and after having had the opportunity to construct their own ideas about religion and social roles.[29] Hence, they come to their wedding relatively informed about feminist notions and about the sort of changes that could be made to the traditional ritual. Their relatively old age at the time of marriage provide them the maturity, strength, and crystallized opinions that enable them to enter into an extensive negotiation about their marriage.

The flip side of this coin is that the older age of these women may have also been a factor in these brides' ability not to be seduced to the "all or nothing" paradigm, hence choosing one system value over the other. This "all or nothing" view is typical of young adults and teens. It is not accidental that the social revolutions happening in the 1960s (e.g., the civil rights movement, Malcolm X, the veterans movement, the feminist movement) were led by young people and students.[30]

Research shows that young women who lived in the tension of modernity and religion tend to either leave religion or give up modern and feminist values and notions.[31] As opposed to these young women who try to avoid the conflict of living in a complex world by choosing one world over the other, the brides in my research, perhaps because they were older, came to their marriage with a complex consciousness that had ripened over a long time. Hence they were able to contain this complex reality and live within both value systems while consistently maneuvering between them.

Third Resource: A Defined Identity—Between a Feminist and a Religious Identity

"I AM DEFINITELY A FEMINIST"

Another resource that stood out was the bride's feminist identity or feminist consciousness. One of the definitions of feminist consciousness or "gender consciousness" is an "identification with women, recognition of the interests and problems women share, and support for collective efforts to realize women's interest and alleviate their problems. . . . [G]ender consciousness clearly refers to the nontraditional conception of women's role typically associated with feminism."[32] The reason a feminist identity or feminist consciousness is so powerful is because it challenges the social system of gender power relations as well as contains "a shared group identity, and a growing politicization resulting in a social movement."[33] Therefore, it has the potential power to create changes in these relations.

The women I interviewed differed from each other regarding the strength of their feminist consciousness and, accordingly, the strength of their identification as feminists. When I approached the women about being interviewed, some of them hurried to clarify that they do not identify themselves as feminists. However, during the interview, a strong feminist identity or consciousness clearly emerged. It seems that there was a gap between the women's self-identification as feminist and their willingness to identify themselves publicly as feminists. This might have to do with the negative and hostile attitudes of society generally and their society in specific in regard to the notion of feminism and feminists themselves. It is not surprising then that some of the brides interviewed for my research differentiated between their feminist consciousness and their identity as feminist, while others strongly owned their feminist identity, like Oshrat, who proclaims, "I am definitely a feminist." Nevertheless, in both cases the women expressed their feminist notions and values.

Research has demonstrated that while feminist opinion (some might refer to this as feminist consciousness as well) and feminist identity are two concepts that relate to each other, they are not always identical to each other.[34] The willingness to embrace a feminist identity publicly is related to a higher level of feminist consciousness. When women are willing to label themselves as feminists, they also tend to take upon themselves feminist activism — participating in more public activities that relate to women's issues and rights.[35]

Hence, the women in my study who embraced their feminist identity were those who challenged the traditional ritual most aggressively and most politically; that is, I identified a relationship between the depth of the feminist identity and the radicalism of the changes to the ritual. In this sense, these brides used this personality resource that enabled them to challenge the wedding ritual and, therefore, the religious system in an extensive way. This is opposed to women who clearly had a feminist consciousness but refrained from identifying themselves as feminist.

"TRADITION DOES A LOT FOR ME"

The flip side of having a strong feminist identity is embracing one's religious identity on account of the feminist identity. Identifying with tradition enabled some of the brides to remain comfortable with refraining from change on some fronts or accepting tradition for what it is when changing it was impossible or too difficult. Some of my subjects expressed their feeling that religious life is a package deal, with more benefits than disadvantages on the whole; they spoke of being part of a dynasty, and of doing what their grandmothers and grandfathers had done; they spoke of the historical significance of tradition as something empowering for them. Ella put it this way: "Tradition does a lot for me, and tradition has a lot of power. That is the main thing for me."

When some of the brides had to choose in different instances between the "hierarchical meaning structure" and the "feminist meaning structure" for their wedding ritual, they deliberately chose the first meaning structure. In these instances, they emphasized the different elements of the rituals that they felt they could identify with. Hence, embracing the religious identity enabled them to stay within the given structure without challenging it.

This strategy isn't typical of Jewish women only. Women from different religions often express their identification with their tradition, stating that generally religion is good even when it has the negative attribute of discriminating against them. They deal with this cognitive dissonance by reframing and reinterpreting the negative elements in their religion in a more positive light. This conception enables them to continue on with their religious life.[36] It seems then that some of the brides I interviewed, in certain circumstances, chose to stress their feeling of overall satisfaction with the religious experience they live in. Therefore, they are willing to ignore certain aspects of gender discrimination that exist in the tradition.

Thus the uniqueness of most of these brides was in their ability to maneuver between embracing their feminist identity and their religious identity, choosing accordingly in each instance between the feminist meaning structure and the hierarchical meaning structure.

Fourth Resource: Emotional Managements—Between Negative and Positive Management

Another resource that enabled these brides to navigate the continuum of change and tradition was the emotional management these brides conducted within themselves. According to Arlie Hochschild, "emotional management" is what we do to our emotions to tailor them for particular situations. When there is a conflict between circumstances and ideology, women and men alike tend to resort to a strategy of emotional management to enable them to act appropriately according to the convention of one's gender and culture.[37] Due to social constructions, education, and culture, the way women manage their emotions is different from how men do so. Women are socially constructed to master their feelings of anger and aggression and work on positive emotions and on the appearance of "being nice girls," while men are constructed to mask feelings of fear and vulnerability.[38]

However, in the case of these women, they were able, on the one hand, to embrace their emotions of anger, enabling them to enter the negotiation on the wedding ritual. On the other hand, these women were able to repress feelings of anger when they felt that the expression of anger would be unproductive, and instead to reinforce feelings of happiness and love.

Based on my research, I would argue that in order to bring about change to the religious framework and start negotiations with the husband, family, and rabbis, the emotional management that my subjects needed to employ was in the nature of *embracing the negative emotions of anger, disappointment, frustration, and stirring up.* These women expressed negative emotions concerning the gap between their feminist values and the hierarchical wedding ritual in which men are more legally powerful and performatively visible compared to women. Embracing their feelings of anger allowed these brides to use this resource to justify their need for change.

Orly Benjamin, in her research about emotional management, refers to anger as a powerful resource that enables one to enter a negotiation in a hierarchical system. She calls this process "unsilencing," the process in which the understanding of oppression defeats the traditional understanding in any given situation, to the extent that the new interpretation can be voiced.[39]

Anger is therefore a significant resource used in order for one to create change. It is particularly significant for women, since women usually find it hard to express anger.[40] According to Hochschild, the reason for this is because anger is perceived as sabotaging the attachment with others, which is counter to how women construct their identity in relations to others.[41] Harriet Lerner explains that from a social perspective it is useful for women to distance themselves from feelings of anger and do positive emotional management, because Western culture does not look kindly upon "angry women."[42] Angry women are perceived as a threat because the anger signals the need for change to the status quo. According to Lerner, even when society is empathetic to the goals of equality, they perceive "angry women" as an annoyance to society. For women, "the direct expression of anger, especially at men, makes us unladylike, unfeminine, unmaternal, sexually unattractive. . . . Even our language condemns such women as 'shrews,' 'witches,' 'bitches,' 'hags,' 'nags,' 'man haters,' and 'castrators.'"[43]

Women are thus socialized to believe that conflict with men or with male frameworks is the wrong approach and instead they must learn to sublimate anger into positive emotions.[44] Women (like other oppressed groups) lack the expertise in dealing directly with conflict, since culturally these emotions and the behavior that is associated with conflict were suppressed within them.

Acknowledging this social construction helps women to understand the uniqueness of the resource of engaging in negative emotional management, especially in the context of their wedding, when women are expected to be the model of femininity. Yet, although a resource, women's anger did not always guarantee their success in changing the ritual. Many times they found themselves giving up or compromising on their wishes in spite of their anger toward the religious system. This complexity is expressed in Michal's interview when she states, "I am exhausted," or Tehila's interview when she says, "One needs to be a real fighter to make a change." Yet the significance of negative emotional management and, specifically, the ability to embrace feelings of anger is that, at least in regard to some situations, these women were able to start a negotiation on the hierarchical meaning structure and, thus, a process of actual change.

"IN THE NAME OF LOVE"

The flip side of this coin is a capacity to repress feelings of anger and engage in *positive emotional management.* Women used this resource in order to help them to remain within the traditional religious framework. They did this by putting aside feelings of anger, insult, and hurt and emphasizing feelings of joy, love, and excitement.

One might ask: if positive emotional management is what women are constructed to do, how then can engaging in positive emotional management be a resource? It is my belief that in the case of my brides, it becomes a resource because the women who choose to engage in positive emotional management do so consciously, compared to other women who might be doing this as a default reaction. The brides in my study have a feminist awareness and realize the problematic aspects of the ritual and the religious system as a whole. Therefore, choosing to put aside their frustration and anger in regard to some or most of the elements relating to the wedding is, in this context, a resource that helps them to stay in the religious system, rather than leaving it. Ella expresses her positive emotional management in the following way:

> What really excited me was that I was getting married; the rest is not that significant.... You see *I don't have a lot of anger*, and I think you need to be

smart about it. . . . That is, I chose a rabbi who understands my questions and where I am coming from with these questions. But *it is a shame if your starting point should be that of anger.* There are enough ways today to be creative and deal with this anger.

Michal, another bride interviewed after her marriage, also talks about her positive feelings that enabled her to make at least some peace with the ritual:

> I am not a person who likes to surrender, but today in the structure of my life and in the structure of making peace within my house I need to reach compromises that are difficult for me but that I reach them in *the name of love* I guess, kind of.

While Ella stresses again and again her lack of anger and the different ways she deals with her questions that enable her to make compromises, Michal stresses her love, which helped her to give up on her desires regarding religion, in general, and specifically in reference to her wedding, although it is important to note the hesitation in her words when she says "I guess" and "kind of." Both women refer to the positive emotional work they do in order to maintain their life with their spouses and the tradition.

Fifth Resource: Egalitarian Couple-hood

Many of the women used their husbands-to-be as their allies and as a social resource. As with the other resources, this was sometimes used to initiate change and sometimes to make peace with and accept the problematic elements of the wedding.

THE PERSONAL IS POLITICAL

In some cases the future husband became someone who supported the brides in their efforts to challenge the religious establishment. In this regard, the brides and their grooms became a coalition, a united front in the face of their families and the officiating rabbis. Thus these brides were able to create changes in the wedding ritual either because their spouses shared the wish to challenge the wedding ritual, since they viewed themselves as obligated to feminist values, or because they agreed to cooperate with their brides' wishes, even if they felt that this was not their initial agenda.

These women felt that they had an egalitarian couple-hood, and perhaps because of that, they wanted to make a change on the social level. They not only wished to express their egalitarian couple-hood in a public way, but they also wished to express their political and social ideas about gender equality and tradition. Moreover, the brides who used their grooms to create a partnership to help them change the ritual were not afraid that their grooms would use the power given them by the ritual in the event the couple ended up divorcing. Regardless, they still harnessed their grooms to affect a type of social change that they did not necessarily see as relevant to their own lives. They did this by signing privately or publicly a prenuptial agreement that serves as a legal strategy of resistance. In this regard, the personal became political.

According to Orly Benjamin, the estimation of the chances for cooperation affects the estimation of the risk involved in the woman's speaking up about gender issues and, thus, the chances of her moving from a stance of silence to a stance of voicing her wishes. However, within heterosexual frameworks, cooperation will not take place until the structure of male dominance based on male rights is challenged by an alternative masculinity based on caring.[45]

The women who chose to use the resource of creating a coalition with their "egalitarian spouse" could do so because their men had given up on the "structure of male dominance," as Benjamin puts it. These men chose to give up on their powerful stance in order to create a wedding ritual that expresses both an egalitarian and mutual relationship.

Although most of the coalitions were done with the spouses, some of the coalitions also involved one or more parents who stood in opposition to the rabbi. Others used their rabbi as part of a coalition to stand opposite the parents who were resistant to wedding changes; the rabbi was used to convince them that there is no halakhic problem with the change the couple wished for. Some brides used their girlfriends who had done similar changes as additional allies and as a support peer group. It seems that the more people the brides had in their coalitions, the easier, more productive, and more radical their negotiations and, therefore, actual changes were.

THE PERSONAL IS PERSONAL

Unlike women who used their spouses as a resource to affect social and political change, there were brides who used the same resource to avoid making a change and hence separated the personal from the political. The saying "The personal is political," which has became a motto for many feminist women, seemed irrelevant to them. This stance explains why most of the brides did not end up signing a prenuptial agreement, which can be viewed as the most radical action in regard to undermining the legal construction of the traditional wedding ritual. These women used their partners to emphasize that the equality of their own relationships did not need expression in the marriage ritual. They argued that the ritual does not express their own relationships, and that was precisely why they could accept the ritual as it is, in spite of its inequality. They felt that their husbands would not abuse the power the *kiddushin* act gave them and so were not concerned about the existence of this power. They stressed the mutuality of their relationship and their feelings of assurance in their marriage and in the character of their husbands. Vered and Rivki express this stance when they say:

> Then and also today I feel that the marriage is more important then the wedding.... *Essentially we have a strong egalitarian relationship* ... and I also think that I told you that you need to choose what you are going to argue about. *It was more important to me that the content of our marriage will be more significant than the external elements.* (Vered)

> It [the element of the *kiddushin*] did not bother *us.* The element of acquisition did not bother *us* because it was clear that *we have a very equal relationship that stems from [a mutual] agreement.* It was clear that he wasn't buying me ... that it is a ritual which is based on an ancient time like any other halakhah that *we* are committed to, and we interpret it. (Rivki)

Both Vered and Rivki use their egalitarian relationship to explain why they have not entered the negotiation of changing the legal construction of their wedding ritual with all its legal implications. Some brides, like Vered, emphasized that the egalitarianism in their marriage is expressed in the essential and the significant parts of their day-to-day life rather than in the wedding ritual. Others, like Rivki, moved to talk in the plural voice — us — when they described their relationship in the context of the marriage ritual. Arlie Hochschild refers to this type of speech maneuver and argues:

> Marriage both bridges and obscures the gap between the resources available to men and those available to women. Because men and women do try to love one another — to cooperate in making love, making babies, and making a life together — the very closeness of the bond they accept calls for some disguise of subordination. There will be talk in the "we" mode . . . and the idea among women that they are equal in the ways that "really count."[46]

Indeed many of my brides created a discourse that used the plural form to emphasize the personal sphere and to decrease the importance of the ritual and, thus, the public sphere.

Conclusion

In this chapter I have built a model that refers to social, personal, and intellectual resources that women drew upon either to change gender relations and religious symbols or to remain within these power relations. These resources were used by the brides as a flexible currency, using some more than others and making concessions and exchanges.

Ultimately, what carries the day is the combined effect of the umbrella resource — the ability to contain dissonance — with the other five resources. This exceptional combination of resources can also explain why it is specifically the religious modern women who initiate this phenomenon of challenging the traditional wedding ritual as opposed to ultra-Orthodox women or secular women. The latter, who might have a feminist consciousness, lack commitment to or involvement in a traditional religious framework. Thus, these women do not feel a need to change the religious world, since they feel it is not relevant to their lives. Furthermore, even if they wanted to effect change, they lack the religious literacy that is needed to negotiate the boundaries of the religious system. The converse is true as well — that is, having religious knowledge, like many ultra-Orthodox women have, will not initiate change when there is no feminist consciousness. In addition they lack the specific type of religious knowledge that can create change. Ultra-Orthodox women who learn are still prohibited from learning Talmud, thus they are barred from the literacy and social power that are allowed for men only. The way these women learn, as opposed to how the women in my research learn, does not elevate them to a point that makes them wish to change the system. They accept a priori the social structure as it is, and their limited religious literacy does not change that.[47] This is why it is specifically those women who find themselves at the junction of modernity and religion who have the power to create change from within.

Finally, I wish to refer to the continuum of the categories of the symbolic "Woman" versus the agency of "women" with which I started my article. Susan Sered claims that "[a]s women become less 'physical' or less 'gendered' — that is as they become older or more educated, they acquire more agency and lose their magnetism as objects of symbolization. In other words, the power to determine the ontological status of oneself or of others is a reflection of access to social resources."[48] This might explain in part why the brides in my study were able to act as social agents. On the one hand, these brides, just by being brides, symbolize the idealized "Woman." On the other hand, the fact that they were married comparatively late, possessed higher general and Jewish education, and had access to other resources rendered them as "women" — social agents of change and renovation of the Jewish ritual and tradition.

While some feminist scholars might criticize these women for staying within the religious system with its patriarchic and hierarchical construction, I find immense power in these women in their ability to constituently move between the two poles: acceptance and tradition versus rejection and change. This constant maneuvering required not only a significant amount of emotional strength, but also a remarkable ability to use one's different social, intellectual, and personal resources in a complex way — a way that enabled them to live with the cognitive dissonance that characterizes parts of their life.

Finally, further research is required to see if these resources are indeed a model that can be generalized and made applicable for studying different women in different religious contexts who maneuver between tradition and modernity.

Notes

1. Arlene Elowe MacLeod, "Hegemonic Relations and Gender Resistance: The new Veiling as Accommodating Protest in Cairo," *Signs* 17:3 (1992): 533–34.

2. Although I assumed that these women would define themselves as feminist to some degree, I tried to refrain from using this definition when I first approached them, knowing that some of them would reject their identification as feminist, as I will elaborate later on in this chapter.

3. These neighborhoods are the venue of several liberal Jewish study centers and of various types of social, religious, and spiritual activities. Their populations include a sufficient concentration of immigrants from English-speaking countries to constitute a reference group for the women I studied. Many of the religious Jews in these neighborhoods could fairly be characterized as liberal Orthodox, in that they seek to challenge some aspects of Orthodoxy while remaining within the halakhic framework. In this chapter, "halakhah" refers to Jewish law as interpreted by Orthodox rabbis, which is the halakhah that the women I studied had to challenge, resist, and adapt in order to formulate the type of wedding rituals they desired.

4. Although there is a tendency to view Israeli feminism as a by-product of American feminism, Israeli feminism (religious and nonreligious) stands today in its own right and has unique characteristics that are related to the Israeli society on its distinctive challenges and social constructions.

5. There is no civil marriage in Israel, so that matrimony, for all sectors of the population, is governed by religious law (Orthodox Jewish, Moslem, or Christian). However, Israel does recognize civil marriages performed outside its borders. Nevertheless, even if these women get married in a civil court outside of the country, in case of divorce they still need to abide by the religious law and go through the Israeli rabbinate, since there is no civil divorce in Israel today.

6. Some of these ritual acts are considered halakhic requirements (according to Jewish law), such as the act of *kiddushin*, and some are considered only a custom, such as circling the groom by the bride. However, in many cases the rabbis viewed the different traditional acts in different ways. According to what the brides told me, while one rabbi thought that the act of covering the bride is a custom and can be modified, another saw it as a halakhic requirement and did not allow making any changes to it. Moreover, when these women wished to change some elements of the wedding ritual, some rabbis admitted to them that while there is no halakhic problem with their wish, they would not allow them to perform the change because of political and social concerns.

7. For feminist perspectives on the traditional wedding ritual, and specifically on the legal and cultural implications of *kiddushin* as an act of acquisition, see Judith Wegner, *Chattel or Person? The Status of Women in the Mishnah* (New York: Oxford University Press, 1988); Orit Kamir, *Feminism, Rights, and Law* (Tel Aviv: Ministry of Defense Press, 2002), 137–51 [in Hebrew]; Susan Aranoff, "Two Views of Marriage — Two Views of Women: Reconsidering *Tav Lemetav Tan du Milemetav Armelu*," *Nashim: A Journal of Jewish Women's Studies and Gender Issues* 3 (2000): 199; Susan Okin, "Marriage, Divorce, and the Politics of Family Life," in *Marriage, Liberty, and Equality: Shall the Three Walk Together*, ed. Tova Cohen (Ramat-Gan: Bar-Ilan University Press, 2000): 7–26; Rachel Adler, *Engendering Judaism: An Inclusive Theology and Ethics* (Philadelphia: Jewish Publication Society: 1998), 169–208; Susan S. Sered, Romi Kaplan, and Samuel Cooper, "Talking about Miqveh Parties, or: Discourses of Gender, Hierarchy and Social Control," in *Women and Water: Menstruation in Jewish Life and Law*, ed. Rahel R. Wasserfall (Hanover: University Press of New England: 1999): 139–65.

8. An *agunah* is a woman whose husband has disappeared or is otherwise unable to give his wife a *get*. A *mesurevet get* is a woman whose husband abuses the power given to him by the halakhah and refuses to grant her a *get*.

9. Kamir, *Feminism, Rights, and Law*, 142–46.

10. See Irit Koren, "In a Bride's Voice: Religious Women Challenge the Wedding Ritual," *Nashim: A Journal of Jewish Women's Studies and Gender Issues* 10 (2005): 29. In this article I also describe in depth the ways these women interpret and change different elements of their wedding ritual.

11. The Hebrew text of the prenuptial agreement can be found on the following website: http://www.youngisraelrabbis.org.il/texts/heskem-mavo%203.05.pdf (last entered May 3, 2010). This prenuptial was created by Rabbi Elyashiv Knohl, Rabbi David Ben Zazon, and the rabbinical court advocate Rachel Levmore, with the cooperation of other lawyers, rabbinical court advocates, and women organizations such as Kolech (the Orthodox feminist alliance). In addition there are six other prenuptials that have been presented as well. To learn more about them, see Ruth Halperin-Kadari, *Prenuptial Agreements* (Ramat-Gan: Bar-Ilan University Press, Rackman Center for the Advancement of Women's Justice, and the Center for Justice for Women, 2008). However, as far as I know, the "Agreement for Mutual Respect" is the most popular agreement in Israel. This is perhaps because it was advocated by Kolech, which has been becoming more and more powerful and vocal in the modern religious society in the last decade.

12. According to halakhah, for a Jewish couple to get divorced, the man must give the woman a *get* (writ of divorce) of his own free will, and she must accept it.

However, the prenuptial agreement represents an attempt to balance the unequal power relations between the couple and to change the halakhic reality in which only a husband has the legal right to decide whether to grant a *get*. These legal agreements came about because of the difficulties and the harsh confrontations that *agunot* and *mesuravot get* have faced in the rabbinical courts. According to the Israel Women's Network and the women's organization Mavoi Satum, there are as many as several thousand *mesuravot get* in Israel, in addition to some thirty *agunot* in Israel alone. See "Get FAQ," Mavoi Satum, accessed September 21, 2011, http://www.mavoisatum.org/page81.html?.

13. Susan Starr Sered, "Religiously Doing Gender: The Good Woman and the Bad Woman in Israeli Ritual Discourse," *Method & Theory in the Study of Religion* 13:2 (2001): 156.

14. Susan Sered, "Women and Religious Change in Israel: Rebellion and Revolution," *Sociology and Religion* 58:1 (1997): 1–2.

15. Ibid.

16. Sered, "Religiously Doing Gender," 160.

17. Ibid.

18. Elliot Aronson, "The Theory of Cognitive Dissonance: A Current Perspective," in *Advances in Experimental Social Psychology*, vol. 4, ed. Leonard Berkowitz (New York: Academic Press, 1969), 1–34.

19. See Leon Festinger, *A Theory of Cognitive Dissonance* (Stanford: Stanford University Press: 1962), 1–31; Joel Cooper, *Cognitive Dissonance: Fifty Years of a Classic Theory* (Los Angeles: SAGE, 2007), 2–3.

20. Elizabeth Weiss Ozorak, "The Power, but Not the Glory: How Women Empower Themselves through Religion," *Journal for the Scientific Study of Religion* 35:1 (1996): 17–18.

21. Tehila is referring here to the following article: Tamar Ross and Yehuda Gellman, "The Impact of Feminism on Jewish Orthodox Theology," *Multiculturalism in a Democratic and Jewish State*, 443–464 (Menachem Mautner, Avi Sagi and Ronen Shamir eds. Ramot Press Jerusalem, 1997) (in Hebrew).

22. In Jewish history there are few examples of knowledgeable women who knew Torah, but this was the exception, and these women were perceived as deviant from the norm.

23. Amos Funkenstein and Adin Steinsaltz, *The Sociology of Illiteracy* (Moscow: Ministry of Security Press, 1997) (in Russian).

24. Ellen M. Umansky, "Feminism and the Reevaluation of Women's Roles," in *Women, Religion, and Social Change*, ed. Yvonna Yazbeck Haddad and Ellison Banks Findly (Albany: State University of New York Press, 1985), 492.

25. Tamar El-Or wrote two important works on religious women's education and literacy. The first deals with ultra-Orthodox women, and the second deals with Modern Orthodox women, who are closer to the constituency I researched. To learn more, see Tamar El-Or, *Educated and Ignorant: On Ultra-Orthodox Women and Their World* (Hebrew title: *Maskilot Uvurot: Me-Olaman shel Nashim Harediyot*) (Tel Aviv: Am Oved Publishers, 1992) (in English, Boulder: Lynne Rienner Publishers, 1994), 94–95; Tamar El-Or, *Next Year I Will Know More: Literacy and Identity among Young Orthodox Women in Israel*, trans. Haim Watzman (Detroit: Wayne State University Press, 2002), 29–32.

26. See Margart Bryant, *The Unexpected Revolution* (London: University of London Institute of Education, 1979); Anne Scott-Firor, *Making The Invisible Woman Visible* (Urbana: University of Illinois Press, 1984); Linda Kerber, *Women of the Republic: Intellect and Ideology in Revolutionary America* (Chapel Hill: University of North Carolina Press, 1980).

27. The ability of these women to appropriate the religious knowledge for themselves is particularly impressive due to the fact that women in the five largest religions (Judaism, Christianity, Islam, Hinduism, and Buddhism) were excluded from formal religious knowledge from the moment that this knowledge became sacred. In all these religions there was a split created between the private sphere, to which women were limited, and the public sphere, which was tied to power and authority. Although some reforms have been made in different streams of these religions, still most of the religious knowledge and education are exclusively for men. See Ursula King, "World Religions, Women and Education," *Comparative Education* 23:1 (1987): 35, 47.

28. It is amazing to see the amount of materials that comes up when one googles "religious single women." These materials include rabbinic responses, forums, and documentary films that portray this phenomenon. This amount of material can testify to how much this subject has become a painful and loaded issue in the religious society.

29. To learn more about the ways the experience of singlehood in these neighborhoods influence and form the identity of these religious modern women, see Chagit Achituv, "The Challenge of Singlehood: Does Defining the Phenomenon of Singlehood as a 'Problem' Answer a Social Need?" *Deot* 17 (2003): 28 [in Hebrew]; and Cheftzi Shtol, "'And Even Though It Is Delayed He Will Come . . .': The Experience of Singlehood within Religious Modern Women," in *To Be a Jewish Woman: Proceedings of the First International Conference on Women and Their Judaism*, ed. Margalit Shilo (Jerusalem: Urim, 2001), 214–27 [in Hebrew].

30. Debra Renee Kaufman, *Rachel's Daughters: Newly Orthodox Jewish Women* (New Brunswick: Rutgers University Press, 1991), 17, 21–22.

31. The relationship between the ability to live in a complex world that entails both sets of values and one's age can be demonstrated by the phenomenon of secular women who choose to enter the religious Orthodox world. In research about women who became religious (*ba'alot teshuvah*) it was found that most of the women who began their journey to the Orthodox world (64 percent) were in their *late teens or in their early twenties.* The women claimed that the reason they chose to embrace the Orthodox movement rather than more liberal forms of Judaism was exactly because Orthodoxy represented for them a defined authority that is not relational to modern realities. Orthodoxy attracted these women specifically because it presented itself with defined moral values and with a supposedly *one and only truth of existence.* Thus the attraction to Orthodoxy was due to the fact that it does not try to balance both worlds. See Kaufman, *Rachel's Daughters.*

32. Laurie A. Rhodebeck, "The Structure of Men's and Women's Feminist Orientations: Feminist Identity and Feminist Opinion," *Gender and Society* 10:4 (1996): 386.

33. Judith M. Gerson and Kathy Peiss, "Boundaries, Negotiation, Consciousness: Reconceptualizing Gender Relations," *Social Problems* 32:4 (1985): 317, 326. To learn more about feminist consciousness or gender consciousness, see also Patricia Gurin, "Women's Gender Consciousness," *Public Opinion Quarterly* 49 (1985): 143; Patricia Gurin and Hazel Markus, "Cognitive Consequences of Gender Identity," in *The Social Identity of Women*, ed. Suzanne Skevington and Deborah Baker (London: Sage Publications, 1989), 152–72; Patricia Gurin and Aloen Townsend, "Properties of Gender Identity and Their Implications for Gender Consciousness," *British Journal of Social Psychology* 25 (1986): 139.

34. Rhodebeck, "The Structure of Men's and Women's Feminist Orientations," 387.

35. Alyssa, N. Zucker, "Disavowing Social Identities: What It Means When Women Say, 'I'm Not a Feminist But . . . ,'" *Psychology of Women Quarterly* 28 (2004): 423, 431–32.

36. Ozorak, "The Power but Not the Glory," 24.

37. Arlie Russell Hochschild, "Ideology and Emotion Management: A Perspective and Path for Future Research," in *Research Agendas in the Sociology of Emotions*, ed. Theodore D. Kemper (Albany: State University of New York Press, 1990): 121–22.

38. Ibid., 163.

39. Orly Benjamin, "The Power of Unsilencing: Between Silence and

Negotiation in Heterosexual Relationship," *Journal for the Theory of Social Behavior* 33:1 (1993).

40. Ariella Friedman, *Annie Oakley Won Twice: Intimacy and Power in Female Identity* (Tel Aviv: Hakibbutz Hameuchad, 2001) (1996) [In Hebrew].

41. See Carol Gilligan, *In a Different Voice: Psychological Theory and Women's Development* (Cambridge, MA: Harvard University Press, 1982); and Hochschild, "Ideology and Emotion Management." While some claim that this is an essentialist view, I understand Gilligan and Hochschild not to be essentialists but rather to focus on the social constructions that make women perceive themselves and act in certain ways.

42. Harriet Lerner, *The Dance of Anger: A Woman's Guide to Changing the Patterns of Intimate Relationships* (New York: Harper & Row, 1985), 2.

43. Ibid.

44. Ibid., 1–3.

45. Benjamin, "The Power of Unsilencing," 15.

46. Hochschild, "Ideology and Emotion Management," 169.

47. El-Or, *Next Year I Will Know More*, 246–47.

48. Sered, "Women and Religious Change in Israel," 160.

MICHAL RONESS

Chapter Nine The *Yoetzet Halakhah* Avoiding Conflict While Instituting Change

Modern Orthodoxy,[1] like most other religious communities, has been affected by the feminist movement in modern times. As in the secular community, Modern Orthodox women are now more learned and more active in the community.[2] Stages in a woman's life are now openly celebrated in the Modern Orthodox community, and there is a growing demand by women to be more active in spiritual ceremonies, especially those involving prayer.[3] Religious women are now also taking leadership roles not only in the secular professional community but also in the religious community. While the highest status for a woman was once leading a girls' high school or being an active *rabbanit* (wife of a rabbi), today women can become *toanot*,[4] trained experts who argue on behalf of women in the rabbinical family courts in Israel, or *yoatzot halakhah*, female halakhic advisors on the laws of family purity.[5] The combination of higher-learning institutions for women and more active roles in the religious community has led to tremendous changes in the status of women.

Many feminist changes in the Modern Orthodox world have drawn widespread opposition and conflict within the community. As Sylvia Barack Fishman has described, there is an "increasing troubled dynamic between Orthodox Jews who are committed to preserving a more traditional status quo and those women, men and rabbis who want to expand women's spiritual expression."[6]

Aryeh Frimer has noted that "there is hesitancy in the Orthodox community to adopt or even tolerate practices such as women's Megillah reading and women reciting the mourner's prayer."[7] An example of a feminist change that caused a great deal of opposition and conflict is the women's prayer groups and *aliyyot* (reading from the Torah in a quorum of men).[8] According to Frimer, the rabbinic world is seriously split on the question of the advisability of such prayer groups for a variety of *hashkafic* (ideological) and public policy grounds. Not only has there been outspoken opposition to prayer groups that allow women to be called to the Torah, there is an abundance of literature for and against the attempted institution of this change.[9]

Opposition to feminist developments is not surprising, as most social change is met with resistance by those who wish to ensure the status quo. This is especially true in a traditional religious society, where religious leaders object to any change that would threaten existing religious norms.

In contrast to other transformative initiatives, the introduction of the *yoetzet halakhah* did not draw a great deal of attention and opposition. As noted by Graetz, "the graduates are being accepted with very little fanfare and even the Ultra-Orthodox rabbinic community seems to welcome them."[10] This limited opposition and relatively subdued reaction to the *yoetzet halakhah* is not due to the limited importance of the change. In some ways, the *yoetzet halakhah* is challenging the rabbis' authority and the Orthodox status quo more than any other feminist initiative. Sylvia Barack Fishman has written, "Perhaps the most revolutionary development in this area has recently taken place in Israel. . . . [W]hile the program was launched quietly and discreetly, Orthodox authorities and laypersons alike recognize the momentous nature of the change it represents."[11]

The purpose of this article is to understand the strategy implemented to ensure the peaceful acceptance of the *yoetzet halakhah* within the Modern Orthodox community. Through the prism of conflict theory on the nature of change processes and trust building, we will analyze what attempts were made to avoid and contain conflict. What steps were taken in order to engage the trust of potential opponents to the institution of the *yoetzet halakhah*, and how did these steps succeed in limiting the conflict? Through the case study of the *yoetzet halakhah*, we will attempt to understand how acceptance of social change can be maximized and how the acceptance of this change differed in Israel and America.

Laws of Family Purity and the Role of the *Yoetzet Halakhah*

The laws of family purity are detailed intricate laws that relate to the woman's status during menstruation and for the seven clean days following menstruation. Jewish law requires husband and wife to abstain from all physical contact during this period, and only once the woman has immersed herself in a *mikveh* (ritual bath) can they reunite. A Jewish religious girl is often oblivious to these laws (apart perhaps from the fact that she knows that her mother immerses) until a short time before her marriage, when she learns these laws in order to begin fulfilling them. The laws of family purity can be daunting — to say the least — at the beginning of marriage. The laws relate to the most intimate issue of a woman's sexual relations with her new husband, and often an Orthodox girl who has grown up in a modest surrounding where these issues were not discussed in the open may find it difficult to adapt to this new reality. Although a woman may become used to the laws of family purity and become more acquainted with the details through experience, each new stage of life brings with it more challenges in this area. Whether it be going to the *mikveh* after childbirth in order to be able to resume sexual relations after postpartum bleeding, dealing with spotting during nursing, or adapting to the new status of menopause, each new stage brings with it new halakhic questions and challenges.

Traditionally, a married woman would refer to her rabbi (or she would send her husband to refer to the rabbi) or the rabbi's wife with her questions regarding questions of family purity. "For reasons of modesty, women do not wish to, and often will not, discuss a family purity question with a man. The consequences of a question not asked can range from improper observance of the halakhah to marital anguish and even to infertility."[12] If a woman is hesitant to ask a rabbi a question in this area, she may decide to abstain from marital relations rather than have to deal with the details of the question. In some cases, her decision could result in her abstaining from relations at the time of ovulation, thus inhibiting the chances of becoming pregnant. In other cases, extending the days of impurity where husband and wife are not allowed to have relations (due to the reluctance to ask a rabbi) can result in unnecessary strains on the marriage. The days of separation can cause frustration, anxiety, or even resentment between the couple.

In order to deal with this situation, Rabbanit Chana Henkin developed the Keren Ariel *Yoatzot Halakhah* program in 1997, which trains women with a background in advanced Judaic studies to become experts in the laws of family purity in order to answer women's questions in this field. Rabbanit Henkin is the founder and dean of Nishmat — The Jerusalem Center for Advanced Jewish Study for Women and the wife of Rabbi Yehuda Herzl Henkin.[13] Her position as a respected educator and pioneer in women's Jewish education enabled her to initiate this revolutionary program. She is currently not associated with the feminist Orthodox organizations such as Kolech or Jewish Orthodox Feminist Alliance (JOFA), and therefore the Modern Orthodox rabbinic world was not suspicious of her intentions when establishing the program.

This two-year program includes more than one thousand hours of textual study of classic rabbinic sources, including Talmud, *Rishonim*, *Shulhan Arukh*, and contemporary responsa. The course of study is supplemented by biweekly lectures in areas of behavioral and medical sciences that relate to the application of these laws in a modern society — gynecology, fertility and reproductive technology, sexuality, prenatal testing, and psychology — given by professionals in the various fields.

An example of the type of conversation that a *yoetzet halakhah* may have with a woman has been described by Rachelle Sprecher Fraenkel:

> On the line is a young woman, postpartum. After three long months, she finally got to the mikvah last night. Today she is already seeing stains and is concerned about her *halakhic* status. The oral contraceptive she recently started taking is throwing her system out of whack. The frustration that has built up during the long separation is evident in her voice. Our experience shows she might be facing an uneasy period of stains, doubts and breakthrough bleeding until her body adapts to the hormones associated with her contraceptive. I investigate the details of her current situation. To my satisfaction, I am able to tell her she is still *tehorah*. I prepare her for the coming period. Experience has taught us that when a woman's expectations are realized, her level of frustration and stress are lower. There are also a few pieces of good *halakhic* advice that could prove highly beneficial to help her avoid problems. She is glad to refresh her memory and we review together the relevant laws and advice.[14]

Over sixty women have graduated the program since its inception. As of now, the *yoatzot halakhah* are being consulted by women through the Nishmat Women's Halakhic Hotline[15] or the Nishmat Internet site[16] on thousands of questions regarding not only the laws of family purity but also questions pertaining to fertility, contraception, and women's health and halakhah. In America, there are a number of *yoatzot halakhah* who have official positions in the community,[17] and the rabbi of the synagogue encourages his congregants to bring their questions to the *yoetzet.* Only if there is a need for a halakhic decision (rather than a consultation) will the question be referred to the rabbi. In Israel, it is less common to have a *yoetzet* officially connected to a synagogue; this is probably because the synagogue plays a less central role in Orthodox life.[18] In Israel, apart from working on the hotline and Internet site, the *yoatzot halakhah* teach preparatory classes on the laws of family purity to future brides, run refresher courses, and serve as informal consultants on family purity issues in their communities.

Change Processes and Conflict

The institution of the *yoetzet halakhah* is an example of social change within the religious community. In order to understand how the potential conflict resulting from this change was dealt with or avoided, we must first deepen our understanding of the different stages that take place when change occurs. Following our understanding of the change process, we can analyze the different measures of conflict reduction implemented in this case.

Kurt Lewin[19] defined a process of change as one composed of the following three stages: unfreezing of the reigning status quo, movement in a new direction, and then refreezing the new status quo.

In order to *unfreeze* the current situation, an openness toward something different must be developed.

First, the awareness of the need for change must be cultivated. The motivation for creating a change must be achieved. Information obtained about the system from outside the system is a common way to increase people's understanding of the need for change. Social feedback is ambiguous and can be interpreted in many ways. Interpretation is influenced by factors such as personal needs and experiences, and the context within which the source of feedback occurs.

When a system faces a change, there are driving forces that promote the change and restraining forces that work to oppose it. In order to increase the driving forces, tension must be created. However, the tension must be dealt with productively in order to be able to cause the change to ensue.

The next step involves *movement* in the religious system, which may be met with some degree of resistance. Resistance is the mobilization of energy to protect the status quo in the face of real or perceived threats to it. Resistant behavior is intended to protect the system from the effect of the real or imagined change.

Following the change in the system, the actions and processes that support the new level of behavior must be *refrozen*. This refreezing provides resilience against forces encouraging old patterns and behaviors. The degree of commitment to the new, changed state will determine whether the change will be adopted into the new status quo.

Over the years there has been criticism of Lewin's model for being linear and static. It ignores organizational politics and conflict and focuses on change driven from the top rather than from the grassroots and day-to-day actions of the members of the organization.

Lewin's conception of freezing and refreezing sees the organization as a static entity, ignoring the fact that organizations are fluid bodies with many players and various stages of change overlapping and affecting each other in a complex myriad of events. Sometimes rational and other times irrational decision-making processes and political struggles can obstruct the planned approach that Lewin has prescribed.[20]

Nonetheless, Lewin's model allows us to clearly define and map out the foundations that allowed for the acceptance of the *yoetzet halakhah* within the Orthodox community. Indeed, as the change becomes a more accepted part of society, so too the complexity of this change emerges and the other influences such as the effects of the grassroots influence on the *yoetzet halakhah*'s position, the political influences, and coalition building between rabbis and *yoatzot halakhah* can be analyzed as well.[21]

In the case of the *yoetzet halakhah*, Rabbanit Chana Henkin recognized that there was a need to integrate women into the halakhic system regarding laws of family purity. Many observant women do not consult a rabbi with an intimate question. Many women decide the issues for themselves — some stringently, others leniently. Unwarranted leniency may not be in accordance with halakhah, and unnecessary stringency can come at the expense of marital harmony.[22]

The need for the change was discussed in correspondence in the Jewish magazine *Jewish Action*, where the claims were made that there is no need for a *yoetzet halakhah* and that women do feel comfortable approaching rabbis with their intimate questions. However, as Joel Wolowelsky points out, "Clearly the program has spoken to some need, as otherwise these *yoatzot* would have no 'customers.'"[23] The need for the change can be measured by the response of the community in utilizing the new service of the *yoetzet halakhah*.[24]

The recognition that there was a need for a change in the Orthodox community led to the opening of the *yoatzot halakhah* program. As in any change in a traditional religious society, there has been resistance to this change. Resistance can be undesirable, but it can also have a potentially constructive role. Resistance naturally emerges as part of the change process. A necessary prerequisite of successful change is the mobilization of the forces that oppose the change. The change can be successful if the conflict is managed correctly. There are two options in how to deal with the conflict impending from the attempt to institute change. One option is to ignore it and try to overcome it through forcing the change on the parts of the community who oppose it. The other option is to increase the resistant group's understanding of the suggested change and attempt to get the opposing forces to participate in its planning and implementation. Understanding the need for the planned change and participation in or influence on the process will allow the resistant forces to feel invested in that change. This was the strategy that was adopted in securing the accreditation of the *yoatzot halakhah*. Rabbanit Henkin attempted to proactively include the rabbis and even get the support of rabbis who were expected to oppose the change.

On completing the *yoatzot halakhah* program, each woman undergoes a series of intense oral examinations with four rabbis. Each rabbi sits with the candidate for forty-five minutes, grilling her with questions on the material covered in the program. The questions can relate to textual passages that were part of the material studied or to practical issues that the *yoetzet* may face in the future. One of the rabbis who is on the examination board appears to be especially skeptical of the possible effects of the *yoatzot halakhah*. It is possible that if he were not involved in the examination process, he may have even opposed the *yoatzot halakhah* program. This is apparent from his questions in the examination where he not only tests the *yoetzet halakhah*'s knowledge but also her motivations and intentions. When testing me, he asked me what

I planned to do with my new title, and he warned me to refer to the rabbis with any questions that were posed to me. Integrating this rabbi as one of the examiners of the program allows him to address his reservations and to personally monitor the process to make sure it does not exceed acceptable parameters. His involvement also indicates his endorsement to other similarly skeptical members of the rabbinate.[25]

Through reflecting on the process of the accreditation of *yoatzot halakhah*, we can identify certain factors that diminished resistance to this innovation and contained the possibilities for future conflict. The following guidelines emerge:[26]

1. Base the logic for the change on objective reasons, rather than on personal ones. Rabbanit Henkin has written, "Our major concern must be the *Halakha*. Not for the purpose of empowering women, but enabling women to observe mitzvoth meticulously, to blossom with the full richness of the fabric of the religious experience."[27]

The purpose of the *yoetzet halakhah* is to assist Orthodox women who are challenged by keeping the laws of family purity. It was not developed in order to allow learned women to achieve status and authority in the Orthodox community. Although this is one of the offshoots of the program, a woman who wishes to become a *yoetzet halakhah* in order to advance her personal learning and status will not be accepted to the program.

2. Have regard for established group or organizational norms. The *yoetzet halakhah* is aware of the norms in the area of the laws of family purity and does not attempt to supersede or replace the rabbis in this field. It is possible to categorize the halakhic questions posed to the *yoetzet* into two groups:[28] (a) Questions that have a clear halakhic ruling and are probably cited in the sources, but the questioner is unaware of the sources or does not have access to them. For women who do not feel comfortable referring their questions to a rabbi, the *yoetzet* can provide the answer because of her experience and knowledge in the field. (b) Questions that relate to a personal situation and the answer needs to be decided based on the specific details. In this case, often the *yoetzet* will tell a woman, "For this question you need to refer to a rabbi." Then she will offer the woman to mediate between her and the rabbi and say, "Would you like me to ask the rabbi for you?" The *yoetzet* may feel more comfortable discussing the question for a third party rather than a woman asking a personal question for herself. Because of her learning and experience as well as her access and rapport with the rabbi, the *yoetzet* also has the ability to enter into a halakhic dialogue with the rabbi regarding the details of the question. This possible advantage is counterbalanced by the fact that the introduction of a mediator between the rabbi and the woman involved can distance the rabbi from his client. The additional link in the chain may distance the rabbi from the direct encounter with the woman's emotional predicament.[29] The *yoetzet halakhah* decides, based on her knowledge and experience, if the question has clear halakhic precedents that have been previously dealt with in the halakhic literature or if it is a unique and novel case where the supervising rabbi needs to be consulted in order to rule, based on his greater experience and knowledge.[30]

3. Advocates should agree on the rationale of the proposed change and should choose the least provocative formulation of this rationale. At the beginning of the institution of the *yoatzot halakhah*, there was some confusion as to their title. This was a result of the different perceptions of the role of the *yoetzet halakhah*. Some referred to them as *poskot* (halakhic decisors) or *toanot halakhah* (rabbinic adjudicators). The first article to be written about these women in the Israeli media[31] wished to give the article an attractive headline. Rabbanit Henkin insisted that the title not be provocative. After negotiation, it was decided that the article would be titled "*Yoatzot Halakhah.*" Since then Rabbanit Henkin[32] has explained that the title — halakhic consultants or advisors — was selected to convey that these women are not rendering original halakhic rulings. For new rulings, they refer to recognized halakhic authorities. The title of these women was especially designed to avoid conflict and express the rationale of the role of the *yoetzet halakhah*. She is not a rabbi nor a halakhic authority. She is a woman well-learned in the laws of family purity and therefore trained to be a consultant on halakhah for other women.[33]

4. Observe existing norms for interacting with authority. The technique of the *yoetzet halakhah* has been a possible source of opposition. Some have leveled the criticism that halakhic questions (especially those pertaining to the laws of family purity) should not be asked on an anonymous telephone hotline or through Internet e-mails and that this is not the normal interaction for halakhic questions. The response to any given halakhic question may differ depending on the specific background of the questioner and her personal experience and situation. This is difficult to measure on an anonymous phone call. There is much debate regarding the responsa to anonymous halakhic questions.[34] The establishment of the phone hotline and e-mail questions was a risk because it opened the *yoatzot halakhah* to criticism from those who saw it as an illegitimate form of answering halakhic questions. Defenders of this decision would say that the benefit of helping people who would otherwise not ask the question at all outweighed the possible criticism and opposition that it may have spurred.

5. Involve those most affected by the change and keep parts of the system stable. This is seen in the reverence given to the rabbinic authority by the *yoetzet halakhah*. Even though a woman answering halakhic questions directly to women is an innovation, the authority of the rabbis in these issues remained stable. The *yoetzet* refers to the rabbi for any question she may have, and the *yoatzot halakhah* have frequent meetings with the rabbis of the hotline in order to remain informed about the rabbinic position of every issue they deal with. The relationship the *yoetzet halakhah* has with the rabbis affects their attitude toward this new position. Some rabbis may see the *yoatzot halakhah* as a threat to their position and authority within the community. The involvement and influence of the rabbis on the *yoatzot halakhah* ensured that the institution of change did not circumvent the agents who may feel most threatened by the change.

6. Introduce change incrementally. When smaller changes are introduced, there is a better chance that they will be successfully accepted and ensure the possibility of moving on to other changes in the future. The conflict management specialist Roger Fisher discussed fractioning conflict as an attempt to deal with conflict more successfully.[35] Also described as incrementalism, this approach attempts to break a larger conflict into manageable pieces. Agents of change will work on resolving smaller parts of the conflict before attempting to deal with larger issues. Participants experience constructive resolution and enhance parties' confidence as they progress to working on resolving larger issues.

This approach is evident in the authority given to the *yoatzot halakhah*. When the program first began, the *yoatzot halakhah* were not trained to determine the status of stains.[36] Rabbi Yaakov Warhaftig explained that this omission in the *yoatzot halakhah*'s training did not stem from a halakhic limitation. A woman is permitted to determine the status of her personal stains, and there is no halakhic obstacle for her to determine other women's stains were she to have the required training. The procedure of showing stains to a rabbi is one of the most difficult parts of keeping the laws of family purity. Reactions of women to this procedure can range from shock that a rabbi looks at a woman's dirty underwear, refusal to take a stain to a rabbi and a preference for making a decision on her own, to an agreement (often grudgingly) to take the stain to a rabbi despite the embarrassment and unpleasantness. Many husbands are set the task to take the stain to the rabbi — not that this combats the embarrassment for the husband (or his wife).[37] I believe that a rabbi looking at a woman's stain on her undergarment is like any professional dealing with intimate situations. However, just as many women today prefer to consult with a female gynecologist, so many Orthodox women would prefer to consult with a woman regarding the status of her stains.

Rabbi Warhaftig's reasoning for not training the *yoatzot* to determine the status of stains was simply to avoid conflict. In order to fractionalize the opposition to *yoatzot halakhah*, the decision was made to allow the *yoatzot halakhah* to be fully integrated into the Orthodox community, and only when women answering questions regarding stains was fully accepted did women undergo the necessary training. The program for the *yoatzot halakhah* includes small workshops regarding the status of stains but does not include the intense experience required to train in this field. This decision was clearly to incrementalize the change in the community, and only once trust and confidence in the *yoatzot halakhah* existed would they be trained in this field.

This approach of incrementalism has limited the authority of the *yoetzet halakhah*. Many *yoatzot halakhah* were frustrated at this limitation and felt that one of the greatest needs of women today was to have a woman available to whom they could refer these embarrassing questions. Women who will not ask a rabbi questions feel that they reach a dead end when the *yoatzot halakhah* responds to a questioner that she must bring this question to a rabbi. As the *yoatzot halakhah* become more experienced in the field, these situations become less common. However, the current framework of the *yoatzot halahka* is restricted due to the limited halakhic experience that they have and the concentration of their studies to the laws of family purity without the broader view of other halakhic fields.

However, the success of this approach of incrementalism is now apparent, as some *yoatzot halakhah* have undergone the training necessary to determine the status of stains. Although still not part of the official training program, there is now no opposition to this training, and the heads of the *yoatzot halakhah* program feel that training in the status of stains is acceptable for the *yoatzot halakhah* and one that the Orthodox community can withstand.

Dealing with Resistance to Change

In order to sustain social change and refreeze it as part of the status quo, there is a need for commitment by a critical mass of people in the community. When instituting the change, motivation needs to be created, resistance needs to be overcome, and then commitment needs to be generated. Focusing attention on those resistant to change often emphasizes their influence on the change itself. When dealing only with the resistant forces, the degree of attention and support needed by the individuals and groups who are less resistant becomes underemphasized. When instituting change, those who are motivated to accept the change or be part of the change need increased support, attention, and resources in order to strengthen these foundations. It may seem redundant or a waste of energy to preach to the converted, but it can play a valuable role in helping spread positive energy for change. This effort has more chances for success than trying to weaken the negative energy against the change.

When creating the *yoatzot halakhah* program, there was no attempt to win over the ultra-Orthodox community. The learning of Talmud and primary halakhic sources is still unacceptable in most ultra-Orthodox communities. How much more so would they object to women taking positions of authority and answering halakhic questions directly to other women. Were the *yoatzot halakhah* to try and gain endorsement from ultra-Orthodox rabbis, they would be met with great resistance, vocal opposition, and possible excommunication from the religious community. As a strategy to avoid this conflict, the *yoatzot halakhah* did not focus or emphasize these resisting forces. Instead, the *yoatzot halakhah* focused on the Modern Orthodox community, which already accepted learning Talmud by women and was therefore less opposed to a woman being in the position to answer halakhic questions pertaining to family purity. The result of this strategy has been the weakening of opposition in general to the *yoatzot halakhah*. There has been little negative publicity toward the *yoatzot halakhah* in the ultra-Orthodox community, and few of the rabbis who do not endorse the program have publicly denounced it. This does not prove that the entire Orthodox community has accepted the *yoatzot halakhah* nor that there is no resistance to it. However, it does signify the success of the avoidance of public, broadcasted conflict. Not only have outrage and possible bans from the ultra-Orthodox community been avoided, but there is preliminary evidence that ultra-Orthodox women also call the Nishmat hotline. While calls are anonymous and most women do not identify themselves or to which community they belong, some aspects of the questions indicate that some callers are from the ultra-Orthodox community. If a woman asks, "Do ultra-Orthodox rabbis agree with this halakhic ruling?" or "What would an ultra-Orthodox rabbi say in this case?" then this is a good indication that the caller identifies with the ultra-Orthodox community.

Building Trust in Order to Avoid Conflict

Following the broader discussion of the effects of social change and the different components inherent in dealing with change processes, we will now focus on one of the main parameters that can determine the successful containment of opposition to change. Trust has been identified as a key element of successful conflict resolution and prevention. Trust is a belief in the other, the tendency to attribute virtuous intentions to the other, and willingness to act on the basis of the other's conduct.[38] Distrust is not the absence of trust but is rather the fear of the other, a tendency to attribute sinister intentions to the other, and a desire to protect oneself from the effects of another's conduct.

When instituting change in a religious community, the level of acceptance will depend on the amount of trust the agents of change have acquired. In the case of the *yoatzot halakhah*, trust needed to be won from three potential groups:

1. The rabbis — the spiritual leaders who would give halakhic legitimacy to the *yoetzet halakhah* and her status as a legitimate authority to answer questions on family purity.
2. Orthodox women — the clients of the *yoetzet halakhah*, who would need confidence in the *yoetzet halakhah*'s halakhic knowledge and Orthodox

religious commitment in order to confide in her with personal halakhic questions.

3. The husbands of those women — in order to comply with the halakhic answers their wives would receive from the *yoetzet halakhah*.

All three groups would need to have confidence in the *yoatzot halakhah*'s commitment to Orthodox halakhic values and their identification with its fundamental social structure. The women would also need to have confidence and trust that the *yoatzot halakhah* understands their question and situation and is an authoritative source on this issue. The rabbis, however, may be more concerned with the *yoatzot halakhah*'s motives and may fear a slippery slope toward feminist changes that could undermine their halakhic authority and perhaps lead to the demand for the ordination of women. The husbands of women consulting the *yoatzot halakhah* may share this fear, although their rabbi's endorsement would probably be enough to grant her legitimacy.

Trust can be divided into two major types: deterrence-based trust and identification-based trust.[39] Deterrence-based trust is when individuals fulfill their commitments because they fear the consequences of not acting in accordance with their promises. Trust is sustained to the degree that the deterrent is clear, possible, and likely to occur if the trust is violated. In addition to the fear of punishment for violating the trust, the trust is maintained for the rewards derived from preserving it. Deterrence-based trust can be increased by repeated interactions where both parties are aware of the benefits of the relationship and what one can gain from the other. The trust is affected by the degree of interdependence and possible alternative relationship. If personal reputation is at stake in the relationship, then short-term gains from untrustworthy acts will be balanced against the importance of maintaining a good reputation.

Identification-based trust is the full internalization of the other's desires and intentions. Parties effectively understand, agree with, and endorse each other's wants. This trust is based on mutual understanding and will develop especially when there is collective identity with collective intentions between the parties. When there are shared core values, beliefs, and concerns, then this trust is strengthened.

We will only take a brief look at the building of trust between the women and the *yoetzet halakhah*, for this trust, although integral to the success of the *yoetzet halakhah*, does not have the potential for conflict as does the relationship between the rabbis and the *yoetzet halakhah.* The trust between the women and the *yoetzet halakhah* is identification-based trust. A woman calling the Nishmat hotline is met with the calming voice of an understanding Orthodox woman intimately familiar with many of the same experiences as the questioner. Both women have the same desires and intentions when discussing the laws of family purity. They want to know the halakhah in order to keep it to the letter of the law, yet they also want to have an empathetic ear to understand the challenges and issues the woman is facing. I can speak personally of how true this is from my experiences before I became a *yoetzet halakhah.* When first married, I would sometimes ask questions of my rabbi. However, when I would refer my question to a *yoetzet halakhah* on the Nishmat hotline, I could feel the difference. The woman I spoke with understood exactly the situation I was describing. I could tell by her responses that she had herself experienced a similar thing. I trusted her response because I knew she understood my question. This was not the case when speaking to the rabbi. Often, I would get off the phone from the short (sometimes embarrassing) conversation not sure if he had understood what I had said.

This is also evident in the length of questions to rabbis and the *yoatzot halakhah.* Often the duration of the phone call to the rabbi is only a few minutes. The woman describes her situation and her question, and the rabbi responds with his answer. There is very little dialogue or exchange. When a woman asks a *yoetzet halakhah* a question, the average conversation is ten to fifteen minutes.[40] The question can be followed up with a discussion about how the woman feels about the halakhic response and what the consequences of the situation will be for the woman. These conversations are important from the halakhic perspective as well, as information may be revealed that was integral to the question but the woman did not realize that it was necessary or helpful to provide these details. The security and relaxed tone of the conversation not only build confidence between the questioner and the *yoetzet,* but also allow the issue to be dealt with more comprehensively. As one *yoetzet* described, "I so want to help, to give the desired answer, the one that will make the woman happy. But one must stay composed — empathetic, but a bit detached — in order to stay objective. It is a matter of trust, and these women rely on us. Our halakhic responsibility is to see the situation as a whole, to consider all circumstances, but to remain impartial and trustworthy."[41]

The trust achieved between the rabbis and the *yoetzet halakhah* is a much more challenging test. Most Orthodox rabbis approach the *yoetzet halakhah* with suspicion and distrust. Rabbis feel threatened by the feminist threats of female rabbinic ordination, fearing that Orthodox halakhic values are at risk. Orthodox rabbis are immediately wary of a woman who wishes to institute a change in traditional halakhic norms, especially when it relates to or has possibilities of impeding upon the rabbis' own authority. Against this backdrop of distrust, the *yoetzet halakhah* had to develop the rabbis' trust not only in order to overcome any objection but also to receive their endorsement.

The trust between the *yoetzet halakhah* and the rabbi is composed of both deterrence-based and identification-based elements. It is easier to build deterrence-based trust first, and then, as the relationship is strengthened and both parties begin to have confidence, they can start to build a relationship based on identification. After proving to the rabbis that her major concern is the integrity of the halakhic system and its observance, the *yoetzet halakhah* could progress to build a relationship based on common goals and objectives.

The deterrence-based trust between the rabbis and the *yoetzet halakhah* stems from the desire of the Orthodox *yoetzet halakhah* to be endorsed by the Orthodox rabbis. Unlike members of some women's prayer groups who do not feel the need for rabbinical endorsement, the institution of the *yoetzet halakhah* was dependent on such endorsement. Rabbanit Henkin chose Rabbi Yaakov Warhaftig,[42] a *rosh kollel* (head of a male institute for advanced Talmud studies), to head the program. In addition to receiving the endorsements of Rabbi Yehuda Herzl Henkin (also a leading Modern Orthodox rabbinic scholar) and Rabbi Warhaftig, Rabbinit Henkin involved other leading rabbis by having the oral examination administered by outside examiners including heads of three different learning institutions who specialize in the laws of family purity. The certificate conferred upon the *yoetzet halakhah* is signed by five leading Israeli Orthodox rabbis. The *yoetzet halakhah* knows that she has been entrusted by these rabbis to answer questions by women on halakhic issues of family purity.

The program was also endorsed by leading American rabbis. At the graduation of the first *yoatzot halakhah* in 1999, Rabbi Norman Lamm[43] publicly declared, "We are still at the beginning of the movement. A movement I hope will take root and flower." Rabbanit Henkin was conferred an honorary doctorate in 2001 by Yeshiva University for her pioneering work on behalf of women's Torah education. This honor, conferred four years after the establishment of the *yoatzot halakhah* program, was a sign of how her program and the *yoatzot* have been accepted.

This trust is in some ways deterrent-based in that if the *yoetzet halakhah* violates this trust by going beyond her authority or exceeding halakhic limits, she will lose the rabbis' trust and their endorsement. Every *yoetzet halakhah* is required to log every question and response she gave during her shift on the hotline. The hotline coordinator (herself one of the more experienced *yoatzot*) goes through the entries in the database and when necessary will discuss the question and answer with the *yoetzet* in order to clarify any errors for the future. The costs and benefits of consistent action by the *yoetzet halakhah* are clear to both the rabbi and the *yoetzet.* The rabbis have given their endorsement for the program despite the fear that the *yoetzet halakhah* may exceed her authority or cause others to go the next step toward female rabbinic ordination. However, they take that risk in order to allow women to answer women on these intimate issues. The rabbis realized the need and benefits of women trained to answer women on these sensitive issues. They recognized that by allowing women into this area of authority, they were also increasing the accessibility of these laws to women and allowing them to observe the laws in a more committed way.

The *yoetzet halakhah* embraces the endorsement of the rabbis, which gives her legitimacy in her community, while being aware that if she violates their trust, she will lose her legitimacy and therefore her authority in the Orthodox community.

Because the trust is deterrent-based, the rabbis impose safeguards against potential threats. One such safeguard is the duty of deference to rabbinic authority for halakhic rulings. As is stated in the text of the certificate, "if a novel decision is needed she will turn to a recognized decisor."[44]

Other safeguards include inquiry into the devoutness of the *yoetzet.* This is seen in the criteria for acceptance to the program:[45]

1. Personal halakhic observance and lifestyle
2. Commitment to disseminating family purity
3. Absence of extraneous motivations

4. Strong background in learning Talmud
5. Teaching or leadership skills

Another safeguard has been to limit the authority of the *yoetzet halakhah*, not because of internal halakhic restrictions but rather to maintain the trust of the rabbis, as seen in the limitation discussed earlier of not initially preparing the *yoetzet* to deal with the evaluation of stains.[46]

The identification-based trust between the *yoetzet halakhah* and rabbis stems from the common desire for women to feel comfortable and encouraged to ask halakhic questions regarding family purity laws. By having shared goals and ideals, they can work together in a relationship to achieve these goals. Identification-based trust is increased when both parties share the same concerns and are motivated by the best interests of their community. Identification-based trust has a strong emotional component and is affected by the circumstances under which the parties meet and the mood at the time that the parties encounter each other.

The effect of circumstances is evident in the contrast of the feminist developments in Israel and America. The rabbis in Israel encountered the innovative idea of the *yoetzet halakhah* following the flourishing of women's learning in Israel. The opening of higher Torah learning to women in Israel predates the Israeli Orthodox feminist movement. (The first *yoetzet halakhah* program was opened in 1997, and the Orthodox feminist movement in Israel, Kolech, was established in 1998).[47] Women's learning was an accepted idea in Israel, and the authenticity of the religious motivation of the institutions and the women learning in them was not called into question. It was almost a natural step for women to progress to being involved in the halakhic process, especially in the area of sexual intimacy. It was against this background that the rabbis in Israel were asked to deal with this initiative. The mood at the time was not one of suspicion, and therefore trust was more likely to be built between the parties than distrust.

In contrast, in America, Orthodox feminists focused upon women's prayer and upon changing synagogue ritual to be more inclusive of women. The motivations of the *yoatzot halakhah* were questioned much more intensely in America, and the fear of the slippery slope toward women rabbis was much more apparent than in Israel. Rabbanit Henkin notes that the difference between the two settings enabled the *yoatzot halakhah* to be more accepted in

Israel, and unlike in America, a relationship of trust was built between the rabbis and the *yoatzot.*[48]

Elements of trust and distrust may coexist because they relate to different experiences with the other or knowledge of the other in varied contexts. The rabbis in Israel could have trusted the women's learning institutions and the development in that field without extending that trust to the *yoatzot halakhah* — a much more radical change with possibly more wide-reaching consequences. The level of trust involved in a relationship can sometimes be related to the chronic disposition of the parties.[49] The situational parameters and the history of the relationship can affect the amount of trust, especially at the beginning. Due to the profound distrust of feminist movements in the Orthodox community, the *yoetzet halakhah* was definitely beginning on the left foot.

What can be done in order to restore or even establish identification-based trust?

1. Exchange information about perceived violations of trust. Identify and understand the act of any violations. An explanation as to the motivation of the violation or how the act was perceived can assist in clarifying any misunderstandings.
2. Reaffirm commitment to the ideals and beliefs that make up the shared values in the relationship. Affirm the goals and the commitment to the relationship. Strategies to avoid misunderstandings and miscommunications can be instituted for the future.

In order to lower distrust, the parties should openly acknowledge and discuss areas of mutual distrust. If any violations of the trust are inconsistent with the core beliefs and values of the relationship, then the relationship is in danger of being discontinued.

There are four suggested ways to repair trust when it is endangered and there is a risk of an escalating conflict between the parties:[50]

1. Address the behavior that is causing distrust. Actions of unreliability or antagonistic activities could lead to distrust.
2. Apologize. Give an account of the trust violation. Acknowledge responsibility and express regret. Commit to alternative behavior in the future.
3. Agree to procedures for monitoring to ensure commitments are kept.

4. Minimize vulnerability or dependence on the other party when distrust develops. Identify alternative ways to have needs met.

An example of a test of trust took place at a recent meeting between a group of *yoatzot halakhah* and Rabbi Warhaftig, the head of the program. One of the *yoatzot* communicated a message from a leading rabbi that he was unhappy because he had heard that the *yoatzot* were answering questions on the hotline regarding the colors of blood stains.[51] This rabbi was expressing his feeling that there had been a violation in the trust he had in the relationship because the *yoatzot* were not fulfilling the halakhic requirements as he saw them. However, this violation of trust did not cause him to publicly denounce the *yoatzot halakhah* or take action against them. Instead, he chose a path of clarification and perhaps even warning. The response of Rabbi Warhaftig was to clarify the issue with the group of *yoatzot halakhah* and set down clear guidelines of how to deal with such questions. The strength of the identification-based trust allowed a confrontation between this rabbi and the *yoatzot halakhah.* Although violations of identification-based trust can directly challenge a person's most central and cherished values, the strength of the trust in the relationship allowed for a conflict to be avoided and the violation to be dealt with swiftly and hopefully effectively.

In this example, the trust was repaired through steps 1 and 2. Although there was no public apology (and the rabbi did not demand one), the issue was dealt with in order to repair the trust between this rabbi and the *yoatzot halakhah.*

An example of the third step of repairing or maintaining trust is the database of all answers given on the hotline and the supervision of these answers. This process ensures the commitment of the rabbis to the system, knowing that there are checks and balances and the *yoetzet halakhah* is trustworthy when using her authority.

The existence of trust makes conflict resolution easier and more effective. However, trust is the first casualty in a conflict. Breaks in trust have a spiral effect in that they cause conflict and thus increase distrust. If the parties are motivated to sustain the relationship, there will be considerable attempts to rebuild the trust, and the relationship will not be abandoned at the first sign of distrust.

The fourth suggested step in repairing trust is irrelevant to the case of the *yoatzot halakhah.* Because the *yoetzet halakhah* is committed to remaining in the Orthodox framework, they do not wish to have any alternative to the support of the Orthodox rabbis. Without the endorsement of Orthodox rabbis, they have no raison d'être.

Conclusion

Through the *yoatzot halakhah*, women have begun to exercise a new authoritative role within the Orthodox community, but nonetheless, this novel participation of women in the halakhic discourse did not draw the conflict that could have been expected. The institution of the *yoatzot halakhah* program was met with surprisingly minimal opposition in the world of Modern Orthodoxy, this despite the fact that other initiatives led by feminist religious women caused great opposition and even fury within the community. In the public eye, the *yoetzet halakhah* was viewed differently than other similar initiatives in that it was not labeled as a feminist endeavor.[52]

I have suggested that the avoidance of conflict succeeded because of the building of trust between the *yoatzot halakhah*, the community, and the rabbis. The resistance was dealt with in a way that was designed to avoid the possible opposition and outcries against these women. Rabbanit Chana Henkin was careful to receive endorsement of the rabbis for this social change, thus ensuring their support within the community. She was also careful when accepting women to the program, choosing candidates who would not only succeed in the role but also would not attract opposition from critics. The fractioning of the potential conflict allowed the gradual management of opposition within the community.

The *yoatzot halakhah* program has only celebrated ten years since its inception. Many Orthodox women have still not had contact with a *yoetzet* or even heard of their existence. Time will tell whether the *yoetzet halakhah* becomes an official part of the Modern Orthodox community and a more recognized communal position. The efforts taken to avoid conflict will contribute to their ongoing success. As long as these efforts continue and the trust between the rabbis and the *yoatzot* is valued, there will be an increased chance that the *yoatzot halakhah*'s activities will become more widespread.

The *yoetzet halakhah* is an example of how innovative changes can be made within the halakhic framework without causing public and destructive opposition. Perhaps in time, it may be possible to apply the test case of the *yoetzet halakhah* as an example of how to institute change in the Modern Orthodox community while successfully avoiding conflict.

Notes

1. Modern Orthodoxy is a subgroup within Orthodoxy that synthesizes Torah traditionalism and modern secular behavior. Other subgroups include ultra-Orthodoxy, which is a right-wing branch of Orthodoxy characterized by its fundamental worldview and opposition to connections with the secular world. Recently, other subgroups have evolved, such as Central Orthodoxy (a mix between Modern and ultra-Orthodoxy), Orthoprax (Jews who engage in the practical Orthodox way of life but do not necessarily subscribe to their beliefs), and Open Orthodoxy (a more left-wing liberal approach to the Orthodox way of life). See Adam S. Ferziger, *Exclusion and Hierarchy: Orthodoxy, Nonobservance, and the Emergency of Modern Jewish Identity* (Philadelphia: University of Pennsylvania Press, 2005).

2. For a full discussion on the sociological developments of feminism in the Orthodox world, see Sylvia Barack Fishman and Steven Bayme, *Changing Minds: Feminism in Contemporary Orthodox Jewish Life* (New York: American Jewish Committee, 2000). For an analysis of the theological aspects of these developments, see Tamar Ross, *Expanding the Palace of the Torah: Orthodoxy and Feminism* (Hanover, NH: University Press of New England, 2004).

3. Sylvia Barack Fishman, "Comparative Reflections on Modern Orthodoxy and Women's Issues," *Edah Journal* 1:2 (2001).

4. For more on the *toenet rabbaniti*, see Nava Bak and Yedida Goldman, "Resting our Case: *Toanot Beit Din*," *Amit* 72:1 (2000): 38–40; and Ronen Shamir, Michal Shitrai, and Nelly Elias, "Religion, Feminism and Professionalism: The Case of Rabbinical Advocates," *Jewish Journal of Sociology* 38:2 (1996): 73–88.

5. The translation of the term *yoetzet halakhah* is "a halakhic advisor." In order to avoid confusion in this article, I have used the Hebrew plural of this term, *yoatzot halakhah*, when referring to more than one *yoetzet halakhah*. For an explanation on why this term was chosen, see below.

6. Fishman and Bayme, *Changing Minds*, 8.

7. Aryeh A. Frimer, "Guarding the Treasure," *BDD—Journal of Torah and Scholarship* 18 (2007): 66–106.

8. For an in-depth analysis of women's issues and modernity, see Joel B. Wolowelsky, *Women, Jewish Law, and Modernity: New Opportunities in a Post-Feminist Age* (Hoboken: KTAV Publishing House, 1997).

9. For writings in favor of the new practice, see Daniel Sperber, "Congregational Dignity and Human Dignity: Women and Public Torah Reading," *Edah Journal* 3:2 (2003); Mendel Shapiro, "*Qeri'at Ha-Torah* by Women: A Halakhic Analysis," *Edah Journal* 1:2 (2001). For an example of writings against the practice, see Eliav Shochetman, "*Aliyat Nashim leTorah*," *Sinai* 135–136 (2005): 271–349; Gidon G. Rothstein, "Women's Aliyyot in Contemporary Synagogues," *Tradition* 39:2 (2005): 36–58. It is interesting to note that in a response to Mendel Shapiro's article in the *Edah Journal*, R. Yehuda Herzl Henkin (one of the supervising rabbis of the Nishmat hotline) has objected to the practice of women's *aliyyot* in a minyan, even coining the practice as non-Orthodox.

10. Naomi Graetz, "Women and Religion in Israel," in *Jewish Feminism in Israel: Some Contemporary Perspectives*, ed. Kalpana Misra and Melanie S. Rich (Hanover, NH: University Press of New England, 2003): 17–56. The acceptance of the *yoetzet halakhah* in the ultra-Orthodox community is still highly questionable. Following the graduation of the first *yoatzot halakhah*, in an article in the English *Yated Ne'eman* newspaper (Moshe Schapiro, "Orthodox Institute Holds Graduation Ceremony for Female Rabbi," *Yated Ne'eman*, Oct. 21, 1999) wariness of this new position and the fear that it was a cover for the ordination of women rabbis was expressed. Apart from limited opposition in the media and blogosphere, to the best of my knowledge, there has not been a public condemnation or excommunication by ultra-Orthodox rabbis.

11. Sylvia Barack Fishman, "Women's Transformations of Public Judaism: Religiousity, Egalitarianism and the Symbolic Power of Changing Gender Roles," in *Who Owns Judaism? Public Religion and Private Faith in America and Israel*, ed. Eli Lederhendler (New York: Oxford University Press, 2001), 131–55.

12. Chana Henkin, "Women and the Issuing of Halakhic Rulings," in *Jewish Legal Writings by Women*, ed. Micah D. Halpern and Chana Safrai (Jerusalem: Urim Publications, 1998), 278–87.

13. Rabbi Yehuda Herzl Henkin has published four volumes of halakhic responsa, *Benei Banim*, and is the author of *Equality Lost: Essays in Torah Commentary, Halakha and Jewish Thought* (Jerusalem: Urim Publications, 1999), *Responsa on Contemporary Jewish Women's Issues* (Jersey City, NJ: KTAV Publishing House, 2003), and *Understanding Tzniut* (Jerusalem: Urim Publications, 2008).

14. Rachelle Sprecher Fraenkel, "A Primary Address for Women," *JOFA Journal*, Winter 2006: 13, 16; available at www.jofa.org/pdf/06jofajournalwinter.pdf, accessed January 2, 2010.

15. Nishmat Women's Halakhic Hotline is a telephone hotline on matters of laws of family purity, in operation since December 2000. Since its inception it has received over eighty thousand calls. The hotline is conducted in Hebrew and English, six hours a day, 6:00 p.m. through midnight and on Friday mornings. A different *yoetzet* answers the phone each day, typically handling up to twenty-five calls. A rabbi is on call when a halakhic decision is needed.

16. www.yoatzot.org. The website is in English and features articles and examples of other questions previously asked on the site. There is also an option to send an e-mail question to the site, and a *yoetzet* will send a response within twenty-four hours. There are current plans to launch the Hebrew *yoetzet* site in the coming months. For an analysis of the questions asked through the Internet, see Deena Zimmerman, "'So She Can Be as Dear to Him as on Their Wedding Day?' Modern Concerns with *Hilkhot Niddah* as Demonstrated by Anonymous Email Questions," in *Rabbinic and Lay Communal Authority*, ed. Suzanne Last Stone (New York: Yeshiva University Press, 2006), 225–41.

17. Bracha Rutner is a *yoetzet* for Riverdale Jewish Center, New York, and Shayna Goldberg is a *yoetzet* at Congregation Ahavath Torah, New Jersey.

18. Chana Henkin, "New Conditions and New Models of Authority: The *Yoatzot Halakhah*," in *Rabbinic and Lay Communal Authority*, 87.

19. Kurt Lewin was a German-American psychologist who was one of the first to study group dynamics and organizational development. His model of change referred to all social systems and is appropriate to be applied in the case of the *yoetzet halakhah*. For more on the model, see Kurt Lewin, *Group Decision and Social Change*, in *Readings in Social Psychology*, ed. Eleanor E. Maccoby (New York: Holt, 1958): 197–211.

20. Bernard Burnes, "Kurt Lewin and the Planned Approach to Change: A Re-Appraisal," *Journal of Management Studies* 41:6 (2004).

21. For a recent analysis of these complexities, see Orit Avishai, "*Halakhic Niddah* Consultants and the Orthodox Women's Movement in Israel," *Journal of Modern Jewish Studies* 7:2 (2008).

22. Chana Henkin, "*Yoatzot Halacha:* Fortifying Tradition through Innovation," *Jewish Action* 60:2 (1999).

23. Joel Wolowelsky, "Rabbis, Rebbetzins, and Halakhic Advisors," *Tradition* 36:4 (2002): 54–63.

24. Sprecher Fraenkel, "A Primary Address for Women."

25. This appraisal is based on my personal experience with this rabbi and discussions with my colleagues. He has not expressed these feelings publicly.

26. Eric C. Marcus, "Change Processes and Conflict," in *The Handbook of*

Conflict Resolution: Theory and Practice, ed. Morton Deutsch and Peter T. Coleman (San Francisco: Jossey & Bass, 2000), 366–81.

27. Chana Henkin, "Women and the Issuing of Halakhic Rulings."

28. This does not include the category of questions related to women's health.

29. This position was voiced by Norma Baumel Joseph, an Orthodox feminist, in a discussion on the pros and cons of the *yoetzet*'s role as a mediator between the rabbi and a woman at the conference "Untying the Knots: Theorizing Conflicts between Gender Equality and Religious Law" at the Hadassah-Brandeis Institute at Brandeis University in Waltham, MA, on April 15, 2008.

30. For a more in-depth analysis of the scope of the authority of the *yoatzot halakhah*, see Tova Ganzel, "The Rabbi, the Posek and the *Yoetzet Halakha*," in *Rabbis and Rabbinate: The Challenge*, ed. Yedidia Stern and Shuki Friedman (Jerusalem: The Israel Democracy Institute, 2011).

31. This article appeared in the national religious newspaper *Hazofe*, Shabbat Supplement Aug. 27, 1999, 8–9.

32. Chana Henkin, "New Conditions and New Models of Authority," 89.

33. For the difference between the role of the *yoetzet*, rabbi, and *posek*, see Ganzel, "The Rabbi, the *Posek* and the *Yoetzet Halakha*."

34. For an analysis on the issue of answering anonymous halakhic questions through the Internet, see Azriel Weinstein, "Mara D'atra," *DAAT* 16 (2003): 8–10.

35. For an overview of fractioning conflict, see Heidi Burgess, Guy Burgess, and Michelle Maiese, "Incrementalism," Beyond Intractability: A Free Knowledge Base on More Constructive Approaches to Destructive Conflict, accessed March 17, 2008, www.beyondintractability.org/essay/incrementalism.

36. When a woman sees a stain on her underwear and if she is unsure if the color is one that renders her impure, she will show the underwear to the rabbi in order for him determine the status of the stain and therefore her status regarding physical relations with her husband. Training to determine the status of colors is through experience called *shimush*. The rabbi will spend many hours with a more experienced rabbi seeing thousands of examples of stains and learning the nuances of which colors are acceptable and which are not.

37. Some rabbis avoid this embarrassment by placing a box outside their house in which people can place envelopes with the cloths and their phone number in order for the rabbi to call and give the answer.

38. Roy J. Lewicki and Carolyn Wiethoff, "Trust, Trust Development and Trust Repair," in *The Handbook of Conflict Resolution*, 97.

39. Ibid. This division is based on the following article: Debra Shapiro, Blair H.

Sheppard, and Lisa Cheraskin, "Business on a Handshake," *Negotiation Journal* 8:4 (1992): 365–77. In their article they also refer to knowledge-based trust, which is less relevant to the case of the *yoetzet halakhah* and therefore not discussed here.

40. Deena R. Zimmerman, "The Nishmat Taharat Hamishpacha Hotline: Women Helping Women," *Le'ela* 51 (2001): 17–20.

41. Sprecher Fraenkel, "A Primary Address for Women," 16.

42. Rabbi Yaakov Warhaftig is a *rosh kollel* in the Harry Fischel Institute for Talmudic Research in Jerusalem. He has headed the *yoatzot halakhah* program since its inception in 1997.

43. Rabbi Dr. Norman Lamm served as the president of Yeshiva University during the years 1976–2002.

44. The complete translated text of the certificate is as follows: "The modest and learned woman of good character whose fear of Heaven precedes her wisdom [name] was tested by us and by a special committee of rabbis and found to be proficient in the laws of *Niddah* and immersion. In response to the needs of our generation and in order to distance many women from sin, we hereby support her and agree that she serve as a primary address for women who will wish to turn to her in these matters for guidance in the way of Torah and fear of Heaven; if a novel decision is needed she will turn to a recognized decisor."

45. Chana Henkin, "New Conditions and New Models of Authority," 89.

46. Ibid., section 6.

47. For an extensive article on women's leadership and the feminist movement in Israel, see Tova Cohen, "Female Religious Leadership: Modern Orthodoxy in Israel as a Case Study" [Hebrew], *Tarbut Domocratit* 10 (2006): 251–96.

48. Chana Henkin, "New Conditions and New Models of Authority," 87.

49. Lewicki, "Trust, Trust Development and Trust Repair," 94.

50. Ibid., 112.

51. The color of the stain can determine whether the stain renders a woman *niddah* (the status of ritual impurity) or not. Traditionally, the decision of the type of color of a stain is decided when the rabbi actually sees the stain and is not decided based on the description of the woman.

52. As Rabbanit Henkin has noted, the *yoetzet halakhah* is not a feminist enterprise, since feminism is perceived both as anti-family and anti-religious.

FATOU KINÉ CAMARA

Chapter Ten The Temple for Women Initiates Project
A Framework for Culturally Meaningful Feminist Expression in Rural Areas

We can do something other than look to Saudi Arabia or the West, we can look to the interior of Africa, its culture, its spirituality.

— *Sembene Ousmane, Senegalese writer and filmmaker*

Introduction

My paper is based on the realization I have made as a feminist activist in a country where 94 percent of the people are officially Muslims[1] that it is possible to improve people's understanding of each others' rights and responsibilities without embarking into a discourse challenging mainstream religious norms. In Senegal (as is the case in sub-Saharan Africa in general) the majority of people continue to believe in the taboos and prohibitions set up by their ancestral pre-Islamic and pre-Christian religion. Therefore when one speaks in a positive way about indigenous traditions, most people listen with interest and pride. The project of setting up a Temple for Women Initiates in Baback Sérères,[2] a Senegalese village where people follow different religions (Moslem, Catholic, Indigenous), was born from this idea that the revitalization of the pre-Islamic and pre-colonial Black African culture is the best way to circumvent religious fundamentalisms.

The young people of the village of Baback Sérères held a meeting on October 15, 2007, to discuss the project of a Temple for Women Initiates. In a letter summarizing the views expressed in that meeting, they wrote the following:

> Culture, which can be defined as the ways of doing things, the way of life, the beliefs, in short the ways in which a group sees the world, occupies a major place in the life of people. However the phenomena of Westernization, combined with the attempts at Islamization, have caused the negation of the existence of Black-African cultures. Without culture it is impossible to reach development.[3]

Issa Laye Thiaw, the main promoter of the Temple for Women Initiates project, is the son of a high priest of the indigenous religion; he is also from an ethnic group, Seereer, with a long-standing tradition of resisting conversion to Islam and the Christian religion. He made the following statement:

> Since Islamization and Christianization, Africans do not respect nature. Conversion starts with a change of mindsets, and as soon as that happens, any further change is accepted. Each religion has plundered the tradition of its community of birth. Where Islam was born, women had little if any rights; Islam has led us to the marginalization and inferiority of women.[4]

Senegal is, according to its constitution, a secular state. Nonetheless, Islam has been officially used as a way to deny women equal rights. The Family Law contains a section called *Des Successions de Droit Musulman* ("Muslim Inheritance Law"). However, there is no section for "Christian Inheritance Law" or "Indigenous Inheritance Law." Muslim Inheritance Law, as codified in Senegalese Family Law, consistently discriminates against women; women systematically get half of what their male counterparts are given, for no other reason than that they are females. For instance, when legitimate heirs are not all of the same gender, females receive only half of what the males get (Article 637, *Code de la Famille*).[5] On the other hand, when it comes to monetary duties, equality is granted to women regardless of Islamic laws: duty to give alimony to their siblings and parents in need (Article 263), duty to take part in home and family maintenance (Articles 151, 155, and 375, §2), and duty to pay damages to the spouse in the event of a divorce suit in which the woman is found guilty.[6] Doudou Ndoye (Senegalese barrister, former minister of justice, and leader of a political party) notes the following (in an article in which he nevertheless sings the Senegalese Family Law's praises):

> The former president of the National Assembly, General Practitioner Amadou Cissé Dia, made a recent narrative of the position of President Leopold Sédar Senghor on the elaboration of the Family Law, specifying that President Senghor conveyed to him that it was necessary to secure the religious leaders' approval and leave the Islamic concepts undisturbed but that unilateral repudiation was to be banned from our ways. (Ndoye, 2001, 11)[7]

Lip service is paid to "modernity," while the greater concern for the Muslim leaders' support is unashamedly made clear. Most articles of the Family Law, which came into force in 1973, were copied out of the Napoleonic Civil Code (except, of course, the articles that refer to polygamy) (Pisier and Brimo, 2007). However, so far all the attempts of abrogating the gender-based discriminatory articles have been successfully opposed in the name of "our Muslim tradition." Article 152 of the Family Law elevates the husband to the status of lord and master of his wives and children. He is allowed up to four wives (Article 133), none of whom has a say in the matter. As the legally appointed head of the family (Article 152), the husband is given the exclusive right to choose the matrimonial home, and his wife/wives cannot live anywhere else without his permission or a decision of justice allowing it (Article 153). The father has exclusive parental authority (Article 277, §2). Children are legally bound to be given their father's family name (Article 3); the child bears its mother's family name only in cases of illegitimacy (Article 4). At the same time, paternity suits are prohibited (Article 191). Women do not have the right to terminate an unwanted pregnancy (abortion is a criminal offense under Article 305 of the Penal Code; it is also a criminal offense under Article 306 to advocate freedom of choice). Whenever female rights organizations campaign for the abolition of these rules, Muslim lobbies defend them in the name of Islam.

Due to the constant reference to "our Muslim tradition" and to the official statistics as to the number of Muslims in Senegal, it is important to give a brief historical perspective of "our tradition" concerning Islam. Islamic movements did not have a strong hold in West Africa until the nineteenth century. Islam spread in West Africa along the trans-Saharan trade routes. Members of the aristocracy and of the merchant elite converted to Islam, but the people in their overwhelming majority retained their indigenous

African religion. The series of *jihad* (holy war) that led to Muslim states in several parts of West Africa in the early nineteenth century did not foster mass voluntary conversions to Islam. In Senegal, the military defeat of the "pagan"[8] aristocracy and their troops (the *ceddo* warriors), followed by the destruction of the indigenous political structures that empowered women to the point of making them heads of state (the *lingeer* of the Seereer and Wolof kingdoms),[9] is what paved the way to the Muslim brotherhoods' emergence as the sole guiding lights and refuge for the people now under a brutal foreign rule (Gellar, 1982, 6–9; Cruise O'Brien, 1977, 47–71 ; Dia et al., 2005, 17–21; Camara and Seck). The marabouts (Muslim leaders) and the French colonial authorities had no interest in keeping alive the memory of the female leaders who used to rule the country.[10] They were equally indifferent, if not hostile, to indigenous law. As for the indigenous religion, it was rejected on both sides (Muslim and French) as satanic, pagan, primitive. In spite of these persisting labels, indigenous law and the indigenous religion are still very much alive in Senegal, particularly in the Seereer and Joola communities. Senegal's first president, famed poet L. S. Senghor (1906–2001), who was a Catholic raised by missionaries and who belonged to the Seereer ethnic group,[11] wrote the following:

> As today a Muslim Head of State will consult the "sacred wood," and offer in sacrifice an ox or a bull, I have seen a Christian woman, a practising medical doctor, consult the Sereer "*Pangool*" (the snakes of the sacred wood). In truth, everywhere in Black Africa, the "revealed religions" are rooted in the animism which still inspires poets and artists, I am well placed to know it and to say it. . . .[12]

Commentators on Senegalese politics and post-independence history regularly marvel at the fact that the Catholic president Leopold Sédar Senghor's strongest allies were the prominent Muslim leaders in Senegal. In fact, it was an alliance of mutual interest that dates back to colonial times (and that alliance is still on). While religious leaders preached obedience to the authorities, they could develop their respective religious brotherhoods without trouble from the state's authorities, who even lent a hand when needed.[13] Christian missionaries were allowed to settle in places peopled in majority by those who had not yet converted to Islam (Dia et al., 2005, 55–59). It is said that during colonial times, some of the holy places that were open indigenous sanctuaries were turned into Christian places of worship. Consequently, churches and mosques, the spiritual strongholds of patriarchal ideology, are all over the country, but there is not one brick and stone edifice built to call attention to, and muster respect for, the religion of the land. Those that existed of old are now desecrated ruins that hold the interest of only a limited number of scholars and archaeologists. The same can be said about cemeteries. With the exception of Ziguinchor (in Southern Senegal), the cities that were created, implanted, or developed by the French, during colonial times, do not have cemeteries reserved for the indigenous religion followers. Land has been earmarked for Christian cemeteries and graveyards for Muslims. This has forced many Senegalese men and women to convert to one of these two religions in order to have a decent burial at their death. Cemeteries play an important role in religious propaganda, as do mosques, churches, and temples, hence the importance of building a temple for the women initiates as a way to promote respect for them and the spiritual values they stand for. Women initiates are female elders who have gone through the various stages of traditional education, which is called initiation. The purpose of the temple is to be a place of learning (a philosophical college) as well as a cultural center open to visitors and researchers. It is to the description of this project, carried by a whole village, men and women alike, without reference to religious faith, that I will devote the second part of this chapter. In the first part I will give an overview of the indigenous religion and of the matriarchal system it stems from.

Insights on the Indigenous African Religion: The Matriarchal and Spiritual Foundations

Matriarchy is one prominent trait of the indigenous African culture (C. A. Diop, 1959). It was at the roots of the sociopolitical system, it ruled the economy and the family, and it also shaped Africans' religious beliefs prior to the introduction of Islam and the Christian faith on the continent. Matriarchy does not mean dictatorship of women over men. It is a system where women are valued for their practical experience, their spiritual knowledge, and their body's sole ability to host and give birth to life and then produce life-sustaining nourishment (milk). That was just one way among many others to express love for femininity. The feminization of spirituality was another facet of matriarchy.

"MOTHER POWER": THE LITERAL AND POLITICAL MEANING OF MATRIARCHY

Literally "matriarchy" means "Mother power"; politically it means a system that promotes gender equity, female heads of state, and female community leaders.

The Literal Meaning of Matriarchy

The term "matriarchy" is composed of the Latin word *mater* (meaning "mother") and of the Greek suffix *arkhè* (which means "power"). Thus, *mater arkhè* means literally "Mother power." Accordingly, a matriarchal society is a society where the maternal values of caring, courage, compassion, nurturance, well-being, and fertility (prosperity) are predominant. In matriarchal societies, woman is the seat of power, the provider of riches, the giver of life, the healer, the embodiment of justice (e.g., the goddess Maât in Egypt, the sacred principle of Truth and Fairness). Historical evidence proves that empowering women, as was the case in ancient Egypt, ancient Nubia, and other African empires (Ghana, Mali, Jolof, Kongo), never meant the cruel rule of women over victimized men. As a matter of fact, matriarchy cannot be defined as the opposite of patriarchy, in terms of it being a system where one gender (here the female one) oppresses the other. Ifi Amadiume accurately points out the following facts about the matriarchal system:

> It is not the direct opposite of patriarchy, or an equivalent to patriarchy, as it is not based on appropriation and violence. The culture and rituals of matriarchy did not celebrate violence; rather, they had a lot to do with fecundity, exchange and redistribution. (Amadiume, 2001, 196)

In order to know how a matriarchal system functions, it is best to study it instead of just assuming that a system based on empowering women will be no different than a system that is based on male power. For instance, the matriarchal system that ruled ancient Egypt meant a gender-sensitive governing system, family laws respectful of women's, mothers', and children's rights, economic empowerment of women, and freedom of beliefs. Ifi Amadiume summarizes the essential features of a matriarchal society:

> Patriarchy and matriarchy are social and political ideologies which directly decide the role and status of women in society; how society is to be orga-

> nized; and how social subjects are to relate to one another. They are also ideologies which decide the degree of violence and abuse of human rights that is permissible in society. Matriarchy as was constructed by African women, had a very clear message about social and economic justice. It was couched in a very powerful goddess-based religion, a strong ideology of motherhood, and a general moral principle of love. (Amadiume, 2001, 101)

In the African agriculturist communities, women were the ones who were entrusted with seed selection, the actual planting of crops, and processing raw material into edible food; men would be in charge of clearing a field and helping at harvest (Ki Zerbo, 2003, 121). Matriarchy is therefore a tribute to the capacity of women to ensure food security, proper health care, and spiritual protection to the entire community. Whereas the patriarchal regime has its origin in harsh nomadic life where women's economic contribution is fairly inexistent, the matriarchal regime is tied to agricultural and sedentary life (C. A. Diop, 1996, 130). In his paper "Rural Women in the Socio-political Transformations," Gidbon Mutiso from Kenya supports that thesis by outlining the weight put on women's spiritual knowledge:

> There is enough oral history from the old people to suggest that the agriculturalist peoples who migrated from area to area gave women extremely significant places in the rituals connected with the settling of new areas. The woman was the one to appease the Gods so as to seek favour for the productivity of the new area. By extension following this line of logic, one can hypothesise that since women were the intermediaries with the Gods and furthermore since self-sufficiency in crops was necessary, it is possible that they utilised this structural position to acquire more socio-political rights (and duties) than has been suggested by colonialism research. (Mutiso, 1975, 528)

The Social and Political Meaning of Matriarchy

In many Black African states and communities, women used to be the land managers and the ones who would take food surpluses and the manufactured goods to the various markets. In Black Africa, marketplaces were essentially run by women. And women were the major traders, travelling sometimes very long distances to sell their goods.[14] Because they were essential in the food production chain, in the distribution circuits, and in the accumulation of household wealth, women (old, young, single, married) were greatly respected. Initiation, the indigenous African way of imparting precious knowledge, relayed the importance of the matriarchal system. Although matriarchal societies are not segregated societies, at some point girls and boys undergo separate initiation rites. In the Seereer communities, *kumax yaay no juul* presides over the training of men initiates, and *jooj maad no gulook* takes over the training of women. Men's initiation training is called *ndut*, meaning "bird's nest," (Dione, 2004, 12), and women's initiation training is called *ngulook*, "marriage ceremony" (B. S. Diouf, 2004, 215; Faye, 2006, 110). This organization along gender lines existed at all levels. In the pre-colonial Wolof and Seereer kingdoms for instance, national coordination was ensured at the top by the *lingeer* (elected queen / female head of state) for the women, and for the men, by the elected king (called *maad* or *buur* in the Seereer kingdoms; *buurba*, *brak*, *dàmmeel*, or *teeñ* in the Wolof kingdoms). Thus, from the base to the top, the gender duality was acknowledged in a way that guaranteed both sexes equal rights and opportunities. Indigenous African theology made sure to entrench the gendered organization of the society and the preeminence of the female element in initiatory teachings.

Education based on the method of initiation uses the ambiguity of words to deliver a multilayered message. Hence the first meaning will be clear, simple, and immediately accessible. The second meaning will only be accessible to those with specific background knowledge. The third meaning will be so enshrouded in symbolism that only insiders will be able to get it. The same word could therefore lead to different directions. The following example explains how initiates fashioned sentences with double or triple meaning, in this case relating to the Seereer take on "Mother power":

"*O loq O yaay fïsu saax it*"

—Simple translation: literally, "The borders of the country are traced using a branch of *yaay*" (shrub whose scientific name is *Combretum glunosicum*).

—Legal translation: "The country is governed by the rules of the maternal lineage" Playing on the ambivalence of the term *yaay* (which also means "mother"), it is declared simply that the matrilineal system governs the country (B. S. Diouf, 2004, 210).

— Esoteric translation: "Sorcery is transmitted by the mother" (because in a matrilineal system everything you inherit, be it goods or titles, you inherit from your mother, including spiritual superpowers).

Drums also conveyed coded messages. In the Seereer kingdoms, a drummed message opening all public celebrations reminds all that Siga Bajaan, a woman, was the first head of state:[15] "'*Siga Bacal, ten eetu maat, maat a guutin a roof*' 'Siga wide hips[16] has founded the state, the state improved after her'" (B. S. Diouf, 2011, 21).

Given the fact that one sentence could carry more than one meaning, it is interesting to note how the word *maat* in Seereer takes its full meaning when one compares it with the meaning of the same word in ancient Egyptian. In Seereer, *maat* means "(state) power" (B. S. Diouf, 2011, 23).[17] In ancient Egypt, *Maât* is the sacred power of Justice (Truth and Fairness), which is symbolized by a female figure, the "Goddess" named Maât. The land of the Pharaohs also attributed the origin of state power to a woman, the Great Mother Isis, whose Egyptian name Ast means "throne, seat, or abode" (Redd, 2002, 162). Isis is also credited for giving men the laws they need to govern themselves in peace and fairness (Diodorus Siculus, first century BCE).[18] Thus it appears that the drummed message about Siga Bajaan is more than a simple reminder that there was once a queen bearing that name. The drummed message recalls and summarizes the matriarchal roots of the Seereer political system. The idea that women deserve respect because they are the ones who organized the community and designed the concept of a state based on *Maât* (Truth and Fairness) is quite literally drummed into people's minds. It is a known fact that in many African kingdoms the female chief of state (usually, but not always, the queen mother) enjoyed a higher respect and had more political power than the king. In the family circle also, the female elements (older sisters, mothers, first wives) wielded more authority than the male ones (Camara and Kandji, 2000).

The Cultural Commission's report (Abidjan Colloquium) underlined the fact that social changes due to external factors took place within the African traditional society and led to various transformations. In a paper entitled "The Matriarchal System as a Proof of the Social Role Played by the Woman in African Traditional Society," Senegalese jurist Siga Sow says, "First colonization, then Islam and Christianity have modified the pattern of matriarchy. Add to these factors the new forms of trade, the cash economy and the modern school which tend to destroy the former image of the woman in Senegal."[19]

One must stress the influence of colonialism and foreign religions (Islam and Christianity). It led to serious misrepresentations of Africa's indigenous religion. It is currently being called everything (paganism, idolatry, polytheism) but what it really is: the religion of the all-loving Mother God, unique Creator and universal life and love giver.

GOD IS A MOTHER: THE SPIRITUAL MEANING OF MATRIARCHY

Although God is not given a gender and is defined as the inaccessible one, indigenous African theology relies on the mother figure to convey the idea of a caring, compassionate, generous, all-loving, and all-powerful God. Amateurs of African art are quite familiar with sculptures portraying a Black woman, totally naked or bare breasted, holding on her knees a suckling infant (in ancient Egypt's art that image is famous as Isis and infant son Horus). Those sculptures emphasize on purpose the role of mothers as the prime nurturers who lavish on their children a love that is similar, as much as such a comparison can go, to the love God has for the whole Creation. It is in that sense that the indigenous African Creator-God is a Mother.[20] However, the male part of the Creator is not put aside, but every time it is outlined, a woman figure appears to serve as counterpart. The female element is what makes the male element come to life, and it is that duality working together that creates life. Therefore, woman is essential in the indigenous religious discourse as both Mother God and God's counterpart. The Divinity is thus made inseparable from the Woman. Such a theology explained and justified women holding the highest offices in the indigenous religion's "clergy" or performing the most crucial rituals. They are priestesses, high priestesses, and prophets. That fact has been documented all over Africa and the Caribbean and as far back as ancient Egypt.

In its conclusions, the colloquium on "The Civilization of the Woman in African Tradition" states that according to ancient myths, the creation of the woman is linked to the origin of death. It is when death appeared in the world that God created the woman so that life would not die forever. Since this time, says the legend, men die but life still goes on. The African woman appears therefore as the giver of life, the savior, and the nurse. The Egyptian legend of Isis and Osiris relates the same myth of Woman being the Savior and the one to guarantee resurrection from the dead and protection from the evil forces of Chaos, Disorder, and Sickness. Accordingly, the African indigenous religion is totally and unequivocally non-misogynistic. Furthermore, indigenous African theology relies on the mother figure to convey the idea of Creation and of the parentage of all God's creatures because "in the beginning was Mother" (Mutiso, 1975, 527).

God is the One who gave birth to Earth, Moon, and Sky. In ancient Egypt theology Nuut is the Universal Mother who swallows the Sun each night and gives birth to it each morning. Nuut is the Primordial Mother; she gave birth to the first human couples, who acquired godlike status as the First Ancestors (Isis, Osiris, Nephtys, and Seth). For Babacar Sédikh Diouf, a Seereer who specialized in researching data linking the Seereer ethnic group to the ancient Egyptians,[21] the strategy used by the woman to impose herself appears clearly: imaginations had to be struck. And that is why in Egyptian antiquity, the goddess NT (NuuT) was given the title "Mother of the Universe," while Roog, the name that Seereer give to God, reveals itself as meaning "Mother" This femininity of God is confirmed in the everyday language when the Seereer say, speaking about men, "*Nqoox paal, yaay um Roog*" ("The black bull's mother [is] God"). In order to tighten his demonstration that for the Seereer "*Roog* is a She,"[22] Diouf gives as further proof the following prayer little boys murmur when they go to bed at night (B. S. Diouf, 2004, 210–11):

Danaas	I am going into sleep
Nqoox paal	(Me) black bull
Yaay um Roog	My mother is Roog
Daapaam lanq	Earth is my bed
Hakandu bil	Rock is my pillow
Hulwa Roog	Sky is my blanket
Dingoor juwaam	Ocean is my fence
Wegoor njelem	Strong iron is my door

In the religion of the Mother God, women are not stigmatized through an emblematic Fallen Naked Woman who is the cause of all evil. The patriarchal tales of Genesis are the total opposite of the African ones. African sacred stories do not bring the woman out of any man's or god's body part, be it its head (like the Greek goddess Athena)[23] or its ribs (like the biblical Eve, created for and named by Adam). In the African Creation stories, man and woman are created by the Primordial Mother. They are the First Twins, hence the special status of twins and of twins' mothers in many Black African communities.

The ancient Egyptian genesis even goes so far as to state that man was created for woman, and for love:

> In a papyrus dating from the time of the Ramesside dynasty (13–12th century BC) God proclaims: "I am the one who has made the primeval waters in order for the Celestial Cow to come into existence. I am the one who has made the Bull for the Cow in order for the joy of love to come into the world." (Al Assiouty, 1989, 239–40)

Respect for woman is not linked to her being veiled; the African religion unashamedly uses the sexual organs of the human body to celebrate, emphasize, and explain different aspects of theology. Indigenous African religion spirituality does not separate the body from the soul, nor does it set one higher than the other. The human body is flaunted and revered as a temple. It is a temple of the spirit that gives it life, and as such one has a duty to keep it clean, beautiful (with ornaments, ointments, tattoos), and healthy. A healthy body hosts a healthy soul and vice versa. That is why a sickness is always seen as a sign of something being wrong in the realm of the spirits. Traditional healers cannot conceive limiting their treatment to the body; the soul also has to be cured of what ails it. Even after death the body has to be treated with love and care; cremation is not documented as an indigenous African practice. Love and respect for the body also explains the fact that total or partial nudity was accepted in many African communities, up until colonization; Christian missionaries and Muslim religious leaders put an end to it. They brought to Africa the ideology of the sinful body and of the sinful women who lead men to their ruin if they are not put under tight male control. They also misrepresented the indigenous religion, labelling it as pagan, superstitious, or satanic practices, conveniently forgetting in the process that the African religion is based on the belief of a one God Creator.

THE AFRICAN RELIGION: A NONTOTALITARIAN GENDER-SENSITIVE MONOTHEISM

The African indigenous monotheism is not only non-misogynistic, it is also nontotalitarian. Whatever name it is given (voodoo, fetishism, animism), the indigenous African religion, as illustrated by the ancient Egyptians' religion, is a true monotheism, because it is founded on the belief of a one God Creator

(Obenga, 2004, 60–73; Thiaw, 1992, 59–68; B. S. Diouf, 2004, 205–21; Sylla, 1978, 45–46). However, the belief in one God Creator does not entail an interdiction to give prayers and offerings to the spirits of one's ancestors and to the guardian spirits of the land. While God's uniqueness is unquestioned, its remoteness from humans is strongly outlined, hence the need for enlightened humans to address their prayers, wishes, and woes to intermediaries who will help them control their destiny. There are different kinds of intermediaries: some are human (priests, prophets, medicine men and women, sightseers), others are the dead ancestors' spirits and the invisible forces present in nature — animals, trees, rocks, rivers (Dia et al., 2005, 84–86, 90–93; Diatta, 2005, 87–89). Because such intermediaries (and their place of residence) are countless, the African religion developed into a nontotalitarian monotheism: for God is unique but God's emissaries and intermediaries are plenty. Consequently every community, every individual is free to choose their path and their messenger to the divine. Such theological principles quite effectively preclude the use of religion as a way of justifying wars against "nonbelievers," "hypocrites," or "infidels."'

Spirits being essentially invisible to the naked eye, it takes a special kind of knowledge (which can be enhanced through initiation) to be able to locate them and interact with them. But as they are potentially everywhere, it is best to treat everyone and everything with respect. This is particularly illustrated in old fairy tales that tell the stories of discarded objects, powerless-looking people, or apparently harmless animals who eventually reveal themselves as powerful spirits in disguise out to test humans' kindness, honesty, or prudence.

The African religion is also based on the belief that everything that exists has a life of its own and the ability to feel and suffer like you and me. Animals, plants, soil, "inanimate objects" feel. We must therefore respect and love all those with whom we share the earth. These kinds of beliefs prompt those who hold them to treat nature and their environment with care and respect. The following examples were given me by Issa Laye Thiaw:

- When you eat under a tree, you want to give it its share, which you deposit at the foot of the tree.
- After a busy morning of toil, when the farmer sits in the shade, he must also put his hoe in the shade and not let it lie in the sun. If he forgets to do that he will be reminded with these words [he told me in Wolof, Senegal's

most widely spoken local language]: "Da fa am bàkkan ni yow." ("It has life — the ability to feel — just like you.")

- When the hoe falls from your hands, we say: "Do not pick it up immediately. It is tired. Let it rest."[24]

The African religion promotes a deep-rooted respect for nature and its inhabitants. Large trees are elevated to the status of sacred trees (e.g., the baobab). Gratitude and respect for animals, and for what each of them can teach us or help us with, are ingrained with the totem system: each clan has an animal it honors and protects (i.e., ancient Egypt's sacred animals; Camara, 2004, 162–93). It is all these rules, entrenched in the indigenous African spiritual beliefs, that the project of a Temple for Women Initiates aims to shelter. Building a temple will serve as a way to ensure a larger respect for and a greater protection of this knowledge and its holders.

The Objectives of the Construction of a Temple for Women Initiates

The project of the Temple for Women Initiates aims at developing the culture and the spiritual values of the Seereer. For the project's initiators, learning the moral values and spiritual knowledge that have been bequeathed by the ancestors will help promote the emancipation of Senegalese women. The temple will constitute a step toward a better life for women, and particularly rural women, at various levels: symbolic, legal, practical.

SHOWCASING WOMEN AS SPIRITUAL LEADERS AND EXTENDING RESPECT TO THE INDIGENOUS RELIGION

Women occupy the most predominant places in the indigenous religion's "clergy." Initiated women perform the most important rituals and prayers for prosperity, fertility, and protection from disasters (Société Africaine de Culture, 1975, 597). Such is not the case in the "revealed religions." Up to this day, in Senegal, there is not one female imam in any mosque or one female priest in any Catholic church, nor is there any female pastor of a Protestant temple. All prayers in churches, temples, and mosques are led by males, a fact that is not lost on those who are quick to deny women a leadership role in the public arena. They use that factor as God-given proof that women cannot claim equal rights with men, who have been appointed their leaders by God Himself. Consequently, from a feminist point of view, it is quite significant to put forward the fact that the indigenous religion, far from denying women equal standing in the spiritual leadership hierarchy, rests principally on female spiritual leaders. Seeing women in the role of spiritual leaders of their community enhances respect for them and for women in general.

There used to be in each Seereer village a queen, the *maad No ngulook* (the ruler of young brides). She had the privilege to keep the bowl, *roon*, or calabash, *saxal*, that contained the objects symbolizing femininity. The temple will thus have a *maad No ngulook*, or "mother superior," who will be charged to chair all the activities of the center and to act as the legal representative of the temple in legal matters and official ceremonies and gatherings. Besides showcasing women in a leadership role, the temple's aim is also to enforce respect for the indigenous religion, in conformity with the constitutional principle of respect for all religions.

The Temple for Women Initiates will give the constitutional principle of freedom of religion and state's respect for all religions effective meaning and substance. The Constitution of Senegal proclaims in its preamble the principles of philosophical and religious freedom. Article 1 of the Constitution specifies that the Republic of Senegal is secular and democratic and that it respects all beliefs. Article 17 recognizes the religious institutions as means of education, and subparagraph 2 of Article 19 states the following: "The religious institutions and communities have the right to develop without obstacle. They are released from the supervision of the State. They regulate and manage their business in an autonomous way." Thus respect for all religions is a constitutional principle, but nothing is done to enforce respect for the indigenous religion. Respect for everyone's religious beliefs does not seem to extend to the indigenous religion.

The methods employed to supplant African religion and the values it carried were (and still are) intimidation and negation of or contempt for the indigenous religion. The promise of heaven and the threat of hell are powerful tools used to move converts away from their ancestral beliefs, which are depicted as satanic practices. These facts have a negative impact on the holders of the oral tradition, who no longer dare to express openly the lessons of old times.

Building a temple for these holders of the oral tradition will give them that courage. In his exposé justifying the building of a Temple for Women Initiates, Issa Laye Thiaw points out the fact that the Seereer are a classic victim of this situation. Not only have they lost their ancestral religion, but in so doing they have contracted an inferiority complex, which has robbed them of the courage to face the apostles of the "revealed religions." Rejuvenating and modernizing initiatory teachings will go a long way to restore respect for the positive ways and values of old.

COLLECTING AND SHARING ANCIENT ESOTERIC TEACHINGS

> The temple is thought of as a shelter for Seereer culture and oral knowledge where holders of ancient knowledge will gather and share their knowledge among themselves and with others.

Stepping past the temple threshold should mean stepping into a very ancient culture. Consequently the temple will be built in accordance with the typical model of the old Seereer habitat. It will be composed of twenty-two houses and a large general-purpose unit, which will be used as conference room. Each house will bear the name of an old village. The people of each one of these villages will be solicited to name a delegate to the philosophical college that will be housed at the temple. The members of the philosophical college will be the women of knowledge from the village of Baback Sérères and neighbourhood villages. Women from other places and men of knowledge will be asked to join as honorary members. The college will be a place where ancient knowledge will be discussed and recorded by the members themselves, who will have ownership rights on all the written, filmed, or recorded material they produce. Researchers and scholars coming to them for information will have to sign agreements protecting their ownership rights. Thus, while making available their knowledge to outsiders, the guardians of the ancient oral tradition will be protected from plunder by unscrupulous researchers who do not share with their informants the royalties they get from the books they write or the health product they market thanks to the valuable information they were given.

The goal of the procedure asking villages to name delegates to the college is to collect the esoteric teachings inherited from the ancestors. That will enable the members of the philosophical college to store, in books, films, and recordings, the initiatory secrets of the targeted zone. Setting up alongside the philosophical college an Academy of Old Tales serves the same purpose. The creation of such an academy, located at the temple, will make it possible to collect and preserve this invaluable cultural inheritance. That will be done by organizing meetings where tales will be told and recorded (with the agreement of the storyteller), which will enable the managers of the temple to collect and store the old tales, which tend to disappear. Tales contain useful information and hold the spiritual and literary heritage bequeathed by the ancestors. The existence of such an academy of the storytellers will make it possible to penetrate the heart of Seereer culture. To encourage the narrators, gifts will be allotted to those who tell the best legends.

Storytelling plays an important part in the moral and intellectual training of young people. This popular literature belongs to the Seereer spiritual heritage, whose conservation is a peremptory necessity. Issa Laye Thiaw, the main initiator of the project, specifies that telling tales was a field mostly reserved for old women. The researcher believes that is why women have a positive image in the Seereer tales.

Building the temple following the model of the ancestral habitat will also serve as an illustration of the "course" on Seereer habitat and traditions, which will be delivered to the visitors of the temple. The temples of old were not only places of worship, they were also places of healing and learning. Accordingly, the objective of the Temple for Women Initiates is to offer the community a variety of services, some of which are lucrative, in order to make it possible for the temple to be self-sustaining. Hence, in order to improve the quality of health care offered to rural women, joint consultations by traditional healers and doctors will be held as a regular activity of the temple. Visits from environmentalists, veterinarians, and so on will be encouraged. Human rights associations and jurists will devise with the members of the temple the ways and means to most efficiently address issues of gender violence, child abuse, and equal rights and opportunities.

In order to make enough money to keep the project self-sustaining, some of the rooms of the temple will be rented to participants at the seminars and conferences held in the temple. Rooms for tourists will also be made available. A showroom will be set up where CDs, DVDs, books, and artefacts produced at the temple or in collaboration with the initiated women will be sold.

The initiators of the project plan to rejuvenate the initiation rites that were the base of the moral and spiritual formation of the children of the community. In the Seereer *Kaamee* or *Seh-seh* language, the place where those rites took place is called *ndut*, "the bird's nest." The initiatory enclosure was seen as the most favorable place to impart to the neophytes the literary and spiritual heritage bequeathed by the old ones.

The transformation of the temple into a summer camp during a few weeks each year will be used to supplement the education of children with the teaching of gender equality, children's rights, and respect for nature through initiatory tales, legends, role plays, traditional songs, and ritual dances. Children from different areas will meet and learn about each other under the supervision of the women of the temple, who will teach them the rudiments of Seereer culture in a festive way. They will also be taught to read and write in their own language.

Conclusion

The existence of the Convention on Cultural Diversity (CDD) represents a new and important platform for promoting culture in the wider context of sustainable development.[25] However, the principles the CDD stands for need to be acted upon in order to give them a meaning that goes beyond the moral stance. The Temple for Women Initiates project gives the CDD such a meaning.

For the promoters of the Temple for Women Initiates project, the first challenge is to successfully lobby national authorities into assuming responsibility on the matter by taking practical steps to ensure that Africa's specific cultural heritage holds its own in the face of the Middle Eastern and Western civilizations' rival attempts to pose themselves as the unique conveyors of a universal message. M. André Youm, the head of the village of Baback Sérères, has officially written to the president of the rural council (*conseil rural*) of Notto Diobass, a letter dated October 18, 2007, to inform him of his decision to allot one hectare of land to the project. So the Association of the Women of Baback have the support of the village's chief and the land on which to build the temple. All they need now is the money to build it. The project has been sent to several government agencies and a few nongovernmental organizations, but the best answers the promoters of the project have received so far are messages of encouragement. However, perseverance being at the heart of all successful endeavours, the promoters of the project are in the process of identifying ways to bring private donors as well as funding agencies to show a true interest in building a Temple for Women Initiates in the Senegalese village of Baback Sérères.

Appendix: The Letter of the Young People of the Village of Baback Sérères

The project called the Temple for Women Initiates falls under a particular context. Threatened by modernization, the Seereer culture is one of the pillars of African civilization, which today tends to disappear. At the current hour, the need for revalorization of this culture, in particular in Jobaas, is posed with acuity. The project is born out of this point of view. Its aim is to make tradition known through the image of the Seereer woman.

Culture, which can be defined as the ways of doing things, the way of life, the beliefs, in short the ways in which a group sees the world, occupies a major place in the life of people. However the phenomena of Westernization combined with attempts at islamization have caused the negation of the existence of Black-African cultures. Without culture it is impossible to reach development. This is an idea that has the support of many researchers, such as those who have pondered the question of African unity, and also of humanitarians interested in what guarantees wellbeing.

Thus to concretize or materialize this idea, various ethnic groups feel the need to act. The values that characterize the Seereer culture, especially its matriarchal side, are enough to give us the model of society we all wish for. The pilot project (TWI) suggested by the AFI, the Association of the Women of Joobas, relates to the importance of culture and its development. The study of the project was the framework of a dialogue between Issa Laye Thiaw and a restricted group of students. According to the participants, the realization of this project could allow the rebirth of certain values and open up new life-style opportunities to women as suggested by the reference document. The participants proposed that dwellings be built to shelter the initiates. These infrastructures could be implemented in each village centre. Knowing that tradition requires a house with two doors, these new infrastructures can be built according to this traditional model. For the success of this project, participants in the debate propose the adoption of a participatory step in the phase of formulation and realization of the project, the women having to be integrated into the decision-making processes and in the planning. The site of the granaries and choosing the tree that would serve as palaver tree were among the questions that were raised. According to certain points of view, the orientation towards the east was favoured for the site of the granaries. The latter were always placed in front of the houses. For certain questions such as the ones about the palaver tree, or the appropriate site for the temple, the participants suggested the matter be investigated with old folks.

With regard to the implication of women, let us note that a process of elimination of illiteracy will have to be set up for better conveying certain messages. As to the place of men within the temple, the debate was focused on two types of status. One is the "yimbir" whose role is to guard the women's privacy during the initiatory phases. The other is the "bidjo" who protects the girls against intruders at the time of ceremonies such as the "minams," the "riiti," etc

Sereer who have jealously guarded culture are now the victims of a phenomenon of alienation which is depriving posterity of its sources, and of its reference marks.

In way of conclusion, the participants salute the initiative and declare their readiness to take an active part in the project. For them, the realization of this project could play a major role in promoting Seereer culture throughout the world.

The youth of the village
Done at Baback, the 15-10-2007

Notes

1. Muslim, 94 percent; indigenous beliefs, 1 percent; Christian, 5 percent (mostly Roman Catholic). "CIA World Factbook 2004/Senegal," accessed March 1, 2008, http://en.wikisource.org/wiki/CIA_World_Fact_Book,_2004/Senegal.

2. Baback Sérères is located in the region of Thiès. For a map of Senegal, see "CIA World Factbook 2004/Senegal," accessed October 3, 2011, http://en.wikisource.org/wiki/CIA_World_Fact_Book,_2004/Senegal.

3. See the full letter in the appendix at the end of this chapter.

4. Conversation on African religion at my home, Dakar, March 26, 2008.

5. The case of the heir of indeterminate gender, the hermaphrodite, is naturally examined in great detail, under Article 597. An expert will be called to determine which is the predominant gender, and if that cannot be established, "the hermaphrodite will receive half of what he would have been entitled to had he been

of the male sex added to half of what he would have been entitled to had he been of the female sex."

6. See Fatou K. Camara, "Women and the Law: A Critique of the Senegalese Family Law," *Social Identities Journal for the Study of Race, Nation and Culture* 13, no. 6 (November 2007): 787–800.

7. "*L'ancien président de l'Assemblée nationale, le docteur Amadou Cissé Dia, a fait une narration récente de la position du Président Léopold Sédar Senghor à l'occasion de l'élaboration du Code de la famille, précisant que le Président Senghor lui avait fait savoir qu'il est nécessaire d'obtenir l'approbation des chefs religieux et ne pas toucher aux concepts de l'Islam, mais la répudiation unilatérale doit être bannie de nos usages.*" He cites as a source the *Sud quotidien* newspaper edition of June 23, 2001.

8. "Pagan" was the term used by the French and by the Muslim warriors who declared holy wars on the territories they wanted to conquer. Actually some of the kings and people they declared pagans were Muslims, only they were Muslims who did not care for Sharia and kept on indigenous practices and beliefs.

9. In the Wolof and Seereer pre-colonial kingdoms, a female head of state, the *lingeer*, was designated each time a new king was elected (Dieng, 1993, 15). Her political power was greater than that of the king (Bamba M'Bakhane Diop, *Lat Dior et l'Islam*, 24; Samb, *Cadior ak Amary Ngoné Sobel*, 36–37; Barry, 1985, 263, 275). Women were also made governors (i.e., a provincial chief appointed by the king). Women governors bore the title of *jee* (Dieng, 1993, 381, 451).

10. In 1855 the kingdom of Waalo, then headed by the *lingeer* (title of the female head of state) Ndatte Yàlla, was the first kingdom to be annexed by the French. Direct rule over most of Senegal was achieved in 1886, with the defeat of the armies of the last Wolof kingdom, Kajoor, and the death of its *dàmmeel* (title of the male head of state) Lat Joor. For the story of Lingeer Ndatte Yàlla (in French), visit "Ndatté Yalla et la stratégie de conquête du pouvoir," accessed October 3, 2011, http://www.sengenre-ucad.org/TexteNdate.htm.

11. Ethnic groups in Senegal are as follows: Wolof, 43.3 percent; Pulaar, 23.8 percent; Seereer, 14.7 percent; Joola, 3.7 percent; Mandinka, 3 percent; Soninke, 1.1 percent; European and Lebanese, 1 percent; other , 9.4 percent. "CIA World Factbook 2004/Senegal," accessed March 1, 2008, http://en.wikisource.org/wiki/CIA_World_Fact_Book,_2004/Senegal.

12. "*Si aujourd'hui tel chef d'Etat musulman consulte le 'bois sacré,' offre en sacrifice un bœuf ou un taureau, j'ai vu telle chrétienne, docteur en médecine et pratiquante, aller consulter les 'Pangool' (les serpents du bois sacré) sereer. En vérité, partout en Afrique noire, les 'religions révélées' sont enracinées dans l'animisme qui inspire encore*

aujourd'hui, poètes et artistes, je suis bien placé pour le savoir et le dire . . ." (Pierre Alexandre, *Les Africains* [Paris: Lidis, 1982], 6).

13. "Although the marabouts resisted cultural assimilation, they were very much involved in Senegalese colonial politics, offering their support and that of their following to Senegalese citizen politicians in exchange for certain favors — e.g. government subsidies for building mosques, jobs and trading licenses for their faithful followers, and redress against abuses perpetuated by the colonial administration. . . . [I]n addition to preaching obedience to the colonial authorities, the marabouts urged their *talibés* (disciples) to grow peanuts for the market in the new areas where they were settling. The French were delighted with this practice, as it promoted the expansion of peanut production, the foundation of the colonial economy. Because of its interest in extending peanut production, the colonial administration granted many prominent Mouride and Tijani marabouts large tracts of land that became peanut estates and often supported the marabouts in their disputes with Fulbe herders, who were fighting to retain control over their traditional grazing lands that were being taken over by the peanut farmers" (Gellar, 1982, 13).

14. See in Société africaine de culture, *The Civilization of the Woman in African Tradition* (Paris: Présence Africaine, 1975): Awe Bolanwe, "The Economic Role of Women in a Traditional African Society: The Yoruba Example"; Aïcha N'doye, "Initiative and Creative Powers of the Woman in a Traditional Economic Life: The Senegal Example"; Jeanne Nzaou-Mabika, "Initiative and Creative Ability of the Woman: The Gabon Example"; and Anastasie Beugré and Djama Séry, "The Woman in the Economy of the Traditional Societies of the Ivory Coast." All four papers put forward the major role of women in production of goods (from agriculture, crafts, and industries) and distribution of the surplus products by trade.

15. A long-standing Seereer tradition traces the origins of centralized political power to a woman called Siga Bajaan (Bajaal or Bacal). Her legend is summarized in this popular Seereer sentence: "*Siga Bajaan fertu maat né*," "Power started with Siga Bajaan" (Gravrand, 1983, 267).

16. According to Babacar Sedikh Diouf, "Bacal" was not the queen's surname but an alias meaning "wide hips," a criterion of beauty (B. S. Diouf, 2011, 20).

17. "Ce même terme 'maât' fossilisé dans le message tambouriné de Siga Bacal, reste encore actif dans la langue seereer avec le même sens de gouvernance de participation sur la base des quatre principes indispensables au 'vivre ensemble': Amour, Vérité, Justice et Paix, enfants de la responsabilité et de la liberté" (B. S. Diouf, 2011, 23). My translation: "The same word 'maât,' fossilized in the drummed

message about Siga Bacal, is still active in the Seereer language with the same sense of participative governance on the basis of the four principles essential to 'living together': Love, Truth, Justice and Peace, the children of responsibility and freedom."

18. Diodorus Siculus gives the following testimony: "Isis also established laws, they say, in accordance with which the people regularly dispense justice to one another and are led to refrain through fear of punishment from illegal violence and insolence" (*Library of History*, Book1, Section 1, VIII: http//:remacle.org/bloodwolf/historiens/diodore/livre1.htm [accessed February 28, 2011]).

19. Siga Sow, "The Matriarchal System as a Proof of the Social Role Played by the Woman in African Traditional Society," in *The Civilization of the Woman in African Tradition*, Société africaine de culture, 337.

20. The place of women in African traditional religion and in ancient Africa's religious art is particularly well documented in these papers, the titles of which say it all: "Egypt's Isis: The Original Black Madonna," by Eloise McKinney-Johnson; "African Goddesses: Mothers of Civilization," by Runoko Rashidi; "The Image of Woman in African Cave Art," by Rosalind Jeffries; "Black Madonnas of Europe: Diffusion of the African Isis," by Danita Reed. All four papers are published in Ivan Van Sertima, ed., *Black Women in Antiquity* (New Brunswick, NJ: Transaction, 2002).

21. Cheikh Anta Diop has established facts that confirm his thesis that Seereer originate from ancient Egypt (*Nations nègres et culture* [Paris: Présence Africaine, 1979]), 392–401).

22. Seereer, as many African languages, does not have gender indicators such as "he, she, her, his."

23. Greek mythology describes the goddess Athena as being the daughter of Zeus, and only by him; Athena was not generated by any woman. She leaped from the head of Zeus, already adult, dressed with her armor.

24. Conversation on African religion at my home, Dakar, March 26, 2008. From childhood Issa Laye Thiaw was instructed in Black African values and the secrets of the initiates through his father, who was a high priest of the indigenous faith. He then trained at the École Franco-Arabe of Dakar, at the École Normale of Tunis, at the École Pratique des Hautes Etudes of la Sorbonne, Paris. He was senior researcher at the Centre d'études des civilisations, Dakar. He is a retired teacher of classical Arabic. He spent many years in the Arab and Islamic countries, where he studied the Muslim religion. He is the author of *La femme Seereer* (Paris: L'Harmattan, 2005).

25. The CDD was adopted on October 20, 2005, by the UNESCO General Conference (148 countries approved it, while 2 countries — the United States and Israel — voted against it and 4 abstained). The CDD entered into force in March 2007, following its ratification by a sufficient number of countries.

References

Al Assiouty, Sarwat Anis (1989). *Origines égyptiennes du Christianisme et de l'Islam, résultats d'un siècle et demi d'archéologie.* Paris: Letouzey et Ané.

Amadiume, Ifi (1997). *Reinventing Africa, Matriarchy, Religion, Culture.* London & New York: Zed Books.

Barry, Boubacar (1985). *Le royaume du Waalo: Le Sénégal avant la conquête.* Paris: Karthala.

Camara, Fatou Kiné (2007). "Le Code de la Famille du Sénégal ou de l'utilisation de la religion comme alibi à la légalisation de l'inégalité de genre." *Genre, inégalités et religion. Actes du premier colloque inter-Réseaux du programme thématique Aspects de l'État de Droit et Démocratie.* Paris: Éditions des Archives Contemporaines — AUF, 459 pages.

Camara, Fatou K. (2007). "The Three Most Important Features of Senegal's Legal System That Others Should Understand." Website publication, October. http://www.ialsnet.org/meetings/enriching/camara.pdf.

Camara, Fatou K. (2007). "Women and the Law: A Critique of the Senegalese Family Law." *Social Identities Journal for the Study of Race, Nation and Culture* 13, no. 6, November, 787–800.

Camara, Fatou K. (2004). *Pouvoir et Justice dans la tradition des peoples noirs.* Paris: L'Harmattan.

Camara, Fatou K., and Saliou S. M. Kandji (2000). *L'union matrimoniale dans la tradition des peuples noirs.* Paris: L'Harmattan.

Camara, Fatou Kiné, and Abdourahmane Seck (2010). "Secularity and Freedom of Religion in Senegal: Between a Constitutional Rock and a Hard Reality." *Brigham Young University Law Review*, no. 3, 859–84.

Corrêa, Sonia, in collaboration with Reichmann Rebecca (1994). *Population and Reproductive Rights, Feminist Perspectives from the South.* London: Zed Books.

Cruise O'Brien, Donald (1977). "Amadu Bamba le saint fondateur des Mourides du Sénégal." *Les Africains*, tome 2. Paris: éditions Jeune Afrique.

Desroches-Noblecourt, Christiane (1986). *La femme au temps des pharaons.* Paris: Stock.

Dia, Ousmane, et al. (2005). *Les religions au Sénégal, Les Cahiers de l'Alternance*, no. 9. Dakar: Fondation Konrad Adenauer (FKA) et Centre d'Etudes des Sciences et Techniques de l'Information (CESTI).

Diatta, Nazaire (2005). "Le sacré chez les Joola." *Les religions au Sénégal, Les Cahiers de l'Alternance.* Dakar: FKA and CESTI, 87–89.

Dieng, Bassirou (1993). *L'épopée du Kajoor.* Paris: Agence de coopération culturelle et technique (ACCT); Dakar: Centre africain d'animation et d'échanges culturels (CAEC), éditions Khoudia, IFAN Cheikh Anta Diop.

Diodorus Siculus. *The Library of History*, book 1, chap. 8, "Beginning." http://penelope.uchicago.edu/Thayer/E/Roman/Texts/Diodorus_Siculus/1A*.html (accessed February 25, 2011).

Dione, Salif (2004). *L'appel du Ndut.* Dakar: IFAN/Enda-Editions, Collection Patrimoine no. 1–2.

Diop, Bamba M'Bakhane (no date). *Lat Dior et l'Islam.* Dakar: self-published (he is the grandson of Lat Dior, the last king of Kajoor who fought the French colonial troops).

Diop, Cheikh Anta (1996). *Towards the African Renaissance: Essays in African Culture and Development 1946–1960.* London: Karnak House.

Diop, Cheikh Anta (1979). *Nations nègres et culture.* Paris: Présence Africaine.

Diop, Cheikh Anta (1959). *L'Unité culturelle de l'Afrique Noire — Domaines du patriarcat et du matriarcat dans l'antiquité classique.* Paris: Présence Africaine (2e édition 1982).

Diouf, Babacar Sédikh (2011). "Dualité de genre et tradition." *Combats pour la parité — Actes du séminaire d'élaboration d'un modèle de loi sur la parité.* Dakar: COSEF et AECID, Dakar, 19–24.

Diouf, Babacar Sedikh (2004). "Le Sérere, paganisme polythéiste ou religion monothéiste." In *Pouvoir et Justice dans la tradition des peuples noirs*, Fatou Kiné Camara. Paris: L'Harmattan, 205–21. http://cosef.org/IMG/pdf/COSEFPublicationIMPRIM_DV_25mars.pdf (accessed January 27, 2012).

Diouf, Madior (2005). "La tolérance religieuse reflet de l'aspiration d'une nation à la démocratie dans l'œuvre de Birago Diop." In *La tolérance religieuse, reflet de l'aspiration d'une nation à la démocratie.* Dakar: Fondation Konrad Adenauer, 10–15.

Faye, Louis Diène (2006). *Education et mariage — Le monde seereer.* Dakar: NEAS, les Nouvelles Editions Africaines du Sénégal.

Gellar, Sheldon (1982). *Senegal: An African Nation between Islam and the West.* Boulder, CO: Westview Press.

Gomez-Perez, Muriel (direction) (2005). *L'islam politique au sud du Sahara identités, discours et enjeux Hommes,* Paris: Karthala.
Gravrand, Henry (1983). *La civilisation sereer — Cosaan.* Dakar: Les Nouvelles Editions Africaines.
Ki Zerbo, Joseph (2003). *A quand l'Afrique? Entretien avec René Holenstein.* Paris: Éditions de l'Aube, poche essai.
Laboratoire Genre (no date). "Ndatte Yalla et la stratégie de conquête du pouvoir." IFAN, université Cheikh Anta Diop. http://www.sengenre-ucad.org/TexteNdate.htm (accessed January 27, 2012).
Mutiso, Gidbon (1975). "Rural Women in the Socio-political Transformations." In *The Civilization of the Woman in African Tradition*, Société africaine de culture. Paris: Présence Africaine, 526–54.
Ndoye, Doudou (2001). "La famille sénégalaise et le droit moderne." *Revue internationale de droit africain EDJA* 48 (spécial droit de la famille en Afrique): 5–12.
Obenga, Théophile (2004). *African Philosophy — The Pharaonic Period: 2780–330 BC.* Dakar: Per Ankh.
Otayek, René, et al. (1993). *Le radicalisme islamique au sud du Sahara, da'wa, arabisation et critique de l'Occident.* Paris: Karthala.
Pisier, Evelyne, and Sara Brimo (2007). *Le droit des femmes.* Paris: Dalloz.
Redd, Danita (2002). "Black Madonnas of Europe: Diffusion of the African Isis." In *Black Women in Antiquity*, edited by Ivan Van Sertima. New Brunswick, NJ: Transaction Publishers, 162.
Samb, Kany (no date). *Cadior ak Amary Ngoné Sobel.* Dakar: self-published (one of Senegal's best-known *griot* — oral tradition holder).
Société africaine de culture (1975). *The Civilization of the Woman in African Tradition.* Paris: Présence Africaine. Meeting organized by the Society of African Culture, Abidjan (Ivory Coast), July 3–8, 1972.
Sylla, Assane (1978). *La philosophie morale des Wolof.* Dakar: IFAN/Université de Dakar.
Thiaw, Issa Laye (2005). *La femme seereer.* Paris: L'Harmattan.
Thiaw, Issa Laye (1992). "La religiosité des Seereer, avant et pendant leur islamisation." *Ethiopiques: Revue trimestrielle de culture négro-africaine, Actes du Colloque des Journées Culturelles du Sine*, "La civilisation sérère d'hier à demain," Fatick, 10–12 mai 1991, 59–86.

LIST OF CONTRIBUTORS

Fatou Kiné Camara is an associate professor of law at the University Cheikh Anta Diop in Dakar, Senegal. She is the Secretary General of COSEF (Conseil sénégalais des femmes/Council for Senegalese Women), an association that works to promote the role of women in politics. She is also deputy secretary general of AJS (the Association of Female Jurists of Senegal), an association devoted to the establishment of gender equality and children's rights, as well as providing legal assistance, advice, and training to citizens in need. As a professor of law, she publishes extensively on "taboo" human rights subjects in Africa (right to abortion, discrimination against homosexuality, conjugal rape, child trafficking in the name of religion, and language rights). In November 2010, she was awarded the Prix des Droits de l'Homme du Cinquantenaire des Indépendances (Human Rights Prize for the Jubilee of the fifty years of independence of former French colonies in Africa) by the Académie des Sciences d'Outre-mer and the Secrétariat du cinquantenaire des Indépendances (France).

Lisa Fishbayn Joffe is director of the Project on Gender, Culture, Religion, and Law at the Hadassah-Brandeis Institute of Brandeis University. The Project focuses on identifying and disseminating innovative theoretical approaches to the reconciliation of conflicts between women's rights and practices rooted in cultural and religious norms. She writes on issues of gender and multiculturalism in Jewish family law and African customary law. She has been a visiting scholar at the Centre for Applied Legal Studies at the University of the Witwatersrand and at Harvard Law School and a lecturer in law at the Faculty of Laws, University College London. She was a member of the Pan Commonwealth Expert Group on Gender and Human Rights. She is co-editor of the Brandeis Series on Gender, Culture, Religion, and Law.

Pascale Fournier is University of Ottawa Research Chair in Legal Pluralism and Comparative Law, associate professor, and vice-dean of research at the University of Ottawa, Faculty of Law (Civil Law Section). Professor Fournier received her LLB from Laval University (1997), her LLM from the University of Toronto (2000), and her SJD from Harvard Law School (2007) as a Trudeau Scholar. Her scholarship focuses on comparative family law, Charter issues, Islam and Judaism in Europe and North America, criminal law and cultural diversity, and critical approaches to law. Her current research project, funded by the Social Sciences and Humanities Research Council of Canada, investigates the migration of two forms of religious divorce (the Jewish *get* and the Islamic *talaq*) in Canada, France, Britain, Germany, and Israel and explores through field interviews the effects of such migration on Jewish and Muslim women. In 2008, she served as expert consultant for the United Nations Development Programme on issues of gender and Islamic law in Tunisia, Egypt, Malaysia, and Nigeria. Her publications were selected by the Harvard-Stanford Junior Faculty Forum (2008), the Québec Bar Foundation prize for "best law review article" (2009), and the Canadian Association of Law Teachers Scholarly Paper Award (Honorable Mention, 2010). Her book *Muslim Marriage in Western Courts: Lost in Transplantation* was published in 2010 by Ashgate Publishing. Since 2011, she has served on the Younger Comparativists Committee (YCC) of the American Society of Comparative Law (ASCL).

Irit Koren has a PhD in gender studies from Bar-Ilan University. She is the author of the book *You Are Hereby Renewed Unto Me: Gender, Religion and Power Relations in the Jewish Wedding Ritual* (Hebrew University Magnes Press, 2011), and also of the book *Aron Betoch Aron* [Altering the Closet: Stories of Religious Homosexuals] (Yediot Acharonot, 2003). Dr. Koren was a visiting scholar at Rutgers University as well as a postdoctoral fellow at the Institute for Israel and Jewish Studies at Colombia University. Her research focuses on the intersection of gender and Jewish studies, with a particular emphasis on the challenges faced by women at the juncture of tradition and modernity. Koren has taught at many institutions both in Israel and in New York.

Rashida Manjoo holds a part-time post as a professor in the Department of Public Law at the University of Cape Town and is the UN Special Rapporteur on Violence against Women. She is the former Parliamentary commissioner of the South African Commission on Gender Equality (CGE), a constitutional body mandated to oversee the promotion and protection of gender equality. Prior to being appointed to the CGE, she was involved in social context training for judges and lawyers, where she has designed both content and methodology during her time at the Law, Race, and Gender Research Unit, University of Cape Town and at the University of Natal, Durban. She has held numerous visiting professorships, including most recently at the University of Virginia. She served as the Des Lee Distinguished Visiting Professor at Webster University, where she taught courses in human rights, with a particular focus on women's human rights and transitional justice. She was the Eleanor Roosevelt Fellow with the Human Rights Program at Harvard Law School (2006–7) and also a clinical instructor in the program in 2005–6.

Likhapha Mbatha is the director of the National Movement of Rural Women of South Africa (NMRW), an organization that was started as a reaction to forced removals in North West, Mpumalanga, and other parts of South Africa. Before joining the NMRW in April 2009, she worked as a researcher at the Centre for Applied Legal Studies and part-time lecturer on customary law at University of the Witwatersrand in Johannesburg. Her research interests are customary law (marriage, inheritance, and traditional authorities), human rights, and land. She has publications on customary marriage, inheritance, land, and local government.

Linda C. McClain is Paul M. Siskind Research Scholar and professor of law at Boston University School of Law. She writes and teaches in the areas of family law, feminist legal theory, and gender and law. She is currently a faculty fellow in the BU Department of Theology Religion Fellows Program. Her book *The Place of Families: Fostering Capacity, Equality, and Responsibility* (Harvard, 2006) offers a liberal and feminist perspective on the relationship between family life and the polity and on a number of contested issues of family law and policy. She is co-editor (with Joanna Grossman) of *Gender Equality: Dimensions of Women's Equal Citizenship* (Cambridge University Press, 2009). She is currently completing two books, *Rights, Responsibilities, and Virtues* (with James Fleming), and *What Is Parenthood? Contemporary Debates about the Family* (co-edited with Daniel Cere), an interdisciplinary volume forthcoming with NYU Press.

Martha Minow is Dean and Jeremiah Smith Jr. Professor of Law at Harvard Law School. She is the author of many influential books and articles, including *Making All the Difference: Inclusion, Exclusion, and, American Law*; *Not Only for Myself: Identity, Politics and Law*; *Between Vengeance and Forgiveness: Facing History after Genocide and Mass Violence*; and *In Brown's Wake: Legacies of America's Educational Landmark.* One of her books, *Partners Not Rivals: Privatization and the Public Good,* considers the role of religious groups and other nongovernment entities in the privatization of education, criminal justice, and legal services. Her scholarship includes articles about the treatment of women, children, persons with disabilities, and members of ethnic, racial, or religious minorities.

Sylvia Neil lectures in law at University of Chicago Law School. She is founder and chair of the Project on Gender, Culture, Religion, and Law at Brandeis University and is co-editor of its book series (Brandeis University Press). She is an adjunct professor at Northwestern University School of Law and has taught courses on religious liberty, gender, jurisprudence, and legal writing. Neil, who began her legal career as a poverty law litigator, served as associate dean at the University of Chicago Law School. Previous to that, she was regional legal and executive director of American Jewish Congress. She is on the national advisory committee of Human Rights Watch Women's Rights Division, WomenOnCall.org, and Jewish Funds for Justice. She has been a consultant to not-for-profit and civic institutions and has served on various boards.

Michal Roness has been a *yoetzet halakhah* (rabbinical law advisor) since 2005 and is on the roster of Nishmat's Golda Koschitzky Halachic Hotline, answering questions regarding the laws of family purity. She holds an MA in conflict resolution from Hebrew University and works as the program coordinator in the Conflict Management and Negotiation Program at Bar-Ilan University.

Ayelet Shachar is Canada Research Chair in Citizenship and Multiculturalism and professor of law, political science, and global affairs at the Faculty of Law of the University of Toronto. She has published and lectured widely on citizenship theory, immigration law, multiculturalism and women's rights, family law and cultural difference, and law and religion in comparative perspective. Professor Shachar is the author of *Multicultural Jurisdictions: Cultural Differences and Women's Rights* (Cambridge University Press, 2001) and *The Birthright Lottery: Citizenship and Global Inequality* (Harvard University Press, 2009). She is the recipient of excellence awards in three countries (Canada, Israel, and the United States) and has recently served as the Leah Kaplan Visiting Professor in Human Rights at Stanford Law School and the Jeremiah Smith Jr. Visiting Professor of Law at Harvard Law School.

Susan Weiss is the founder and executive director of the Center for Women's Justice in Israel. Susan has been actively working to find solutions for the problems of Jewish women and divorce for over twenty years, first as a private attorney, then as the founder and director of Yad L'Isha from 1997 to 2004, and now as the founder and executive director of CWJ. She initiated the innovative tactic of filing damage cases against recalcitrant husbands in the Israeli civil courts, is an editor of *The Law and Its Decisor* (a quarterly journal published by Bar Ilan University Law School), and has written extensively about Jewish women and divorce. She is an attorney with an MA in sociology and anthropology and is currently a doctoral student at Tel Aviv University.

INDEX

Page numbers in italics refer to tables.